LOOKING INTO PICTURES

LOOKING INTO PICTURES

AN INTERDISCIPLINARY APPROACH TO PICTORIAL SPACE

edited by
Heiko Hecht
Robert Schwartz
Margaret Atherton

A Bradford Book
The MIT Press
Cambridge, Massachusetts
London, England

This book was set in Times New Roman on Quark by Asco Typesetters, Hong Kong.
Printed and bound in the United States of America.

Library of Congress Cataloging-in-Publication Data

Looking into pictures : an interdisciplinary approach to pictorial space / edited by Heiko Hecht, Robert Schwartz, Margaret Atherton.
    p.   cm.
"A Bradford book."
 Includes bibliographical references and index.
 ISBN 0-262-08310-8 (alk. paper)
 1. Picture perception—Congresses. 2. Perspective—Congresses. 3. Picture interpretation—Congresses. I. Hecht, Heiko. II. Schwartz, Robert, 1940–
III. Atherton, Margaret.
BF243 .L66   2003
152.14—dc21   2002070319

10 9 8 7 6 5 4 3 2 1

Contents

Contents

Acknowledgments

The last half of the twentieth century witnessed revolutionary changes in the study of perception. The assumptions underlying the earlier perception paradigm—(1) the eye as camera, (2) the visual image as a picture, and (3) perception as primarily the result of interpreting static pictorial cues—have all been severely challenged. The implications of this paradigm shift for the study of picture perception, however, have not been well explored.

The editors thought the time was ripe for an in-depth, interdisciplinary examination of this issue. Aided by a grant from the Zentrum für interdisziplinäre Forschung (Center for Interdisciplinary Research; ZiF) in Bielefeld, Germany, we contacted many of the most prominent philosophers and psychologists in Europe and North America who are actively engaged in research on pictorial representation and picture perception. We asked them each to write a chapter on the topic "reconceiving pictorial space" (as described in the introduction) and to participate in a conference to discuss their work. Just about everyone contacted agreed on the need and importance of the project and also agreed to write a paper. Subsequently, chapter drafts of the participants were circulated, and a weeklong meeting was convened at the ZiF in the summer of 2000 to discuss and debate each person's position.

We thank the staff at the ZiF for their excellent administrative support. Johannes Roggenhofer, director of the ZiF, as well as Michael Kubovy and William Epstein participated in the conference discussions, and without their input the book would not be the same.

Introduction

Once Kepler correctly characterized how light reflected from objects projects a pattern of rays on the retina, a close relation between pictorial space and perceived physical space became a guiding presupposition of most work in the theory of vision. Given that the stimulus for vision is an image, a picture of the world the light rays "paint" on the retina, perception of the spatial layout must somehow depend on processing this image. We see the world through, or on the basis of, "picture images." The link between pictorial and physical space became even tighter as a result of the Renaissance development of systems for perspective rendering. Pictures constructed according to the rules of perspective seemed to mirror, and hence resemble, what they depicted. In the case of trompe l'oeil, viewers could not even tell the difference between the two. Perspective pictures were thought, therefore, to provide a correct, perhaps the only correct, way to represent physical space pictorially.

If any of this was in doubt, the subsequent invention of the camera clinched the case for allying pictorial and perceived space. Photographs, it was widely thought, represent space as it "really" is. Moreover, the similarities between the eye and the camera are striking. As the camera focuses light through a pinhole and lens onto a flat piece of film, so the retinal image is a projection of the world through a lens and pinhole (iris) onto the two-dimensional retinal surface. In both cases the projections follow the path of linear perspective. Thus, the "eye as camera" metaphor was born, and it came to dominate and set the problematic for the study of perception. As influentially formulated by Hermann von Helmholtz (1894) in the late nineteenth century, the goal of perceptual psychology was to find the rules of inference our visual system uses to derive a unique 3-D interpretation from the 2-D retinal image.

By the middle of the twentieth century, many of the assumptions underlying the "eye as camera" metaphor, however, came under serious attack. Philosophers questioned the very coherence of the notion of a sensory "picture," an uninterpreted phenomenal entity, standing as an intermediary between our perceptions and the physical world. Meanwhile, in the psychology of vision, theorists, building on the pioneering work of James J. Gibson (1950, 1966, 1979), began to propose models of spatial perception at odds with the whole conception of vision as a process of inference from a static pictorial image.

Amidst all these changes, however, one fundamental assumption has continued to play a prominent role in both the philosophical and psychological studies of picture perception. The idea that perspective pictures are special, the true way to represent space, although periodically challenged, has not been displaced. When philosophers talk about pictures and how pictures differ from languages and other forms of representation, it is almost always photographs or perspective renderings they have in mind. Similarly, in psychology, the study of picture perception tends to center on phenomena largely concerned with the viewing of perspective pictures. The special status accorded perspective pictures in vision theory is further highlighted when one considers that many experiments aimed at studying nonpictorial spatial perception are not actually conducted in real physical environments. Subjects, instead, are provided perspective pictures, or their computer screen equivalents, to view.

By contrast, theory and practice in artistic circles have evolved along a rather different path. Although the influence of perspective doctrines on post-Renaissance Western art was profound, artists eventually felt themselves needlessly constrained by its demands. Twentieth-century Western art has seen a veritable explosion of alternative schemes for depicting space. Today, the idea of there being only one legitimate way to represent space in artistic renderings, the one the post-Renaissance tradition favored, seems old-fashioned if not, as some contend, an outright matter of cultural bias or chauvinism. Surprisingly, philosophical and psychological work on picture perception has been relatively unmoved by these shifts in artistic practice and attitude. But the rationale for this steadfast adherence to traditional commitments is open to question.

As noted, the supporting "eye as camera" metaphor that has served to underpin the paradigm is no longer sacrosanct. In addition, other arguments commonly used to justify according perspective pictures special status, have also come under attack. For example, a number of influential writers in psychology and philosophy have argued forcefully that appeals to the notion of "resemblance" fail to explain either the character or uniqueness of perspective representation. Some theorists, in fact, have gone on to argue that perspective representation itself depends on conventions and so is best understood as a form of symbolization, on par with languages, music notation, maps, graphs, and the like.

All volume contributors were asked to consider what, if anything, recent developments in their area of specialty entailed about the relationship between pictorial and perceived physical space. More particularly, they were asked to consider such questions as these: Is the traditional conception of the nature of pictorial space still adequate, or must it be reconceived? Are vision scientists justified in substituting perspective pictures for real objects and environments in their studies? Are these setups, in Gibson's terms, "ecologically valid"? Given the pervasiveness of nonperspective renderings, not only in art but in advertising, scenic design, instructional displays, and so many other areas, does it make sense to treat these forms of picturing as of only marginal interest? Might a reconception of pictorial space, then, enable vision science to contribute more to our understanding of this wider realm of pictorial representations? And what might the implications of such a reorientation be for work on computer-generated "virtual reality" environments?

Finally, any reconception of "pictorial space" is sure to have profound implications for the conduct of experimental research in picture perception. For the assumptions of the traditional paradigm not only have shaped the theories developed; they have largely determined the very problems considered suitable or important to study. For example, much contemporary work in picture perception is devoted to testing and accounting for the effects that alterations in viewing angle, height, motion, and distance have on the way we see pictures. These experiments, however, tend to hinge crucially on features of perspective pictures and the geometry of the light rays such pictures project. Accordingly, the rationale for the studies, as well as the explanations proffered, depend on assumptions about the relationship between perspective renderings and perceived space. But if the account of pictorial space and pictorial representation were to change, what types of experimental methods and measurement devices would be most suitable to explore the domain?

The papers of the contributors fall into three natural groups: the dual nature of picture perception, the status of perspective, and exploring pictorial space.

I   THE DUAL NATURE OF PICTURE PERCEPTION

In addition to representing people, places, and things, pictures themselves are physical objects, with their own size, shape, color, and location. For the most part observers are well aware of these properties. Thus, the perception of pictures appears to be different in important ways from the perception of ordinary objects and spatial layouts. Any satisfactory theory of pictorial space must take into account this dual nature of picture perception. And any reconception of pictorial space must do so as well. The chapters in part I offer competing views on this distinctive aspect of picture perception.

In chapter 1, Richard Wollheim elaborates his influential thesis that pictorial representation is to be understood in terms of a phenomenal notion of "seeing-in." He claims that this account provides a natural framework for handling the dual nature (or "twofoldness") of picture perception. Wollheim also argues that his seeing-in approach better explains pictorial representation than other prominent theories do, in particular inference and illusion models. For Wollheim, representational content is set by the intentions of the artist and revealed to observers by what they are able to "see in" the picture.

Rainer Mausfeld, in chapter 2, holds that picture perception does not present a separate or special explanatory problem. Rather, the duality of picture perception is symptomatic of the perceptual system's wider capacity to handle what Mausfeld terms "conjoint representations." Building on a basic theoretical model in which sensory inputs compete to trigger representational primitives of the perceptual system, Mausfeld proposes that the duality of picture perception is one of a number of cases that can be explained by hypothesizing that more than one primitive is triggered. Mausfeld discusses many other cases that might exemplify a similar mechanism, for example, color and brightness, which, as primitives result in the simultaneous perception of surface illumination and ambient illumination. Mausfeld concludes by using the theoretical apparatus he has set up to give a new interpretation of Irvin Rock's "proximal mode."

In chapter 3, H. A. Sedgwick links the dual nature of pictures with the fundamental distinction between direct and indirect perception. Building on Gibson's ideas, he argues that indirect perception is reducible to direct perception. But Sedgwick allows that at present the latter theory is far from adequate. The dual nature of pictures will remain problematic, therefore, until a better account of direct perception is at hand. Summarizing a series of Gibsonian-inspired experiments, Sedgwick provides striking evidence that "cross-talk" between directly and indirectly specified aspects of pictures can explain most of the "errors" found in recovering physical space from pictures.

Reinhard Niederée and Dieter Heyer argue, in chapter 4, that we should not take the dual aspects of picture perception as a kind of two-stage process. Instead, the duality reflects two aspects of a single unified perceptual process, the nature of which has implications beyond the case of pictures. Their proposal is that the duality of picture perception is an indication of the visual system's capacity to manage ambiguity. This sort of ambiguity, they claim, is found not only in picture perception but also in ordinary vision. Here, too, ambiguity is frequently preserved rather than reduced to a single consistent scene. Using concepts such as Sedgwick's cross-talk, they demonstrate the functioning of interactive processes that require the presence of both elements and conclude that perception can profitably be considered a complex phenomenon, more like a language than a simple presentation of what is out there.

In chapter 5, Mark Rollins begins by explaining why strategic design theory (SDT) is taken by many to provide a serious alternative to Marr-style computational models of vision. This "bag of tricks" account appeals to a variety of flexible, context-sensitive, task-specific operations that do not require highly articulated representational structures. Rollins explores the implications that adoption of such an SDT approach has for a range of issues in picture perception, in particular the issues related to direct versus indirect perception. Among the other topics he examines are the issues of conceptual versus nonconceptual content, and recognitional (seeing-in) versus conventionalist accounts of representation.

II THE STATUS OF PERSPECTIVE

The dominant view of pictorial space gives pride of place to perspective renderings. But given the dual nature of picture perception, it cannot be claimed that seeing even the most accurately constructed perspective picture is the same as seeing that which it represents. In addition, we know that people on an everyday basis deal perfectly well with a myriad of pictures that violate the canons of perspective. So wherein lies the special status of this system of depiction? A common answer is that these renderings provide a true or realistic rendering of space. But this response will not be satisfactory unless it is backed up by a plausible analysis of the idea of one representation of pictorial space being correct or more accurate than another. The chapters in part II discuss the justification for claims about the special status of perspective.

Chapter 6, John Willats's chapter, serves as a bridge between parts I and II. Willats reprises the old question of whether the rules of pictorial representation are mere convention or immutable natural law. His answer is that the duality of pictures is mainly an outcome of the method used to describe the representational system. In this way, he seeks to relate the phenomenal duality of picture perception with the supposed unique status of perspective renderings. One outcome of his analysis is an explanation for why line drawings, which violate almost every rule of perspective, look as convincing as they do.

Robert Hopkins argues in chapter 7 that the question of whether perspective is conventional is itself unclear, and he offers a more precise statement of the issue. Hopkins then presents his own account of pictorial representation in terms of "seeing-in" as experienced resemblance of visual form. One major challenge resemblance theories face is that they have trouble accounting for the wide range of pictorial renderings that do not seem to resemble what they represent. Hopkins counters this objection by loosening the seeing-in criterion. This move also provides room for conventional factors to play a role in assessing resemblance. Nevertheless, Hopkins concludes that these compromises do not undercut his central claim that perspective picturing is special and nonconventional.

In chapter 8, Klaus Sachs-Hombach sets out to develop a principle for distinguishing pictures from linguistic and other symbolic forms. He, too, rejects a conventionalist theory in favor of a resemblance-based account of pictorial representation. The principle that evolves from his study is "A sign is a picture if the perception of the essential properties that the sign vehicle has in relevant respects is identical to the perception one would have of the corresponding properties of some other object under a certain perspective and if this perception is constitutive for the interpretation of the sign." The chapter is an attempt to explain and justify the ideas proposed and appealed to in this definition.

Klaus Rehkämper in chapter 9 defends the view that linear perspective can be identified as the correct way to represent the world pictorially, because it captures the way the visual system sees the world. Like Sachs-Hombach, he is concerned with addressing problems raised by Nelson Goodman's claim that linear perspective represents conventionally rather than representing by some natural relation. Rehkämper suggests that

Goodman's argument embodies a confusion of the relationship between the picture and its object with the relationship between the picture and an observer of that picture.

In chapter 10, Patrick Maynard illustrates the consequences of what he identifies as a fallacy: the fallacy that a linear projection is a depiction and hence that a theory of linear projection is a theory of depiction. He urges the theoretical importance of recognizing that linear perspective is no more than a technological tool that can be used to make pictures. Moreover, as essentially a matter of geometry, the tool has precisely nothing to say about vision or subjectivity. Maynard urges development of an independent theory of depiction, one that recognizes we have a more complicated task and even a more complicated spatial task than merely relating something two-dimensional to something three-dimensional.

III EXPLORING PICTORIAL SPACE

However one settles the theoretical issues in parts I and II, there remains the practical problem of applying the answers in the conduct of experimental research. Alternative conceptions of pictorial representation and pictorial space structure the problem space, the evidence sought, and the methods of collecting, measuring, and interpreting the data. Just how these matters play out will, of course, vary somewhat with the topic of concern (e.g., size, shape, and distance recognition). The chapters in part III explore several core empirical issues against the background of concerns discussed in the previous parts.

James Cutting's chapter, chapter 11, provides a transition between parts II and III. Cutting proposes solutions to a variety of theoretical questions about perception and perspective. He suggests that all perceived space has an inherent ordinal metric, thereby reuniting the dual aspects of pictures and creating an elegant synthesis of direct and indirect perception. By distinguishing between close personal space and a farther vista space, Cutting puts pictures in their (vista) place, which amounts to a perceiver mode where would-be spatial distortions are no longer an issue. He also offers us a new explanation of why line drawings work as well as they do.

In chapter 12, Jan Koenderink and Andrea van Doorn offer an in-depth analysis of the problem of measuring pictorial space, exploring along the way why common alternative attempts to measure a space that is nonphysical have gone wrong. Their own nonreductionist approach is unconventional and constructive. Koenderink and van Doorn first discuss their development and use of a number of methods to access observers' implicit knowledge of pictorial space. Then, on the basis of evidence from their empirical studies of surface relief, they derive a formal description of pictorial space as distinctly different from Euclidean space.

Sheena Rogers, in chapter 13, puts forth and defends the thesis that a realist theory of picture perception is problematic. Relying on ideas associated with ecological approaches to vision, she questions the doctrine that if the same information is available in pictures as is in a real scene the picture must look real. Moreover, she provides a body of empirical data showing that this need not be so. Similarity does not suffice for realism. Rogers also offers an explanation of why pictures may "lie" to us and why trompe l'oeil is so powerful.

In chapter 14, John Kennedy, Igor Juricevic, and Juan Bai set out to solve a mystery that can be called the "aggravated underspecification problem." A full-fledged rendition, such as a photograph, already underspecifies the rendered scene because the picture is necessarily less complex. Simple line drawings substantially widen this gap. How is it, then, that we readily see faces, objects, and so on, in a few marks on a piece of paper or even in one continuous pencil line? The visual system apparently finds an empirical solution to a problem that has no theoretical solution. The authors attempt to solve this mystery by studying the significance of lines and borders in pictures. They show that the empirical solution is found, in part, by interpreting borders as edges of surfaces. The ecological view reflected in Kennedy and his coauthors' argument supplements Koenderink and van Doorn's attempt to use image statistics as an explanation for this mysterious ability of the visual system. It also contrasts with Willats and Cutting's solutions to the same problem.

Hermann Kalkofen also provides reasons to believe there is no easy relationship between pictorial space and physical space. He guides us through a number of neglected examples of pictorial representations that do not presume one point of view at one time. These representations embody numerous inconsistencies, and yet we are able to make good sense of them. Once you take these sorts of examples into account, it becomes clear that standard attempts to deal with the representation of space from a single viewpoint merely scratch the surface of the problem of perceiving pictorial space and point the way to further work to come.

We hope that the reader will not only enjoy the diverse discussion of pictorial space found in this collection, but that the volume's chapters will be an inspiration to continue the theoretical and empirical work advanced.

PART I

THE DUAL NATURE OF PICTURE PERCEPTION

Chapter 1

In Defense of Seeing-In

Richard Wollheim

1

When we look at a picture, by which I mean a representational picture, we see something in it. That is my starting point. So when we look at Édouard Manet's *Emilie Ambre* (figure 1.1 and color plate 1), we see a woman in it. In saying that we see a woman in it, I refer to a certain feature of our perception of pictures, and this feature has important theoretical consequences. Because of this feature what two well-known groups of theorists find to say about pictorial perception is false. It is not the case that the representational content of Manet's painting, or the fact that it represents Madame Brunet, is something that we infer from our experience of the marked surface: for we also have an experience, a visual experience, of her. Furthermore it is not the case that the visual experience we have of Madame Brunet is such that, in the absence of information to the contrary, we would believe that we were seeing her face to face. When we look at the painting, we see Madame Brunet, but the way we see her, or the mode of perception, is such that we say that we see her in the picture. So, representational content is experiential, but it is not the product of illusion.

Is there something that we can say directly about that feature of picture perception, or seeing something in a picture, which carries with it this double load of theoretical consequence?

I believe that we can, and, to pick out this phenomenological feature, I have, for a number of years, used the term "twofoldness." When I look at the Manet, my perception is twofold in that I simultaneously am visually aware of the marked surface and experience something in front of, or behind, something else—in this case, a woman in a hat standing in front of a clump of trees. These are two aspects of a single experience. They are not two experiences: they are not two simultaneous experiences, as I used

Figure 1.1
Edouard Manet, *Emilie Ambre*. Philadelphia Museum. See plate 1 for color version.

to believe, nor are they two alternating experiences, as Ernst Gombrich has claimed in *Art and Illusion* (1956).

It should not be hard to see how twofoldness refutes the two theories of representational content that I have referred to. That, in looking at Manet's Madame Brunet, I experience a woman in a hat falsifies the inferential view, and that I am visually aware of the marked surface refutes the illusion view.

If we use the term "seeing-in" to identify the appropriate perceptual mode to adopt toward representational pictures when we view them as representational pictures—as opposed to some other way, such as regarding them exclusively as paint samples or exclusively as props in some game of memories—then my further claim is that twofoldness is an essential feature of seeing-in. (In contrasting viewing pictures as representations and viewing them some other way, I am leaving open the question whether, once we have succeeded in seeing something that was intended to be a representation as a representation, we are able to view it any other way. I have serious doubts on this score.)

2

If we think of twofoldness as built into seeing-in, then we can use the notion of seeing-in in two different ways.

In the first place, we can use the notion of seeing-in to provide a definition of a representational picture. A representational picture is a picture that requires, or calls for, seeing-in. What frees this definition from triviality is that although representation can be explained through representation, we do not need representation in order to identify seeing-in. On the contrary, seeing-in precedes representation both logically and historically. We can see things in objects that were neither intended to be, nor are believed by us to be, representations. Looking at a stained wall in *Chicago 1948*, we can see in the wall a boy carrying a mysterious box (figure 1.2). And I am sure that our ancestors engaged in such diversions before they thought of decorating the caves they lived in with images of the animals they hunted.

Understood in this way, or through the perceptual skill of seeing-in, the category of representational picture includes both figurative and abstract pictures. It does not however include all figurative and abstract pictures, for there are two comparatively restricted groups of pictures, one figurative and one abstract, that do not, for what are complementary reasons, call for twofoldness, and hence are not representational. On the figurative side, there are trompe-l'oeil pictures (figure 1.3), for they do not call for awareness of the marked surface; and, on the abstract side, there are those pictures which aim at flatness (figure 1.4), for they do not call for us to experience one thing in front of the other.

Second, we can use the notion of seeing-in to identify the representational content of a picture. A painting represents whatever can be correctly seen in it.

The point of "correctly" is to indicate that, whereas with nature, there is no impropriety in anything that we may happen to see in, say, a stained wall, and with a Rorschach test the only impropriety is to insist on seeing nothing rather than something in the fabricated inkblots put in front of us, there is, once representation arrives on the scene, one thing, just one

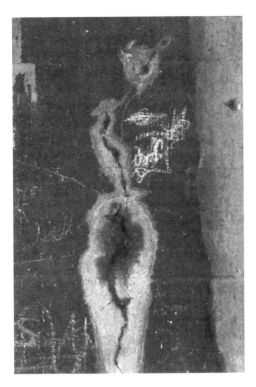

Figure 1.2
Aaron Siskind, *Chicago 1948.*

thing that we do right to see in its surface. We do wrong—though the wrong may be committed in play or jest, and not in error—if we see anything else in its surface. When Marcel Proust went to the Louvre and saw his friends from the Faubourg in the paintings of the old masters— for instance, the Marquis du Lau in a remarkable double portrait by Domenico Ghirlandaio (figure 1.5)—he was playing a game, and the game was to see what he was not supposed to see. Once seeing-in is transposed from nature to art, or at least to artifactuality, it gains a standard of correctness.

I would make a further claim to the effect that this standard is set by the fulfilled intentions of the artist. And the intentions of the artist are fulfilled when, working under the causal influence of certain psychological factors, which have come to be called in this particular theoretical context "intentions," he has so marked the surface of his painting that it is possible for

Figure 1.3
Alexandre I. Leroy de Barde, *Reunion of foreign birds placed within different cases.*
Nineteenth-century watercolor. Inv.: 23692. Photo: Michèle Bellot. Copyright
© Réunion des Musées Nationaux / Art Resource, NY. Louvre, Paris, France.

Figure 1.4
Barnett Newman, *Vir Heroicus Sublimis*. 1950–51. Oil on canvas, $7'11\frac{3}{8}'' \times 17'9\frac{1}{4}''$ (242.2 × 513.6 cm). The Museum of Modern Art, New York. Gift of Mr. and Mrs. Ben Heller. Photograph © 2001 The Museum of Modern Art, New York.

a properly sensitive, properly informed, spectator to have an experience that tallies with those factors. "Tally" here is a broad term, and its specific application depends on the type of psychological factor, or intention, that is seeking fulfillment. When the artist has a representational intent, which is our current concern, this intention is fulfilled when it is possible for a properly sensitive, properly informed, spectator to see in the surface that the artist has marked the object that he intends to represent. Likewise the artist's representational intentions are unfulfilled when it is impossible for an appropriate spectator to see that object in the picture. What makes what an appropriate spectator can or cannot see in a picture relevant to fulfillment of the artist's representational intention is that experiences of seeing-in "tally with" representational intentions.

3

Within the account that I have offered of how we identify a painting's representational content, there is a point that needs elaboration. I have equated a painting's representational content with what can be correctly seen in it, and I have equated what can be correctly seen in a painting with an experience that conforms with the artist's intentions. In other words, the artist's control over the content of the picture that he is making is

Figure 1.5
Domenico Ghirlandaio (1448–94). *Portrait of an old man and his grandson.* Copyright © Alinari / Art Resource, NY. Louvre, Paris, France.

limited in this respect: that it is out of the things that can be seen in his picture that his intention determines what the picture represents. If something cannot be seen in a painting, it forfeits all chance of being part of its content.

So the question arises, How can we determine, for a given picture, whether something can be seen in that picture? What are the limits of visibility in a picture?

The question is clearly ambiguous between an extensional and a nonextensional reading. Since there is little doubt but that when we ask whether something can be seen in a picture, the "something" is clearly to be understood in a nonextensional way, we should reformulate the question thus: How do we determine, for a given picture, the range of things that something that can be seen in that picture can be seen as?

One proposal for answering that question is this: In a given picture, we pick out a certain object that can be seen in it. Let us imagine that we merely pick it out as "that thing." Then people in turn propose various concepts that apply to the thing in question, and what we have to decide for each such concept is whether it affects how we see the object or whether it merely affects what we say about it. If for a given concept, and the concept could be one that had independently occurred to us, the answer is positive, then we can see the object as falling under that concept. If the concept is f, then we can see the object as f, and fs are visible in that picture.

In an article of recent years, I applied this test for visibility in a picture in the following way: We look at a painting showing a figure seated amongst classical ruins (figure 1.6), and someone starts to ask questions of us, to which we must answer, Yes, or No. So, for example, Can you see those columns as having been thrown down? Yes. Can you see those columns as having been thrown down hundreds of years ago? Yes. Can you see those columns as having been thrown down hundreds of years ago by barbarians? (with some difficulty) Yes. Can you see them as having been thrown down hundreds of years ago by barbarians wearing wild asses' skins? (with little difficulty) No. Though we are perfectly ready to believe that the barbarians whose handiwork our eyes are prepared to acknowledge in this picture did indeed wear wild asses' skins, there is no way in which this belief, or the concept that figures in it, can help us to structure our perception of the painting, or can affect how we see the columns. So, of the range of concepts put to us in this test, it is the only one that is not instantiated by something visible in the picture.

Those who are impressed by the modularity of the faculties are likely to resist this test and what it is supposed to show, but to them all I can say is that, whatever credence we might give to the role of modularity in perception in general, there is obviously a level of complexity above which it doesn't apply, and there is reason to think that picture perception lies outside its scope. The reason can be brought out by our considering pictures of women. Now, of some of these pictures, such as Manet's *Emilie Ambre,* when we further ask, What woman is it of? there is an answer to this ques-

Figure 1.6
Nicolas Poussin, French, 1594–1665, *Landscape with Saint John on Patmos*, 1640, oil on canvas, 100.3 × 136.4 cm, A. A. Munger Collection, 1930.500 © The Art Institute of Chicago. All rights reserved.

tion, whereas with the rest, such as Manet's *La Prune* (figure 1.7), there is no answer to this question. To generalize, some pictures are of particular things or events, and others are of things or events merely of some particular kind.

The explanation for why we classify the two paintings in different ways is not that there is in reality such a person as Madame Brunet and that Manet painted his painting by painting her, whereas there is no particular person whom *La Prune* represents, though all this is in fact true. For, in the first place, I believe (contra Nelson Goodman) that we should put Jean-Auguste-Dominique Ingres's *Jupiter and Thetis* in the same category as Madame Brunet even though Jupiter and Thetis are not real persons. Second, to invoke this kind of explanation at this stage would be to go

Figure 1.7
Edouard Manet, *La Prune (Plum Brandy)*, c. 1877, oil on canvas, .736 × .502 (29 × 19$\frac{3}{4}$); framed: .876 × .641 × .057 (34$\frac{1}{2}$ × 25$\frac{1}{4}$ × 2$\frac{1}{4}$). Collection of Mr. and Mrs. Paul Mellon. Photograph © 2001 Board of Trustees, National Gallery of Art, Washington.

into reverse about how a representational picture comes by its content. Accordingly, if we really do think that there is a division within paintings of the kind I propose, according to which *Emilie Ambre* and *Jupiter and Thetis* lie on one side of the line and *La Prune* lies on the other, this must be because there is a difference, a perceptual difference, between an experience of a painting that we would naturally report by saying "I see a particular woman in that picture" and an experience of a painting that we would more naturally report by saying "I see merely a woman in that picture." And, if this is so, then one experience must be laden with referential thought and the other laden with nonreferential thought, and this would in turn show that, in the domain of picture perception, perception exemplifies a rather remarkable degree of permeability by thought.

4

I return to the claim that when I look at a picture appropriately, the twofoldness that qualifies my perception is not a matter of my having two experiences, each one of a familiar kind, which can also be had outside the aegis of seeing-in. Rather I have one experience with two aspects, and this is distinctive of, if not unique to, seeing-in.

I have said that some philosophers deny or have denied this idea outright. But other philosophers, and also (or so it seems to me) some perceptual psychologists with interests in this area, in effect assume its falsity. Whether this is so or not, let me set up a straw man who does assume two separate experiences, and I want to consider how this assumption can grossly distort something that he might be inclined to think of as "the problem of picture perception."

If someone holds that looking at a picture is not characterized by twofoldness but is constituted of two paired experiences, each of a kind familiar to us from outside the perception of pictures, one of which presents the viewer with something two-dimensional, the other with something three-dimensional, then the person is likely to think that the problem of picture perception is how to explain the occurrence of a problematic experience, that is, the experience of something three-dimensional when confronted solely by a two-dimensional surface. That being so, the natural next step is to look for the explanation of this experience within the experience paired with it: namely, the experience of looking at the marked surface, and seeing it as such.

5

Our straw man goes wrong in locating the explicandum of his inquiry where he does. For, when we look at, say, *Emilie Ambre,* it is not the case that we have an experience of the sort that would, in the absence of ancillary evidence to the contrary, lead us to believe that we were seeing *Emilie Ambre* face to face. But might our straw man not yet be right in what he takes to be the explicans? He might be. It might be the case that, whenever we saw something in a marked surface, we were led to do so by a prior experience of the surface for the duration of which we inhibited ourselves from seeing something in it. But I am skeptical that this is so: I cannot readily believe that every occasion on which we see something in a marked surface is preceded by our seeing that surface without seeing anything in it. So the latter kind of experience cannot furnish an explanation of the former kind.

A different kind of explanation of why we see something in a marked surface, though the two can get confused, is an appeal not to some way in which we see the surface but to some way in which the surface is. The way the surface is, in such cases, is not necessarily something of which we are aware, but, unless it were as it is, we would not see in it what we do.

It is sometimes argued that, in any account of what we see in a surface, there is no room for any feature of the surface to play a role unless this feature is itself visible. But this betrays a confusion between two kinds of account. For it is certainly the case that in an *analysis* of what it is to see something in a marked surface, a feature of the surface of which there is no awareness is out of place. This is because an experience can only be analyzed in terms of constituent experiences. But when it comes to an *explanation* of what it is to see something in a surface, the situation is different. For we can explain an experience in terms of other experiences, but also in terms of features of the environment to which the experience is sensitive, even though the person might have no awareness of them as such. In the second case, the explanation does not double as an analysis.

6

If we do think that it is possible in principle to explain how we see a woman's head in a painting by citing objective features of the painted surface, it is important to recognize that because of the vast diversity of ways in which a woman's face can be represented or the vast diversity of painted surfaces in which a woman's face can be seen, the explicandum in such cases will be not something of the generality of the representation of a woman's face but something of the particularity of Raphael's depiction of a woman's face, or Guercino's depiction of a woman's face, or Picasso's depiction of a woman's face, or Willem de Kooning's depiction of a woman's face. Some might feel that this would leave the central question of representation, why these are all representations of the same thing, unanswered. But anyone sensitive to what a painter is doing when he paints a woman's face might prefer not to raise this question.

Chapter 2

Conjoint Representations and the Mental Capacity for Multiple Simultaneous Perspectives

Rainer Mausfeld

Mens videt, mens audit: Cetera surda et coeca.
It is the mind that sees and the mind that hears;
the rest are deaf and blind.

—Epicharmos[1]

Commonsense taxonomies were, inevitably, the origin from which the natural sciences, at their earliest stages of development, derived their categorizations of phenomena. This can be witnessed by the classical division of physics into, for example, optics, acoustics, theory of heat, and mechanics. During the process of its theoretical development, physics became increasingly divorced from these kinds of classifications and rather grouped phenomena in accordance with its own internal theoretical structure (the classical theory of heat, for instance, disintegrated into statistical mechanics, on the one hand, and electrodynamics, on the other hand). In perceptual psychology corresponding pretheoretical classifications of phenomena are mirrored in the standard textbook organization in terms of salient perceptual attributes, such as color, depth, size, or form. In this field, it will likely prove to be more difficult than it was in physics to dispense with commonsense classifications of phenomena and to instead follow lines of theorizing that are traced out by the development of successful explanatory accounts. This difficulty is due to the power that the phenomenal appearance exercises over our way of theoretically grouping perceptual phenomena. Although we are well aware that commonsense taxonomies are an inapt guide for the endeavor to achieve, within the framework of the natural sciences, a theoretical understanding of the mind, we are held captive by the appearances. We are inclined to believe that perception works in the way it phenomenally appears to us and that a theoretically fruitful classification of phenomena basically follows our commonsense psychological intuitions. It was such pretheoretical commonsense taxonomies that in perceptual psychology brought forth subfields such as picture perception or color perception.

For someone, like me, who is working in the field of color perception, picture perception does not appear as a natural field of inquiry, all the more so because hardly any other two fields in visual perception are as remote in their approaches and their theoretical frameworks as picture perception and color perception. Nevertheless, I believe that phenomena in these fields share, on a more abstract level, structural similarities that appear to point to deeper principles of our mental architecture. This is hardly surprising, because there is no reason to expect that classes of perceptual phenomena that arise in the context of certain artifacts, such as pictures, and classes of phenomena that pertain to certain phenomenal attributes, such as color, will survive as theoretically useful categories when more successful explanatory accounts of perception have eventually been developed. Rather, such accounts would result in a classification of phenomena that is determined by the actual internal principles underlying perception, whatever these may turn out to be.

The most promising general approach to perception appears to me to be one that follows ethological lines of thinking. Such approaches have, notably when couched in computational terms, already yielded intriguing explanatory frameworks of promising range and depth. From an ethological perspective, the core task of perceptual psychology is to investigate the structure of perceptual representations and the nature of the representational primitives on which it rests. With respect to color perception, such an approach has brought forth what I believe to be interesting theoretical speculations about the nature of the representational primitives and about the internal structure they give rise to. The internal principles that are suggested by these speculations and that we are only beginning to understand are fairly general ones that crosscut commonsense categorizations of phenomena. Although not much is presently known about the structure of the representational primitives to which these principles refer, some of their general properties are suggested by interesting structural similarities that certain phenomena from various domains in cognitive science appear to share. Among these phenomena is our ability to perceptually deal with the so-called dual character of pictures. This ability is, I believe, part of a general structural property of our basic cognitive architecture that refers to the handling of *conjoint representations over the same input*. In various domains and at different levels of the cognitive system, we can encounter phenomena that are likely due to the internal handling of multiple conjoint and often competing representations. From this point of view, picture perception and its dual character are a special instance where we exploit these given capacities in the context of human artifacts. Before arguing for this view in greater detail, I will briefly delimit the topic of my inquiry.

In picture perception, more than, say, in research on stereo vision or color coding, the tension looms large between what are to be considered universal and what cultural and conventional aspects, a tension that mirrors and maintains the time-honored distinctions that placed physis and ethos, nature and convention, essential and accidental properties in well-nigh irreconcilable opposition to one another. The corresponding issues are a matter of much debate between—to use some fashionable jargon—universalists and cultural relativists. Outside some areas of vision and language, little of substance is presently known about where to draw a dividing line between universal aspects and aspects of cultural variation, individual plasticity or learning history. However, the entire idea of cognitive science rests on the assumption that *some such* distinction can be drawn at all. This also holds for inquiries centering on picture perception. The perception of pictures, on the basis of multiple pictorial components of very different status, involves highly complex interactions of our perceptual faculty and various interpretative faculties, which are presently not well understood. These interactions give rise to a high degree of cultural variation. I shall deliberately ignore the cultural dimension of picture perception and, with respect to the so-called dual character of pictures, focus on structural elements of perception that seem to be part of our basic cognitive endowment.

2.1   THE DUAL CHARACTER OF PICTURES

Pictures and pictorial representations, though highly impoverished two-dimensional abstractions of what is depicted, can evoke strong perceptual impressions of objects, spatial relations, or events within us. A dominant theme in the field of picture perception has been the issues centering on notions of perceptual space and the extent to which corresponding percepts can be evoked by features of pictorial representations, notably through linear perspective (cf. Haber 1980; Rogers 1995). During the Renaissance an increasing interest emerged in techniques of linear perspective. This was motivated by the artists' desires to imitate nature and to achieve "visual truth" in their paintings. This idea gave rise to related inquiries into artistic techniques for the evocation of space and, in particular, into techniques for creating geometrically correct two-dimensional pictorial representations on a canvas of the three-dimensional layout of the pictured scene. In such investigations, as Martin Kemp observed, "the eye figures little, the mind features even less" (1990, p. 165). Rather, what was to be accomplished was "the demonstration of an internally consistent system of the spatial elements in a picture and, above all, a proof that the system rested upon non-arbitrary foundations" (ibid., p. 11). The canvas was regarded as a window, often referred to today as an "Alberti window," through which the painter views the world and that intersects the painter's visual cone (Lindberg 1976). This conception gave rise to the idea that a realistic appearance of depth and space can be achieved in pictures by mimicking the exact geometrical relations in the structure of light that reaches the eye from a three-dimensional scene. Consequently, a system of construction rules, in the sense of artistic-engineering techniques for the purpose of creating, on a flat canvas, pictorial representations that induce a strong appearance of depth in the observer, gained prominence in Renaissance art.[2] Although these artistic techniques later joined with ideas on geometrical processes of image formation in the eye, their use and development were primarily shaped by considerations internal to the complex variety of cultural purposes underlying artistic productions. However, for the endeavor to imitate nature and to achieve visual truth in two-dimensional representations of the world, the importance of rules for linear perspective is on a par with those for simulating the effect of lights and the interaction of light and objects by using spatial pigment patterns on a flat surface (Schöne 1954). It is a historically contingent development of art history that resulted in linear perspective, rather than other aspects, first gaining prominence in the context of artistic attempts to imitate nature.

The notion of a *dual character of pictures* basically refers to the phenomenon that pictures can generate an in-depth spatial impression of the scene depicted while at the same time appearing as flat two-dimensional surfaces hanging on a wall. Albert Michotte (1948/1991) recognized the challenge that this kind of phenomenon poses for perception theory.[3] A description in terms of a perceptual conflict between the perceived flatness of the picture's surface and the perceived depth of what is depicted captures only a small fraction of the perceptual enigmas involved. By careful phenomenological observation when viewing pictures, one can easily gather indications of how difficult it is to precisely describe what the percepts are and thus what the perceptual achievements are in these situations.[4] I will deliberately leave out many of the problems that we encounter in describing exactly the percepts or the perceptual achievements in corresponding situations of viewing pictures. I will, rather, distinguish only two general problems to which the notion dual character of picture seems to refer, which I will address in turn. The first is the problem of cue integration with respect to depth or, more generally, spatial representations.[5]

The second is a problem that seems to me to be even more complex and much deeper, namely, the problem of what I refer to as conjoint representations over the same inputs and our ability to smoothly handle them. By conjoint representations I will, in an intuitive and tentative way, denote two or more representational primitives of the same type or of different types that exploit the same input properties in different and interdependent ways. The special case of *competing* conjoint representations is furthermore characterized by the property that the parameters of one representational primitive that relate to a certain aspect of the input are antagonistically coupled with parameters of the other representational primitive that refer to the same aspect. As an illustration think of a surface viewed under some chromatic illumination: the incoming color signal is internally exploited in terms of two components, that is, "surface color" and "illumination color" (to be understood as internal and not as physical concepts); the extent to which a "surface" representation exploits the incoming color signals in terms of its color parameter antagonistically constrains the values that an "ambient illumination" representation can assign to its color parameter, and vice versa.

The two issues of the integration of conflicting cues with respect to a specific representational primitive, on the one hand, and a dual representation that results from conjoint representations over the same inputs, on the other hand, are often conflated.

2.2   CONFLICTS IN CUE INTEGRATION WITH RESPECT TO DEPTH OR SPATIAL REPRESENTATIONS

The lines along which we can theoretically explore the dual character of pictures considered as a case of cue integration are comparatively well explored in visual psychophysics. Although problems of cue integration are intricate enough we have both a wealth of experimental results and subtle mathematical-modeling tools, such as the Bayesian framework, which has proved a fruitful basis for dealing with these issues. All this is well known, and I will only briefly review some of the relevant evidence in order to better differentiate the second problem of conjoint representations from issues of cue integration.

We know from psychophysics that the depth one experiences, that is, the apparent variation in surface relief and the relative location of objects in 3-D space, is constructed from multiple sources of evidence. These cues can carry different weights with respect to internal spatial representations, weights that can be but are not necessarily in line with natural ecological constraints. For instance, occlusion carries a strong internal weight but provides only weak constraints for spatial representations, namely, that the depth on one side of the border is greater than on the other side. Another example is shading, which provides information about the surface normal at each location. Even cues that are unrelated to depth per se can be used to disambiguate other cues, such as spatial frequency content for 3-D-shape-from-texture cues. If different sources of evidence favor different and mutually incoherent spatial representations of the same input, the visual system often has some kind of default preference for solving this cue conflict. It does this without providing any phenomenal access to alternative representations. A case in point is the Ames room, where systematic manipulations in linear and texture perspective cues result in estimates of depth and size based on a cue integration that vetoes or ignores cues of familiar size; the cue integration seems rather to be in line with internal heuristics such as "lines that are nearly parallel in the image are parallel in 3-D," or "lines that meet at a common vertex in the image also meet at a common vertex in 3-D."

In picture perception we find a plenitude of ways to evoke space and depth on a two-dimensional surface that mirror the plenitude of depth cues. We encounter a similar situation for the integration of *conflicting* cues, namely the integration of stereo disparity information and various monocular depth cues.[6] Although the depth information of the picture surface is perfectly in line with the depth information from the frame or the surrounding wall, the scene depicted can invoke the impression of being phenomenally extending in depth.

In principle we could conceive a visual system that integrates these cues in such a way that the stereo information completely dominates and, in the case of incoherence, vetoes monocular information, which phenomenally would result in a reduction of the—already not very strong—3-D vividness of the scene depicted to zero, that is, a flat picture without any indication of surface orientation or relative 3-D locations of objects. Interestingly enough, our visual system uses almost the opposite strategy: it is a well-known result from visual psychophysics that monocular cues often dominate the resulting 3-D interpretation over stereopsis, even at close range where stereopsis is most accurate. I will mention only a few corresponding studies. For instance, in a pioneering study, Walter Schriever (1925) found that perspective alone as well as occlusion could overrule disparity information. Schriever also made a wealth of careful observations about attentional effects and vagueness and instability, as well as individual differences. Mümtaz Turhan (1937) found that in center-surround situations, brightness gradients of opposite direction can result in perceptual impressions that violate the physical depth relations of infield and surround as provided by disparity information and motion parallax (infields whose brightness gradient has the same direction as that of the surround appear to lie in the same depth level as the surround, whereas they appear to lie in a different depth plane and often look bent in the case of opposite brightness gradients). Turhan observed that physically incompatible depth interpretations of the infield can occur at the same time and often are accompanied by some kind of vagueness of the perceptual impression.

John Yellott (1981) showed that an inside-out face—a mold of a face—looks right side out as long as shading is present, despite the presence of contradictory disparity information as provided by a random-dot stereogram projected onto the surface of the mask. If the mold is presented solely as a random-dot stereogram with no shading, it is seen inside out, that is, consonant with the disparity information. Another interesting example is provided by Kvetoslav Prazdny (1986), who described a random-dot stereo cinematogram that portrays a flat object in front of a background that changes its two-dimensional shape consistent with a three-dimensional rotating wire object, while at the same time the binocular disparities are incompatible with the relative depth information specified by the image motions. Due to the appearance of three-dimensionality in these displays he concluded that the kinetic depth effect effectively vetoes the stereo disparity cue with respect to the shape of the object (however, disparity determined the position of the object with respect to the background).

A particularly effective demonstration of the monocular influence over stereo information was provided by Kent Stevens and Allen Brookes

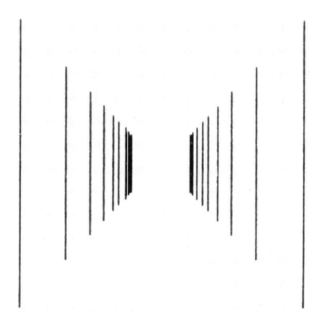

Figure 2.1
Stimulus configuration used by Stevens and Brookes (1988). The lines are stereoscopically presented as being coplanar, that is, they increase linearly in disparity
from left to right. The 3-D impression, however, is of a corridor extending in
depth, as suggested monocularly.

(1988; see also Stevens, Lees, and Brookes 1991). The lines in the stereoscopically presented figure 2.1 are coplanar, that is, they increase linearly
in disparity from left to right. The 3-D impression, however, is of a corridor extending in depth, bordered on either side by columns of vertical
lines or stakes. In the stereo-apparatus the innermost lines on either side
of the vertical meridian had stereo disparities of ± 11 minutes of arc; the
outermost lines had disparities of $\pm 51'$. It is remarkable that the line
with $-11'$ disparity appeared more distant than the line of disparity $+51'$.
Stevens and Brookes found empirical evidence that stereopsis extracts
3-D surface information only where the second spatial derivatives of disparity are nonzero, corresponding to loci where the surface is curved,
creased, or discontinuous.

We now can directly apply their result to the situation of picture perception. A picture hanging on a wall has no local disparity differences over
the picture surface but only a continuous uniform gradient of disparity

indicating a flat although extended surface. Accordingly, because of the specific properties of the human visual system for integrating binocular and monocular sources of depth evidence, as exemplified by Stevens and Brookes's results, stereopsis is particularly weak under these conditions. Our phenomenal spatial impression is therefore—in the presence of monocular depth cues such as occlusion, texture, shading, or perspective—determined by these monocular cues. Thus, in picture perception, we take advantage of the internal coding property that depth is derived from disparity only where the surface exhibits continuous curvature or sharp discontinuities, because some binocular disparity information must be discounted in picture perception to interpret drawings at all.

I will not dwell further on the cue integration aspect of the dual character of pictures (for a more recent study of cue integration with respect to depth, see Landy et al. 1995). What I wanted to show is that the conflict between stereo information and monocular depth cues, as well as the corresponding observation that the flatness of the picture plane does not impede the depth impression of the scene depicted, is simply a special case of the specific way our visual system integrates disparity information with other depth cues, as mirrored in a great variety of psychophysical results.

2.3 CONJOINT REPRESENTATIONS IN PICTURE PERCEPTION

I will now turn to the second aspect of the notion of dual character of pictures, namely, the issue of conjoint representations over the same input and our ability to handle them smoothly. This issue is much more puzzling and much less understood than the conflicting cue aspect. I shall first describe the corresponding kind of phenomenon, as referred to in the literature on picture perception. Like the cue integration aspect, it is, in my view, not specific to picture perception but rather a general and essential property of our cognitive organization.

In picture perception, we can simultaneously have the phenomenal impression of two different types of objects, each of which seems to thrive in its own autonomous spatial framework,[7] namely, on the one hand, the picture surface as an object—with corresponding object properties such as orientation or depth—and, on the other hand, the depicted objects themselves with their idiosyncratic spatial properties and relations. We seem to have two mutually incompatible spatial representations at the same time; at least in the sense that they are available internally and we can, without any effort, switch back and forth between them.

Before venturing some more speculative ideas about some general properties of our cognitive architecture on which this ability rests, I will list some observations concerning this dual nature of pictures that I consider to be of particular relevance.

In an aside, in order to avoid potential misunderstandings I would like to emphasize that pictorial art in general cannot simply be understood as a kind of frozen optical array or a static boundary case of the optical structure of the input from a scene. Pictorial art is much richer than naturalistic artistic productions and serves a great many different symbolic functions. Pictures are not surrogates for scenes, nor can they be subjected to a criterion of some absolute notion of veridicality (whatever that means) with respect to the scene depicted. Thus, those aspects of picture perception that we potentially can understand from core perceptual principles—and, as I said in the beginning, it is only this part that I will address here—are, from the perspective of cultural studies, the least interesting aspect of picture perception. What we usually refer to when we talk about picture perception are symbolic interpretations at various levels and thus aspects that pertain to highly complex interactions of our perceptual faculty and various interpretative faculties. Within the framework of the cognitive sciences we virtually know next to nothing about the cognitive principles underlying these achievements. Let us look at four types of observations that are of particular theoretical relevance:

1. A continuous path of transitions exists from a view of a real 3-D scene to a scene as depicted (or abstracted) on a canvas.

We can easily construct a continuous path from the view of a real 3-D scene to a real 3-D scene viewed as a kind of frozen Alberti window to a photo of this frozen optical array and to a highly reduced drawing of the relevant contours of the scene. This allows us to experimentally investigate all sorts of transitions and boundary conditions in picture perception.[8]

2. We can phenomenally accentuate one or the other aspect and switch back and forth in an effortless way.

This aspect is phenomenally so conspicuous and striking that we usually do not pay much attention to it. It is at the core of what we mean when we refer to the dual nature of pictures. Though such switches are correlated with depth aspects, they actually pertain to the entire perceptual organization of the visual field and thus to attributes such as shape, or shading and brightness gradients. A wealth of observations pertaining to this kind of phenomenon have been reported in the literature, a wealth that contrasts oddly with the silence about what to make of these observations theoretically.

Ernst Gombrich (1982) made the important observation that one has to achieve the proper mental attitude to take full advantage of the capacity to switch back and forth between the reality of the picture as an object and the reality of the depicted objects. Because of this, people at earlier stages of cultural development regularly seem to have problems seeing what is depicted in a photo. For instance, Jan Deregowski, Muldrow, and Muldrow (1972) reported that people from a remote Ethiopian tribe when presented with a drawing of an animal would pay attention to the characteristics of the drawing paper but would ignore the picture; they exhibited a complete inattention to the content of the representation while concentrating on the medium. Several others have reported essentially the same observation. When people at earlier stages of cultural development regularly have problems in seeing what is depicted on a photo, they have not yet attained the ability to exercise what Gombrich called the proper mental attitude and thus cannot fully exploit a given cognitive capacity in the case of previously unknown artifacts. However, as Margaret Hagen and Rebecca Jones concluded from a review of corresponding studies, "this coexistence of information poses few problems even for the naive observers when pictures represented only single solid objects. There is no evidence whatsoever that any group of people see pictures of faces, cups, hunters, antelopes or elephants as flat 'slices of life,' as it were" (1978, p. 192). Many other interesting regularities were found with respect to the ability to simultaneously handle both types of reality, as it were. For instance, outline drawings present fewer difficulties than photos to naive observers; thus contour information seems to be of greater importance than texture.[9]

Corresponding observations are, of course, not confined to picture perception, but pervade psychophysics and perceptual psychology. For example, in the study mentioned previously, Stevens and Brookes (1988, p. 383) made the observation that experienced stereo observers can also discern the true stereo depth of the component lines with scrutiny, as if they can selectively disregard the monocular depth interpretation.

3. The "realities" of pictures as objects and depicted objects bear different amounts of internal computational relevance and phenomenological vividness.

We can switch back and forth between these two kinds of spatial representations, but this is not a switch between a 2-D representation (within some 3-D representation) and a different full-fledged 3-D representation. Rather, the spatial representation of the scene depicted is phenomenally quite shallow. In a sense we could regard it as a phenomenal analog to David Marr's $2\frac{1}{2}$ D spatial representations, that is, what we perceptually experience are local surface orientation, distance from viewer, or discontinuities in depth and discontinuities in surface orientation, without either the phenomenological vividness or the other internal properties of a full-blown 3-D representation. There are, of course, several other aspects that are responsible for the reduced 3-D vividness of the scene depicted, notably a lack of cues provided by motion, and the ranges of color and luminance contrast, which are much narrower than those of real scenes.

Even if we attend to the two-dimensional picture surface we may experience the depicted object, say, a line drawing of a cube, in a mandatory way as three-dimensional, and yet this 3-D spatial representation lacks other crucial elements of a full-blown 3-D representation; for instance, it would hardly fool us into trying to grasp and rotate the cube.[10] Both types of representation exhibit therefore quite different kinds of anchoring within the internal computational structure, and we can safely conjecture that we have specific mechanisms subserving "flat" representations by ignoring certain aspects of 3-D structure. Pieter Saenredam's *Interior of the Saint Jacob Church in Utrecht* (1642; figure 2.2 and plate 2) may serve as another illustration. In this case the conflict with size relations in the spatial representation of the picture viewed within the environmental context already suffices to divorce the—otherwise mandatory—3-D interpretation of the scene depicted from other internal-coding properties of full-fledged 3-D representations.

4. The two representations are not independent but interlocked.

When we look at a picture like the one displayed in figure 2.2, it seems that we can achieve a kind of autonomous spatial representation of the scene depicted that is detached from the normal spatial representation of our environment, including the picture surface plane. In other words, we seem to use our faculty for spatial representations to emulate certain of its achievements in a restricted local framework.[11] As a result, the internal output of such an emulation is a partly autonomous, though comparatively faint, local spatial representation within the canonical spatial representation of our environment. In fact, both representations are nevertheless internally interlocked; just *how* they are interlocked is poorly understood. I will mention only two observations in this regard: first, in many cases, we can experience that—at least locally—the spatial vividness

Figure 2.2
Pieter Jansz Saenredam, *Interior of the Saint Jacob Church in Utrecht*, 1642. Bayerische Staatsgemäldesammlungen, Alte Pinakothek, Munich. See plate 2 for color version.

gained by one aspect is lost by the other. Second, as Hagen and Jones (1978, p. 194) also pointed out, "the space behind the picture plane is not completely separated from the space of ordinary environment which surrounds the picture." For instance, Deregowski, Muldrow, and Muldrow (1972) observed an interesting effect of a horizontal versus a vertical presentation of a picture of a profiled standing buck. When the picture was presented lying flat on the ground, most observers reported that the buck was lying down; when it was presented vertically, they reported that the buck was standing up.

The proposals and corresponding observations by Maurice Pirenne (1970), James Farber and Richard Rosinski (1978), Michael Kubovy (1986), and others that the surface characteristics of the picture have to be available internally, in order to allow some kind of compensation process that corrects distortions caused by an inappropriate viewing geometry, also indicate that both representations are interlocked in complex and poorly understood ways. In other areas, such as color or brightness perception, we have a better theoretical understanding about how conjoint representations are interlocked.

The structural perceptual properties that we can identify in theoretical analyses of phenomena centering around the dual character of pictures cannot simply be regarded as kinds of "perceptual irregularities" that are due to encountering an artifactual situation. Rather, these phenomena seem to point in a particularly conspicuous way to a general perceptual capacity to deal with conjoint representations.

2.4   TRIGGERING AND PARAMETER SETTING: THE DUAL FUNCTION OF SENSORY INPUTS WITH RESPECT TO REPRESENTATIONAL PRIMITIVES

In perception theory we can roughly distinguish three aspects of architecture with respect to the relation of sensory inputs and internal representations: (1) Several kinds of input properties are exploited by the same kind of internal representation (e.g., computational theories of cue integration), (2) the same input property is independently exploited by several representations (e.g., in bees, color vision proper and wavelength-dependent behavior coexist and subserve independent representations,[12] cf. Goldsmith 1990), and (3) the same type of input property is exploited by conjoint representations over the same input (i.e., the *same* input can give rise to several *different* but interlocked output codes and to multiple simultaneous layers of representation). This last type of architecture can be expected to play a prominent role in highly versatile and complex perceptual systems that have to simultaneously subserve a great variety of tasks. Such systems must internally have the outputs of many subsystems available for purposes of a great variety of higher-order representations and thus have to provide computational means to handle conjoint representations over the same input.

In this section, I will briefly sketch a theoretical perspective on the structure of perceptual representations that I believe to be promising, both theoretically and empirically, for attempts to deal with conjoint representations. This approach is inspired by two general perspectives, which are related in some of their core ideas. The first perspective refers to the ideas underlying classic ethological approaches, notably of Jakob von Uexküll, Konrad Lorenz, and Nikolaas Tinbergen, and by the extension of these ideas to richer and more complex functions (e.g., Wehner 1987; Marler 1999; Gallistel 1998) than those studied in earlier years under the heading of "innate release mechanism."[13] An ethological perspective has, in its basic theoretical assumptions, also gained support from computational approaches. The second perspective is Noam Chomsky's (e.g., 2000) *internalist* inquiry into the nature of language and mind (which adhere to the maxim that in rational inquiries into mental phenomena there is no reason to deviate from the methodological principles routinely employed in other domains of the natural sciences with respect to other "natural objects"; a maxim that should be uncontroversial, yet, in the cognitive sciences, assumptions to the contrary still remain highly influential). Needless to say, the theoretical picture of the basic principles underlying perception that has been emerging in corresponding studies is still very skeletal and, of necessity, has to be based on considerable theoretical speculation. Yet, an ethology-inspired internalist approach, which focuses attention on the structure of the representational primitives underlying perception, seems to provide a promising framework for asking novel and potentially fruitful questions about the internal architecture of perception. Such an approach is also less susceptible to the *physicalistic trap* (Mausfeld 2002), which, in the history of perceptual psychology, has often hindered the asking of appropriate questions.

In perceptual psychology, a wealth of empirical and theoretical evidence has been marshalled by Gestalt psychology, Michotte's "experimental phenomenology",[14] ethology, studies of the newborns and young children, and computational approaches, evidence indicating that the structure of internal coding is built up in terms of a rich set of *representational primitives*. According to the theoretical picture that has emerged from corresponding studies, perception cannot be understood as the "recovery" of physical world structure from sensory structure by input-based computational processes. Rather, the sensory input serves as a kind of sign for biologically relevant aspects of the external world that elicits internal representations on the basis of given representational primitives. (Thus, even "highly impoverished" sensory inputs can trigger perceptual representations whose "complexity" far exceeds that of the triggering stimulus and whose relation to the sensory input can be contingent from the point of physics or geometry.) Although the sensory input is a causally necessary requirement for perceptual representations, the perceptual computations triggered are under the control of an internal program based on a set of representational primitives. They are representation driven rather than stimulus driven.

With respect to human perceptual capacities, this theoretical perspective and the evidence on which it is based suggest distinguishing, as an idealization, a sensory system from a perceptual system.[15] Whereas the sensory system deals with the transduction of physical energy into neural codes and their subsequent transformations into codes that are "readable" by and fulfill the needs of the perceptual system,[16] the perceptual system contains, as part of our biological endowment, the exceedingly rich perceptual vocabulary in terms of which we perceive the "external world" (whose relevant aspects pertain not only to physical and biological aspects but also to mental states of others). Furthermore, the perceptual system provides the computational means to make these perceptual concepts accessible to higher-order cognitive systems, where meanings are assigned in terms of external world properties. The sensory system interfaces directly with the motor system (this interface is evolutionarily an old one) as well as with the perceptual system, whereas the perceptual system interfaces with the motor system and higher-order cognitive systems. Because the sensory system provides, in terms of its physicogeometrical vocabulary, the cues that the perceptual system exploits in terms of its conceptual structure, issues of cue integration directly refer to the structure of the interface between the sensory system and the perceptual system. In contrast, issues of conjoint representations refer to structural properties of the perceptual system itself.

Although we are still far from having a clear theoretical picture of the kind of primitives that underlie perceptual representations, primitives such as "surfaces," "objects,"[17] or—as temporal analogs to "objects"—"events" (to be understood as *internal,* and not as physical concepts) seem to be among the fundamental pillars of the internal representational structure of perception. These primitives determine the data format, as it were, of internal coding. Each primitive has its own proprietary types of parameters, relations, and transformations that govern its relation to other primitives. The data structure for the internal representational primitive "surface,"[18] for instance, can be expected to include a set of free parameters, which refer to attributes such as "color," "depth," "texture," "orientation," and so on (again to be understood as *internal,* and not as physical attributes) and may also include specific primitive relations (which may correspond to, e.g., "junctions" and "edges" of various sorts, "concavities" and "convexities," "gaps," or "holes").

The values of the free parameters, which lie in a specific region of the corresponding parameter space, have to be determined by the sensory input (and are probably modulated by factors such as "attentional weight"). The sensory input thus serves a dual function: first, it provides triggering cues for which primitives are to be activated, and thus selects among potential data formats in terms of which input properties are to be exploited. Second, it triggers processes that result in a specification of the values of the free parameters of the activated representational primitive. Both aspects have to be dynamically interlocked. On the one hand, values can only be assigned to free parameters once the data format has been determined; on the other hand, the activation of a specific data format requires that the values assigned to the free parameters be in a permissible range and lie in a specific region of the corresponding parameter space (if certain types of parameters belong to more than one representational primitive, their values are likely constrained differently). For example, the wavelength information in a sensory input appears to be exploited by (at least) two different types of representational primitives, which we can tentatively refer to as "surface" and "ambient illumination" (again, to be understood as internal, *not* as physical concepts). The two data formats to which these primitives give rise both include a free parameter for "color."[19] Accordingly, we have to distinguish different types of "colors," depending on the particular primitive to which they belong. Colors that are attached to the representational primitive "ambient illumination" subserve a different function and exhibit different coding properties than colors attached to the representational primitive "surface" (cf. Mausfeld 2003). The values of the two different kinds of free parameters, which both contribute to the phenomenal attribute of color, are likely to be subject to different types of constraints.

Although the properties and interdependencies of the free parameters of representational primitives have to mirror, with respect to the perceptual system as an *entirety,* biologically relevant structural properties of the external world, empirical evidence strongly suggests that they are codetermined by internal aspects, such as internal functional constraints or internal architectural constraints, such as legibility requirements at interfaces. The complex and up-to-now poorly understood interdependencies of free parameters contribute to the fact that representational primitives defy definition in terms of a corresponding physical concept (even in the sense of the latter providing necessary and sufficient conditions for the former); rather, representational primitives have their own peculiar and yet-to-be identified relation to the sensory input and may also depend intrinsically on other representational primitives, in a way that cannot simply be derived from considerations of external regularities, however appropriately we have chosen our vocabulary for describing the external world.[20]

In inquiries into the nature of representational primitives, we can and, taking a specific subsystem of the organism as the unit of analysis, should actually avoid any notions of the "proper" object of perception and the "true" antecedents of the sensory input, among the infinite set of potential causal antecedents (though such notions are, of course, an indispensable part of both ordinary and metatheoretical discourse). The only physics of the external world that figures in a formal theory of visual perception is the physicogeometric properties of the incoming light array. In terms of these properties, we can completely characterize the relation of representational primitives to the sensory input, and thus their "proximal semantics," as it were, which can extensionally be understood as the equivalence classes of the physical input situations by which they were triggered. The proximal semantics of the perceptual system is, in other words, defined by its relation to the sensory system. The proximal semantics (as a purely syntactically defined feature) as well as structural relations among representational primitives are given by design and are thus essentially impervious to change by experience.

What is modifiable by experience are the values of certain parameters, the latitude of which is determined in a highly specific way that is proprietary to a structure of perceptual representations. Characteristic examples are provided by Hans Wallach and Eileen Karsh (1963), who showed that disparity-related parameters can be recalibrated by the kinetic depth effect, when disparity and motion provide inconsistent shape information, and by Joseph Atkins, Jozsef Fiser, and Robert Jacobs (2001), who showed—with respect to perceiving depth or 3-D shape from 2-D displays in which disks moved horizontally along the surface of a cylinder and exhibited corresponding gradients of texture element compression—that the differential weighting in the integration of visual cues is recalibrated by the corresponding correlations with haptic cues. In animal ethology, illustrative examples are the mechanisms by which birds learn to sing a song appropriate to their species and region (Marler 1999) or the learning of the solar ephemeris by bees, as part of a sun compass mechanism (cf. Gallistel 1998). In these cases, a structure of corresponding representational primitives has to allow for parameters whose values are based on a "calibration or checking procedure to insure that the values of those symbols do in fact accurately represent the values of the real world variables to which they refer" (Gallistel 1998, p. 10). For instance, a sun compass mechanism "has built into it what is universally true about the sun, no matter where one is on earth: it is somewhere in the east in the morning and somewhere in the west in the afternoon. Learning the solar ephemeris is simply a matter of adjusting the parameters of this universal ephemeris function so as to make it fit the locally observed motion of the sun" (Gallistel 2000, p. 1183). In the case of the human perceptual system, the ontogenetic plasticity, provided by specific structures of representational primitives, cannot, of course, be understood solely on the basis of physical considerations of this kind.

With respect to the structural interdependencies of the free parameters that are potentially involved in a certain input situation, we can, for the purpose of our discussion, distinguish the case dealing with how different parameters of a specific type of representational primitive are interlocked in a certain situation from the more complex case dealing with how parameters of the same type are interlocked in conjoint representations.

When different aspects of the visual input are exploited by the *same* type of representational primitives, for example "surface" representations, we can encounter situations involving competing interlocked parameters, say for size and distance,[21] orientation and form, or motion direction and form (which can phenomenally be mirrored in multistable or vague percepts). A change in the value of one type of parameter, say for coding depth, can, even in cases of otherwise identical stimulus conditions, require strong changes in other types of parameters, say for coding motion direction or 3-D form. The demonstration by Erich von Hornbostel (1922) using a wireframe cube is a particularly striking classical example showing that a change in parameters for motion direction—and a concomitant change in depth parameters—constrains form parameters in a way compatible only with nonrigid transformations of form (see also Wallach and Karsh 1963; Wallach, Weisz, and Adams 1956).

Similar observations have been pervasively made with respect to other attributes (e.g., Schwartz and Sperling 1983; Dosher, Sperling, and Wurst 1986; Kersten et al. 1992). For instance, motion can codetermine color in various ways (Hoffman 2003; Nijhawan 1997), and Ken Nakayama, Shinsuke Shimojo, and Vilayanur Ramachandran observed that "[i]f perceived transparency is triggered, a number of seemingly more elemental perceptual primitives such as color, contour, and depth can be radically altered" (1990, p. 497). In many of these cases we do not know yet whether we are dealing with the problem of how the different free parameters of a *single* representational primitive are interlocked, or with the problem of how representational primitives of the same (or similar) type are interlocked. As a rough experimental diagnostic, one might conjecture that cases in which small changes in a relevant attribute of the input cause radical changes in other attributes indicate situations in which several representational primitives are involved.

Representations that form a conjoint structure are of particular theoretical interest in the present context. In the case of conjoint representations the same aspects of the visual input are simultaneously exploited by two or more representational primitives of the same type or of different types, whose parameter spaces overlap.

In sufficiently complex perceptual systems with a high degree of representational versatility a given (and sufficiently rich) sensory input is not likely to elicit only a single representational primitive but rather to trigger conjoint representations. Conjoint representations require special mechanisms and computational means to handle the interlocked way in which they exploit the same input.

2.5   CONJOINT REPRESENTATIONS AS A GENERAL STRUCTURAL PROPERTY OF OUR BASIC COGNITIVE ARCHITECTURE

In picture perception, a physicalistically misconstrued framing of the problem of the dual nature of pictures highlighted an interesting class of phenomena while it at the same time obstructing the way to theoretically deal with these phenomena in a fruitful way. Once general properties of such phenomena are explored on a sufficient level of abstraction, it becomes obvious that cognitive science teems with corresponding phenomena, which witness, it seems to me, our cognitive capability to simultaneously handle conjoint representations over the same input. First, I will illustrate corresponding phenomena with some examples from visual psychophysics, where one can find a plenitude of corresponding examples indicating that a given sensory input triggers conjoint representations. Afterward, I will briefly turn to more complex domains, where I must inevitably resign to point out, in a more or less allusive manner, some structural similarities with respect to the issues under scrutiny. For each of these examples, I will first try to identify potential candidates for representational primitives that are integrated in an interlocked way with respect to the same input and then provide, in an unsystematic manner, some observations that speak in favor of corresponding candidates.

Examples from Visual Psychophysics

Depth   We presently do not know much about the representational primitives underlying representations for space and depth. The available evidence suggests that there are, in addition to "surfaces," probably several quite different representational primitives whose data format is primarily determined by some depth-related parameters.[22] Representational primitives for local or distant "ambient space,"[23] or for dealing with "flat" spatial situations could be regarded as candidates for these representational primitives. Three observations may suffice to illustrate corresponding issues.

1. In a picture, we can see an object as partly occluded but still intact. This can be interpreted as a case of a 2-D surface representation competing with a shallow 3-D object representation. Even a simple figure-ground situation, such as Edgar Rubin's vase, exhibits a very flat 3-D appearance; the "perceived depth separation between figure and ground has not been well understood," as Naomi Weisstein and Eva Wong (1986, p. 33) rightly noted.

2. Even when cues carrying a strong internal weight, such as occlusion, are violated in a way that is globally incoherent with an interpretation in terms of a physically distant scene, representational primitives with depth-related free parameters can still be activated and provide an impression of space and depth. Reńe Magritte's 1965 painting *Le blanc-seing* (depicting a lady on a horse within an assemblage of trees) may serve as an

illustration of this. In this painting, occlusion cues that are globally incompatible are provided by locally switching foreground and background, without, however, entirely blocking a depth interpretation (though the resulting impression is a peculiar one). This applies even more so for cues that do not seem to carry a strong internal weight, such as *linear* perspective or global 3-D incoherence of local depth cues (as in so-called impossible figures). Also in this case, a shallow 3-D object representation may compete with a 2-D surface representation.

3. Often representational primitives of the same type seem to be involved in conjoint representations within different frames of reference, as it were. In picture perception, the representational primitive "surface" is involved both with respect to the perception of the picture surface plane and with respect to the perception of the scene depicted. In this case, different "surface" representations compete for the depth information that is provided by the incoming sensory input. In the context of picture perception, the visual system seems to have a preference for assigning the differential depth information that is available in the incoming light array to the scene depicted. If the canvas itself exhibits (suitably chosen) differences in physical depth, the physical depth signal of the medium, that is, the canvas, tends to be internally assigned to the scene depicted. Consequently, the canvas itself looks flat while the picture undergoes corresponding "distortions." Striking examples are provided by the paintings of Patrick Hughes (cf. Wade and Hughes 1999).

Color and Brightness As depth-related parameters appear, in a highly tangled way, in multitudinous internal representations, it is difficult to identify, in a specific case, the conjoint representations involved. The situation is less complicated when we are dealing with color- and brightness-related parameters. Here, phenomenological observations on the interplay of surfaces and (chromatic) illumination as well as corresponding physical considerations provide a rich source for theoretical conjectures about basic conjoint representations. They suggest that the perceptual attributes "color" and "brightness" are part of the data format of two different but interlocked representational primitives.[24] They can figure as free parameters with respect to the representational primitive "surface" as well as the representational primitive "ambient illumination." Both representational primitives thus form a conjoint representation with respect to the free parameters "color" and "brightness." The corresponding regions in the parameters spaces of these two representational primitives overlap. The visual system then has to provide computational means to deal with sensory inputs that are compatible with different parameter combinations in this joint region.[25]

The interplay of the two representational primitives involved is phenomenally mirrored in many peculiarities that are characteristic for color appearances under (chromatic) illumination. Of particular interest among these is what Hermann von Helmholtz called seeing two colors "*at the same location* of the visual field one behind the other" (1867, p. 407) and what Karl Bühler referred to as "locating colors in perceptual space one behind the other" (1922, p. 40; cf. Fuchs 1923a). For instance, in a room illuminated by a reddish light, we can "see" both the color of the object (e.g., "white" wall) and the color of the illumination, though there is, as David Katz observed, a "curious lability of colors under chromatic illumination" (1911, p. 274). Similar observations hold, with respect to brightness, for the appearance of surfaces on which a shadow is cast. I will briefly mention a few other observations that seem to be of relevance for attempting to understand the internal structure underlying color and brightness perception.

1. The dual nature of color coding that results from the exploitation of the input by two different kinds of representational primitives is perceptually mirrored in what, since Katz's (1911) groundbreaking work, has been called "modes of appearance," in particular a "surface color" mode and an "aperture or light color" mode. This descriptive taxonomy, which itself is in need of explanation by some deeper principles, has unfortunately often been called upon as an explanation itself, thereby confusing the observation with its explanation.

2. The phenomenal dissociation of brightness and grayness also suggests different representational primitives in which "brightness" figures as a parameter. Since Hering, is has been well known that even for achromatic colors at least a bidimensional account is necessary, as can be witnessed by appearances such as luminous gray. With respect to painting, the difference between a "brightish white" and a "whitish bright" is crucial and has been recognized as such since painters became interested in representing the effects of light (Schöne 1954, p. 203).

3. The Mach card or Ewald Hering's "stain versus shadow" demonstration *(Fleckschattenversuch)* are typical classical phenomena that demonstrate how certain attributes can modulate the relation between different representational primitives that exploit a given sensory input. In Hering's demonstrations slight changes in figural characteristics of the Alberti

window, namely, masking of the penumbra of a shadow by a dark line, are sufficient to induce a switch to a "surface" representation that completely exhausts the information related to brightness. This is even the case when the physical construction of the situation—that is, light source, shadow-casting object, and the process of drawing the boundary—is completely transparent to the subject. The available perceptual and cognitive "interpretations" are completely overruled by a single geometric characteristic.[26]
4. The coding properties pertaining to a representational primitive "ambient illumination" (or transmission medium) resemble, and are probably related to, coding properties of the "ground" in figure-ground segmentations (cf. Kaila 1928).

Surfaces and Objects   Representational primitives of "surfaces" (cf. Nakayama, He, and Shimojo 1995) and "objects" seem to be among the pillars of the internal conceptual structure of the perceptual system. Hence, it is likely that they themselves are differentiated into families of corresponding primitives that are intertwined in complex ways. From the many types of observations that pertain to this issue I will, in an unsystematic way, mention only three examples.

1. There are situations where we can simultaneously see two surfaces at the same "location" of the visual field. For instance, looking out of a train window at dusk, we can simultaneously see a red hat on the hat rack and a green tree at the same location in the window. In psychophysics we can find, as Franz Faul (1997) did with respect to chromatic transparency, transitions between transparent and opaque representations of surfaces, or, as Patrick Cavanagh (1987) found, conditions under which surfaces are simultaneously opaque and transparent.
2. With respect to conjoint "object" representations striking phenomena can be encountered in cases where representational primitives that refer to different levels within some "hierarchy of organization" are involved, as in the previously mentioned case of so-called impossible figures. An example of other phenomena that can be interpreted along these line are those, referred to as *object superiority effects,* that show that coding properties, such as threshold, detection, or identification performance, with respect to elements of the same local stimulus configuration, depend critically upon whether this element is an essential part of an "object" representation (Gelb 1921; Lenk 1926; Weisstein and Harris 1974; Gorea and Julesz 1990). On a more abstract level, the process of reading itself seems to be based on an exploitation of a corresponding capacity.

3. The most general class of phenomena that are likely to be caused by conjoint representations are those traditionally referred to as phenomena of figure-ground ambiguity. The Gestaltists rightly stressed that the figure-ground organization, which refers to internal, mental aspects, not to aspects of the sensory input, belongs to the most fundamental aspects of perception.[27] They also observed that different figure-ground organizations for identical sensory inputs would give rise to strong changes in a variety of other factors such as thresholds or perceptual attributes (e.g., Fuchs 1923b; Gelb and Granit 1923). Within the framework put forth here, a change in the figure-ground organization for the same input is regarded as the phenomenal effect of the working of more basic principles that refer to the structure and interplay of competing conjoint representations.

Examples from Other Areas of Cognitive Science

Properties of the architecture of internal representations that have to do with conjoint representations become even more important when the faculties in question have to fulfill, on the basis of a given sensory input, more complex achievements, such as the perception of emotional expressions or the ability to impute mental states to self and to others. As not much is presently known about the specific data format of representational primitives underlying visual representations, this situation vastly deteriorates when we turn to other areas of cognitive science, beyond vision and language. I will therefore resign myself to listing a few instances that appear to me to share, with respect to the issue of conjoint representations, interesting structural similarities. If these similarities are not merely superficial but rather are grounded in deeper structural properties of our cognitive architecture—and I think there are good reasons to assume so—their careful disclosure would facilitate the identification of theoretical issues that are of great relevance to cognitive science.

Language and Meaning   Our ability to internally handle conjoint representations appears to be mirrored in various ways in language use. Corresponding conjectures appear to gain some plausibility when we deal with how we linguistically handle what is provided by our perceptual system. Many of the examples from visual psychophysics mentioned earlier implicitly bear on this issue. A more explicit example is provided by the way in which we can simultaneously handle deictic-versus-intrinsic, and object-centered versus viewer-centered frames of reference when we are talking about spatial relations (cf. Levelt 1984; Jackendoff 1987).

With respect to language and meaning, observations of "conflicting perspectives" abound. Although they are undoubtedly of great theoretical importance, it is not easy to assess whether and to what extent an analysis in terms of conjoint representations is appropriate in these cases (and, more generally, how to conceive of the relation between the "internal semantics" of the perceptual system and the lexical semantics in the Chomskyan sense). Because the structural similarities between these two cases appear striking to me, I will, all the same, briefly mention two of them.

In the semantics of natural languages (in the Chomskyan sense of I-languages), the internal conditions governing the meaning of words can encompass simultaneously mutually exclusive aspects of concreteness and abstractness to which we can refer, in using the word, at the same time. "The notion *book* can be used to refer to something that is simultaneously abstract and concrete, as in the expression *The book that I'm writing will weigh 5 pounds*" (Chomsky 1995, p. 236). It seems to be a pervading characteristic of natural languages that "a lexical item provides us with a certain range of perspectives for viewing what we take to be the things in the world" (Chomsky 2000, p. 36) and that "quite typically, words offer conflicting perspectives" (ibid., p. 126). For example, "I can paint the door to the kitchen brown, so it is plainly concrete; but I can walk through the door to the kitchen, switching figure and ground. The baby can finish the bottle and break it, switching contents and container with fixed intended reference" (ibid., p. 128).

These and other observations probably point, or so I believe, to interesting similarities between the structure of the lexicon and the structure of the representational primitives of the perceptual system. In language, lexical items provide us with a certain perspective for viewing what we take to be the things in the world; they are "like filters or lenses, providing ways of looking at things" (ibid., p. 36). The same characterization applies, on this level of abstraction, to the perceptual system. Its fixed set of representational primitives provide, as a perceptual ontology, as it were, a set of concepts or a perceptual vocabulary by which the signs delivered by the sensory system are exploited in terms of notions such as "surface," "physical object," "intentional object," "potential actors," "self," "other person," or "event" (with respect to a great variety of different categories and time scales), with their appropriate attributes such as "color," "shape," "depth," or "emotional state" and their appropriate relations such as "causation" or "intention." In this regard, the structure of the perceptual system seems, in humans, to resemble more the structure of language (more precisely, the structure of the lexicon of I-language) than the structure of the sensory system.[28]

The rich conceptual structure of the perceptual system, which extends far beyond physical aspects of the external world, links the signs provided by the sensory system to the conceptual structure of language and of other cognitive systems. The structure of the lexicon, where "notions like actor, recipient of action, instrument, event, intention, causation and others are pervasive elements of lexical structure, with their specific properties and interrelations" (Chomsky 2000, p. 62), seems to partly mirror (and extend) the conceptual structure of the perceptual system. The representational primitives of the perceptual system and their structure have, in a cognitive system as complex as ours, to ensure an appropriate fit of data formats at the corresponding interface. The property of the lexicon that its items typically offer *conflicting perspectives* on what we take to be the things in the world probably has its counterpart, so I'm inclined to speculate, in the structural organization of the perceptual system in terms of conjoint representations of its representational primitives.

Another, and even more complex, case in point is the use of allegories in oral or written expositions. Their specific properties, as well as the ranges within which they can be employed, probably also reflect the capacity to handle conjoint representations, which bear, respectively, on the relation of medium and message, as it were. Allegories provide a way of expressing something differently from the literal meanings that are used *(aliud dicitur, aliud demonstratur)*. For all relevant elements of the exposition they provide two interpretations at the same time, one literal interpretation *(sensus litteralis)* and one actually intended more abstract interpretation *(sensus allegoricus)*. One has to understand both at the same time. The literal meaning serves as a kind of semantic medium to trigger the intended superordinate meaning. Similar considerations apply to allegorical meaning in pictorial art, as illustrated in figures 2.3 and 2.4.

Here, the visual input is exploited by representational primitives that deal with concrete physical objects, as well as by other representational primitives that deal with the perception of social relations and that read through this level of representation and exploit the input in more abstract terms. In the pictures displayed, these abstract terms refer to the "nature" of social order, as it were.

The allegorical character of figure 2.4 may appear less obvious, because the objects that figure in the literal interpretation, which refers to people in the Russian concentration camp Kolyma, belong to the same category

Figure 2.3
Pieter Brueghel the Elder, *The Big Fishes Eat the Small Fishes*, 1557, copperplate
engraving, FM 1365, Rijksmuseum, Amsterdam.

Figure 2.4
Gerd Arntz, *Kolyma,* 1952, linocut, private collection.

as the ones that figure in the actually intended interpretation, which refers to the threatening of the individual by the terror of the state.

The pictures displayed demonstrate again that we cannot understand the use of allegories solely in terms of representational primitives. Rather, highly complex interactions of our perceptual faculty and various interpretative faculties are involved, about which we presently know next to nothing, within the framework of cognitive science.

Pretense Play   In pretense play, which is a case of *acting as if,* in which the pretender correctly perceives the actual situation, we are also dealing with a case where the same situation is simultaneously exploited by two different representational structures. These structures compete, because, as Alan Leslie put it, "typically the pretense representation contradicts the primary representation" (1987, p. 415). (This contradiction, however, always remains, as Johan Huizinga (1938/1986) noted in another context, constantly fluctuating.) The structural similarity between drama, as a special case of pretense play, and the dual nature of painting was emphasized by Michotte and Michael Polanyi. In the "duplication of space and time that occurs in theatrical representation," Michotte noted, "the space of the scene seems to be the space in which the represented events are actually taking, or have taken, place and yet it is also continuous with the space of the theatre itself. Similarly for time also, instants, intervals, and successions for the spectators belong primarily to the events they are watching, but they are left nevertheless in their own present. A further peculiar phenomenon that vividly confirms the unreal character of the representation concerns the way in which an interval, which really lasts usually a matter of minutes or seconds, comes by this process of transportation to have the apparent significance of days, months, or even years" (1960/1991, p. 191 f.). And Polanyi (1970a, p. 231) observed that "the painting's self-contradictory flat-depth has its counterpart here in equally paradoxical stage murders and other such stage scenes.... Art appears to consist, for painting as for drama, in representing a subject within an artificial framework which contradicts its representational aspects."

In infant development spontaneous pretense play emerges at a quite early stage (at about twelve months), and quickly reaches a state, at about the age of three, where children are able to engage in complex fantasies involving imaginary objects, animals, or people. Furthermore, children are also able to understand the pretense play of other (e.g., Harris and Kavanaugh 1993).

An explanatory account of pretense play poses, as Leslie (1987) rightly observed, deeper puzzles than reality-oriented play, which responds to an object's actual properties or expresses knowledge about its conventional use: "How is it possible for a child to think about a banana as if it were a telephone, a lump of plastic as if it were alive, etc. If a representational system is developing, how can its semantic relations tolerate distortions in these more or less arbitrary ways. Indeed how is it possible that young children can disregard or distort reality in any way and to any degree at all? Why does pretending not undermine their representational system and bring it crashing down?" (Leslie 1987, p. 412). Unlike the cases of the dual character of pictures or the dual nature of color coding, pretense play cannot be understood by referring to an "ability to coordinate two primary representations" (ibid., p. 414) of the same situation. Rather, pretend representations "are in effect not representations of the world but representations of representations" (ibid., p. 417), which makes pretense play a case where a primary representational structure (which deals with how the situation is actually perceived) competes with a superordinate representation or *metarepresentation* (which deals with what the pretense is).

Imputing Mental States to Others and Perspective Taking   A perceptual system by definition serves to couple the organism to biologically relevant aspects of the external world. For an organism with a mental structure as rich as ours the relevant aspects of the external world pertain not only to physical and biological aspects but also to the mental states of others. The world as we conceive it comprises not only objects and surfaces with their perceptual attributes but also emotional states and intentions of others. From an ethological perspective one can reasonably expect that there is, with respect to the architecture and functioning of the perceptual system, no fundamental difference between perceiving aspects of the physical world and aspects of the mental states of others. In either case the sensory input serves as a sign for biologically relevant aspects of the external world that elicits internal representations on the basis of given representational primitives.

Evidently and not unexpectedly, the capability to mentally interact with others is part of the newborn's biological endowment that quickly matures to a state where the child can impute mental states to oneself and to others. The ability to mentally interact with others rests on representational primitives (whose nature is still at the boundary of scientific elucidation) that have their proprietary ways of exploiting the sensory input. It

Figure 2.5
Sergei Eisenstein, *Potemkin,* 1926, still from the "Odessa steps" sequence, New York, the Museum of Modern Art, Film Stills Archive.

is an essential characteristic of the way these primitives exploit the sensory input that they go "beyond" those physicogeometrical properties of the sensory input that are exploited by primitives dealing with the physical world. They go beyond what may be called *physical surface characteristics* of the situation encountered and bear on a more abstract construal of this situation. We can see the eyes of a person and the direction of that person's gaze, and we see a person's face and simultaneously see that person being angry or fearful. Figures 2.5 and 2.6 may illustrate this, both with respect to a static 2-D representation of a real face and a drawing that depicts a culturally shaped abstraction of a face.

From the rich empirical evidence that is available I will only mention one experiment on complex imitation behavior, by Andrew Meltzoff (1995). Meltzoff investigated, in a suitably constructed and controlled experimental setting, whether eighteen-month-old infants interpret "behavior in purely physical terms or whether they too read through the literal body movements to the underlying goal or intention of the act" (ibid., p. 839). In the critical test situation infants were confronted with an adult

Figure 2.6
Pablo Picasso, *Weeping Woman,* 1937, etching, aquatint, and drypoint on paper,
Paris, Musée Picasso. © Photo RMN—Gérard Blot.

who merely demonstrated the "intention" to act in a certain way, using entirely unfamiliar objects, but never fulfilled this intention. The adult tried but failed to perform a specific target act, so the end state was never reached and thus remained unobserved by the child. For instance, for the object pair that consisted of a horizontal prong that protruded from a gray plastic screen and a nylon loop, the experimenter "picked up the loop, but as he approached the prong, he released it inappropriately so that it 'accidentally' dropped to the table surface each time. First, the loop was released slightly too far to the left, then too far to the right, and finally too low, where it fell to the table directly below the prong. The goal state of draping the nylon loop over the prong was not demonstrated" (ibid., p. 841).

The recorded responses of the infants, namely, the number of children who produced the target act, capitalized on toddler's natural tendency to pick up behavior from adults and to reenact and imitate what they see. Interestingly, "infants were as likely to perform the target act after seeing the adult 'trying' as they were after seeing the real demonstration of the behavior itself" (ibid., p. 845). They did not reenact what the adult literally did but rather what he intended to do (they did not produce the target acts when the physics of the situation, i.e., the movements that are traced in space, were performed by an inanimate device). The type of interaction exemplified in this experiment gives rise to a situation that triggers representational primitives that deal with mental interactions and with the perception of mental states of others. In such situations a kind of *reading-through* with respect to the physical surface characteristics is made possible, which allows the system to organize these characteristics in terms of more abstract mental representations.

A similar reading-through with respect to physical surface characteristics underlies mirror self-recognition. This is an achievement that can only occur when corresponding representational primitives for a self-representation are available, which are interlocked with those that deal with the physical surface situation. Whereas most monkey species under most conditions do not show mirror self-recognition (Tomasello and Call 1997, p. 336), in humans the relevant representational primitives underlying mirror self-recognition have matured by the age of about twenty months.

There are many other cases of highly complex mental achievements, such as the development of the appearance-reality distinction in young children (e.g., Flavell, Flavell, and Green 1983), whose structural

Figure 2.7
Enrico Baj, *I funerali dell'anarchico Pinelli,* 1972, etching and aquatint, private collection. It depicts the "defenestration" of the Italian anarchist Guiseppe Pinelli
from the Milan police headquarters on December 15, 1969, after the bomb attack
by right-wing extremists at the Piazza Fontana.

properties probably can abstractly be described in terms of (unknown)
conjoint representations, which also may compete for the same input. An
important class of representational primitives that have to be assumed as
an internal representational skeleton for perception are also those that
deal with dynamic situations or temporally organized events with respect
to various types of "objects" (e.g., Zacks and Tversky 2001). With respect
to picture perception this can be illustrated by the etching displayed
in figure 2.7, where the scene depicted is perceived as a single moment
within a sequence of events, and the time slices *not* depicted are as important for what is perceived as the one that is depicted.

Structural similarities between these cases appear to suggest that conjoint representations and corresponding transformational structures for
properly handling them internally are a fundamental property of our perceptual system. On higher levels of the cognitive system, this property may
have its counterpart in our pervading capacity to simultaneously take
conflicting perspectives in "looking at things and thinking about the
products of our minds" (Chomsky 2000, p. 36). Although an attempt to
fit the aforementioned pieces into the theme of conjoint representations is,
inevitably, already highly speculative, with respect to the perceptual system, our general capacity to handle simultaneous, conflicting perspectives
will almost certainly lie beyond the reach of such attempts. As Chomsky

put it: "What we take as objects, how we refer to them and describe them, and the array of properties with which we invest them, depend on their place on a matrix of human actions, interest, and intent in respects that lie far outside the potential range of naturalistic inquiry" (2000, p. 21). With respect to those aspects that we hope are within the reach of naturalistic inquiry we can, in situations of poor theoretical understanding, only entrust ourselves to Helmholtz's guiding principle that "order and coherence, even if they ground on untenable principles, are to be preferred to the disorder and incoherence of a mere collection of facts" (1867, p. VI).

Whatever the specific nature of the representational primitives of the perceptual system turns out to be, their categorical character necessitates, from a functionalist point of view, additional general mechanisms for handling continuous transitions in the sensory input, as well as for providing, whenever appropriate, smooth transitions between internal categories. Corresponding questions are of particular relevance with respect to conjoint representations. I will therefore briefly address this issue using examples from visual perception.

2.6   VAGUENESS, SMOOTH TRANSITIONS BETWEEN REPRESENTATIONAL PRIMITIVES, AND THE NEED OF A "PROXIMAL MODE"

The relation of representational primitives to the sensory input has, in an idealized way, been described in preceding sections in terms of the equivalence classes of physical situations by which they are triggered, or, equivalently, in terms of equivalence classes of output codes of the sensory system. However, such an idealization is evidently inappropriate, because it would result in a cognitive architecture with functionally undesirable properties. Instead, we have to assume, in line with empirical evidence, that the equivalence classes of physical situations by which representational primitives are triggered have "fuzzy boundaries," which, in general, yield smooth triggering characteristics both with respect to the relation of a single representational primitive to its triggering class of inputs as well as with respect to transitions between representational primitives that exploit the same input. Because triggering a representational primitive is tantamount to exploiting the sensory input (or the output of the sensory system) in terms of a specific data format with a specific set of free parameters, corresponding "smoothness" requirements apply, as a rule, to the mappings of physical input features to values of the free parameters.

Usually, in a given input situation (which can also include dynamic sequences of inputs) there is a latitude whose extent is determined by the structure of the joint parameter spaces involved, as to which representational primitives could be triggered and which values could be assigned to their free parameters; a latitude that corresponds to an ambiguity about which of potential external situations could have given rise to the sensory input. By way of illustration, think, with respect to distance and size, of the Ames room, or, with respect to surface color and illumination color, of a white wall under reddish illumination and a reddish wall under white illumination that both give rise to the same sensory input. In such cases the visual system often exhibits a preference for some "default interpretations." These preferences can be expected to partly mirror different probabilities with which a certain sensory input can be caused, under "normal" ecological conditions, by different external scenes. However, such ecological probabilities do not solely or even predominantly determine "default interpretations," as the cases of the Ames room and the Hornbostel demonstration illustrate. Rather, internal constraints that result from various kinds of stability requirements are, in cases where different combinations of values can be assigned to the free parameters, likely to play a crucial role in singling out default interpretations.

Choices between potential values of the free parameters could be made by a strategy by which global changes, following small variations in the input (or in the vantage point), in the representational primitives triggered and in the values of their free parameters are, intuitively speaking, kept at a minimum, particularly at the interfaces of the perceptual system with the motorial system and with higher cognitive systems. By such a strategy global stability of superordinate representations could be maintained. Such a strategy would protect the system from settling, under "impoverished" situations, on some definite interpretation that would have to be changed to an entirely different interpretation following a small variation in the input. In input situations whose properties are compatible with various combinations of values of the free parameters (of representational primitives of the same or of different types), transitions between different interpretations often appear to be to some extent receptive to modulations by attentional mechanisms.

Color perception appears to be a particularly conspicuous case of conjoint representations. Because the same characteristics, with respect to color or brightness, of a light array reaching the eye can be physically produced in many different ways (e.g., by either a certain interaction of physical surfaces and light sources or, using a slide or a CRT [cathode-ray tube] screen, by light sources alone). Representational primitives that subserve different distal interpretations, as it were, compete, on the basis of relevant cues, for the same input. These different but interlocked representational primitives, in which "color" and "brightness" figure as free parameters, were referred to earlier as "surface" representation and "ambient illumination" representation. Phenomena related to color and brightness perception provide rich evidence for the way transitions between representational primitives are handled internally. In the classical literature, corresponding observations were carefully described and their importance was properly acknowledged, despite the fact that a suitable theoretical framework for dealing with them was lacking. Katz, Adhémar Gelb, Hans Wallach, and many others described a plenitude of situations in which "very small changes in external stimulus conditions or in internal modes of perceiving" are accompanied by continuous transitions between conjoint representations, or—as Gelb put it with respect to color —between internal states that are "of essentially different nature" (1929, p. 600). For example, Turhan (1937, p. 46) observed that, under his experimental conditions, brightness gradients can simultaneously give rise to two incompatible percepts, one of a curved surface (as would result from an "interpretation" of the sensory input in terms of a specific nonhomogeneous illumination) and another one of a slanted flat surface (as would result from an "interpretation" of the same sensory input in terms of a homogeneous illumination). However, the triggering strength of the sensory input does not suffice to tighten an unambiguous "interpretation" in terms of either of the representational primitives involved. The internal vagueness with respect to the representational primitives involved is, as Turhan noted, perceptually mirrored in a peculiar impression of perceptual vagueness and indeterminacy.

In color perception, we can deal with the interplay of the conjoint representations involved—more specifically, with the relation between the corresponding free color parameters—in terms of the idealized functional goals of illumination invariance and scene invariance of the surface color at a scene location. Because the same sensory input can be compatible with quite different combinations of values of the free parameters (which mirrors the different ways in which the input could have been causally generated) and thus give rise to different functional achievements, the system has to guarantee smooth modulations, under small input variations, of the relations between the representational primitives involved and thus to provide at least a partial compensation between the relevant free parameters. A simple observation that witnesses a corresponding property is provided by the fact that, for instance, a green light (or a greenish ambient illumination) and an olive-green surface, whose colors are yielded by free parameters of different representational primitives, exhibit some phenomenological similarity, although the classes of appearances these two primitives give rise to could, in principle, have been completely divorced from each other.

An important consequence of the requirement of ensuring smooth transitions between conjoint representations is the existence of what is called a "proximal mode" in perception. The existence of a proximal mode is, as Rock noted, "not merely of interest as a phenomenological nicety but rather has important ramifications for a thorough-going theory of perceptual constancy" (1983, p. 254). Evidently, once we have attained the ability to exercise a suitable "mental attitude," we can perceptually detach certain attributes from their "frame of reference" as given by a specific representational primitive in which these attributes figure. For instance, a coin lying on the ground at some distance from the observer and being viewed at a slant is perceived as being circular in shape and of its usual size. Still, we can also see it, in the proximal mode, as an elliptical shape of diminutive size. In the same vein, railroad tracks that recede from the observer toward the horizon are perceived as being parallel. Still, we can also see them, in the proximal mode, as converging toward the horizon. Attributes that figure in both types of conjoined representations can, apparently, be dissociated from aspects that are proprietary to each of the representations involved. Thus, the existence of a proximal mode helps to protect the system from adopting a behavior where small continuous changes in the input result in abrupt changes in internal representations.

It is important to note that only those aspects necessitated by corresponding continuity considerations are accessible to a proximal mode. There is no proximal mode in the sense of a measurement device misconception of perception, or in the sense of the (entirely obscure) notion of a kind of retinal seeing (there is, for instance, no proximal mode for a veridical seeing of isolated elements of so-called geometrical illusions). Rather, what can figure in a proximal mode is entirely determined by the structure of conjoint representations involved.

In color perception, for instance, the proximal mode percept corresponds to that combination of potential values for the free color parameters of both representations involved that is determined by the internal assumption of a "canonical" or default situation, which, in this case, would correspond to a spatially homogeneous illumination that does not chromatically deviate from a "normal" one. The small decontextualized color patches underlying colorimetry are, with respect to the representational primitives involved, a degenerate situation that is closely related to the proximal mode. Because such isolated patches proved very useful for investigations into functions of the sensory system that pertain to color, they often are misleadingly regarded as the building blocks of color perception. In terms of the representational primitives involved, these isolated patches correspond to in-between stages of *internal* vagueness—which is not to be confused with perceptual vagueness (there is no perceptual vagueness in these cases)—where the system has not yet been able to settle on a data structure in terms of these primitives.

The percept yielded by the proximal mode is sometimes referred to as the "local color quale." In many situations, one can focus attention on the local color quale as such, or on color as a property of surfaces (cf. Arend and Goldstein 1987); for instance, a spot appearing gray when seen in the first mode of attention may appear as a shadowed part of a white object or a illuminated part of a black one in the second mode. Situations like these, in which it is possible to produce, by slight changes in the mode of attention, transitions where the "surface gains in whiteness to the same extent that the illumination looses brightness" are, as Gelb rightly noted, of "particular theoretical importance" (1929, p. 600). As in picture perception, where we can, with respect to depth, simultaneously have the phenomenal impression of two different types of objects, each of which seems to thrive in its own autonomous spatial framework, we can also, with respect to color or brightness, encounter situations where we seem to have two mutually incompatible representations at the same time, between which we can, to a certain extent, switch to and fro.

With respect to depth, it is much more difficult than it is with color to identify representational primitives in which depth figures as a parameter and that are interlocked to form conjoint representations. For biologically crucial internal attributes such as "depth," the corresponding spatial representations are based on a high redundancy from many subsystems in order to guarantee a stable representation even in situations where internal and external conditions deteriorate. In the case of depth, it is particularly difficult to distinguish (1) cases of cue integration with respect to the same instance of a representational primitive, say, a specific "surface" representation, (2) cases in which several representational primitives of the same type are interlocked or compete (e.g., several "surface" representations in a transparency situation), or (3) cases in which representational primitives of different types are interlocked in conjoint representations. The requirement of smooth corresponding transitions is, however, of importance in each of these cases.

Potential candidates for different and probably conjoint representations in which "depth" figures as a parameter are, on the one hand, those that deal with the (entirely relative) spatial layout of a scene (e.g., those underlying the kinetic depth effect) and, on the other hand, those that deal with egocentric distance in a full-fledged ambient 3-D space. There also seem to be specific mechanisms subserving "flat" representations by ignoring certain aspects of 3-D structure. For many tasks and operations, the availability of a full-fledged 3-D representation is not necessary or can even be an impediment. Nevertheless, the visual system cannot simply discard the corresponding information but has to keep it available internally, because slight changes in the retinal input might require access to 3-D representations. As in the case of color, this handling of multiple representations can phenomenally be either imperceptible or it can be mirrored in multistability or in perceptual vagueness. All of these phenomenal accompaniments can be encountered in picture perception just as much as in other areas of perception. Picture perception is not special, neither with respect to this property nor with respect to other perceptual principles. Like all perceptual tasks that involve human artifacts, it rests on and exploits the complex interactions of given perceptual structures and—most notably in the case of nonnaturalistic paintings—of various interpretative faculties, whose properties are at present only poorly understood. Among these properties is the ability to phenomenally access the different "layers" of conjoint representations or to exercise attentional control over them, within the narrow constraints set by the system. Artifacts depend on human intentions, and their use is therefore subject to interpretation; this holds for TV screens, microscopes, books, or pictures. One has to understand what they were designed for; nevertheless, they exploit given capacities. From the perspective of the cognitive sciences, picture perception does not constitute a domain of phenomena bound together by some domain-specific explanatory principles. Only when we have become aware that a classification of phenomena in terms of "picture perception" relies on a pretheoretical commonsense taxonomy can phenomena of picture perception prove fruitful for directing our theoretical attention to structural properties of our mental architecture that we otherwise find difficult to notice because they are an all pervading property of the way we are designed.

ACKNOWLEDGMENT

I should like to thank Franz Faul and Johannes Andres for comments on an earlier draft of this chapter.

Notes

1. Diels (1922, fragment 12, p. 123).

2. Also, pictorial devices—flattening techniques (Willats, 1997)—have been developed to control the perceptual balance between the flatness aspect of the picture and the depth aspect of what is depicted, such as accidental alignments between two or more parts of a scene and the position of the viewer, the use of mixed and mutually inconsistent perspectives, or obtrusive surface marks.

3. These phenomena could, from a physicalistic perspective, be described as a kind of discrepancy between what is physically there, namely, a flat surface, and the perceptual impression evoked. However, framing the problem this way amounts to conflating the level of the physical generation process of the sensory input with the level referring to perceptual mechanisms by which this sensory input is exploited (cf. Mausfeld 2002).

4. Phenomenological observations that appear particularly salient or enigmatic do not necessarily have a particular relevance for perception theory. Although phenomenological observations of various kinds are of prominent heuristic importance for perception theory, they do not carry a kind of "epistemological superiority." Phenomenological observations do not provide "direct access" to the nature of representational primitives; rather, they result from an interplay of various faculties, including linguistic and interpretative ones. Thus they are, within a naturalistic inquiry into the principles of perception, on a par with many other sources that provide relevant facts and observations.

5. The notion of "representation" is burdened with a high degree of ambiguity due to its multifarious meanings. Many corresponding locutions in this chapter, such as *pictorial representation,* refer to ordinary discourse. With respect to these, I do not attach much importance, in the present context, to carefully distinguishing different meanings. In the context of explanatory frameworks for certain phenomena, however, I use the notion of "representation," for example, in the terms *spatial representations* or *surface representations,* to denote elements of postulated internal structure that are part of an inference to the best explanation. In the context of perception theory, this neither involves particular ontological commitments nor any reference to the external world. More concretely, a "surface" representation is not, in any meaningful sense, to be understood as a representation *of* physical surfaces. Dispensing with notions of "reference," "truth," or "veridicality" within explanatory frameworks of perception theory is, as Chomsky (1996, 2000) has argued most convincingly and adamantly with respect to naturalistic inquiries of the mind, entirely in line with standard methodological principles of the natural sciences.

6. Demonstrations for different kinds of situations of conflicting depth cues have been provided, for example, by Hornbostel (1922), in his striking demonstration that the image of a rotating wire cube viewed in a mirror undergoes a dynamic nonrigid transformation (cf. also Adams and Haire 1959); by Ames (Ittelson 1952); by Epstein (1968), Gillam (1968), Youngs (1976), Rogers and Collett (1989), and Trueswell and Hayhoe (1993); and by Koenderink, van Doorn, and Kappers (1994).

7. This is conspicuously illustrated and symbolized by Magritte's painting *La condition humaine,* which plays with the many different levels involved.

8. The most extreme versions are trompe-l'oeil paintings that aim to induce the viewer to perceive the painted object as reality. Such illusionistic effects only work in cases where the painted 3-D perspective is as shallow as possible, which explains the highly restricted pictorial themes of trompe-l'oeil paintings (cf. Mauries 1997).

9. Polanyi (1970a) and Pirenne (1970) introduced the terms "focal" versus "subsidiary awareness" to deal with these observations. Focal awareness refers to the subject represented, and subsidiary awareness refers to the characteristics of the surface of a picture.

10. For similar reasons, Michotte (1948/1991, p. 181) emphasized the distinction between "phenomenal three-dimensionality" and "phenomenal reality." He argued that "three-dimensionality and reality are different properties of our perceptions and must be considered as *independent dimensions* of our visual experience.... By *reality* we mean an empirical characteristic, the potential for being manipulated. By *three-dimensionality* we mean another empirical characteristic, the capacity for being matched to the volume of a substantial object" (ibid).

11. Even *within* a single picture, different and globally incoherent local spatial representations can be elicited. This was deliberately employed to create certain aesthetic effects, as in Piero della Francesca's painting *The Resurrection of Christ* (see Field 1993) or paintings by de Chirico.

12. The action spectra for wavelength-dependent behavior underlying bees' celestial orientation and navigation depend on more than one pigment, without exhibiting metameric classes, whereas trichromatic color vision is exclusively employed in feeding and recognition of the hive.

13. Interestingly enough, Gombrich (1982) also explicitly based his position on ethological arguments.

14. Michotte was particularly sensitive to the problem of meaning in perceptual theory, which he regarded as being intrinsic to the structure of primitives that underlie perceptual organization and that "prefigure" the phenomenal world: "Our research suggests that this primitive structure occurs in the form of a world of 'things' that are separate from one another and are either passive or else animate bodies ultimately endowed with specific "vital" movements.... This possibly throws some light on the origin of these concepts, but we ought to stress the biological importance of such spontaneous organization of the phenomenal world since only such organization could enable the individual (whether human or ani-

mal) to adapt its reactions before any individual experience had the opportunity to provide it with any structure" (Michotte 1954/1991, p. 45).

15. This distinction is different in character from widely made distinctions between so-called earlier or lower-level systems and higher-level systems. The latter basically correspond to the sensation-perception distinction as used by Spencer, James, Wundt or Helmholtz, which refers to an alleged hierarchy of processing stages by which the sensory input is transformed into "perceptions." In contrast, the present distinction refers to two categorically different types of structures and is more in line with corresponding distinctions by Descartes, Cudworth, or Reid (cf. Mausfeld 2002, appendix).

16. Computational approaches of the kind pioneered by Marr almost exclusively deal, with respect to this distinction as I conceive it, with the sensory system; they have revealed that it has a much richer conceptual structure and greater computational power than previously assumed.

17. Among representational primitives pertaining to "objects" there are, as corresponding evidence suggests, not only those that pertain to "physical objects" of various types but also a great variety of specific types that pertain to intentional physical objects or to biological objects.

18. Again, the internal concept "surface" is assumed to be entirely determined syntactically, that is, by its data structure and the kind of transformations and relations that operate on it. It is not, in any meaningful sense, a *representation of* physical surfaces. I use the term *surface representation* only as a convenient abbreviation for a postulated representation (whose nature we presently only poorly understand), whose properties seem to be conveniently describable, at the metatheoretical level of the scientist, in terms of perceptual achievements related to actual surfaces.

19. More precisely, the two different parameters involved can be regarded as pertaining to the same attribute, if they figure as parameters of the same type in some superordinate structures and computations. Again, a label such as "color" serves only as a convenient metatheoretical characterization of a certain type of parameter.

20. Because of these interdependencies of free parameters, attempts to identify the representational primitives of the structure of perception and their "data structure" by investigating attributes like color or depths in isolation are doomed to fail (apart from lucky coincidences). They are just as futile as it would be to try to determine a *n*-dimensional manifold from a random sample of one-dimensional projections.

21. Even in cases of physically identical input situations, perceptual properties that have usually been regarded as predominantly mirroring properties of input channels, such as discrimination, critically depend upon the settings made for conjoint parameters. A case in point is the observation, known as the Aubert-Förster phenomenon, that discrimination for objects that subtend the same visual angle is better when the object is perceived as a small one at near distance than when it is perceived as a large one at greater distance.

22. Jan Koenderink argued that "the notion of a depth map as summary representation of pictorial relief is hardly tenable." He concluded that it is likely "that mental structure contains various (perhaps mutually inconsistent) fragments of data structures and that only the execution of particular tasks may perhaps draw on a variety of them and lead to some degree of coordination" (1998, p. 1083).

23. The Ames room demonstration also suggests that an "ambient space" representation is triggered according to its own rules and has, in cases in which different combinations of values can be assigned to free parameters, its proprietary "default interpretations," even if these result in ecologically odd parameter settings for "object" representations pertaining to objects located in this ambient space. (In the Ames room, a person who walks along the wall opposite the observer, which physically recedes in depth from the observer, appears to shrink in size.)

24. "Color" presumably also figures as a free parameter in a variety of superordinate primitives that pertain to more complex, biologically relevant aspects of the external world, such as those pertaining to "edible things" or to "emotional states of others."

25. Mausfeld and Andres (2002) found evidence that second-order statistics of chromatic codes of the incoming light array differentially modulate, by a specific class of parametrized transformations, the relation of the two kinds of representational primitives involved.

26. For recent demonstrations that bear on these issues see, for instance, Adelson (1993), Knill and Kersten (1991), or Buckley, Frisby, and Freeman (1994).

27. Problems of figure-ground segmentations are also a "major obstacle in developing computational theories," as Weisstein and Wong (1986, p. 61) noted, because basic elements that are used in standard computational theories for the extraction of surface properties are themselves dependent on figure-ground segmentations. Figure-ground segmentation itself is a most fundamental variable that determines and influences perceptual attributes such as color or depth. Surfaces that are linked up as "background" can even survive inconsistent disparity information, as Belhumeur (1996, p. 342) showed by a stereogram in which we perceive a continuation of a background object behind foreground strips, even if this is not consistent with the actual disparity relations for a part of the background section.

28. If, to some interesting extent, this should indeed turn out be the case, comparing the functioning of the perceptual system with language, as notably Descartes and Cudworth did (cf. Mausfeld 2002, appendix), would not merely be an illustrative or pedagogical metaphor but rather a *theory-constitutive metaphor,* which invites exploring "the similarities and analogies between features of the primary and secondary subject, including features not yet discovered, or not yet fully understood" (Boyd 1979, p. 363).

Chapter 3

Relating Direct and Indirect Perception of Spatial Layout

H. A. Sedgwick

3.1   DIRECT AND INDIRECT PERCEPTION

Pictures are made and used for many purposes. In my work, and in this chapter, I focus on just one of these purposes, which is to afford the accurate perception of the three-dimensional layout of a scene. This purpose may be linked to, and in part derived from, many other purposes—aesthetic, narrative, historical, architectural, navigational, instructional, and so on—that give it a social setting and significance, but I shall not pursue those links here. To say that the purpose is accurate perception implies that we have knowledge of the true layout of the scene, to which an observer's perception of its representation can be compared. The scene represented may actually have existed at one time, as in a photograph; it may be pure invention, as in a 3-D computer graphic; or it may be some combination of invention and reality, as in an architectural drawing. But it is, in all the cases I am considering, precisely specifiable. I refer to this represented scene as the virtual scene.

It would go beyond my purpose, and my competence, to pursue in this chapter philosophical questions concerning what is real and how we know it to be so. Instead, I shall adopt a naive realism that assumes the existence of a real world that surrounds us and that we perceive, more or less, when we look around. Following James J. Gibson, I shall refer to our perception of this real world, or scene, as direct perception. Gibson, and I, then refer to our perception of a virtual scene that is represented to us in a picture as indirect perception. These two terms, "direct" and "indirect," are to be understood in relation to each other. They refer to two different situations for perception. Direct perception is perception "without intermediary agents," to quote a dictionary definition (*Webster's College Dictionary* 1992); it is looking directly at the scene itself rather than looking at a representation of it. Indirect perception refers to looking at a virtual scene through the intermediary agency of a representation. Gibson put it bluntly: "Direct perception is what one gets from seeing Niagara Falls, say, as distinguished from seeing a picture of it" (Gibson 1979, p. 147).

Making pictures is, or can be, an art, but making accurate pictures of three-dimensional scenes is also a technology. This technology has been developing for a long time and is continuing to develop rapidly, so the variety of pictorial representations available to us is now immense. Thus we have not just one kind of indirect perception but rather a multidimensional continuum of kinds of indirect perception.

One source of variation comes from the kind of information that is provided to specify the represented scene. We may have one or more kinds of pictorial information, such as perspective, shading, texture gradients, and so forth, as are found in paintings and photographs; motion information, as is found in movies and television; stereoscopic information, as in stereograms; or interactive information, as in displays contingent on eye, head, or body movements or on simulations of any of these.

A pictorial display is itself an object in the real space of the observer. So a second source of variation is in the kind of information available to specify the display itself. Such displays are most typically presented on a flat surface of some sort (although the variations from this are highly interesting), such as a canvas, a photographic print, a projection screen, or a computer or television monitor. The information specifying this surface may include the oculomotor adjustments of accommodation and vergence, the stereoscopic disparity of the frame or surface of the display, motion parallax, and so on. In some situations efforts may be made to minimize this information, such as fixing the position of the head, limiting vision to one eye, or requiring the observer to look at the picture through a pinhole.

A third source of variation is in the interface between the display and the surrounding environment of the observer. Any representation of a virtual space is always embedded in the real space of the observer. We may ask, How much of the field of view is taken up by the display—only a few degrees, as in some computer displays, or a wide angle, as in Cinerama or IMAX movies? Is the real environment also visible or is it concealed? Does the display attempt to be immersive (perhaps with haptic feedback or vestibular stimulation)? To what extent are the exploratory movements of the observer allowed or inhibited? How casual or controlled is the presentation of the display?

In one corner of this multidimensional continuum of possibilities, we have displays that do their technological best to duplicate the perceptual experience of direct perception. These are the so-called virtual reality displays. They have many limitations now, but it would be foolhardy to try to define limits on how close they can eventually come to complete success. I think this corner, pushed to whatever limits we imagine may be possible for it, is a useful reference point in thinking about the relation between indirect and direct perception.

What would be the opposite corner of this multidimensional continuum? The minimal pictorial display? It is not easy, nor for my purpose is it important, to pin this corner down, because there are various plausible candidates. A simple pencil sketch, a patch of texture, the motion of a few points of light, a few lines seen stereoscopically—each of these is capable of producing some perception of three-dimensional space. The assertion that I want to make is that, whichever of these corners we start from, there is a continuous, seamless path (actually many paths) connecting this corner of our continuum to the opposite corner.

Thus it seems to me that if we are going to make categorical statements about pictorial representation and about indirect perception, then these statements need to be broad enough to include this entire continuum from the simplest sketch to the most complex virtual reality.

To define direct perception as looking at the real layout of the world and indirect perception as looking at the virtual space of a representation leaves open the question of how different these processes are. The most parsimonious hypothesis is that they are fundamentally the same. Such a hypothesis is implicit in the research of many vision scientists, who increasingly are using pictorial displays as a convenient way of studying direct perception, although without always paying sufficient attention to the current limitations of such displays, as Jan Koenderink has very eloquently noted in a recent editorial (1999; also see Hurlbert 1998). Thus we can try to understand indirect perception and direct perception in the same terms. Only if this effort fails do we need to postulate perceptual processes or mechanisms that are unique to indirect perception.

3.2   THE PROBLEM OF DIRECT PERCEPTION

To attempt to understand indirect perception in terms of direct perception implies that we must first understand direct perception. This is an unfortunate implication in that we are still far from such an understanding. This is not just a matter of clearing up the details. There is disagreement, as well as some lack of clarity, about the most fundamental issues in direct perception.

For example, we may ask what the most appropriate way is to describe or characterize what we see when we look at a three-dimensional scene. There is what I shall call the "standard model," which goes back at least as far as Descartes. According to this standard model, what we see in the first instance is the angular direction and distance from ourselves of every point in the scene. David Marr referred to such a description as a "viewer-centered" representation of the scene (Marr 1982). Our more complex perceptions are then built up from this basic information. We determine the size of a surface, for instance, by geometrically combining its angular extent (determined by differences in direction) with its distance. The three-dimensional shape and slant of surfaces are determined in a similar fashion. The perception of angular direction is not regarded by this model as being much of a problem, because angular direction can be directly related to the optical projection on the retina, combined with the rotational posture of the eye in the head. The perception of distance, however, is a major problem because the projection of a point onto the retina is the same whatever the point's distance. Recovering the point's distance from its projection thus seems almost an impossibility; it almost seems that any distance is as good as another, making distance completely ambiguous. The standard solution is the list of cues to distance—accommodation and vergence of the eyes, stereopsis, motion parallax, and so forth.

There has been dissatisfaction with the standard model for some time, but that dissatisfaction has grown more acute and widespread in the past few decades, and the search for alternatives has been increasingly vigorous and productive (reviewed in Sedgwick 2001). Proposals have been made, for example, that the geometry of three-dimensional perceptual space is non-Euclidean, is affine, or is ordinal. Although each of these descriptive systems may give us some useful angle on the character of direct perception, it seems unlikely to me that visual space perception by biological organisms, such as ourselves, adapted to our particular environmental niche, is going to be adequately described by any geometry that is abstract, fixed, and universal.

In what follows, I'll briefly describe three hypotheses about direct perception, and for each hypothesis I'll try to describe some of its implications for our understanding of indirect perception.

3.3   THE GROUND THEORY OF SPACE PERCEPTION

The first hypothesis, proposed by Gibson in 1950 (Gibson 1950, p. 6), is that, instead of space per se, what we perceive is the layout of connected surfaces that compose our visible environment. The foundational surface of the environment, for terrestrial animals such as ourselves, is the ground plane. Except for things that float or fly, everything ultimately is supported by the ground and so is connected through the ground plane to everything else. Gibson proposed that rather than seeing distance through empty space we see distance along the ground plane. This conceptual shift resolves the apparent ambiguity of space perception. Increasing distance along the ground plane is projected as increasing angular height in the optical projection, which Gibson called the optic array. This angular height in the optic array, together with the height of the eye above the ground plane, thus unambiguously specifies distance along the ground. Gibson referred to this hypothesis as the "ground theory" of space perception and saw it as a radical departure from the standard model of space perception.

What Gibson did not know was that the same hypothesis had been proposed, and discussed in some detail, almost 1,000 years earlier by the Arab philosopher and scientist Alhazen, whose great work on optics only began to appear in English in 1989 (Alhazen 1039/1989), ten years after Gibson's death. Alhazen made the observation that the distances of objects are uncertain if they are seen protruding above the top of a wall, so that their bases are not visible, and he argued that distance can only be perceived between objects that are visibly connected by a surface such as the ground. I do not yet know the history of this idea during the 600 years between Alhazen's death in 1039 and the publication of Descartes *Optics* in 1637 (Descartes 1637/1965), but I see no trace of it in the standard model, described earlier, that Descartes advocated.

We must qualify this ground theory hypothesis somewhat because binocular vision and stereopsis allow us to see the sizes and distances of objects floating in empty space with some accuracy, especially if they are fairly close to us. But this is a limited qualification. Research done by Barbara Gillam and me (Gillam and Sedgwick 1996; Gillam, Sedgwick, and Cook 1993; Sedgwick and Gillam, submitted), as well as by some other groups (Glennerster and McKee 1999; Mitchison and Westheimer 1984), shows that if an object floats in front of a background surface, rather than in empty space, then stereopsis is used to relate the object to this background surface rather than to the viewer.

The relation between direct and indirect perception is much more straightforward from the standpoint of the ground theory than from that of the standard model. Because the standard model posits distance perception through empty space, from the eye of the observer to the object, it has traditionally been forced to rely heavily in its theorizing about space perception on stereopsis and the oculomotor adjustments of the eyes. But because these are precisely the forms of information absent from paintings, photographs, and other nonstereoscopic pictorial representations, an explanatory gulf is opened up between the direct and indirect perception of space. The ground theory, in contrast, is right at home in pictorial representations of space. As is clear in the first Western work on the subject, written by Alberti in 1436 (Alberti, 1436/1972), the successful representation of spatial relations depends on the accurate construction of the ground plane. Without a connected layout of three-dimensional surfaces, pictorial representations tend to collapse onto the picture surface. Some modern artists, such as Wassily Kandinsky, have done fascinating experiments on the creation of three-dimensional impressions from abstract objects floating in empty space, but much of the fascination comes from the lability and ambiguity of these impressions. Recently, Jan Koenderink, Andrea van Doorn, and their colleagues have performed a series of careful and very interesting experiments on the perception of representations of sculptural objects floating in empty space. They have found that the perceptions of such objects are stretched and even sheared in ways that appear to be essentially arbitrary from one observer to the next (Koenderink, van Doorn, and Kappers 1995; Koenderink, van Doorn, Kappers, and Todd 2000a).

Our predisposition to perceive the environment as a layout of connected surfaces underlies the effectiveness of simple presentations such as line drawings. A horizontal line across the middle of the page is sometimes enough to invoke the perception of the ground plane. A complex architectural space of connected surfaces can be evoked by a few converging and parallel lines.

In complex scenes, not everything rests directly on the ground or floor. Instead, a lamp may rest on the table, or a book may rest on a shelf attached to the wall. But the wall extends down to the floor, as does the table, so that ultimately everything that does not float or fly is supported by the ground. To apply the ground theory of space perception to complex environments, it must be generalized to include such scenes. For some time I have been interested in what I refer to as the "nested hierarchy of contact relations," which establishes the spatial layout of scenes through complex sets of connected surfaces (Sedgwick 1987a; Sedgwick 1987b; Sedgwick 1989).

Jeanette Meng and I have investigated observers' ability to perceive spatial relations in such situations (Meng and Sedgwick 2001). Using computer graphics, we asked observers to move a marker along a track on the ground until its distance to the observer matched that of a cube resting on a block that in turn rested on the ground (figure 3.1). Holding the cube and the top of the block constant, we varied the block's point of optical contact with the ground. In this way we progressively increased the perceived distance of the block. The perceived distance of the cube also increased appropriately, showing that its perceived location relative to the ground was effectively mediated by the block on which it rested.

In another experiment we varied the height of the block and with it the height of the cube in the image plane. If observers were influenced simply by the "cue" of height in the image plane, this should have increased the perceived distance of the cube, but it did not. Because the base of the block, where it made contact with the ground, did not change, the perceived distance of the cube did not change either. The observers' distance settings did become more variable, however, reflecting the increased separation between the ground and the cube's surface of support.

Recently (Meng and Sedgwick 2002) we have looked at a somewhat more complex situation, in which the cube rests on one block and the marker and its track rest on another. When the two blocks are the same height, the variability of distance settings is reduced, suggesting that observers establish a shortcut directly between the tops of the two blocks, based on the coplanarity of the two surfaces, rather than relating the cube and marker through the ground. These exploratory experiments are just a beginning. If we wish to apply Alhazen's and Gibson's ground theory to the perception of complex spatial layouts, either real or virtual, much more work remains to be done.

3.4   ENVIRONMENT-CENTERED PERCEPTION OF SPATIAL LAYOUT

The second hypothesis I wish to discuss holds that direct perception is primarily environment centered (Sedgwick 1983). By "environment centered" I mean that what is most salient in our perception of spatial layout is how

Figures 3.1a and b

In this experiment using computer graphics, observers moved a marker along the track on the ground until it appeared to be at the same distance as the small cube resting on top of the block. In the two conditions shown here, the positions of the cube and of the top of the block were held constant in the image while the block's pictured contact with the ground was varied by decreasing (from a to b) the vertical dimension of the block. The perceived distance of the cube was effectively mediated by the changing distance of the block, as specified by the location of the bottom of the block relative to the ground. Reproduced and modified with permission from Meng and Sedgwick 2001; original displays were in color.

objects' surfaces are related to the principal surfaces of the environment. In contrast, the standard model is viewer centered, meaning that spatial layout is perceived primarily in relation to our own viewpoint.

Let us first consider how this distinction applies to the problem of size and distance. In the standard, viewer-centered model, the perceived size of an object is based on its perceived distance from the observer. This implies that perceived size and perceived distance should vary together; for example, errors in perceived distance should be reflected in errors in perceived size. This idea, dubbed the "size-distance invariance hypothesis" (Kilpatrick and Ittleson 1953), has been examined empirically many times and is not well supported by the evidence (for reviews, see Gillam 1995; Sedgwick 1986).

In the environment-centered model the perception of size is based on the object's relation to the context provided by the environment. Gibson (1950) provided an example of such contextual information for size, pointing out that surfaces such as the ground are usually textured, with the elements of this texture being uniform, at least statistically, across the extent of the surface. The relative sizes of objects resting at various locations on such a textured surface are specified by the number of texture elements that each object covers. The objects' distances from the viewer are irrelevant to this relationship. In this view, Gibson pointed out, the perceived size of an object is a by-product of the perceived scale of the environment. As Gibson says, "the size of any particular object is given by the scale of the background *at the point to which it is attached*" (Gibson 1950, p. 181; emphasis in original). In addition to texture scale, the scale of the environment is also specified by perspective. For example, on an extended ground plane, the line of sight to the horizon is parallel to the ground and so intersects objects resting on the ground at a constant height (equal to the height of the observer's eye). Thus, the horizon sets a constant scale across the entire ground plane. The relative height of each object is specified by what I refer to as the "horizon ratio relation": the ratio of the object's total optic array projection divided by the projected portion of the object below the horizon (Sedgwick 1973). As with texture scale, this ratio specifies the relative sizes of objects independently of their distances from the viewer.

In the environment-centered model, distance from the viewer's eye has no special significance. Distance is perceived between objects and, as discussed earlier, is perceived along surfaces rather than through empty space. More fundamentally, though, in the environment-centered model distance loses its primacy altogether. What is primary instead is location, the point at which an object contacts a supporting surface. Given the set of contact relations between the objects and surfaces of the environment, distances between locations can be derived as needed (Sedgwick 1983, 1987b).

Finally, let me illustrate this distinction between environment-centered and viewer-centered models with the example of surface orientation. As Gibson and Cornsweet (1952) pointed out, we can define the slant of a surface either relative to the observer's line of sight or relative to an environmental surface such as the ground plane. They referred to these as "optical slant" and "geographical slant," respectively. The properties of these two types of slant differ in important ways. Consider a flat surface slanted relative to the ground, say at an angle of 45°. The geographical (or environment-centered) slant of this surface is a constant 45° along its entire length. It also remains a constant 45° as the observer moves around in the environment. In contrast, the optical (or viewer-centered) slant, where the line of sight meets the surface, changes as the line of sight sweeps along the surface or as the observer moves around.

Surfaces that have the same environment-centered slant are parallel to each other and thus share the same vanishing line in perspective. Each distinct vanishing line in the optic array thus corresponds to a family of parallel surfaces and specifies their environment-centered orientation (Sedgwick 1983).

Marr suggested that the visual system first finds the viewer-centered structure of the environment and then can derive other information, such as parallelism, from it (Marr 1982). Some years ago Steve Levy and I tested this idea, using computer graphics images, by asking observers to adjust the orientation of one surface until it matched either the viewer-centered or the environment-centered slant of another surface (Sedgwick and Levy 1985). We found that observers were more precise in making environment-centered matches. This makes it seem more plausible that environment-centered slant is primary than that it is derived from viewer-centered slant.

What are the implications of the environment-centered model for the relation between direct and indirect perception? It seems to me that it offers us some understanding of the ease with which a representation can embed a virtual space in the real space of the observer. An environment-centered virtual space can be coherent within itself without necessarily being clearly related to, or even commensurable with, the real space of the observer. Virtual objects' sizes relative to the scale of their virtual environment, their locations relative to the layout of virtual surfaces, and the slants of their surfaces relative to the surfaces of this virtual space may all be more salient to indirect perception than these virtual objects' viewer-centered distances or the sizes or slants that could be derived from such distances.[1]

3.5   CROSS-TALK

My third hypothesis concerning direct perception is that the perceived three-dimensional spatial layout of a scene is influenced by cross-talk from the scene's projection in the optic array (Sedgwick 1991).[2]

The recent literature on the perception of distance over the ground offers a good example of what I am calling cross-talk. Suppose that we scatter a number of objects over an open field and then we ask an observer to estimate distances between pairs of these objects. From the viewpoint of the observer, the projection of the ground plane is compressed, so the angular extent of a distance radial to the observer is considerably smaller than the angular extent of an equal distance in the frontal plane of the observer. Charles Levin and Ralph Haber (1993) have shown that this difference in angular extent influences observers' perception of distance, resulting in an underestimation of radial distances relative to frontal distances. The perceived relative distances are a compromise between the true relative distances and their optic array projections. What is critical here is not distance per se but the relation between distance and its projection. Jack Loomis and John Philbeck (1999) have shown that with monocular viewing the effect of compression is invariant when all the distances are scaled up while the same compressive relations are maintained by increasing the eye height proportionally. In all these situations there is good information available for the true distances, but the perceived distances are nevertheless affected by cross-talk from their optical projections.

In direct perception, the effects of cross-talk from the optical projection appear for the most part to be relatively small. When we turn to indirect perception, however, we are introducing a projection surface, such as the surface of a photograph or painting, and the perception of this projection surface, I believe, gives greater salience to the projective relationships, thus increasing the strength of the cross-talk.

Let us consider one example from a study that I did with Andrea Nicholls (Sedgwick and Nicholls 1993a). We used monocularly viewed computer-generated scenes of a rectangle on the wall of a room. The wall was slanted so that the projection of the rectangle was compressed on the surface of the picture. We asked observers for perceptual estimates of the width-to-height proportion of the rectangle in the scene. We held that proportion constant on average over a series of trials but varied the pictured slant of the rectangle, so that the width-to-height proportion of its projection on the picture surface became increasingly compressed. As we increased the compression on the picture surface, observers' estimates of the rectangle in the scene became more compressed. This is a clear example of cross-talk from the picture surface to the perception of the virtual scene.

In another experiment (Sedgwick et al. 1991), we similarly found cross-talk in the indirect perception of virtual size, comparing the relative size of two rectangles. We also found that when we increased the salience of the information for the surface of the picture, by adding a frame and surface texture, we increased the amount of cross-talk from the picture surface to the virtual scene. A related result has been found by David Eby and Myron Braunstein (1995), who showed that adding a frame to a picture diminished the perceived depth within the pictured scene. Koenderink and his colleagues have shown that viewing a picture with both eyes, which provides additional information for the picture surface, rather than with just one eye, also has a flattening effect on the virtual object (Koenderink, van Doorn, and Kappers 1995; Koenderink et al. 2000a).

The hypothesis of cross-talk from the picture surface to the pictured scene helps to resolve an important issue in our understanding of indirect perception. This is the problem of what happens to perceived virtual space when we view a picture from the wrong viewpoint. An essential part of creating an accurate representation of a three-dimensional scene is to choose the viewpoint, the place from which the eye or the camera views the scene (Sedgwick 1980). When the representation, a photographic print, for example, has been created, there is now a point in the real space in front of the photographic print where the observer's eye must be placed to obtain the same view that the camera had. If the eye views that representation from some other viewpoint, the perspective of the photograph now specifies a different virtual space, one that is a distortion of the original virtual space. For example, if the viewpoint is displaced laterally, then the virtual scene specified by perspective is sheared. If the viewpoint is too near or too far, then the virtual space is compressed or expanded, respectively (Sedgwick 1991).

The perceptual problem is that observers tend not to notice these distortions. Someone walking through a photography exhibit tends not to notice distortions of the virtual space of the pictures, even though the point of observation is continually changing. This has led to the suggestion that there is a perceptual compensation mechanism (Pirenne 1970, p. 162). Such a mechanism is hypothesized to recognize that the observer is looking at the representation from the wrong viewpoint and to internally correct for the distortion that this produces. The existence of such a mechanism in indirect perception would, it seems, open up a considerable gulf between indirect and direct perception. There can be no need for such a compensation mechanism in direct perception, because the viewpoint of the observer is always, by definition, the correct viewpoint. Thus this hypothesized compensation mechanism, which would need to be a mechanism of formidable complexity to correctly solve the problem of compensation, would exist for indirect perception alone.

The cross-talk hypothesis offers an alternative to the compensation hypothesis. As the observer moves around, the virtual scene specified by perspective distorts, but the surface of the picture does not change. Thus cross-talk from the picture surface to the perceived scene will tend to have a conservative effect, that is, to reduce the perceived distortions of virtual space. Unlike the compensation hypothesis, however, the cross-talk hypothesis does not predict that there will no perceived distortion. It only predicts that the amount of perceived distortion will be less than what is specified by perspective.

I shall briefly describe one study, done with Nicholls (Sedgwick and Nicholls 1994), that addresses this issue. Using computer-generated scenes with slanted rectangles similar to those I described earlier, we looked at the effect of reducing the size of the picture, which is optically equivalent to viewing the picture from a distance farther than the correct viewing distance. The depth dimension of the virtual space specified by perspective is thus stretched, increasing the optically specified slant and width-to-height proportions of the rectangle on the wall. We found that the perceived proportions of the rectangle did indeed increase, but not by nearly as much as perspective predicted. We were able to account for most of this shortfall, however, with a control condition that measured the cross-talk from the proportions, unchanged by minification, of the projected rectangle on the surface of the picture. When we also included controls for the effects of the smaller angular size of the minified picture and the smaller angular size of the minified rectangle within it, both of which tended to reduce perceived slant, we were able to account for almost all of the discrepancy between the perceived virtual space and the optically specified virtual space. We were able to do this without invoking any special perceptual mechanism to compensate for being at the wrong viewpoint. This, along with a number of other results (Rogers 1995; Sedgwick and Nicholls 1996; Sedgwick, Nicholls, and Brehaut 1995; Yang and Kubovy 1999), suggests to me that the hypothesis of a special compensation mechanism in indirect perception is unnecessary and that we can account for the indirect perception of virtual space, even when seen from the wrong viewpoint, in terms of the same mechanisms, such as cross-talk, that we find operating in direct perception.

Let me briefly sum up. The technology of accurate spatial displays produces an ever-changing, multidimensional continuum of pictorial representations, ranging from the most compelling virtual realities to the simplest pencil sketches.

We may imagine indirect and direct perception as a lock and key. When we have the right theory of direct perception, it may provide the key that opens up our understanding of the whole continuum of indirect perception. I have described three hypotheses about direct perception that may provide a good fit with the problems of indirect perception.

First, direct perception is attuned to the complex spatial layouts of connected surfaces that compose much of our environment. Display technologies have for a long time been well suited to the representation of such layouts.

Second, direct perception is environment centered—attuned to geographical orientations of surfaces, locations of objects on those surfaces, and sizes relative to the scale of the environment. This facilitates the indirect perception of self-contained virtual scenes embedded within the real space of the observer.

Third and finally, there is a dual awareness in direct perception—of the three-dimensional scene and of its optical projection—and the perception of each is influenced by cross-talk from the other. In indirect perception there is a corresponding duality between the perception of the virtual scene and the perception of the picture surface. Cross-talk from the stable picture surface tends to reduce the perception of distortions in the virtual scene when the picture is viewed from the wrong viewpoint.

Notes

1. This is not to deny the possibility of a viewer-centered mode of perception, especially in near space, and in some visual-motor activities, although such situa-

tions can easily be mistaken as viewer centered when they are not. Instrumental vision is rarely exactly viewer centered, where the center is taken to be the nodal point of the eye, or the cyclopean eye of binocular vision. For manual tasks the important relations are between the hands and the object; for locomotor tasks they are between the feet and the goal; for tool-using or vehicular tasks they are between the tool and its object or the vehicle and its goal; and so forth. It may be that such tasks are better understood in environment-centered terms.

2. There is also cross-talk in the other direction: if we try to attend to the scene's projection, our perception is strongly influenced by the three-dimensional scene. In indirect perception, cross-talk from the pictured scene to the picture surface can account for some geometrical illusions, such as the Ponzo illusion (Sedgwick and Nicholls 1993b).

Chapter 4

The Dual Nature of Picture Perception: A Challenge to Current General Accounts of Visual Perception

Reinhard Niederée and Dieter Heyer

4.1   INTRODUCTION

Pictures form a significant part not only of our visually oriented culture but also of the stimulus material employed by perceptual psychologists. Nevertheless, with few exceptions (e.g., Rock 1984), standard textbooks on the psychology of perception tend to ignore the challenging peculiarities of picture perception, and the same goes for mainstream vision science.

One major reason for this is that, first of all, attention is restricted to realistic pictures in the strict sense, based on central perspective, such as Renaissance paintings or photographs. In a second step, then, the perception of these pictures is conceived as being on a par with the perception of a scene as seen through a window. Hence, on this account, the perception of a picture, that is, the perceptual emergence of pictorial space in the observer's consciousness, need not be distinguished in principle from the perception of an everyday scene. Such a conception of picture perception implies that the spatial percept evoked by a flat realistic picture is simply a perceptual illusion, which is not different, in principle, from other well-known perceptual illusions such as the Ames room.

Except for limiting cases such as perfect trompe l'oeil, this is not the case, however. That is, as a rule, nobody misperceives a painted scene as a real one. Rather we speak, without hesitation, of seeing a painting of a scene. As Edmund Husserl (1980), Michael Polanyi (1970b), Maurice Pirenne (1970), James J. Gibson (e.g., 1979), and others have forcefully pointed out, this is due to what is often called the *dual nature* of picture perception: the evoked percept involves *both* the perceived surface of the picture as part of perceived real space and the experience of pictorial space, both aspects being subtly interwoven. If our visual system were able to capture merely one of these aspects, then picture perception as we know it, and along with it the cultural achievements based on it, could not exist. For, if the pictorial surface were invisible, pictures would cause illusions in the strict sense and thus would be difficult to handle as objects in everyday life. Conversely, if just the pictorial surface were visible, then pictures would reduce either to pieces of decoration or to mere carriers of conventional signs.

Contrary to the window analogy mentioned earlier, some authors have in fact argued that it is only the flat material picture object that is *perceived*. The emergence of pictorial space in the observer's consciousness is then counted as a phenomenon fundamentally different from ("direct") perception. For instance, in his early phenomenological writings, Jean-Paul Sartre (e.g., 1940) maintains that the experience of pictorial space is a matter of *imagination* based on the perception of the material pictorial surface (cf. Wiesing 2000, p. 43 ff.). Another widespread move of this kind is to assume a two-stage process, the first stage of which corresponds to the perception of the pictorial surface. This percept is then conceived as being the basis for an intrinsically different additional interpretation process in a semiotic sense, comparable to reading ("reading a picture").

In this chapter, in contrast, a unifying psychological perspective will be taken that understands both aspects of the dual nature of picture perception as genuine and interrelated features of a complex perceptual process, which is to say that both aspects are assumed to rely on essentially the same set of basic perceptual mechanisms. So far as this general assumption is concerned, we thus follow the path already taken by other psychologists of perception, such as Gibson (1979), to mention only one.

To preclude misunderstanding, we would like to add that despite the emphasis placed here on genuinely perceptual aspects, we do not, of course, mean to deny the potential relevance of imagination proper or interpretation (in a semiotic sense) in the context of picture perception. These concepts should not simply be lumped together, however, with the notion of *perception,* even though it must be conceded that the boundary between these concepts seems inherently fuzzy. Furthermore, perceived objects other than pictures may equally well trigger processes of imagination or serve as (more or less conventional) signs in a semiotic sense. These issues will therefore not be discussed here.

From the perspective of visual science, the dual nature of picture perception might at first sight appear to be a marginal, if not an anomalous phenomenon, dependent on utterly artificial stimuli. Even then, vision science would have to meet the challenge posed by this phenomenon. For reasons to be pointed out, we are convinced, however, that phenomena of that kind should not be considered marginal. On the contrary, we believe that general theories of perception will profit substantially from taking such complexities into account from the start. This would require, however, a corresponding modification of standard scene-based overall accounts of perception.

From this very perspective, pictures might indeed turn out to be natural objects of study not only for students of picture perception but for visual scientists in general. To simplify matters, we will restrict attention mainly to realist pictures (central perspective). Mutatis mutandis, our considerations are meant to apply to other cases as well.

4.2   WHERE TO "LOCATE" THE DUAL NATURE OF PICTURE PERCEPTION: A ROUGH SKETCH

As the reader will have noticed, we have been talking about the dual nature of picture *perception* and *not* about a "dual nature" of pictures *themselves*. That is, duality is considered here as a feature of an observer's *percept* caused by a pictorial stimulus—the perceptual experience "of a picture." This duality has its origins in the visual processes underlying the percept. Trivially enough, we will fail to find any such duality in the "world out there," that is, in the physical stimulus itself. Nor would it do justice to the phenomenon at issue just to point at the "discrepancy" between the real physical stimulus, a flat material object, on the one hand, and the "illusory," purely mental, pictorial space evoked by it, on the other.

The Current Standard Framework of Perception

To spell out more clearly what is meant by this distinction, let us first give a rough and simplified sketch of the current standard framework of perception. Its basic ingredients are the following. An observer is facing a physical scene, that is, a spatial arrangement of material objects, illuminated by some light source(s), the so-called distal stimulus. The light is partially reflected (or transmitted) by the objects (surfaces) in the scene. The light pattern reaching the eye acts as a medium between the scene and the observer's eye, where, via the eye's lens, it projects onto the retina creating the "retinal image" (proximal stimulus), or, in the standard case of binocular vision, a pair of retinal images. The two-dimensional retinal image itself must not, of course, be confused with "what is seen" by the observer. Rather, by means of a stimulation of a field of retinal receptors (rods, cones) it serves only as an "input" ("raw data") to a complex visual process. In the course of this process the visual system extracts and integrates *cues* (or, in Gibsonian parlance, picks up invariants) that eventually yield a richly structured conscious "output," the *percept*. At this level, meaningful "wholes" in the sense of Gestalt psychology (e.g., perceived objects), endowed with (perceived) shape, color, size, spatial position, orientation relative to the observer, motion, and so on, are organized into a dynamic, more or less coherent, perceived scene. Note that although the percept is part of our conscious experience, the underlying visual processes (including the relevant cues) for the most part are *not* accessible to consciousness. Needless to say, our present understanding of these processes still is rather fragmentary.

In sum, this scheme assumes that a physical input evokes a conscious experience, the percept. From a functional viewpoint, the latter in turn is usually conceived as a partial 3-D scene-representation, whose components may or may not be "veridical" with respect to the underlying physical scene. As usual in vision science, the term "perception" is employed here, regardless of whether or not veridicality is met; that is, the evocation of a visual illusion by an external stimulus is equally counted as an instance of perception. From a Helmholtzian viewpoint, this process would be described as an unconscious inference yielding the most likely hypothesis about a state of affairs "out there" that could have caused the retinal input.

From the perspective of the scheme just outlined, it is indeed fairly obvious that the notion of duality of picture perception pertains to the visual processes and their "output," that is, to the percept. However, in being centered around the concept of a scene-representation, this scheme, strictly speaking, does not allow for the possibility of this kind of duality.

The Meaning of "Duality"

Unlike the simultaneous awareness of the perceived size and perceived distance of an object, of perceived incident illumination and perceived surface color (e.g., Katz 1935), or of a perceived transparent layer and the perceived object seen "through" it, which in principle fit into the frame of a single consistent scene description, a duality of the kind under consideration does not. For, how could a flat opaque surface on a wall and a transparent opening in that wall with a scene being visible through it coexist at the same location? On the preceding account, however, the system should always come up with a single (most "simple" or "likely") scene description. That is, we should either have (a more or less "veridical") perceptual impression of a surface as part of perceived real space or the illusory impression of pictorial space seen through a windowlike opening. (Here and in what follows the term "impression" refers to perceptual experiences and does not necessarily imply vagueness or the like.) At best, bistability—perceptual switches between the two percepts—might occur, as known from the well-known Necker cube and many other examples. Regarding picture perception, Ernst Gombrich (1960) in fact advocated such a view, insofar as he postulated that we could only attend to one of the two just-mentioned aspects at a time, ruling out a simultaneous coexistence of both perceptual impressions.

Against this position, a number of authors—rightly, we believe—have argued that in many situations we are in fact aware of both aspects simultaneously, this double impression making up what we call a prototypical perceptual experience of a picture (e.g., Polanyi 1970b; Pirenne 1970). What may be shifted is *attention*. Indeed, we are hardly ever simultaneously aware of both aspects in a full-fledged manner, indeed. In many situations, pictorial space is the more salient aspect, but our actions concerning a picture will require an awareness of the picture as a flat object in real space. In fact, even if attention is largely concentrated on one aspect, there often is at least a residual awareness of the other aspect, too. The dynamics of attention certainly needs to be taken into account in this connection, but this is true of perception in general and does not imply bistability as it is experienced, for instance, in the case of the Necker cube.

For brevity, the dual aspects of picture perception at issue will henceforth be called the *planar* and the *spatial* aspects of a picture percept, respectively, even though the planar aspect itself does of course also include a spatial component with respect to perceived real space. It is worth noting that the distinction between planar and spatial aspects of a picture percept involves not only genuinely spatial features but at the same time a duality of aspects pertaining to perceived color. For instance, what looks like a pattern of black, gray, and white patches on the picture surface (planar aspect) may go hand in hand with the perceptual impression of a scene composed of objects of different achromatic colors under certain perceived lighting conditions. As the case may be, this may include perceived shadows, perceived light sources, perceived translucency, or perceived gloss. Of course, the same goes for chromatic aspects of color vision. To our knowledge, this aspect of the duality of picture perception has been largely neglected in the relevant literature (but see, for instance, Schöne 1954, appendix B).

Most important, the spatial and the planar aspects do not simply coexist in parallel but are related to each other. They are experienced as a perceptual unit. Whenever we speak here of one's being aware of both aspects "simultaneously" or "at the same time," this kind of unity is tacitly implied. For this kind of phenomenal binding, too, suitable concepts are missing in the orthodox scheme of perception sketched earlier. Moreover, in most situations there is a notable perceptual asymmetry between the planar and the spatial aspect insofar as only the former is experienced as belonging to perceived "real space." To spell this out, perceptual degrees of "looking real" (cf. Michotte 1948, 1960) and corresponding perceptual hierarchies need to be taken into account, too.

Not all objects called pictures in our culture evoke dual percepts of the kind just discussed. For instance, in Andrea Pozzos's famous ceiling *The Transmission of the Divine Spirit* (1688–1694, Chiesa di Sant'Ignazio, Rome; cf., e.g., Pirenne 1970), the painted pillars appear spatially real from a specific viewing position. That is, only the *spatial* aspect is present in the percept. This is an instance of a trompe l'oeil in the strict sense, where a picture is not seen *as a picture* anymore in that there is no simultaneous awareness of planar and spatial aspects. Note that in our context one had better not speak of a painting itself as a trompe l'oeil but, rather, of a *trompe l'oeil effect.* For we are speaking of a perceptual phenomenon that is also dependent to some extent on *viewing conditions,* such as the position of the observer. Similarly, for instance, a trompe l'oeil effect can sometimes occur if parts of an ordinary realistic painting are viewed monocularly through a reduction tube, or in stereoscopic vision, where two slightly different pictures are presented to the right and the left eye.

At the other extreme, in the twentieth century a number of painters have explicitly aimed at avoiding the impression of a perceived pictorial space, a famous instance being Kasimir Malevich's black square. Again this phenomenon may in certain cases depend on viewing conditions. The impression of a perceptual space may not be present, for instance, when a painting is viewed from a very short distance.

Both extremes mark the poles of a continuum of perceptual experiences. In between these poles we find the dual experience mentioned before. In the present context, we will only speak of *picture perception proper,* if both aspects are perceptually present to some degree.

An Extension of the Standard Scheme

As pointed out before, the orthodox scheme of perception is inadequate for this situation. An appropriate extension of that scheme is outlined in figure 4.1. In this scheme we refer to the standard setting, where the physical *stimulus* consists of a flat pictorial surface.

It is worth noting, however, that the perceptual duality characteristic of picture perception at the level of the *percept* is not necessarily tied to this standard setting. That is, it is not restricted to situations in which the perceived picture plane corresponds to a real surface while the perceived pictorial space is illusory. For such an impression could just as well be caused by other stimuli. In contemporary art, for instance, James Turrell and Amish Kapoor impressively demonstrated how an illusory percept of a planar opaque object on a wall or the ground as part of perceived real space can be evoked by a suitable arrangement of architecture and lighting. Because these illusory surfaces appear more or less homogenous in color, no dual aspect is present in these cases. However, situations are conceivable where an illusory perceived picture plane goes hand in hand with a perceived pictorial space. In principle, even the entire perceived "real space" could be illusory if a suitable (future) binocular virtual reality device were used. At the other extreme, one could think of cases where neither the perceived picture plane nor the perceived pictorial space are illusory. Imagine, for example, an observer standing inside a camera obscura looking at a translucent screen which is located in between the observer and the camera's pinhole (assuming some device which compensates for the optical inversion). In this case the observer will have the proper impression of a picture, with the perceived pictorial space corresponding to the real scene in front of the camera obscura.

These final observations once again sustain our initial claim to the effect that an appropriate account of *both* aspects of the dual nature of picture perception necessitates referring to the *percept* itself. This feature of the percept needs to be carefully distinguished from how—that is, by which *distal* stimulus—it is generated. In consequence, from a psychological viewpoint the emergence of dual percepts can in principle be discussed without wedding it to the notoriously difficult concept of veridicality from the start.

Related Forms of Perceptual Duality

What makes duality phenomena an important topic for general structural accounts of perception is the observation that they are not the least

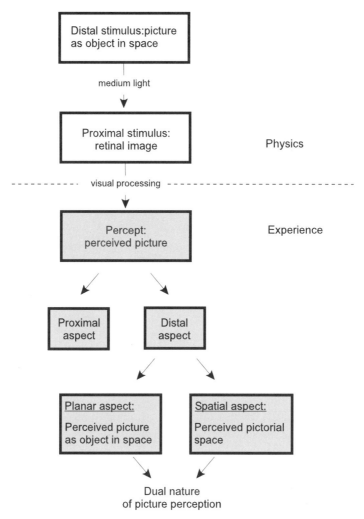

Figure 4.1
Extension of the standard framework of perception for the case of picture percep-
tion. As for the *proximal aspect,* see the section "Related Forms of Perceptual
Duality."

restricted to the case of picture perception. Obvious other examples are mirror images and, in certain cases, perceived illumination patterns such as shadows and slide projections. In the case of a mirror, typically a dual percept is evoked in which the impression of a glossy, metallic, and opaque surface, belonging to perceived real space, coexists with the impression of a spatial configuration "behind the surface," the so-called mirror image. Similar phenomena occur with other kinds of glossy surfaces such as water. Trompe l'oeil–like effects can occur if mirrors are looked at obliquely, meaning that the mirror surface is not perceived, while the mirror image is perceived as a part of real space.

In most situations, perceived shadows on a surface are merely an aspect of perceived illumination. As mentioned before, this phenomenon alone will not count as an instance of duality. Sometimes, however, the shadow additionally takes on an objectlike or even spatial quality, which may then be counted as an instance of duality in perception. The same phenomenon can be encountered with highlights on a surface. A limiting case is a perceived projected slide, where a perceived illumination pattern on the wall may coexist with a full-fledged perceived pictorial space.

Even though the case of mirrors and objectlike shadows exhibits essentially the same kind of perceptual duality found in the case of picture perception proper, there are also some interesting differences concerning the perceptual relation between perceived real space and the respective counterparts of perceived pictorial space (e.g., a mirror image). For in these cases, perceived real-world objects and certain perceived dual-world objects often are linked perceptually in the sense that the latter are perceived as being caused by the former.

Finally, perception in general comprises a kind of duality of aspects, pertaining to the percept, which bears some resemblance to the duality discussed before, even though in some respects it is fundamentally different in nature. These aspects are sometimes addressed as a "proximal aspect" or "painter's mode," on the one hand, and the "distal" or "world aspect/mode," on the other (see, e.g., Rock 1983; Todorovic 2002). Whereas the latter refers to the perceived scene (perceived-objects-in-space), the former is meant to capture aspects of the percept that are thought of as being more closely related to the proximal stimulus. Take, for example, a situation in which an observer is looking at a disk that is tilted relative to the direction of view. The observer will then perceive a tilted circular object (distal aspect) and *at the same time* will have the impression of a more or less elliptical contour (proximal aspect). The latter aspect closely resembles the perceived contour that a corresponding picture drawn in perspective would display. Note that here the planar aspect of the perceived picture is referred to. Nevertheless the proximal aspect should not be identified with the planar aspect in picture perception, because only in the case of a perceived picture do we also have the impression of a planar surface in space. In consequence in a more complete account of picture perception, three aspects could be distinguished: first, the proximal aspect and, second, the distal aspect which, in turn, splits up into the planar and the spatial aspects. The necessity of such a triple account becomes obvious when pictures are looked at obliquely.

4.3   WHEN AND WHY DO DUAL PERCEPTS EMERGE? SOME REFLECTIONS

Having outlined our concept of duality in picture perception and in other perceptual phenomena, we now want to point out why we believe that perceptual duality provides an important clue to our understanding of basic features of perception in general. In particular, we will briefly discuss some ideas about the functional role perceptual duality might play in achieving perceptual stability in the presence of ambiguity. To do so, we first need to take another and slightly more detailed glance at the general scheme of perception discussed earlier.

The Concept and Problem of Inverse Projection

One of the milestones in the development of theories of vision was Kepler's theory of light rays projecting onto the retina, thereby forming the so-called retinal image (cf. Lindberg 1976). By his account, the eye works essentially in the same way as a lens camera. His theory made it possible to integrate earlier theories of vision based on the concept of central projection into a modern optical framework. Before, the theory of central projection had already played an essential role in Renaissance painting, where it achieved an impressively mature state (which, in turn, was foreshadowed by ancient theory and art). Given a real or imagined scene, the goal was to produce a painting that, ideally at least, yielded the same projection to the eye, and hence the same visual impression. In principle at least, this method provides a powerful means to generate *equivalent stimuli,* that is, stimuli that generate identical retinal images and therefore have the same effect on the visual system (when they are viewed monocularly from a specified viewing position and in certain fixed illumination conditions). From a modern viewpoint, the concept of equivalent stimuli refers solely to the physical principles connecting the distal and the proximal stimulus. Although this level of analysis is sufficient if merely the Renaissance painters' goal is pursued, it falls short of providing us with a perceptual theory that allows us to predict *what* is seen when we are looking at a scene or a realistic painting and to explain *why* we see what we see.

The first problem that comes to mind is that, given a retinal image, there is an indefinite number of—equivalent—possible scenes (seen from a fixed viewing position) that could have generated this proximal stimulus. If perception is understood as generating a scene-representation then the question arises, which of these possible scenes should be represented? These scenes might be called the possible *virtual spaces* associated with the proximal stimulus. Of course, this question not only arises in the context of picture perception but applies also to perception in general. Consider, for instance, a cube viewed from a certain position. Usually, we will perceive it as a cube. This cube could now be distorted in many different ways without changing the retinal image. Hence, in all these cases we would have the same percept; that is, we would perceive these objects as cubes. The question now arises of why, given only that proximal stimulus, our visual system generates a representation of a cube rather than a representation of any of the other compatible objects.

If one would now produce an equivalent trompe l'oeil, we would of course also see a cube. What the theory of central projection underlying Renaissance art would then explain is that we perceive the *same* in both situations, that is, when viewing the real cube and the picture of the cube, but not *why* we see a cube at all. For when viewed from a fixed viewing position, the picture (i.e., the proximal stimulus generated by it) is associated with an indefinite number of possible virtual spaces. Although it is fairly unproblematic to speak of *the perceived* virtual (or pictorial) space for a given observer at a given time, it seems unjustified to speak of *the* virtual space of a picture independent of an observer. Unfortunately, many investigators start out with the idea of a fixed virtual space of a picture, directly or indirectly derived from the original scene underlying the picture (e.g., the scene photographed), which is then taken as a standard of reference in their evaluation of the judgments made by their subjects concerning their *perceived* virtual space.

George Berkeley (1709/1975) and other early scholars in the field of vision already clearly recognized the fundamental problem that the just mentioned nonuniqueness throws up for any theory of vision. In computational accounts of vision this difficulty is known as the ill-posedness of the (unconstrained) "inverse projection problem." As for human vision, the situation seems to be even worse insofar as the actual percept need not even correspond to any of the possible virtual scenes associated with the retinal image (leaving aside the question of what correspondence could mean here exactly). As a consequence, a theory of vision has to face the major challenge of spelling out the principles according to which our visual system constructs a more or less well-specified—simplest? most likely?—perceived scene from the proximal stimulus. This includes an analysis of why and how the visual system organizes our perceived world into meaningful wholes, that is, perceived objects, in the first place. For in the light pattern reaching the eye these wholes are not present in any immediate way. So, strictly speaking, the theory of central projection underlying Renaissance art is silent about this construction aspect as well.

What Is Wrong with the Concept of Equivalent Stimuli?

On closer inspection, it turns out that the Renaissance explanation of why realistic paintings work, based solely on the theory of central projection, is in fact insufficient. For the strict notion of equivalent stimuli evoked in this context is not applicable. This is because a painting and a depicted scene hardly ever generate identical proximal stimuli. Ironically, this discrepancy is most obvious in the case of line drawings based on contours, which are commonly used to illustrate the geometry of projection underlying Renaissance art. To understand why we perceive such a drawing in the way we do, we need to go beyond the *physical* notion of equivalence with respect to the retinal images generated. Rather, a *perceptual* notion of equivalence is needed in which the constitution of perceived objects on the basis of their contours plays a central role. In other words, if one does not want to rely merely on the experience that "it works," which may be sufficient for an artist, a theory of vision is needed to understand this weaker notion of equivalence. However, even in seemingly less problematic cases (photography or photorealistic paintings) the strict notion of equivalence typically fails. For instance, the spectral composition and the intensity of the light reaching the eye (from the picture and the depicted scene, respectively) in most cases are clearly different, with contrast being severely reduced in the former case.

Even if it were possible to achieve strict equivalence, the usefulness of this concept is limited from the start because it is restricted to monocular viewing and does not take into account the dynamics of perception. That is, the observer's viewpoint has to be fixed, thereby excluding bodily movements, which are so important in ordinary vision. Even in the case of monocular vision with a fixed viewing position, accommodation introduces a dynamic element, yielding different results for an observed painting and the corresponding scene.

Last but not least, the fact that most realistic paintings evoke a dual percept clearly shows the nonequivalence of the picture and the corresponding scene. For, if they were equivalent, a trompe l'oeil effect would have to occur. In other words, one would have the visual impression of a real scene as viewed through a window. Instead, the visual system comes up with a percept in which two perceived virtual spaces—one of them being the picture plane in a certain position in space—are intertwined, as it were. Why does this happen? Rather than being a nuisance, the aforementioned difficulties turn out to be a clue for our theoretical understanding of the dual nature of picture perception and possibly even of some basic structural features of perception in general.

Cue Integration and Cue Segregation

Before turning to the question just posed, we will first briefly sketch some features of the standard account of depth perception in general and how it is usually applied to perceived depth in pictures. On this account, the perception of spatial features in a scene is conceived as being based on a number of so-called depth cues. Some of them already apply to static monocular viewing, such as shading and cues derived from the geometry of central projection. The latter include occlusion, texture gradients, height in the projection plane, and so-called linear perspective cues (referring to certain linear image elements, such as converging lines interpreted as parallels in space). Other monocular cues involve dynamic components, such as the cue of motion parallax and the ocular-motor cue of accommodation. Finally, we have cues that only work for binocular vision, such as binocular disparity and the ocular-motor cue of convergence. For a more detailed review see, for example, Stephen Palmer (1999).

Considered individually, each of these cues, if applicable at all, tends to yield depth information of only limited reliability and strength. This suggests the assumption, shared by most researchers, that the visual system in one way or another combines various depth cues to create a sufficiently reliable and sufficiently specific scene representation. In the recent computational literature on spatial features of perception this idea has led to various formal models of "cue integration" (see, e.g., Landy et al. 1995, who also review some of these models and related Bayesian approaches).

The idea of cue combination is commonly employed as an explanation for what will be called here the *monocular depth enhancement* in picture perception. This is the well-known observation that in most cases the perceived depth pertaining to perceived pictorial space is markedly more distinctive, or pronounced, when pictures are viewed monocularly, from a fixed viewpoint, and through a reduction tube that shields off the picture frame. (In fact, in many cases a similar phenomenon is found for colors, illumination, and gloss in perceived pictorial space.) Only recently has monocular depth enhancement been studied quantitatively in a series of studies (Koenderink, van Doorn, and Kappers 1995; Koenderink et al. 2001).

The standard explanation for monocular depth enhancement is based on the assumption that under those constrained viewing conditions, conflicting depth cues that under ordinary viewing conditions signal flatness (e.g., binocular disparity, motion parallax) are eliminated. In ordinary viewing, in contrast, these conflicting cues are combined with the static monocular cues responsible for the impression of pictorial space, yielding a single compromise scene representation.

In being confined to the concept of a single scene representation as the outcome of a cue combination process, traditional cue integration theories are by their very nature unable to account for duality phenomena in perception. However, what needs to be accounted for in picture perception is not only the monocular depth enhancement phenomenon but, first and foremost, the duality of picture perception. One could of course contemplate extending the standard account accordingly. Let us roughly sketch one general way of how this could be done. Assume that given a certain proximal stimulus, the visual system encounters a situation in which considerable conflicts between cues occur, and two (or possibly more) sufficiently rich coherent subsets can be found, each of which is apt to trigger a scene representation of its own. Then in certain cases the visual system will constitute corresponding subpercepts that coexist, rather than just form a kind of simple compromise or decide on only one of them. The formation of different subpercepts, each of which involves a process of cue integration, goes hand in hand with a kind of cue clustering we will call *cue segregation*.

These different subpercepts are not simply generated in isolation but there are mutual interactions at various levels of processing. Adopting a term coined by Sedgwick (chapter 3 this volume), we assume a *cross-talk* between those processes. For instance, the reduction of the distinctiveness of perceived depth in ordinary picture viewing (as opposed to static monocular viewing) might be explained by a cross-talk between (processes generating) the perceived picture plane and the perceived pictorial space. The same goes for the often reported inverse phenomenon that in certain situations the planar aspect of a perceived picture seems less vivid in the presence of a perceived pictorial space that involves a strong impression of depth. (Further potential instances of cross-talk are described later on and in chapter 3 in this volume.)

Another kind of interlock between the generated subpercepts is some kind of phenomenal binding, which in the case of picture perception is experienced as the *perceptual unity* of a perceived picture. The perceived pictorial space and the perceived picture plane perceptually belong to each other, as it were. For certain types of duality, the visual system even seems to create a suitable type of gestalt (e.g., "perceived picture"), which due to learning possibly becomes equipped with specific higher-order cues. Furthermore, as already mentioned before, such subpercepts may be experienced as standing in a hierarchical order to each other, only one of them belonging to perceived real space.

Like any other account of perception, this scheme needs of course to be complemented by the concept of attention. In particular, attention may be shifted between different subpercepts, possibly leading to a refinement or enhanced vividness of one subpercept at the expense of another.

Finally, one might contemplate integrating the concept of a proximal mode into our scheme by assuming that it is primarily related to an initial state of processing that forms the basis for the later extraction of cues and precedes the processing of cue integration and segregation. The previous remarks on cross-talk, phenomenal binding, and shifts of attention mutatis mutandis apply here as well.

Needless to say, our proposal of how duality concepts might be integrated into common concepts of cue integration throws up more questions than it is able to answer. Nonetheless, we are convinced that duality phenomena in perception should not simply be neglected and therefore that they should be integrated into concepts of cue integration in one way or another. Maybe, the cue concept will itself eventually turn out to be inadequate, after all, which then would call for a still more fundamental revision of the general conceptual framework under consideration.

Duality in Perception: Functional Aspects

At first sight, duality in perception might look like a defect—at least, when the visual system is viewed from a perspective that emphasizes its representational features. Why should the system come up with two or more different interpretations of the proximal stimulus at the same time? We suggest that duality is one of a variety of strategies our visual systems employs to cope with perceptual ambiguities. In one way or another, these strategies allow the visual system to represent (at the level of the precept) the possibility of certain alternative representations compatible with the proximal stimulus. On the standard account of perception in contrast, the visual system would always have to decide for one specific scene-representation, regardless of what kind of input it gets (even though perhaps nobody actually will maintain such a strict position). When conflicting or insufficient cues are present, this could in certain situations lead to unreliable scene-representations (illusions) or to the oscillation between different scene-representations (bi- or multistability). In fact, our visual system appears to reduce the frequency of risky illusions or confusing multistability by a number of strategies, such as the following ones (cf. figure 4.2):

1. *Perceived occlusion.* Here, we have an overall impression of the partially occluded object (so-called amodal completion; cf. Michotte, Thinès, and Crabbé 1964/1991). At the same time we have the visual impression that the occluded parts are not visible, which leaves open other possibilities of what could be behind the occluding object. Note that we are *not* simply speaking here about the *physical* fact of one object being occluded by another relative to the eye but of *perceived* occlusion.

2. *Perceptual vagueness.* Think, for instance, of an object seen through fog or of the diffuse character of the perceived size and distance of objects far away.

3. *Impossible figures.* Here a visual overall impression emerges that locally conforms to physical scene descriptions but which is globally inconsistent as a global scene description.

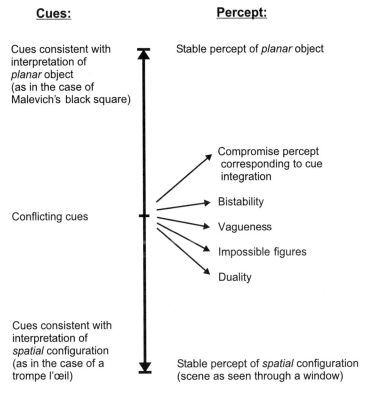

Figure 4.2
Strategies of how the visual system copes with perceptual ambiguities. The two extremes (top/bottom) correspond to two stimuli that evoke different clear-cut percepts. As an example, the case of picture perception is considered. If, now, one proximal stimulus is gradually transformed into the other, conflicting cues will arise. Some of the responses of our visual system are listed on the right.

4. *Interplay between proximal and distal mode*. Think, for example, of a house seen through a window, which at the level of the percept simultaneously appears smaller than the window (proximal mode) and larger than the window (distal mode).

5. *Duality*. Various forms of perceptual duality, such as those discussed earlier (pictures, mirrors, objectlike shadows).

Of course, several of these phenomena, including bistability, may occur in combination. Simple examples are pictures of an object in fog (duality, vagueness) or the picture of a Necker cube (duality, bistability).

These examples suggest that our visual system possesses a rather sophis-
ticated ambiguity management up to the level of the percept, which so far
has hardly been taken into account in a systematic way.

4.4   FURTHER SHORTCOMINGS OF THE WINDOW METAPHOR IN PICTURE PERCEPTION

Let us focus attention again on picture perception proper. As pointed out
before, the classical window analogy is at least incomplete, insofar as it
fails to accommodate the dual nature of picture perception. One might
now contemplate maintaining the window metaphor by applying it only
to the *spatial* aspect of perceived pictures. This would then imply that the
planar and the spatial aspect correspond to different inverse projections.
We will now discuss two phenomena that show that even this more liberal interpretation of the window analogy is inappropriate. Interestingly,
these phenomena seem to be restricted to the case of picture perception
proper, that is, they are not encountered in trompe l'oeil situations. In
consequence, these intricacies seem, indeed, to be intrinsic features of the
dual processing of pictures.

Compensation Hypotheses versus Cross-Talk

First, we will deal with the question of what happens when pictures are
viewed from different positions. For each viewing position, a different retinal image results, each of these associated with a specific set of possible
virtual spaces in terms of central projection. According to the window
analogy, corresponding changes of the perceived pictorial space would
have to occur when the viewing position is changed. There is some evidence that the observed changes in many situations appear to be less than
expected, however. We will call this the *robustness* of perceived pictorial
space (for a review of some of the relevant literature see, e.g., Rogers
1995).[1] According to Pirenne (1970), changes that appear to be in line with
the window metaphor occur in the case of trompe l'oeil (e.g., with Pozzo's
aforementioned ceiling in Sant'Ignazio). When viewed from a viewpoint
other than the station point, drastic distortions may be perceived, which
are much stronger than those ordinarily experienced in picture perception
proper, that is, when a dual percept is evoked (where the station point is
an ideal viewpoint corresponding to the center of projection).

A number of researchers have proposed an explanation of such phenomena in terms of a so-called compensation mechanism (such as Gibson

1947/1982, Pirenne 1970, or Kubovy 1986; for a discussion, see Rogers 1995). In a nutshell, such compensation hypotheses assume several stages of visual processing assumed to work roughly as follows. First, the picture surface and how it is situated in space are determined; building on that, a "correct" viewing position is determined by the postulated mechanism, relative to which the visual system finally constructs the pictorial space. Such approaches appear problematic for various reasons. The theoretical question arises of what the "correct" viewing position should be and according to what principles the visual system should construct such a point. Also, the empirical adequacy of these approaches seems questionable. Ideally, by such an account the visual system would always construct the same viewing position relative to the perceived picture plane and hence the same associated pictorial space. This is obviously not the case. An interesting extreme case is that of anamorphic pictures. Consider, for example, an anamorphotic painting of a skull as in Hans Holbein's famous *Ambassadors* (1533). From the correct station point a skull is seen, whereas from a frontoparallel viewing position we have the impression of a pretty long egglike object. This is clearly at odds with the compensation prediction.[2] Finally, it does not seem plausible that the visual system is endowed with a complex mechanism just for the case of picture perception.

Instead of assuming such a compensation mechanism, we hypothesize that the aforementioned phenomena may to some extent be due to a crosstalk between the processes yielding perceived pictorial space and the perceived picture plane, respectively. In cases where the perceived picture plane—thanks to shape constancy mechanisms—appears more or less invariant, the robustness of pictorial space found in many situations might be due to an influence the latter exerts on the former (for a similar position, see chapter 3 in this volume).

Note that this concept of cross-talk (which without doubt is in need of a much more detailed elaboration) has the interesting property that it could in principle work both ways. Consider, for instance, the example of the anamorphic skull, which on the picture plane corresponds to a long egglike patch. Recall that from the station point, the skull is seen. At the same time it is virtually impossible to see a long egglike patch on the picture plane; instead, a patch whose shape resembles the contour of the skull is seen. This might be due to a reverse cross-talk effect, namely, an influence perceived pictorial space exerts on the perceived picture plane.

Finally, recall that compensation theories usually assume that perceived pictorial space corresponds to *some* scene representation (viz. one of the possible virtual spaces associated with a "corrected" viewing position). In contrast, we assume that due to cross-talk and other factors, "incoherent" perceived pictorial spaces may emerge, that is, spaces that do not correspond to *any* possible scene representation. This incoherence seems to be one of the reasons pictures look "strange" from certain viewing positions. Certain experimental findings reported in the literature (see, e.g., Rogers 1995) may be interpreted this way. Last but not least, such intricacies highlight the fundamental conceptual and methodological difficulties notions of correspondence between the physical world and perceptual experience raise from the start.

Dissociation of Spatial Reference Systems

We now turn to the second feature of picture perception that is not in line with the more liberal reading of the window metaphor. In everyday situations our visual system usually establishes, roughly speaking, an environment-centered spatial frame of reference. This includes the basic orientations of the horizontal and the vertical. In addition we have a perceptual awareness of ourselves as looking at objects from a certain direction. We may, for instance, have the impression of looking down to the floor, which itself appears horizontal. The same thing happens when we are looking through a window. Typically, we then have a unifying reference system that connects the perceived world in front of and behind the window.

The same kind of integration is achieved by our visual system in the case of a trompe l'oeil situation. Imagine, for instance, that we are looking at a trompe l'oeil from the station point. Imagine further that the trompe l'oeil is painted in such a way that in our perception the room we are standing in (along with its floor) continues in perceived pictorial space (i.e., ideally there is no perceptual distinction between perceived real and perceived pictorial space; an example of such a trompe l'oeil is the fresco by Baldassare Peruzzi in the *Salla della prospettiva, Villa Farnesina, Rome* [see Kubovy 1986]). Assume now that the trompe l'oeil was moved up the wall in such a way that its bottom now is above our head. If a trompe l'oeil effect would then still occur, what we would see then—in line with inverse projection—would be a ground plane tilted down toward us. The visual system would maintain a common frame of reference: the perceived ground plane belonging to pictorial space would no longer appear horizontal, and we would have the visual impression of looking at that plane.

Consider now a similar situation, where we look at a picture, but no trompe l'oeil effect occurs. When the painting is now moved up, we typically still have the impression of a horizontal ground plane (in conflict with inverse projection) which appears to us as being seen from *above* while at the same time the picture plane is perceived as being seen from *below*. In other words, we here get a dissociation between the spatial frame of reference pertaining to perceived real space (including the picture plane), on the one hand, and perceived pictorial space, on the other. Metaphorically speaking, it is as if in picture perception proper our visual system takes a separate virtual viewpoint associated with perceived pictorial space (analogous to the "mental eye" in Koenderink et al. 2001). As demonstrated by our everyday experience of looking at a photograph in a newspaper lying horizontally on the table in front of us and many other situations, this phenomenon extends to a variety of possible orientations and positions of the picture plane. Similar remarks apply to perceived size and distance in pictures. The dissociation observed in these cases goes hand in hand with a relative stability of the spatial frames of reference associated with perceived pictorial space, which in turn is an important aspect of the robustness of pictorial space.

4.5 EPILOGUE

The preceding analysis gives only a first impression of the richness of the perceptual phenomena involved in the perception of pictures and, to some extent, mirrors and shadows. Further complexities arise when pictures are painted or projected on curved or transparent surfaces. In those situations sometimes a complex phenomenal interlock between perceived pictorial space and perceived picture surface occurs, which no longer can simply be described as the coexistence of two neatly separable aspects (several examples of this can be found in contemporary art, e.g., in the work of Tony Oursler). Another type of complexity arises when pictures involve multiple perspectives, or when their rendering becomes less realistic, as for example in impressionist art. Last but not least, the dual-ity of the spatial and the planar aspect extends to the dynamic case of motion pictures. Without doubt, a much more refined theoretical account, thorough phenomenological studies, and experimental investigations are needed to obtain a deeper understanding of such phenomena in picture perception.

Once one has an increased awareness of duality in perception, a plethora of analogous phenomena that go beyond the dichotomy of a spatial and a planar aspect attracts one's attention. Suffice it to briefly mention a few examples. First, duality can occur at various levels simultaneously. Think, for example, of perceived pictures in a picture or paintings like Givseppe Arcimboldo's *Summer*. Here one perceives (as a part of perceived pictorial space) a head composed of fruit and vegetables. That is, at the same time a head and an arrangement of fruit and vegetables are seen. Or think of a wooden sculpture of a woman, where, loosely speaking, the impression of a woman and of a piece of wood coexist. In theater the simultaneous perception of an actor on the stage and of a character within the drama "put on stage" may be counted as an instance of dual perception (e.g., Polanyi 1970b). Of course, in all these cases, an additional symbolic aspect can come into play that increases complexity even further. All in all, perception seems to embody some of the complexities typically thought of as being characteristic of language-based cognition. In certain respects, at least, our perceptual experience sometimes seems to resemble a multilayered narration more closely than a straightforward representation of "what there is."

Notes

1. Note that in order to verify "that a change is less than expected," one would, strictly speaking, have to compare the perceived pictorial space with *all* of the possible virtual spaces associated with the retinal image. As a measure of discrepancy one would then have to take the distance to the best-fitting virtual space, as it were. Unfortunately, most studies in the field base this measure only on a single distinguished virtual space associated with the respective viewing position. To this end, a "true" virtual space is singled out associated with a standard viewing position (station point). This true virtual space is then geometrically transformed into "the" virtual spaces for other viewing positions. So far we have not found an adequate justification for this approach.

2. If the visual system were able to reconstruct the correct viewpoint, a skull would be seen in both cases. If, in contrast, the system always picked a virtual viewing position perpendicular to the perceived picture plane, the long egglike object would be seen in both situations.

Chapter 5

Perceptual Strategies and Pictorial Content

Mark Rollins

5.1 INTRODUCTION

Recently in cognitive science there has been a healthy trend toward rethinking some old debates. In particular, the traditional opposition between constructivism and direct realism—the view that perception depends on mental representations versus the view that it does not—has been cast aside by several philosophers and scientists in favor of what can be seen as a hybrid account. Such hybrids go by a variety of names: "animate" or "utilitarian" or "interactive" theories of vision, for instance. (Ballard 1991; Ramachandran 1990). But all are distinguished by their rejection of central ideas in the work of David Marr. Although Marr's "computational Gibsonism," as he called it, is already a compromise, it combines elements of constructivism and direct realism in the wrong way: it restricts the range of knowledge on which the visual system can draw and builds certain assumptions into it. Such constraints have the effect of making the perceiver respond to visual information partly *as if* the response were direct, because no variation is permitted across perceivers. There can be no difference due to background knowledge; thus the response is to some extent determined by causal law. But constraints of that sort merely provide a framework within which elaborate representations are constructed. What is wrong with Marr's compromise, according to recent research, is that it *presupposes* that such rich representations are needed; and some evidence strongly suggests that they are not.

An alternative that has recently emerged makes vision depend on representations but of a rather sketchy sort: "visual semiworlds," as they have been called (Churchland, Ramachandran, and Sejnowski 1994). These are sufficient, it is said, precisely because perception is *not* constrained in Marr's way. The visual system draws upon background knowledge of various kinds, and it collaborates with other sensory systems and motor control: the eyes conspire with the ears and with muscles, tendons, and joints to enable the viewer to take representational shortcuts. The virtue of such a cooperative sensory scheme is that it makes possible *perceptual strategies*. With those in hand, precise computations and representations are no longer required.[1] I shall refer to a theory of this type as a strategic design theory (SDT). The primary question I want to address is how SDT might be applied to picture perception and, in particular, to the perception of pictorial space in the context of visual art.

An Example: Motion Capture

It is well known that a series of flashing lights can produce the appearance of motion. But, as Vilayanur Ramachandran (1990) points out, it is also the case that even if one light is occluded, it will appear to move behind the occluder if it is located properly in the context of other alternately flashing lights. This is an instance of a class of cases that we can call (following Ramachandran) *capture phenomena*: the location of the missing light and its motion from one point to another are captured, as it were, by the other lights, although the absent stimuli cannot be actually registered in perception. Importantly, this effect cuts across different sense modalities: alternating the location of sounds, one of which corresponds to the position of a flashing light, can also produce the appearance of motion to the point behind the occluder. Here the visual information is captured by auditory stimuli.

Motion involves a change of position, of course, and a spatial trajectory from one place to the next. Where the moving stimulus is complex, there is also the problem of defining a spatial register between features of the stimulus at one moment in time and the same features a few moments later. This "correspondence problem" is one, Ramachandran argues, which motion capture is able to sidestep. To cite his central example, if this account is correct, it will not be necessary for the visual system to compute the trajectories of each and every spot on a leopard as it leaps from tree to tree.

It is clear that knowledge plays an important role in these cases; namely, in the assumptions that are needed to disregard information. For instance, as Ramachandran notes, the utilitarian solution to the correspondence problem in motion detection presupposes the knowledge that spots do not normally jump off of surfaces or otherwise move around discontinuously. Such knowledge is part of a conception of the physical world, having to do with properties of surfaces. Nonetheless, there is an important sense in which such assumptions or constraints are *ecologically specific*. Although the constraints may be inherent in either the nature of the task or the visual equipment available to the perceiver, different constraints can be brought to bear by the different strategies employed to perform the task. And the training of the perceiver's abilities in this regard will be context dependent. Thus, which tasks are governed by which constraints can vary from perceiver to perceiver.

In any case, what strategic design theories explicitly deny is that knowledge of this sort can be used to compute or infer exact locations of each and every spot. It may be that the relevant knowledge in this case is really procedural; it involves knowing how to move a cluster of points or regions in space along a trajectory, keeping them together without counting them, in effect. If so, the knowledge need not be encoded (certainly not symbolically) but only have the status of a conditioned (internal) disposition or ability. But even if the knowledge is theoretical, vested in declarative or semantic memory, the point is that it does not specify, nor is it used to compute, all of the possibly relevant details. At any rate, the claim of the hybrid approach is not that no representation is required for perception at all but only that fewer or less complete ones will do. The point is that a perceptual task is performed without a detailed representation of the sort on which Marr-style computation would depend.

What, then, does motion capture have to do with static picture perception of the sort required for visual art? The answer is that in the SDT approach, nature generally favors an economical use of resources. This is apparent in the case of motion capture as a way of handling the correspondence problem, and it will emerge that the same principle in a different form is supposed to be at work when we process the information in a painting or drawing. But before we turn to that, I first want to consider the sense in which SDT might be said to view perception as partly direct.

5.2   WHAT IS A *HYBRID* PERCEPTUAL THEORY?

The claim that picture perception is partly direct means different things to different people. It is sometimes said, for instance, that picture perception, even from a Gibsonian perspective, is indirect, although the processes by which the information in the picture are accessed involve no elaborate internal representations (e.g., Sedgwick, chapter 3 in this volume). But this means only that perception of the depicted scene is mediated by the *picture,* which can itself provide information directly. In the words of a philosopher whose views are congenial to directness: "Pictures are visual prostheses; they extend the informational system … in ways that depend upon and also augment our ability to identify things by their appearance" (Lopes 1996, p. 144). According to this view, pictures are external records of events that make internal records, at least in the form of detailed copies, unnecessary. In this case, when it is said that "picture perception" is indirect, that simply means that objects, scenes, or events are perceived by way of a picture. We can therefore call this the *pictorial surrogate* view.

However, sometimes it is said that picture perception is indirect (according to James J. Gibson), and more is meant than that pictures mediate the pickup of information, which the depicted scene would also contain (e.g., Cutting and Massirioni 1998). The claim, in this case, means that accessing that information in the picture may, in fact, require internal representations. However, based on this view, whether or not that is so will depend on the nature of the picture. Sometimes picture perception will require internal representations, and sometimes it will not. Thus the "picture perception" that is partly direct, according to this use, is really the generic ability and not any particular instance of it; and "partly" means "for some pictures, but not all." Call this the *occasional constructivist* account.

Neither of these views entails a hybrid theory of the sort that I wish to elucidate. Such a theory claims that individual pictures are perceived through a mixture of direct and indirect processes. This view might be taken to apply to all pictures. But it might also be more limited in scope. For instance, we could adapt the occasional constructivist insight—that pictures need not all be perceived using the same processes—but maintain that pictures fall along a continuum, rather than being of two distinct types. Purely direct access and wholly indirect perception would be found at the ends of the continuum, with mixtures of various sorts in between. This would amount to an *occasional hybrid* theory.[2] My focus would then be on the pictures in the middle of the range. Even there, however, there is the need to investigate the sense in which the direct component of perception might be direct.

At first glance, the sense in which SDT treats perception as partly direct seems clear. In positing various ways in which the visual system economizes on resource use, SDT cuts back, in effect, on mental representations. It envisions, for example, replacing the precise delineation of details with spatial tracking of coarsely coded features to resolve the problem of correspondence. It is possible, then, that the "direct component" of SDT is no more than the absence of an elaborate mental representation and the reliance on partial information contained in the momentary glance. Perception would thus be direct just insofar as it is not indirect.[3]

However, even partial representations are internal media that stand between the perceiver and the world, and they can involve a constructive process, even if it only results in relatively simple forms. In any case, the emphasis in SDT on active processes, such as the movements of eyes, head, or body, makes it clear that perception is imagined to be partly direct in a much more positive sense than the absence of elaborate representations would suggest. Directness is identified, perhaps, with the mechanisms by which momentary glances are coordinated (or with their effects on perception), rather than the mere fact that the information they contain is fragmentary and incomplete. This suggests that we can construe the directness of perception according to SDT in the following way: internal representations are required for picture perception, but the roles they play in perception are *both inferential and noninferential* in form. In the discussion that follows, I will explain noninferential operations on representations in terms of perceptual strategies. It is by virtue of these strategic operations that perception is direct. The fact that they can be defined in terms of uses of representations makes SDT a hybrid theory in a very strong sense.

Armed with that interpretation of SDT, then, we should be able to define the issue of hybridity in a clear and precise way. There are, it would seem, two opposing positions. On one hand, there is David Marr's account, which is often linked to Gibson's by virtue of Marr's emphasis on *constraints* on computation. In the words of Michael Kubovy and William Epstein (in press): "According to the approach of Marr and Gibson constraints are neither (1) lodged in the mind nor (2) are they active constituents in the perceptual process. They are the conditions which the world must satisfy if the computational algorithms are to go through." The implication is that perception is direct to the extent that it relies on bottom-up processes, constrained in this way.[4] If pictures do, indeed, come in a variety of types, we might then argue that they vary according to how much weight they require to be assigned to bottom-up, modularized processes, on the one hand, and to top-down, cognitive processes, on the other. For some pictures (those midway along a continuum), both would be given significant weight.

On the other side, there is Ramachandran's SDT-type account, which rejects Marr's stage-based approach and defines a composite theory in terms of an inferential/noninferential process blend. The noninferential ingredient, on this account, is what allows us to employ internal representations that are only partial and incomplete.

Unfortunately, the matter is not as simple as that dichotomy suggests. There are complications on both sides of the fence. For one thing, even proponents of a paradigmatic form of SDT, such as Ramachandran, embrace modularity in a certain sense, at the same time as they are rejecting Marr's modularized computational model. The operations of modules depend on assumptions and constraints. This means that the visual system's instantiation of such constraints does not preclude its reliance on heuristics and strategies. If perception is direct to the extent that it employs processes that are bottom-up, SDT suggests that it can also be direct in another sense, namely, in the noninferential control processes by which its resources are deployed. For SDT in the flesh, the two forms of directness can hand in hand.

On the other side of the fence, there is the theory of James Cutting, which he calls "Directed Vision" (1998). According to that account, information in a scene is actually overspecified: there will be multiple sources from which a perceiver can pick the information up. Thus the relation between information and the properties by which it is specified is not, as Gibson thought, one to one. Nonetheless, the "bottom-up" sense of directness remains in play: whatever the source happens to be, it may provide the information without intervention from cognitive processes. Thus Cutting describes direct specification in a way that suggests a close alignment with Marr: "[I]n many cases the specification of a percept by information can be written as a deductive syllogism.... That is, given certain assumptions (axioms), a definitive conclusion can be drawn" (1998, p. 86). Further, "natural law is followed [in perception] because there is no alternative, and mathematics is used because that is the way perceptual systems work. The natural law and mathematics are deeply ingrained in the nervous system, and their rules constrain and guide perception and cognition" (p. 75). As I have noted, Cutting maintains that the perception of some pictures depends on inference and higher-order cognition, and this opens the door to a Marr-style hybrid account, at least on occasion. At the same time, the many-to-one relation that Cutting describes also implies that perceivers can respond (directly) to the same information in different ways: he speaks of different "styles" by which perceivers may select or integrate information. Although he does not put it this way, here again the two forms of hybridization appear to work together.

That fact is important for an understanding of pictures. In recent years, it has often been argued that what a picture represents depends on what can be recognized in it, using ordinary perceptual abilities (Schier 1986). That is, no special training in the use of pictorial conventions is required.[5] This Recognition theory, as it is called, implies that pictures are individuated by the particulars of the psychological response they tend to generate. What any picture represents, its content in one sense, is determined by what can be seen in it; and what can be seen in it depends on perceptual processes. This is true, presumably, of both the type of object or scene that the picture represents and the particular instance or token of that type: a babe-in-arms, for example, as well as the infant Jesus held by its mother, Mary. Insofar as picture perception is indirect, we are inclined to say that the content of the picture is determined by the content of the internal representations produced in response to it. There is, then, the difficult question of how to individuate those internal representations. But Recognition theory has been endorsed by some psychologists who are friendly to the idea that perception is partly direct (e.g., Cutting and Massironi 1998). If they are right, it must be possible to say how, on a recognition-based account, the content of the picture is partly identified in terms of direct information pickup. Recognition accounts of pictorial content draw on Marr's type of computational Gibsonism. But, as the complexities described make clear, that leaves open the possibility that the directness of picture perception might be understood in more than one way. My interest is not really in the proper use of the term "perceptual directness." My aim is, rather, to indicate the impact on the theory of depiction that exploring the non-Marrian construal of directness might have. What I will argue is that the contributions of the two psychological components, direct and indirect, to pictorial content are not what Recognition theories have taken them to be.

5.3   PERCEPTION AND CONVENTION IN PICTURE RECOGNITION

I begin by recalling Ernst Gombrich's famous claim that "there is no innocent eye." In saying that, Gombrich implies that perception is a matter of convention, in the sense that perceptual categories vary from place to place and that diverse techniques for representing them are taught and learned. Recognition theories have also been used to link perception to convention; but only by inverting Gombrich's idea. They say that *convention depends on perception*. That inversion is motivated by the goal of reconciling a perception-based theory of depiction with Nelson Goodman's idea that art is a language. The claim means more than just that pictorial conventions are learned and applied by means of vision.

Goodman's conventions are formal, of course, in a way that Gombrich's are not. Goodman claims that visual art represents by way of a system of arbitrary symbols that have distinctive syntactic and semantic properties, just as a verbal language does. The knowledge required to decode a picture is thus special and not derived from a general experience with the perceptual world. Indeed, on the conventionalist view, we often learn how to perceive the natural world from looking at pictures, rather than the other way around. Pictures *define* space for us, they do not simply represent it. In Goodman's words: "Nature is a product of art and discourse" (1968, p. 297). However, according to certain recent accounts, the semantic properties of even a verbal language, at least some of them, must be explained in terms of perceptual mechanisms that serve to locate the speaker's *body in space*. And it is the semantic properties of this sort that provide the model for pictorial representation. In light of that, space cannot simply be a pictorial convention, for the relevant conventions presuppose it. Visual art might be a language, but the very properties that make it so must be explained in terms of perceptual psychology.

The idea that convention depends on perception is most apparent in the case of demonstrative reference (Evans 1982; Schier 1986; Lopes 1996). When I refer to "this cup" or "the lamp over there," I must establish perceptual contact with the relevant object, both for myself as the speaker and for listeners with whom I wish to communicate. This requires me to look, point, or nod in a certain direction, thus linking the location of an object to the position of my own body. When a listener looks in that direction, he, too, understands the reference by locating the object and me in relation to himself.

In the case of pictures, even if reference is not exactly of the demonstrative sort, the need for perceptual contact with the depicted object by way of a spatial location is the same. According to Gareth Evans, for example, pictorial reference is mediated by thoughts of a type that depends essentially on early visual processes. In this he is followed by Flint Schier, Christoper Peacocke, and Dominic Lopes.[6] Thus Peacocke describes a role for spatial "scenarios," as conditions on perception that are essentially ways in which a perceived scene is organized in relation to the perceiver's body: what is in front of or behind the perceiver, to the perceiver's right or left. Lopes, for his part, emphasizes spatial "aspects," which are "patterns of visual salience," defined by the perceiver's point of view. Not all aspects are purely spatial, but even those that aren't presuppose and depend upon the spatial organization of the picture. Pictorial reference, on his and Schier's account, is actually established by the causal history of the picture.[7] But the perceiver's understanding of reference is mediated by the totality of features depicted, which are themselves dependent on the spatial aspect that the picture contains. To that extent, pictures function, not so much like names for, or descriptions of, the things they denote, as like verbal pointings to "this" or "that" object, located over "here" or "there." The basic idea is that pictures embody a perspective or point of view that allows some features of the depicted object to be seen and preclude the representation of others.[8]

The central assumption, shared by Peacocke, Evans, Lopes, and Marr, is that the perception of basic spatial properties depends on internal processes that are *nonconceptual* and unaffected by background knowledge and beliefs. There is of course no general consensus about what the term "concept" and cognates like "conceptual" or "nonconceptual" mean. But the basic idea at work in these accounts is that concepts are units of representation that play roles in the construction of propositions and the drawing of inferences that depend upon domain-general knowledge. As such, concepts are interdefined in a holistic framework, stored in semantic memory. But none of that is true of spatial aspect representation. Conceptualization is eventually necessary to establish reference, but that must be "grounded" on nonconceptual perceptual contact via the spatial organization of the picture (Lopes 1996, p. 102, n. 12). That organization is encoded in elements that are unchanged by the higher-order processes to which they contribute; perceptual content is thus *atomistic* rather than holistic at that level.

In conjunction with the appeal to nonconceptual processes, Recognition theories typically posit a stage in the perception of space that is insulated from the effects of conceptual knowledge and beliefs. Early visual processes are cognitively impenetrable and domain specific, in the strict sense described by Jerry Fodor (1983); that is, they are "modular." Moreover, they depend on innate knowledge. This is a point that has sometimes been applied specifically to pictorial space. In the words of Arthur Danto (in press), who defends the modularity thesis: "As a pictorial device, perspective was invented by Brunelleschi, but as a mechanism of optical perception [it] is genetically defined." Techniques for representing space are historical, he argues; but the spatial eye itself is not.

However, the relation of SDT to the modularity thesis is actually complex. These complexities matter, I shall now argue, because it is precisely with regard to the modularity thesis and the reliance on nonconceptual foundations for perception that mainstream Recognition theories go astray.

The Modularity Thesis

The primary problem with construing the directness of perception in terms of the modularity thesis is that the thesis is probably false. At least this is so with regard to the strong version advocated by Fodor. Some suggestive evidence in this regard comes from neuroscience. For instance, it has been shown that there are as many or more lateral and descending connections among functionally and anatomically distinct areas of a monkey's visual system as there are ascending connections (Van Essen and Anderson 1990). Consistent with that fact is the evidence that the responses of cells in area V4 to a visual stimulus can be modified by somatosensory stimuli (Maunsell et al. 1991). Finally, recent brain-imaging studies of humans show that the same areas of visual cortex that are activated by viewing a picture are also activated by remembering it. This suggests that visual processes involved in picture perception, even basic ones, can be affected by information stored in memory (Wheeler, Petersen, and Buckner 2000).

The assumption is that such lateral and descending connections in the brain serve some function in information processing. And the possibility that they serve some function specifically in the perception of visual *representations* is supported by experiments in psychophysics. There the evidence shows, in a variety of ways, that "later" stage processes can affect "earlier" ones. Consider, as an illustration, the fact that face recognition can influence (discernment of) shape-from-shading. A hollow mask viewed from the back is often seen as convex rather than concave; that is, its nose is perceived as pointing toward, rather than away from, the viewer. This is so, even when the mask is illuminated from below rather than above. Because such a change in illumination often transforms the perception of convexity into an experience of concavity when the object is not a face, it can be argued that the categorization of the object as a face must be what blocks the expected effect of shading cues. That conclusion appears to be borne out by a further test in which two identical masks are placed side by side, with one inverted. The assumption is that it is hard to see the inverted mask as a face; thus it should not override shading cues in the way that an upright mask does. And this turns out to be the case (at least up to a certain viewing distance): the inverted mask is seen as concave rather than as convex. Thus, it has been argued that semantic categorization affects shape-from-shading (Churchland, Ramachandran, and Sejnowski 1994, pp. 33–34). In which case, the strong modularity thesis would appear to be false.

To be sure, Ramachandran has also argued that economizing strategies *presuppose* the existence of modules, combinations of which get reinforced for their success in performing a task and become part of an organism's standard repertoire. In that case, what the evidence actually shows is not so much that the modularity thesis per se is false as that the nature of modules and their impact on perception is not what Marr thought it to be. Ramachandran suggests that there may be many such modules, over two dozen in vision, whose functions are even more specialized than Marr's account would lead us to believe. But I am going to argue that even if the modularity thesis is true, that fact does not matter much for our understanding of how pictures represent. That point applies with even greater force, I believe, when there is the kind of proliferation of modules that Ramachandran suggests. Such *designer modules,* as we might call them, essentially undercut the original import of modularity, as providing a fixed, basic set of distinct abilities that can contribute to the performance of various perceptual tasks.

In any case, my claim is that modularity in any form is not able to carry us very far toward a hybrid account and thus does not shed light on the contribution of the direct component to pictures. The weakness of a modularity-based hybrid account appears in two ways. First, the constraints imposed by modules are actually fairly minimal, to the extent that tasks such as picture perception are performed on the basis of perceptual *experience,* that is, conscious central processes on which diverse knowledge is brought to bear. For example, although he defends the modularity thesis, Danto's view is predicated on the assumption that, especially when perceived pictures are works of art, central processes must be brought into play. In contrast to Gombrich, Danto believes that there *is* an innocent eye. It exists in early vision. But for him, there is also a beguiled and jaded eye, an eye of the world, which appears later in the processing stream. And that is what eventually determines pictorial content. Although picture perception depends on a basic perceptual competence that all perceivers have in common, according to Danto, perceptual psychology cannot tell us what the content, spatial or otherwise, of a picture is. It cannot tell us what a picture means. The reason is that most of the content of a picture is, in Danto's words, "invisible." It depends on historical relations that cannot be seen, although they can be understood.

Danto's point is that the content of a picture must be inferred; because history, he says, supervenes on perception through the perceiver's beliefs. But if we agree that this sense is legitimate, then the modularity thesis becomes more or less irrelevant. At higher levels, the constraints on modules can always be superseded. Danto suggests that the modularity of mind insures that there will be something like theory-neutral observations against which to check the visual hypotheses and interpretations that we form when confronted with pictures. But if we think of the constraints imposed by modularity on pictorial content as something like the constraints imposed by observation sentences on scientific theories, then it's clear that their role is not that of elements from which an interpretation is constructed but only that of providing test cases for any interpretation. And there may be many of those interpretations that can pass the test. If so, then this stage-based compromise with Gibson is not very compelling. In the end, it is the indirect component that carries all the explanatory weight.

The second manifestation of the modularity-based hybrid's weakness is that constraints on vision really have more the status of antecedent causal conditions than of premises, the conditions themselves having content, in an inductive inference. And this points to the another reason that a stage-based hybrid account falls short of being a genuine compromise with direct realism. Even if the visual system were modular, the modules could be harnessed together in a variety of ways in the performance of a given perceptual task. That is, modularity does not preclude the possibility that a wide variety of perceptual strategies might be employed in picture recognition; in that sense, the relation between informational arrays and the visual system cannot be one to one.

The Nonconceptual Nature of Spatial Perception

Some of the same problems found with the modularity thesis also arise in regard to the nonconceptual nature of perceived space. Of course, if the modularity thesis is false, that already casts doubt on the possibility that perceptual content is wholly nonconceptual. If perceptual content is nonconceptual, someone might argue, then it is not cognitively penetrable. The reason is that "cognitive penetrability" is defined as the effect of knowledge by way of inference, and knowledge is encoded in concepts. Thus if the evidence shows that perception *is* cognitively penetrable, it should follow that it is concept dependent.[9] However, I think that it is important to say more about the specific nature of the constraints that nonconceptual spatial processes are supposed to impose on picture perception. In general, the motivation for positing such processes is clear: without them, either we must say (with Goodman) that pictorial and perceived space are constructions that depend on acquired concepts and learning, or we must say that they depend on innate concepts.

From the point of view of recognition theory, this amounts to a dilemma. On the one hand, the learning hypothesis is unacceptable, because it flies in the face of what Schier and others take to be the distinguishing feature of picture recognition; what Schier calls "natural generativity." Essentially, the idea is that once a person has been able to recognize an object or scene in one picture, that person can recognize—without any further learning—objects and scenes in all pictures. For this to be the case, presumably, that person needs some sort of foundational perceptual process. Yet, on the other hand, the innateness hypothesis runs afoul of the conceptual holism that Peacocke and others assume to obtain. That is, if any perceptual categories are innate, they cannot be concepts, unless all concepts are innate, because concepts are interdefined in a holistic network. But if that is so, it will be impossible to individuate concepts (and thus to ascribe meaning to words or pictures), because there would be no fixed point of reference from which to begin.

The appeal to spatial aspects, scenarios, and the like is intended to be a remedy for this dilemma. For example, Lopes develops an account of the impact of spatial aspects on the rest of a picture's content in terms of various forms of pictorial indeterminacy. Of special significance here is the distinction between cases in which a picture simply leaves certain features out and cases in which its spatial organization precludes them from being represented. A picture will be noncommittal about the wrinkles and bumps on the man's face, if the artist simply omits them from the picture. In that case, we understand that the man's skin has texture, but nothing is implied about their particulars. By contrast, if not all of the man's nose is visible because of the angle from which the artist has chosen to depict his face, something *is* implied about its particulars, namely, the overall shape and size of the nose. Thus we might say that the range of properties that can be represented in a picture is determined—*controlled* is perhaps the better word—by the spatial aspect it contains.

Moreover, these spatial aspects are supposed to play a central role in the determination of the picture's referent, where it has one, on the model of demonstrative reference. The aspects themselves are defined by causal relations between the picture producer and the objects represented in the scene. These need not be actual causal relations; a painting might embody a point of view that the artist would have, if that artist were to stand in a certain place. But what the picture provides is a representation of the spatial aspects of objects as defined by this perspective. In that case, the picture perceiver is able to gain access to the content of the picture by means of this spatial aspect, which the perceiver can recognize without any reliance on concepts.[10] The net result is essentially a two-factored theory of pictorial content: the reference of a picture is determined by psychological processes, the object of which is itself established by causal spatial relations. The meaning or content of the picture in a larger sense is then a function of higher-order interpretations that draw on background knowledge, vested in a holistic conceptual scheme.

This is a theory of pictorial content that rests on shaky empirical grounds. For example, as Patricia Churchland, Ramachandran, and Terrence Sejnowski (1994) point out, although figure-ground organization is generally thought to precede shape recognition, their model allows for the order to be reversed and for shape recognition to contribute to the identification of figure and ground. Other evidence also suggests that the spatial organization of a picture does not always ground or constrain recognition in the way the Recognition theory seems to imply. For instance, subjects appear to be able to spatially reorganize remembered pictures and, as a consequence, identify new features and new objects in them (Kosslyn 1994). Thus, it cannot be said that scenarios or spatial aspects or perceptual reference frames are always fundamental. Even if spatial properties are somehow encoded preconceptually, that fact does not resolve the dilemma described here.

Moreover, what emerges from these results is that the processing of pictorial space and its relation to the recognition of depicted objects need not be done in a single way; it depends on the strategies available to the perceiver. For example, in some cases, subjects are *not* able to overcome the initial perceptual organization of remembered pictures and so not able to recognize new objects in them (Reisberg and Chambers 1991). However, in those cases, the block can be eliminated if the subjects are allowed to supplement perception or perceptual memory with support from motor control. For instance, subjects can recognize verbal ambiguities from memory (e.g., when the word "life" is repeated over and over in the mind, it comes to be heard as "fly"); but only if allowed to engage in a kind of silent speech. That involves more than simply rehearsing the sounds in the "mind's ear" without speaking. It also includes sending motor commands to the mouth, tongue, and lips without moving those parts of the body in noticeable or sound-producing ways. This is shown by the fact that subjects cannot recognize verbal ambiguities from memory if they are chewing gum. What this suggests is that the perceivers' motor system works together with visual or auditory memory in the performance of the task. That is, perceivers exploit their strategic resources.

5.4   PERCEPTUAL STRATEGIES AND PICTORIAL SPACE

Let us return for a moment to the Recognition theorist's idea that what a picture represents depends on what can be seen in it, using ordinary perceptual abilities, and to the attempt to reconcile that idea with the view that pictorial art is somehow languagelike. Recall that the marriage of perception and convention was supposed to be arranged by grounding pictorial representation on pictorial reference, using demonstrative reference as a general model. The assumption was that spatial layouts relating the scene to the position of a viewer are necessary to establish reference and that these layouts are perceivable without benefit of concepts. Consequently, their perception is not learned and not dependent on background knowledge. But in light of the problems with the modularity thesis and the nonconceptual process claim that I have cited, this marriage of perception and convention is, I believe, on the rocks. So I now want to propose the following change. Insofar as reference does constrain what a picture can represent, the implication of SDT is that reference is established more by *strategic success* in performing a task than by causal relations. What I mean by "strategic success" is not just that a unique computational result is obtained, or even that a goal is achieved or a target is hit. I mean, rather, that establishing reference is done in an efficient way that conserves the resources of the system. This implication is suggested by the various ways in which SDT assigns important roles to attentional control.

For example, Churchland, Ramachandran, and Sejnowski (1994) argue that attention shifts can precede eye movements in tracking a moving object and thus bind the visual stimulus to a location. Although Churchland and colleagues do not describe the mechanisms by which such covert attention shifts might be carried out, an empirically well-grounded model based on brain studies has been suggested by David Van Essen and Charles Anderson (Van Essen, Anderson, and Olshausen 1994; Anderson and Van Essen 1987). Further, Ramachandran and William Hirstein

(1999) argue that the manner in which the information in a picture is processed is, to some extent, the result of innately defined attentional preferences, which have been exploited by artists in various ways. In this respect, picture perception is like the bottom-up location of diagnostic features in nature; for example, the baby seagull's recognition of its mother's food-laden beak by virtue of the stripes on the beak. Moreover, this attentional "glue" is an essential ingredient in perceptual learning. The acquisition of perceptual strategies, Ramachandran and Hirstein claim, is driven to a large extent by the fact of limited attentional resources. Successful perceptual grouping and binding are inherently pleasurable (because of links between the visual and the limbic systems). Thus we are rewarded for economy.

This implies that perceptual reference is grounded on perceptual strategies that depend on attentional and other control mechanisms. In that case, reference is not determined simply by where the gaze is directed (or, with pictorial reference, the direction in which the picture is "looking," i.e., its point of view). Invoking attention in that way invites a theory of reference based on causal relations (and nonconceptual, foundational modes of vision). What SDT implies instead is that pictorial reference depends on the type of attentional strategies it encourages its viewer to use, together with the viewer's own attentional "style," that is, the disposition of her visual system to utilize its resources (modules, subsystems, perceptual categories) in characteristic ways. For reference, SDT suggests, is really referring: it's something that people *do* through pictures and perceptions. It is to that extent an achievement (as philosophers used to say), so the explanation of it must include some account of how it gets done. Goodman himself acknowledged the importance of eye movements in this regard: "The fixed eye," he said, "is almost as blind as the innocent one" (1968, p. 287). But if Goodman's idea is cashed out in terms of SDT, then a picture becomes more like a speech act than a formal symbol: picture perception, like perception generally, has an important *performance* dimension. If art is like a language, it must be so in a different sense than Goodman intended.[11]

What, then, does this discussion have to do with pictorial space? The answer, as I shall now try to make clear, depends on defining the sense in which SDT is partly direct. I have suggested that perception cannot be direct by virtue of hardwired constraints and modularized operations; nor is it direct just because it is, in its early stages, nonconceptual. Nonetheless, I think that the emphasis on the role of spatial aspects and organization in some Recognition theories provides a clue to how perceptual strategies might play a similar role in constraining pictorial content. In the models to which I have previously referred, shifts of attention are a matter of moving the gaze across different regions of space; in that sense, spatial operations contribute to the recognition of objects through the scanning of contours or the location of diagnostic features. Moreover, insofar as eye movements are involved, the process is itself identified with actual changes in spatial position. This is true, by the way, even when the eyes do not move. In the Van Essen and Anderson (1987) model of covert attention shifting, information is literally rerouted so that it flows along a different path in the brain.[12] But beyond that, I think there is a sense in which perceptual strategies contribute to the spatial content of pictures, and their impact does not rest on inference of either the deductive or the inductive type. To show how this is so, I turn now to an example of resource deployment on a neural network model.

This example involves a theory of *concept redeployment* in connectionist terms. The account is motivated by the fact that connectionism does not seem well equipped to explain visual *discoveries*—sudden changes in the perceived identity of an object or, indeed, in the perceived spatial organization of a scene. These changes cannot be easily attributed to the gradual settling of a connectionist system into a stable state through exposure to a training set over time. However, Paul Churchland (1989) has tried to resolve this problem by proposing a model of concept redeployment. Churchland's original goal was to give an account of theory change in science. But what he says can easily be extended to perceptual learning and to the changes that define the history of visual art. The phenomenon of the revelatory experience, the creation of a radically new way of seeing things, is illustrated equally well by the physical theory that treats light as a wave and the perceptual experience in which a figure first seen as a rabbit is now viewed as a duck.

In both cases, what is distinctive is that no new concepts are added to the scientist's or perceiver's store; old ones are redeployed instead. Thus there is no learning in the most familiar sense: no new facts are discovered (although unnoticed features may become apparent), and no new categories are created into which data are put. What makes this sort of concept redeployment a candidate for direct perception is that it results from a change in resource allocation *and nothing else,* just putting your perceptual resources in a different account. These revelatory experiences produce no initial growth of intellectual capital, and thus no higher-order, complex mental representations should be expected to ensue. Although it is easy to think of the process as one of concept association, this is a case in which changes in the strengths of connections among concepts should not be construed as changing the basic conceptual scheme. Instead, the change should be ascribed to *control mechanisms,* routing information along new paths rather than representing it in new forms.[13]

I would argue, then, that Churchland has provided an alternative way to understand the sense in which vision is partly direct, as exemplified by this model of concept deployment. In so doing, he has pointed to a resolution of a certain tension in his own account. According to this account, the visual system encodes information in nonsymbolic, that is, nonlinguistic, forms. We might be inclined, then, to consider perception to be direct simply by virtue of the fact. Indeed, some proponents of neural network models, in which vision depends on connectionist principles, explicitly claim that this is the case. On these accounts, visual processes are similarity based and subsymbolic. As a consequence, the models are said to be Gibsonian in spirit. Although vision is mediated by internal representations, the representations consist of activation patterns in a neural network, for example, "perceptual prototypes" produced by vector coding as parcellated regions in a multidimensional similarity space. In that case, the principles of ecological resonance between an organism and the environment are supposed to extend inward to the brain. In the words of Bechtel and Abrahamsen (1991, p. 268): "The connectionist concept of relaxing or settling into a stable state is reminiscent of the ecological concept of resonating to an invariant." Thus, "as cognitive psychology becomes increasingly connectionist, it may become increasingly ecological as well" (1991, p. 267).

The problem is that, under some construals at least, connectionist prototypes are concepts, they are cognitively penetrable, and they are interrelated in a holistic network. In all of these respects, they differ from the representations of space on which recognition is supposed to depend. Moreover, Churchland, for one, views connectionist vector coding as a form of inductive inference. So to that extent, there can be no straightforward link between directness and nonsymbolic internal representations of a connectionist sort.

However, the tension in Churchland's construal of perception as both direct and inferential can be resolved by relocating the source of the directness in his model. Directness in Churchland's theory of perception is to be found, not in the fact that vision depends on nonpropositional, similarity-based representations but in the redeployments of perceptual categories that I have just described. Those redeployments are driven by attending to certain features of the visual stimulus, and they produce a change in the "tuning" of the perceiver to his environment. Consequently, they affect the "ecological laws" that might apply. In that sense, they contribute to perceptual reference.

As it happens, this model of resource deployment embodies some of the features that proponents of Recognition theories have found attractive. For instance, what Churchland has in mind is a type of discovery that precedes subsequent inductive reasoning. In that sense, a perceptual strategy functions somewhat like a stage in information processing (although not one that is universal or unmodifiable). Similarly, although concept deployments obviously involve concepts, they also do not involve inductive generalization, the formation of new concepts, or explicit thoughts in propositional form. That is, they do not involve the type of concept use that ordinary cognition requires. In that respect, we might speak of them as being "nonconceptual."

The account I have laid out also helps us understand some of the similarities and differences among competitor accounts that are congenial to the notion of perceptual directness. Specifically, the learning that SDT envisions is often more a matter of conditioning or training (e.g., the training of attention) than of deriving conclusions from premises. This is apparent in the emphasis of Churchland, Ramachandran, and Sejnowski (1994) and Ramachandran and Hirstein (1999) on the role of reinforcement learning in establishing perceptual strategies in the brain. This is a form of learning they explicitly contrast with learning of a more cognitivist sort, for which Marr's constraints are said to provide a foundation. Thus it may help distinguish their view from Cutting's, for instance, which posits a mathematical, deductive model for the direct specification of information and allows for higher-order cognition in the perception of pictures of certain types. In the latter case, which involves the elaboration of input and the "building up" of constructions, learning in the sense of stored background knowledge may be brought into play.[14]

Finally, this analysis of attention and other modes of resource control sheds light on what is visible and what is not in a picture. Ramachandran (1990) has suggested that there is a sense in which information that is not explicitly encoded in perception is "captured" by motion and by attraction to diagnostic features. This suggests that although the information is not represented, it remains somehow available, either for the performance of a perceptual task or as a component of perceptual experience. A precise correspondence between each spot on a leopard in different locations is not computed, but information about the spots might be used to identify the animal as a leopard, and perceivers report that they are aware of changes in position of the stimuli that are captured in this way. Thus there is a sense in which such information forms part of the content of perception but content that is *unrepresented.*

In this case, the strategy seems to involve ignoring some information for the purpose of the task, while retaining it implicitly in the following sense: the visual system assumes a rough correspondence between the information that is represented and the information that is not. This assumption allows the perceiver to experience the unrepresented information in some sense, as well as perform tasks that depend upon it. And this is so, even though the information is never explicitly encoded and thus cannot be used to draw the inferences or make the computations needed to produce more elaborate mental constructions. Although the notion of the capture of information is not entirely clear, it invites comparison to the Recognition theorist's claim that spatial organization in a picture can ground a kind of pictorial content that is *implicit,* that is, not simply left out but not delineated either, because it is occluded or because it is not visible from the point of view that the picture contains. I conclude, then, with some brief remarks about how the bearing of perceptual strategies on the unrepresented content of a picture.

5.5   THE UNREPRESENTED CONTENT OF PICTURES

Pictures are, of course, always incomplete. Details are inevitably omitted, but also the point of view and spatial organization of the scene allow some things but not others to be literally seen. It is tempting to say that this is where indirectness intervenes: we fill in the gaps through inference or imagination. This is the constructivist view. It is the sense in which pictorial art contains "invisible" content on Danto's account. We add a layer of conceptualization to our recognition of the type of item denoted by way of a perspective and thus comprehend that there is more to the item than literally meets eye. Indeed, according to this view, we comprehend what more there is in a way that penetrates experience, while leaving the basic elements of the perceived stimulus unchanged. This more inclusive experience then mediates the performance of the task. Our understanding that certain features are likely to lie behind an occluding object in a picture is the product of interpretation. It is constrained by what we see and, in turn, limits our further thoughts about it.

However, I think that the unseen content of a picture can include more than what lies behind the occluder. The reason is that we are constrained in what we can see in front of the occluder as well. As Churchland's example of concept deployment suggests, patterns of information use tend to become ingrained; they dominate and sometimes interfere with our discovery of solutions to perceptual and scientific problems. Breaking their grip often requires deviating from familiar routines or sequences in the processing of information at different points in space; it requires attending to stimuli in a novel way. The performance of a task becomes automatic, and that may prevent us from noticing what is before our very eyes. Moreover, insofar as pictorial content is the product of constraints, these constraints are not construed as representations in the mind or brain. This is as true of perceptual strategies as it is of assumptions that operate in early vision. In that sense, too, perceptual strategies contribute to pictorial content that is unrepresented.

Finally, these patterns of control, these habits or predispositions, contribute to the performance of a perceptual task in a larger sense than just bringing the task to completion. These routines, relative to the perceiver's abilities and level of expertise as they are, affect the speed and efficiency, as well as the reliability, with which the end is achieved. As a consequence, they affect the perceiver's experience: the sense of ease or effort, the feeling of challenge or frustration, that accompanies the performance of every task. Pictorial content, in this sense, too, is only implicit in picture perception. Nonetheless, where the picture is a work of art, it permeates aesthetic experience. It is an important aspect of pictorial content that should not be ignored.

5.6 CONCLUSION

It is sometimes said that the development of linear perspective reflects the emphasis on the importance of the individual that was characteristic of the Renaissance. It emphasized the centrality of the picture's spectator, who could comprehend all with little effort and in a single glance. It was thus the natural complement to voyages of discovery and the conquest of geographical space (Fleming 1986). That tells us little, of course, about how linear perspective actually works and why (beyond the convergence of everything from the picture's point of view on a single vanishing point) it highlighted the spectator. But it does suggest that pictorial space and the appeal of perspective has something to do with mechanisms of perceptual control. What I have argued is that adapting a plausible theory of pictorial representation, Recognition theory, to the various hybrid accounts of perception that have emerged in recent years sheds light on how those mechanisms operate. This light is, I think, more important than the question of what it means for perception to be direct. But by articulating a Recognition theory of this sort, we can also come to better understanding of the differences among certain hybrid theories, which is where the most interesting issues remain to be explored.

Notes

1. It will soon become clear that these are strategies available to the visual system rather than the perceiver. I do not wish to imply by the term *strategy* that optional modes of processing are always selected as a matter of conscious choice.

2. And in either this or its original version, the idea that there are varieties of pictures can be combined with the pictorial surrogate view. The result would be that pictorial surrogacy would then be said to come in a variety of forms.

3. Of course, we then have to define the term "indirect," which is not a simple task (as Schwartz 1994 has shown). I simply stipulate for now that "indirect" perception involves processes that depend on internal *representations;* that it does not matter whether those representations are thought to be neural or irreducibly mental (as perhaps a functionalist philosophy of mind suggests); and that to represent something is to stand for it in some way. Thus perception is indirect if it depends on an internal event that *refers* to the object perceived and if the attribution of properties to that object presupposes the reference.

4. Compare also Stillings et al. (1987, p. 456).

5. However, on this account, pictures need not be perceived exactly as ordinary objects are. There can be significant differences in the ways the standard perceptual equipment is employed.

6. There are significant differences among these thinkers. In particular, Peacocke's view is sometimes treated as *opposed* to a recognition theory of the sort that Lopes endorses because Peacocke makes basic recognition depend on resemblance. But these differences do not affect the point I wish to make here.

7. That is, an accurate understanding of pictorial reference by a perceiver is one that comports with its actual causal history.

8. To this, Lopes adds an important qualification: A picture is not limited to a single consistent point of view, as vision is. It may contain multiple and visually impossible perspectives. Nonetheless, it is essential for Lopes to lay down some constraints on the spatial organization of a picture and its aspects, if he is to be able to distinguish the case of a single picture with multiple perspectives from the case of multiple pictures side by side or in the same frame, each with a single point

of view. This he does in terms of "spatial unity." A picture, he says, "is a representation whose content presents a "spatially unified" aspect of its subject.... [E]very part of the scene that a picture shows must be represented as standing in certain spatial relations to every other part" (1996, p. 126). It is in this sense that space plays a fundamental role for him. This would be true of cubist paintings or impossible pictures, for instance, which contain multiple points of view but not true of a picture postcard showing the various sights of Frankfurt. The former could be related to a single object-centered representation; but the latter could not.

9. However, the converse is not true: perception might depend on concepts, but if those are limited in scope (e.g., the concept of an edge, a line, an angle, etc. in early vision) then perception need not be said to be affected by background knowledge. Conceptualization does not entail cognitive penetration. This assumes, of course, that concepts can be used in relative isolation, which is just the point that some philosophers (Peacocke, for one) deny. To that extent, one's view of the connections between concepts and cognitive penetrability in vision will depend on one's view of conceptual holism. In contrast to the other recognition theorists I have cited, Schier does not seem to take a position on whether perceptual content, in particular spatial content, depends on concepts or not. But for him, in either case, early recognition processes are modular.

10. Of course, being nonconceptual is only a necessary and not a sufficient condition for spatial perception to play the dominant role that it is supposed to play. In Marr's model, shape and line representation involve no concepts either. Lopes thinks that the perceiver-centered perspective is eventually to be translated into an object-centered representation, as Marr has claimed. It is that translation, in fact, that supports the recognition of objects under different aspects. Presumably, as early stages of perception, shape and line recognition also constrain later stages. Nonetheless, initially such information is viewpoint dependent; in that sense, spatial aspects might be said to be fundamental.

11. Of course, the analogy to speech acts is only partial at best. The pragmatics of language depend on more than the mechanics of verbal "gestures," including the intentions of the speaker and an audience as the primary context of speech. But Recognition theory does not claim to explain all of reference in terms of demonstratives, or even all of demonstrative reference in terms of spatial aspects. My claim about perceptual strategies, attention, and referring is intended to be equally modest.

12. It is important for the account I am developing here that such rerouting can also occur in other ways that do not involve shifts of attention. For example, brain-imaging evidence strongly suggests that after even a brief training period, some perceptual tasks become virtually automatic, in the sense that they no longer require attention. When that happens, they appear to be performed by different areas of the brain than when the task was new (Posner and Raichle 1994, pp. 125–129).

13. Churchland's model applies to resources other than concepts, for example, representations of abstract shapes for which we have no labels, as might be produced by early visual modules. I omit here an account of the actual mechanism of

redeployment that Churchland suggests. It involves attaching different operators to inputs or stored information to allow them to be used subsequently in different calculations (Churchland 1992, p. 46). The attachment is not itself part of the calculation, nor are the items to which the operators are attached changed when different operators are used. This appeal to operators may seem to suggest that "deployment" is a kind of inference after all, perhaps on the model of deduction: a literal movement of shapes from one position to another, without regard for their meanings or what they denote. However, the redeployments controlled by the operators will not exemplify rules of inference, such as material implication or negation. A better comparison might be to instructions for arranging pictures in a gallery without regard for either what they represent or for relations among their features, where the features are construed as object parts or governed by combinatorial principles.

14. It is important to note that what are reinforced on these SDT models are strategies, that is, forms of overt behavior and neural response. What gets rewarded is economy in resource use, not the truth of ideas or veridicality of perception. The reward is for doing a task quickly, efficiently, and with little effort, not (just) for getting it right. Of course, accuracy in perception should bring further rewards, and some level of accuracy will be a necessary condition for the selection of a strategy in the species or the strategy's acquisition by an individual. But SDT suggests that we could be rewarded (at least internally) even when we get things wrong, perhaps as a result of imposing a coherent organization on a stimulus. Thus, the appeal to reinforcement learning by Churchland et al. does not mean that theirs is a model of the "association of ideas" that might be treated simply as a form of inductive inference. Robert Schwartz (1996, p. 83) has argued that Cutting's account is hard to distinguish from theories that follow Ramachandran (namely Gilden's 1991). I agree that Cutting's and Ramachandran's approach have important points in common. But I suggest that one important difference, even if it is only a matter of emphasis, is the relative importance their views attach to learning of different kinds.

PART II
THE STATUS OF PERSPECTIVE

Chapter 6

Optical Laws or Symbolic Rules? The Dual Nature of Pictorial Systems

John Willats

Two questions concerning the representational systems in pictures have been widely debated. The first is whether perspective is a uniquely good way of representing shape and space or whether it is just one among a number of equally valid systems, rather as English is just one among a number of languages. The second is whether representational systems are natural or conventional. By "conventional" I do not just mean conventional in the weak sense that it is or has been conventional to use perspective in some cultures but not in others,[1] but in the stronger sense that the relations between the spatial systems in pictures and the scenes they represent are arbitrary and can therefore be determined by cultural conventions rather than natural laws.

In practice these two questions are often confused, because it is often implied that perspective is the best of all possible systems precisely because it is natural—that is, based on the laws of optics. The obvious model here is photography. Because cameras can produce pictures without the intervention of human agency,[2] and because these pictures are necessarily in perspective, it is tempting to think that perspective must be the best of all possible systems. The problem with this is that it suggests that other pictorial systems, especially relatively unfamiliar ones used in other periods and cultures, must somehow be inferior. Much of this confusion can be avoided by asking what it is that perspective is good *for,* and I have argued elsewhere (Willats 1997) that different representational systems are good for different purposes. Perspective, for example, can be good for landscape painting because it gives one a good idea of what a landscape looks like from a particular viewpoint, but orthographic projection is better for engineering drawings—and is universally used for that purpose—because it shows the true shapes and sizes of objects, irrespective of any particular viewpoint. Similarly, railway maps based on topological geometry, such as the map of the London Underground system, are better as route maps than pictures in perspective because the maps show the connections between stations without irrelevant details such as the shapes of the lines or the stations.

There is, however, another more subtle source of confusion concealed in these questions: the temptation to judge representational systems as natural or conventional on the basis of whether they are best described in terms of projective geometry or symbolic rules. "Natural" theories of pictures are derived from the laws of optics, and because the projection of light rays from the scene and their intersection with the picture plane can be described in terms of three-dimensional projective geometry, the argument that pictures are natural has focused on the question of whether the spatial layout of pictures can be described in these terms. Margaret Hagen (1985, 1986) has argued that *all* representational pictures can be regarded as being based on what she calls "natural perspective" because their spatial systems can be described in terms of three-dimensional projective geometry. In contrast, other types of pictures such as Byzantine mosaics and cubist paintings, which are based on inverted perspective and whose spatial systems are difficult to describe in these terms, are often said to be "languagelike" because they symbolize features of the scene rather than represent them optically (Goodman 1968). This analogy is typically used to support the argument that pictures are conventional because linguists generally agree that the relations between the units of language and their referents are arbitrary. As a result, it is tempting to conclude that in the case of pictures whose spatial systems are best described in terms of symbolic rules, the relation between scenes and pictures is also arbitrary. My thesis here is that these two modes of description—in terms of the laws of optics or symbolic rules—are not mutually exclusive but complementary and that in many cases descriptions given in terms of symbolic rules can also be related back to optical laws. However, I shall also argue that in some circumstances one form of description may be more appropriate and revealing than the other.

Take, for example, Giovanni Canaletto's line drawing in perspective of the *Campo di Santi Giovanni e Paolo,* circa 1735.[3] Martin Kemp argues that the spatial system in this and a number of similar drawings "is best explained by supposing that it is based on a camera image" (1990, p. 197)—that is, that Canaletto produced these drawings with the aid of a camera obscura, the forerunner of the modern photographic camera. To support his argument Kemp draws attention to the unusual quality of the line in this drawing: "[I]t traces the perspectival outlines in a summary, freehand manner with virtually no auxiliary construction lines" (1990, p. 197). What Kemp is saying is that Canaletto looked directly at the optical image in his camera obscura and then traced over the outlines of the buildings as they appeared in the image. This method of producing a drawing was not unusual in the eighteenth century. However, pictures in perspective can be and were produced by quite other means: that is, by the use of perspectival rules, such as the rule that lines representing edges in the scene at right angles to the picture plane (the orthogonals) converge to a vanishing point. If Canaletto had used this rule in the production of the *Campo di Santi Giovanni e Paolo,* Kemp suggests, the construction lines derived from this rule would probably still be present in the drawing.

Such rules have a long history. The first known example of a construction rule resulting in a picture in true perspective was given by Alberti in his *Della Pittura* written in 1436 (Spencer 1966) in the form of what he called the *costruzione legittima,* but this replaced earlier workshop rules, such as the rule that the depth of each successive tile in the representation of a pavement should be reduced by one-third, or Cennino Cennini's rule that the moldings at the top of a building should slope downward while the moldings at the bottom should slope upward. Following these earlier rules results in pictures in which the orthogonals converge but not to a single coherent vanishing point. In practice, artists often combined optical methods with the use of perspectival rules: it seems likely that Canaletto would have corrected the composition in his painting of the *Campo di Santi Giovanni e Paolo* by using perspectival rules,[4] even though the original outlines may have been taken from a camera obscura image. In the case of true Renaissance scientific perspective the rules described by Alberti are directly related to the laws of optics. Nevertheless, it may be appropriate to describe the actual processes of picture production for pictures such as the *Campo di Santi Giovanni e Paolo,* in terms either of the laws of optics or the use of symbolic rules, depending on which method, or combination of methods, the artist actually used.

When it comes to picture perception, descriptions based on optics and three-dimensional projective geometry are usually more appropriate, because it is characteristic of pictures in perspective that their two-dimensional geometry is similar to that obtained by projecting the rays of light from a real scene on to a flat surface. Again, definitions of this kind have a long history, from Brook Taylor's (1719) definition of a "Picture drawn in the utmost Degree of Perfection" to James J. Gibson's definition of a "faithful" picture as "[a] delimited surface so processed that it yields a sheaf of light-rays to a given point which is the same as would be the sheaf of rays from the original scene to a given point" (Gibson 1954; quoted in Gibson 1971, p. 28). In other words, pictures in perspective provide us with a view that, at least as far as its geometry is concerned, is similar to what we might obtain from a view of a real scene. On the other hand, we characteristically *recognize* pictures as being in perspective (as distinct from being in some other system) in one of two ways: either by looking to see whether their orthogonals converge to a vanishing point (in the case of pictures depicting buildings or other rectangular objects) or by looking to see whether objects that are farther away in the scene are drawn to a smaller scale compared with objects in the foreground (in the case of landscapes in which there are no obvious straight edges). Here again, as in the case of picture production, descriptions in terms of the laws of optics or symbolic rules may be more or less appropriate, depending on the circumstances.

Similar arguments apply to pictures in systems other than perspective. Perspective is just one among a number of drawing systems that can be defined in terms of either drawing rules or three-dimensional projective geometry: these include oblique projection, the basis of many oriental drawings and paintings, and orthogonal projection, widely used by engineers and architects for their working drawings. In practice, engineers and architects do not derive their working drawings from optical views of objects or scenes but make use of implicit rules of the kind "draw the front faces as true shapes" (for drawings in orthogonal projection) or "draw the side edges using parallel oblique lines" (for drawings in oblique projection). Similarly, although we know little of the working methods of Chinese, Japanese, and Persian artists, all of whom used oblique projection, it seems most unlikely that they used optical methods: in the vast majority of cases real scenes corresponding to these pictures did not exist, and there would have been insuperable difficulties obtaining a view from an infinite, or at least very considerable, distance above the scene, which is what definitions in terms of optics demand. It seems much more likely that these artists made use of implicit symbolic rules (Willats 1997, pp. 198, 199). However, when it comes to picture perception, definitions of these systems based on projective geometry seem more appropriate because all these systems provide at least approximations to views of possible objects or scenes.

Hagen has argued that because oblique projection, orthogonal projection, and their variants can be described in terms of three-dimensional projective geometry, pictures based on these systems exploit what she calls *"natural perspective*, the geometry of the light that strikes the eye" (1986, p. 8). To the extent that such pictures provide at least approximations to views of possible views of objects or scenes this argument has some force but only in relation to picture perception. However, her failure to recognize that these systems can equally well be defined in terms of symbolic rules—rules about the lengths and directions of the orthogonals—has led her to a number of false conclusions.

The first of these is her claim that "there is no development in art" (1985, p. 59), which she applies to both artists' pictures and children's drawings. She was obliged to make this claim because it follows from her contention that "*all* representational pictures from any culture or period in history" and all children's drawings (beyond the scribbling stage) are based on "*natural perspective*, the geometry of the light that strikes the eye" (1986, p. 8). If oblique projection, orthogonal projection, and the like are simply varieties of perspective, and perspective is defined in terms of three-dimensional projective geometry, how can there be any development from one system to another? As Hagen puts it, "is it possible to measure developmental level with a tool that itself shows no development?" (1985, p. 76). The flaw in Hagen's argument is that some periods in art history do show a definite developmental sequence, and this is also true in the development of children's drawings. Moreover, this sequence is not difficult to understand once the projection systems are defined in terms of drawing rules.

Perhaps the most obvious example is the case of children's drawings of rectangular objects such as tables or cubes. Although the details vary somewhat according to the experimental conditions, and the terminology varies from one writer to another, a number of experiments have shown that children's drawing development follows the sequence: topological geometry, orthogonal projection, horizontal and vertical oblique projection, oblique projection, and, finally, some form of perspective (Lee and Bremner 1987; Nicholls and Kennedy 1992; Victoria 1982; Willats 1977). This sequence is easily described in terms of increasingly complex drawing rules. Thus in drawings based on topological geometry there are no orthogonals; in orthogonal projection, the orthogonals are represented by points; in horizontal and vertical oblique projection, the orthogonals are horizontal or vertical; in oblique projection, the orthogonals run at an oblique angle across the picture surface; and in perspective, they are also oblique but converge to a vanishing point. So the rules for producing pictures in these systems are increasingly complex (Willats 1977; 1997). In this case, describing children's drawings in terms of drawing rules provides a convincing interpretation of the developmental sequence, whereas describing them only in terms of projective geometry leaves this sequence inexplicable.

The reasons this sequence occurs are perhaps more controversial, but one factor seems to be that the acquisition of more complex rules is necessary in order to produce drawings that are *better as representations,* in the sense that the objects depicted can more easily be recognized and their three-dimensional shapes can more easily be seen in the drawings (Willats 1997; Wollheim 1977). This argument, however, is best related to picture perception and definitions of the systems given in terms of projective geometry: it is only by the employment of systems later in the developmental sequence, such as oblique projection and perspective, that drawings can be produced that are better as representations, because they show rectangular objects from a general direction of view, and false attachments can be avoided. A "false attachment" in a picture occurs when two features in a scene appear to be touching, whereas in fact they are separated in depth: for example, when in an amateur photograph a tree appears to be growing out of someone's head.

A similar sequence occurred in the development of Greek vase painting. Again, the terminology varies from one writer to another. In their drawings of rectangular objects the development followed the sequence of orthogonal projection, oblique projection, and, finally, a simple form of perspective that developed into more or less true perspective for wall paintings during the Hellenistic period (White 1967; Willats 1997). As with the development of children's drawings, this development is probably best understood in terms of the acquisition of increasingly complex drawing rules, at least so far as picture production is concerned; the impulse behind this sequence was probably, again, the desire to produce drawings that were better as representations. Finally, the change from the use of inverted perspective or incoherent mixtures of oblique projection or naive perspective during the medieval period to the discovery or rediscovery of true perspective at the beginning of the Renaissance was regarded at the time as a definite advance; and as Alberti made clear, this advance was achieved by the use of better rules.

Hagen's failure to recognize that the spatial systems in pictures can also be described in terms of drawing rules leads her to a second false conclusion: the claim that all representational pictures exploit natural perspective. Again, this is mistaken. There are two quite large classes of pictures whose representational systems cannot be defined in terms of the laws of optics but which are, nevertheless, representational in any normal sense of the word. The first class consists of pictures based on topological rather than projective geometry: this class includes many cartoons and caricatures, children's early drawings such as the so-called tadpole figures, early rock drawings, the earliest Greek vase paintings of humans and animals, and some artists' pictures—among them paintings by Henri Matisse, Picasso, and Paul Klee (Willats 1997). A good example is Klee's *Another Camel!* 1939.[5] It is difficult, though perhaps not impossible, to regard drawings of this kind as projections from views of scenes (Bunge 1966, p. 221); they can, however, easily be described in terms of topological geometry. The shapes of the lines in this drawing are wildly distorted, judged in terms of the laws of optics, but Klee has been very careful to preserve the topological connections between the line junctions that denote points of occlusion. As a result, the drawing is easily recognizable as a depiction of a camel, and the three-dimensional shapes of the features in the drawing can still be seen, albeit in a distorted form.

The second class of pictures whose spatial systems are difficult to account for in terms of three-dimensional projective geometry are those in inverted or divergent perspective and pictures containing incoherent mixtures of systems, usually variants of oblique projection. This class includes medieval paintings, Persian miniature paintings, Byzantine mosaics, Russian icon paintings, and many modern paintings, including cubist paintings. Hagen claims that inverted perspective: "was never adopted anywhere with enough consistency to be called a style of spatial depiction.... Whatever the reasons for the occasional appearance of divergent perspective, it is never characteristic of any coherent art style" (1986, p. 149). This is not, however, the case: although inverted perspective is not in itself a consistent system in the way that scientific perspective is a consistent system, its *employment* in Orthodox art was consistent over a period of at least a thousand years.

As with oblique projection and its variants, the spatial systems in all these types of pictures can easily be described in terms of the rules governing the directions of the orthogonals. In inverted perspective, for example, there is a general tendency for the orthogonals to diverge, instead of converge, as they do in scientific perspective. However, these spatial systems cannot be regarded simply as alternatives to scientific perspective, in the way that English and French can be regarded as alternative languages. The human visual system is designed to take in spatial information from scenes, not from pictures, and judged by the standards of optical realism pictures in these systems must be regarded as anomalous. But what could be the reason for the existence of such anomalies?

There appear to be at least four possible reasons for these anomalies. The first, and simplest, is the use of crude or mistaken rules or of incompatible mixtures of rules. For example, the fifteenth-century *Birth of Saint John the Baptist* by Giovanni de Paolo is in a crude form of perspective but also contains incompatible mixtures of oblique projections.[6] Anomalies of this kind often occur during periods of transition when one drawing rule is being replaced by another: in this case, when oblique projection and its variants were being replaced by perspective. Similar anomalies appear in children's drawings, during the transitions between different developmental stages.

Second, as I have argued elsewhere, the anomalies that are so characteristic of Byzantine mosaics and fifteenth- and sixteenth-century Russian icon paintings are not "mistakes" but may have served quite specific theological purposes. Unlike Catholic fifteenth- and sixteenth-century art, and seventeenth-century Protestant art, Orthodox paintings and mosaics were not intended to look optically realistic; rather, they were intended to depict a spiritual world, as opposed to the material world of the senses. Moreover, the flattening of the pictorial space that resulted from the use of such anomalous devices as inverted perspective and false attachment drew attention to the picture as a physical object so that the union of the depicted spiritual world and its material support provided a metaphor for the incarnation (Willats 1997).

Third, many artists, particularly during the twentieth century, used anomalies for expressive reasons. Much of the poetic quality of Marc Chagall's paintings, for example, can be attributed to the fact that they contain mixtures of drawing systems that impart a dreamlike and otherworldly quality to the painting, similar to that found in many icons, and it is surely no coincidence that Chagall was influenced by icon painting.

Finally, a number of modern painters have used anomalies as a way of investigating the nature of painting itself. This seems to have been the impulse behind much of the work of such diverse painters as Juan Gris, perhaps the purist and most technical of all the cubist painters; the surrealist painter René Magritte; and Paul Klee. An adequate account of the anomalies in the work of these painters, however, requires a fuller account of the spatial systems in pictures than that given earlier in terms of topological and projective geometry.

According to David Marr (1982) any scheme for representing shape and space (and this includes pictures as well as scenes) must have at least two components. The first component defines the spatial relations between the units of which the scheme is composed. For example, the shapes of the actual buildings in the Campo di Santi Giovanni e Paolo in Venice might be described in terms of the relative directions of their edges in three-dimensional space, whereas in drawings of this scene their shapes would be represented by the relative directions of the lines representing those edges. I shall refer to the systems that map the spatial relations in scenes into corresponding relations on the picture surface as the *drawing systems*. The second component in Marr's account consists of the units of which such representations are composed: Marr calls these the primitives of the system. For example, a description of the shapes of the buildings in a scene might be given in terms of edges as scene primitives, and the representations of these buildings in a drawing might be made up of lines as picture primitives. I shall refer to the systems in pictures that map scene primitives into corresponding picture primitives as the *denotation systems*. Thus an account of the representational systems in pictures can be given in terms of two mutually dependent components: the drawing systems and the denotation systems. In the drawing systems

spatial relations in the scene	are mapped by the drawing systems into	spatial relations in the picture

and in the denotation systems

scene primitives (such as edges)	are mapped by the denotation systems into	picture primitives (such as lines)

There are five main drawing systems: perspective; oblique projection and its variants; orthogonal projection; inverted perspective; and systems based on topological geometry. In addition, there are three main denotation systems: optical systems; line drawings; and silhouettes in which the primitives are two-dimensional regions. As (with certain restrictions) any of the drawing systems can be combined with any of the denotation systems, this provides quite a rich method of classification that can be used to describe the representational systems in pictures from a wide variety of periods and cultures.

As with the drawing systems, the denotation systems can be defined in terms of either the laws of optics or symbolic rules. In optical systems zero-dimensional dots of tone or color are used to denote the intercepts of small bundles of light rays. Typical examples are television pictures and pointillist paintings. The denotation system in Canaletto's painting of the *Campo di Santi Giovanni e Paolo* can be assigned to this class, although in this case (as in most color photographs) the dots of color are extremely small. In line drawings the picture primitives are one-dimensional lines— normally black lines on a light ground—and examples can be found in virtually all periods and cultures. In the third main class of denotation systems the picture primitives are two-dimensional *regions*. Typically, in pictures based on regions as primitives, the regions denote whole volumes in the scene, although they can also be used to denote regions in the visual field. Regions and volumes have very few shape properties, the most important being that of extendedness: that is, the property of relative extension in various directions in space. In children's early drawings, for example, such as the tadpole figures, round regions are used to denote round volumes such as the head or head/body, and lines or long regions are used to denote long volumes such as the arms and legs.[7] Similarly, in the map of the London Underground, round regions are used to denote the stations and long regions are used to denote the track. Examples of other pictures employing regions as primitives include early rock drawings, such as those of Camonica valley, and some paintings and drawings by Matisse and Picasso (Willats 1997).

Because the tones and colors of the dots of pigment in a photograph or television picture can be directly related to the fall of light, it seems appropriate to describe the denotation systems in these pictures in terms of optics. But can this approach also be applied to line drawings? The problem here is that the array of light given off from a line drawing is usually quite different from that which could be obtained from a real scene. Compare, for example, Canaletto's original sketch of the *Campo di Santi Giovanni e Paolo* and his painting of the same subject. The array of light given off from a painting, even a highly finished painting such as this, can never fully match that given off by the scene it represents, if only because the range of luminance levels in a painting can never be as great as that obtained from a real scene. Nevertheless, the tones and colors in this painting are so clearly related to the fall of light in the real scene that they are better described in terms of optics than symbolic rules. But, equally clearly, this is not true of the lines in the original sketch: most of these lines represent the edges of buildings, edges in what Marr (1982) would call an object-centered description of the scene that exist independently of the fall of light. Thus, although Canaletto may well have derived the drawing system in this picture from a camera obscura image, the denotation system would have been based on an implicit rule: "use lines to denote edges and contours."

Gibson maintained that "there is *no* point-to-point correspondence of brightness or color between the optic array from a line drawing and the optic array from a scene" (1971, p. 28). Certainly, early attempts to obtain line drawings from gray-scale images automatically, by scanning photographs and representing the luminance steps in the image (points where the tonal values change abruptly), are fairly unconvincing (Marr 1982). However, research by Don Pearson, Hanna, and Martinez (1990) suggests that Gibson's assertion that there is *no* correspondence between arrays from line drawings and real scenes may have been unduly pessimistic, because they were able to produce quite respectable line drawings from gray-scale images by using what they called a "cartoon operator" tuned to pick out a combination of luminance steps and luminance valleys. Nevertheless, what works for a computer does not necessarily work for human beings. Many of the mistakes made by amateur artists and art students come about as a result of the temptation to use lines to represent the abrupt changes in luminance values that come about at the edges of shadows, and this is particularly the case in figure drawing. An important part of an artist's training consists of learning to ignore the boundaries of the shadows that often mask the points where contours end and, instead, to use the implicit rule "use lines to denote contours."

Thus when it comes to picture production, the denotation systems in optically realistic pictures are often best described in terms of optics and the fall of light, whereas the denotation systems in line drawings are usually best described in terms of symbolic rules. But if so, why is it that line drawings can look so convincingly realistic? Pearson and colleagues suggest that this might be because the early stages of the human visual system include a feature detector, similar to their cartoon operator, that picks out a combination of luminance step edges and luminance valleys, so although the optic array from a line drawing is not physically similar to that obtained from a real scene, it nevertheless provides an effective perceptual equivalent. If this is indeed the case, it might make sense to describe the perception of line drawings in terms of these features of the optic array, rather than in terms of rules about what lines may and may not denote.

Finally, are the denotation systems in pictures based on regions as primitives best described in terms of optics or symbolic rules? It is not difficult to see how pictures of this kind can be derived using symbolic rules, such as the rule "use a round region to denote a round volume," and it seems likely that children employ implicit rules of this kind as a basis for their earliest drawings. However, it also seems likely that rules of this kind have a "natural" basis in optics, because round volumes will always project a round region in the visual field, whereas a long volume will usually project a long region, except in the unlikely case in which a long region is viewed end-on. In evolutionary terms, such "natural" associations presumably come about as the result of an association between the shape of the object and the view of that object that is most frequently encountered (Willats 1992b). Thus William Stern, commenting on the lines and round regions that children use in their tadpole figures, said: "We call these symbols 'natural' because their meaning does not first require to be learnt (as in the case of letters or mathematical signs) but directly occur to the child, and are used by him as a matter of course. Thus a long stroke is a natural symbol for an arm or leg, a small circle for an eye or head" (1930, pp. 369–370).

By the standards of optical realism and projective geometry, tadpole drawings must be judged to be anomalous, and as adults we do in fact make such judgments when we look at children's early drawings—which is perhaps why they look so puzzling. When we look at tadpole figures we interpret the lines as representing contours, and these lines look "wrong" as the projections of the contours of the human figure. For the child, however, the lines do not represent contours, but form the outlines of regions representing whole volumes. Thus the drawing rules underlying the perception of these drawings by adults are quite different from the rules by which such drawings have been produced. Perhaps an analogy might be drawn here between children's early drawings and their early speech. Although sentences such as "Nobody don't like me" sound wrong to adults, "It is important to understand that when children make such errors, they are not producing flawed or incomplete replicas of adult sentences; they are producing sentences that are correct and grammatical with respect to their current internalized grammar" (Moskowitz 1978, p. 89). I suggest that, in the same way, the drawing rules by which the tadpole figures have been produced are consistent in their own terms; but they are not the rules normally used by adults.

According to Breyne Moskowitz, "Children's errors are essential data for students of child language because it is the consistent departures from the adult model that indicate the nature of a child's current hypotheses about the grammar of a language" (ibid., p. 89). Similarly, the anomalies in children's drawings can give important information about the nature of the drawing rules they are using at each stage in the developmental sequence. The use of anomalous or ungrammatical sentences as a way of investigating the normal adult rules of language is, of course, a standard technique in linguistics, made famous by Noam Chomsky (1957/1971), and a similar technique was used in the so-called picture grammars developed in the 1970s by Max Clowes (1971) and David Huffman (1971), and later by David Waltz (1975). In these grammars the "alphabet" is made up of various types of line junctions, and the "syntax" consists of drawing rules about the ways in which these junctions may and may not be related. These rules are not, however, arbitrary, but are derived from constraints about the nature of the physical world or the laws of optics. One important rule, for example, is that a given line must have the same meaning along its whole length so that a line cannot represent a convex edge at one end and a concave edge at the other. Another rule about the number of surfaces hiding a contour is derived from the laws of occlusion, in which one object may hide another from a particular direction of view. Clowes and Huffman showed that line drawings that satisfy these constraints look "right," while drawings that do not satisfy them look anomalous or "wrong."

Well before the 1970s, however, a number of artists seem to have been engaged in a similar enterprise, using anomalies in painting to investigate the nature of painting itself. Magritte's *The King's Museum,* 1966,[8] for example, contains a very obvious anomaly, and in this case it is fairly easy to see which pictorial rule is being broken. There is nothing odd about the drawing system in this painting, which is straightforward perspective. What is odd is that in one part of the picture the normal rule of occlusion is reversed. This rule says that parts of a scene will be hidden from a viewer at a given point, and that representations of these parts of the scene should be omitted from the picture. In the vast majority of pictures, whether in perspective or otherwise, obeying this rule is so fundamental that we simply take it for granted: as Jan Koenderink (1990) remarked, the representation of occlusion is the most powerful of all depth cues. What Magritte's painting does is to make this rule explicit. Because the normal rule has been broken it has to be formulated in terms of a denotation rule, but in this case the rule is clearly related to the laws of optics.

The main drawing system in Gris's *Breakfast,* 1914 is axonometric projection (a variety of oblique projection popular with the cubists), but this is disguised with diverging lines that give an impression of inverted perspective, and it is combined with a reversed version of atmospheric perspective in which the warmest and most saturated area of color occurs in the background of the depicted scene.[9] These drawing systems are combined with no fewer than four anomalous denotation systems. First, as in Magritte's *The King's Museum,* the normal rules of occlusion are reversed: parts of the scene that would be hidden from the viewer are included, and other parts that would be in view are left out. Second, there are numerous instances of false attachments both within the picture and between features in the picture and edges of the frame, breaking Huffman's constraint that the scene should be depicted from a general position of view. Third, real objects in the scene, such as wood grain paper and real wallpaper, are included in the picture, confounding the distinction between scene primitives and picture primitives. And finally, by using part of a real newspaper in the painting, Gris introduced an alien symbol system—natural language—into the domain of the picture. These last two devices are purely artificial, but otherwise all the drawing systems and denotation systems in this picture can ultimately be related back to the laws of optics, although apart from the use of axonometric projection they reverse the normal rules derived from these laws.

Much of Klee's work, particularly in his later years, sprang from a concern with the rules of depiction. As he said in his diaries: " I have carried out many experiments with laws and taken them as a foundation. But an artistic step is taken only when a complication arises" (Klee 1961, p. 454). Some of these "complications" seem to have been used for expressive purposes, as in his *Naked on the Bed,* 1939.[10] In other paintings and drawings they seem to serve a purely investigatory or metalinguistic function: apart from its playful title, his *Oh! but oh!* 1937[11] could be an essay on the denotation systems in line drawing in the manner of Clowes or Huffman, and in other paintings and drawings, such as *With Green Stockings,* 1939, the two functions seem to have been combined.

With Green Stockings contains four types of pictorial anomalies, all related to the denotation systems in the picture. The first group of anomalies concerns the way the girl's arms, legs, and nose are drawn. In normal line drawings the lines denote edges and contours, as they do here in the outlines of the girl's head, her skirt, and the ball. In other parts of the picture, however, the lines denote either three-dimensional volumes, as in the case of her arms and legs, or a ridge (a two-dimensional surface) in the case of her nose. In the painting (figure 6.1A and plate 3) the anomalous denotation systems used for the arms and legs are highlighted with patches of color: yellow for the arms and green for the stockings. In figure 6.1B these areas are shown using two different tones. Systems of this kind are very rare in adult pictures but common in children's early drawings such as the tadpole figures.

The second group of anomalies violates Huffman's rule that a line must keep the same meaning along its whole length: in Klee's painting this rule is broken in at least six places. One instance of this can be seen in the line that begins in the top of the patch of red paint representing the girl's hair. In its path round the girl's head this line begins by representing the contours of her head, cheek, and chin; then it turns sharply and continues as a representation of her shoulder. Just past this sharp turn, however, at a point marked by the beginning of the patch of yellow paint (1), the line changes its reference and denotes the girl's arm as a long volume. Two more anomalous changes of reference occur in the line that begins at the top right of the painting. At first this line represents the girl's arm as a long volume. Then, just past the edge of the patch of yellow paint it turns and changes twice, representing first the back of her blouse as a contour (2) and then the line of her belt as a long region (3). Finally, no fewer than three anomalies are present in the near-vertical line in the center of the painting. At the bottom of the painting, within the patch of green paint, this line represents her foot and her leg as long volumes. Then, as it crosses the edge of her skirt (4), it represents the contour of a fold in her skirt seen against the skirt as a background. Next, as it passes the line of her belt (5) it changes its reference again, representing the contour of her bodice, but this time against a blank background to the left. Finally, the line changes its reference for a third time (6), and ends by representing the ridge in the girl's neck as she turns her head.

The third group of anomalies in the picture concern the way Klee uses line junctions. In normal line drawings of smooth objects, there are two types of line junctions: T-junctions, which represent the points where contours disappear behind surfaces, and end-junctions, which represent the points where contours end. *With Green Stockings* contains examples of both types of junction, used both anomalously and in the normal way. A normal T-junction occurs at the bottom right of the painting, where the line representing the girl's left leg disappears behind the edge of her skirt. A similar T-junction occurs at the bottom left of the painting, but here the line of the leg, instead of disappearing behind the edge of the skirt, continues in view. We may interpret this anomalous junction in two ways.

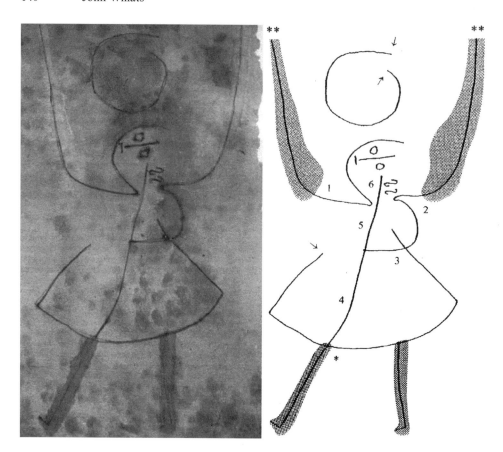

Figure 6.1

(*A*) Paul Klee, *Mit Grünen Strümpfen* (With Green Stockings), 1939, watercolor and blotting paper, 34.9 cm × 21.0 cm (13¾″ × 8¼″), Felix Klee Collection, Berne. © 2001 Artists Rights Society (ARS), New York / VG Bild-Kunst, Bonn. (*B*) Analysis of Paul Klee's *With Green Stockings*. The patches of tone correspond to patches of color in the painting (yellow for the arms and green for the stockings). These patches highlight line segments based on a denotation system in which *lines* denote *volumes*. Numbers 1 through 6 mark anomalous changes in meaning along the lines: for example, 1 indicates the change from a system in which the line denotes a *contour* to a system in which the line denotes a *volume*. The single asterisk marks a false attachment giving rise to an anomalous T-junction. The double asterisks mark false attachments between features in the picture and the picture frame: in this case, the edge of the blotting paper. The arrows indicate anomalous end-junctions. See plate 3 for color version.

The first, and perhaps more obvious way, is to think of the continuation of this line past the edge of the skirt as an example of transparency: we can still see the leg as it passes behind the skirt, as if the skirt were transparent. Alternatively, we can think of this anomalous junction as occurring as the result of a false attachment (see the part marked "*" in figure 6.1B): the line above the edge of the skirt represents the contour of a fold in the surface of the skirt, but this contour is falsely attached to the line of the leg. *With Green Stockings* also contains both normal and anomalous end-junctions. If we follow the line of the contour of the skirt on the right of the painting, up past the point at which it is caught in by the girl's belt, it ends in the normal way. On the left of the painting, however, a similar line simply ends in mid-air (see the "→" symbol). Similar anomalous end-junctions occur in the contours of the ball above the girl's head. In terms of picture perception we can no longer interpret these end-junctions as picture primitives denoting the points where contours end; instead, they simply become marks on the surface of the picture.

Finally, like Gris's *Breakfast*, Klee's painting contains examples of false attachments (see the part marked "**" in figure 6.1B) between features of the picture and the edge of the frame: these occur where the lines representing the ends of the arms just touch the edge of the paper.

I have analyzed Klee's *With Green Stockings* in some detail, and alluded, though more briefly, to the pictorial devices in Gris's *Breakfast*, because these two paintings represent extreme test cases for the argument that the spatial systems in pictures of this kind are "conventional" in the sense that in them the relations between scenes and pictures are arbitrary and symbolic rather than natural. At first glance both these paintings may suggest that this argument is convincing. Clearly, neither of these paintings can easily be accounted for in terms of the laws of optics, or by simply saying that they reproduce the structure of the optic array, or the "light that strikes the eye." Nevertheless, I have tried to show that in neither case are the relations between scenes and pictures arbitrary. Both paintings contain numerous instances of pictorial anomalies, but nearly all these instances can be accounted for by saying that they break or reverse rules derived from optical laws.

My purpose in giving these examples is to show that it is sometimes appropriate to describe the representational systems in terms of the laws of optics, and at other times it may be better to describe them in terms of pictorial rules. Psychologists and theoretical writers on theories of pictures have tended to favor descriptions based on projective geometry and the laws of optics, perhaps because psychologists have concentrated more on picture perception than on picture production. Artists, however, have usually been more interested in the rules involved in picture production, because these are the rules they have to use in their paintings and drawings. Some of these rules, like the perspectival rules about the orthogonals converging to a vanishing point, have been used quite consciously, but it seems probable that many of them operate at an unconscious level, like the rules of language. However, one method of describing the spatial systems in pictures does not preclude the other: both methods are necessary, and this duality seems to be an inherent property of representational systems. Deciding which is the better way to describe these spatial systems ought to depend on the outcome of detailed investigations into the spatial relations between scenes and pictures, rather than on some a priori theory about the general nature of pictorial representation. As Stephen Hawking has pointed out, there were for at least two hundred years two hotly debated theories about light: "One, which Newton favored, was that it was composed of particles; the other that it was made of waves. We now know that both theories are correct ... [and that] for some purposes it is helpful to think of particles as waves and for other purposes it is better to think of waves as particles" (Hawking 1993, pp. 81 and 56). I suggest that something similar seems to be true of the representational systems in pictures.

ACKNOWLEDGMENT

I am grateful to the University of Birmingham, Department of Psychology, for financial help in enabling me to attend the Conference "Reconceiving Pictorial Space" held at the Zentrum für interdisziplinäre Forschung," Universität Bielefeld, at which a shorter version of this chapter was presented.

Notes

1. For example, Hagen regards all the representational systems that can be defined in terms of projective geometry as perceptually equivalent, describing them as varieties of "natural perspective" but argues that: "The selection from among the representational options of natural perspective in terms of bias, preference, value or function is determined by cultural convention" (1986, p. 83).

2. In practice, of course, photography nearly always involves some human intervention.

3. Illustrated in Kemp (1990, fig. 390).

4. Kemp (1990, fig. 278, pp. 145, 146). See also Kemp's account of the working methods of Pieter Saenredam, on pp. 114–116, and see also Willats (1997), on pp. 190–193.

5. Illustrated in Willats (1997, fig. 3.2).

6. Illustrated in Dubery and Willats (1983, fig. 57, p. 54).

7. Children's early drawings are usually composed of marks consisting of lines, but it is crucial to distinguish between the marks in a picture, and the more abstract notion of the picture primitives that these marks represent (Willats 1992a).

8. Illustrated in Gablik (1985, fig. 196).

9. Illustrated and analyzed in Willats (1997, pl. 6, pp. 275–279).

10. Illustrated and analyzed in Willats (1997, pl. 5, pp. 264–267).

11. Illustrated and analyzed in Willats (1997, fig. 12.3, pp. 280–281).

Chapter 7
Perspective, Convention, and Compromise

Robert Hopkins

7.1   THE ISSUE

What is special about picturing in perspective? The question needs clarifying. In one sense, all picturing is perspectival, for there can be no depiction that is not from some point, or points, of view. In another sense, only some pictures are perspectival, or in perspective. In this sense, perspectival pictures are those conforming to the rules of some set of drawing systems. This is the sense relevant here, but it is hard to clarify satisfactorily. One thing is clear: the required conformity is not historical. It matters not how the picture was actually produced but whether the finished product has the features the rules prescribe. The unclarity lies in just which drawing systems are the relevant ones, and what, if anything, unites them as a group. I will try to proceed without addressing these issues, returning to them only at the close of the chapter.

Unfortunately, even granting this omission does not leave our question clear. What sort of "specialness" is at stake? Enthusiasts and skeptics about perspective sometimes frame the issue between them as whether or not perspectival picturing has a special "authority" or "unique validity" (Hyman 1992), but what does this mean? We can make some progress by appeal to the idea of convention, provided we give that notion a clear content. As I will use the term, for a practice to be conventional is for it to be one of two or more equally good solutions to a problem, all of which are available to a given community, which is adopted by each member of that community simply because it is adopted by the others, it being common knowledge that this is so.[1] In order to apply this notion to the matter in hand, we need to specify the problem that picturing in perspective solves. I will make a suggestion on this score at the chapter's end. Given some such specification of the problem, the question of perspective's status as conventional or otherwise will center on whether its solution to that problem is uniquely advantageous.

Is the question, then, whether perspectival picturing is conventional, in the sense defined? Not quite. For the skeptical, conventionalist answer might take a more or a less radical form. We have as yet said nothing about picturing in general. Given a specification of the problem it solves, we can ask of it too whether it is conventional. The two skeptical positions on perspective both hold that picturing in general is a matter of convention. The more radical view is that even given the conventions constituting picturing in general, the further practices definitive of perspectival picturing are themselves a matter of convention. The less radical position is that given those general picturing conventions, perspective is not conventional. That is, given that more general conventional practice, perspectival systems solve their specific problem better than rival solutions. An analogy may help. It is a conventional matter which side of the road we drive on. But, given that practice, it is not a matter of convention which direction one ought to look before stepping out from the curb. If the problem is that of avoiding being run over, the background conventions render one solution better than the alternative and hence not itself conventional. The less radical skepticism about perspective sees it as playing a precisely parallel role. We need to phrase our question so as to leave room for this sort of view.[2]

We can thus formulate the question as follows: Is perspectival picturing (a) a matter of convention; (b) a nonconventional consequence of those practices, themselves conventional, which constitute picturing in general; or (c) neither of the above? As noted earlier, this question is incomplete without specifications of the problems picturing in general and perspectival picturing in particular are, respectively, intended to solve, and without some definition of the different perspectival drawing systems. I think, however, that the question is sufficiently clear for discussion to proceed.

7.2   A THEORY OF PICTURES

I will answer the question by appeal to a particular account of pictorial representation. That account needs more exposition and defense than I can give here (see Hopkins 1998). If it is of interest anyway, that is because it points the way to a compromise between the enthusiastic and skeptical positions on perspective. Even if the account is rejected, perhaps some of its rivals can adopt the structure of that compromise. The compromise emerges in sections 7.5 and 7.6. Section 7.5 shows how the view can accommodate many of the ideas that suggest perspective is a matter of convention. Despite that, section 7.6 explains just what is, on my account, special about perspectival picturing, in terms that are, in one respect at least, as strong as any enthusiast about perspective could want. But to see how this combination of responses emerges, we need first to expound the view. This section does that, and the next two elaborate and reject an objection, one particularly salient here. This objection is that the view seems unable to acknowledge the existence of any picturing other than that in perspective.

The account begins from Richard Wollheim's thought (1987, chap. 2 B) that what is distinctive about pictorial representation is that it engenders a special kind of visual experience. I follow Wollheim in calling this experience "seeing-in." It is a necessary condition on a surface depicting something that that thing be seen in the surface. But the condition is only necessary. What is further required is that something makes it *right* to see that thing there. The requisite "standard of correctness" is supplied either, in the case of nonphotographic pictures, by the intentions of the artist, or, in that of photographs, by some special causal relation between the marked surface and the thing visible in it.

Where I differ from Wollheim is in my account of seeing-in itself. In my view, seeing-in is a form of experienced resemblance. To see something in a marked surface is to experience the marks as resembling that thing in a certain respect. The immediate problem is to say what this respect is, because we might think that the differences between picture and object are at least as obvious as any similarities. It's tempting to think that the picture is experienced as resembling its object in respect to some shape property. But, given the manifest differences in 3-D shape between (most) flat canvases and what they depict, what can this property be? There is an answer to this question. It finds its neatest expression in the work of the eighteenth-century philosopher Thomas Reid.

Reid distinguishes between two properties, which he dubs "real" figure and "visible" figure (1764, chap. 6, sec. 7). The former is just 3-D shape. The latter is in effect the shape things have if we ignore the dimension of depth. It is a matter of the directions of various parts of the object from the point of view. Thus, if I see a long table stretching away from me, different parts of the table lie in different directions from my point of view. For instance, the two distant corners lie in directions different from each other and different from the two directions in which the nearer corners lie. The far right-hand corner lies to the right of the far left-hand corner, and above the near right-hand corner. And the directions in which the two distant corners lie are closer to each other than are the directions of the two nearer ones.[3]

I make two observations about visible figure. The first is that it is a genuine property of things in our environment. For the point of view is just the actual location from which the world is seen, and visible figure is simply a matter of the spatial relations in which parts of the object stand to that location. This is a complex property determined by the object's 3-D shape and orientation to the point of view, but it is distinct from either of these. Reid realized this, despite the misleading contrast with "real" figure, for he described visible figure itself as "a real and external object to the eye" (ibid., chap. 4, sec. 8).

The second observation is that visible figure deserves its name: it is something we see.[4] My comments about the directions of corners of the table do not merely describe how the world is laid out. They also capture how my experience presents that arrangement. I see the directions in which the various corners lie, and see, for instance, that opposite points on the table's long edges lie in directions ever closer together, the farther away from me they are. Of course, as with any property we perceive, our experience can be misleading and will always be imprecise in certain respects. When a half-submerged stick looks bent we misperceive, not just its 3-D shape, but its visible figure too. And no visible figure is perceived with complete precision: there is always a degree of specificity beyond which experience neither represents the object as having this visible figure or as having that one. Indeed, imprecision is an important feature of our perception of this property. For experienced visible figure is only as determinate as the point of view it involves, and in general our visual experience presents the world not from a point but from a zone in environmental space large enough, in binocular vision, to include the actual location of both eyes.[5] But the observation stands: visible figure is seen, albeit with varying accuracy and precision. This is just as well. Visible figure can hardly be central to making and understanding pictures, those representations so closely bound to vision, unless visible figure is something vision makes available.

Reid noted that it is the artist's job "to hunt this fugitive form [i.e., visible figure], and to take a copy of it" (ibid., chap. 6, sec. 7). I more or less agree. For it is possible for a picture to resemble its object in visible figure, even though they differ considerably in 3-D shape. A picture of our table, for instance, might represent the four corners of its top by marks which lie in just the same directions from my point of view as did the corners themselves, when I stood before the table. The marks lie in the same directions, from the relevant point of view, as did the corners, even though, by lying at different distances in those directions, they form a configuration very different in 3-D shape from the table itself. But Reid's formulation is not quite right. What is crucial for pictorial representation is not actual resemblance in visible figure but that the marks be *experienced as* resembling the depicted object in this respect. To experience this resemblance is to see the object in the picture. And provided some intention or causal connection renders it right to experience the picture in that way, it is the picture's sustaining such experiences of resemblance in visible figure that constitutes its depicting that thing. Thus we have the basics of an account of picturing. What are the implications of this view for our question about perspective?

7.3   A CHALLENGE: ACCOMMODATING THE VARIETY OF PICTURES

This issue is best approached through a challenge to the resemblance view. Surely at least some perspectival systems are designed precisely to preserve the visible figure of depicted objects. Consider Alberti's claim that when painters cover a plane with colors, "they should only seek to present the form of things seen on this plane as if it were of transparent glass. Thus the visual pyramid could pass through it, placed at a definite distance with definite lights and a definite position of centre in space and in a definite place with respect to the observer" (1436/1966, p. 51).

Isn't this strikingly reminiscent of my description of how a picture of the table might preserve its visible figure? The only difference seems to be that talk of the visual pyramid substitutes for that of directions from the point of view. Now, whatever Alberti was doing, he was attempting to prescribe how pictures should be fashioned. His injunctions presuppose that not all pictorial representations are this way; otherwise there would be no point urging that they should be. But if pictures fitting his prescriptions preserve visible figure, presumably those that don't fit them will not do so. And if these other pictures don't preserve visible figure, how can they meet the resemblance view's main condition on their counting as pictorial representations, namely, that they be experienced as preserving it? The view purports to be an account of picturing per se, but it seems at best to cover a tiny fragment of the pictorial realm, picturing in Albertian perspective.

Of course, there are other perspectival drawing systems. Perhaps they, or at least some of them, succeed in preserving visible figure too. But this at best goes only a small way toward meeting the challenge posed. For even if all picturing in perspective meets the view's criterion for pictorial representation, that still leaves all other picturing, quite implausibly, excluded.[6] In effect, the resemblance view seems to have taken what is true of a subset of picturing, a subset at best as large as that of all picturing in perspective, and made it definitive of picturing per se. And this leaves it giving implausible answers to the two questions before us. To the question "what is pictorial representation?" it gives an implausibly narrow answer, in effect one applying only to perspectival picturing. If so, it also gives the wrong answer to the question "what is special about picturing in perspective?" For it implies that it is special precisely in being the only picturing there is.

To save the resemblance view, we need first to argue that it covers all the rich variety in ways of picturing. But, having done that, we need also to find some other account of what is special about pictures in perspective. The next section undertakes the first of these tasks. Because its main aim is negative—that the view can evade the current objection—readers more interested in my positive assertions about picturing and perspective may choose to skip this section.

7.4   MEETING THE CHALLENGE

Let us begin by trying to sharpen the challenge. Consider a particular object, say a long table, at a particular distance and orientation. The challenge concerns the range of things the resemblance view can allow to count as pictures of that thing, at that distance and orientation. Only a limited range of marks will preserve the visible figure of the table when so positioned. They might differ in color, texture, and sharpness of line, say, but not in their fundamental positions on the surface. Now, it is true that the view does not analyze depiction in terms of actual resemblance in visible figure—experienced resemblance is what matters. And it is quite possible that picture makers have learned to elicit such experiences even when the resemblances themselves are missing. After all, they have done just that for colors, using context to ensure that a pigment is seen as the color of spring foliage, for all that the two are really rather different in hue. But there are strict limits on such trickery: a pink pigment cannot be seen as resembling one that is lime green, whatever the context. And this is because, generally, our perception of features of our environment is, though not perfect, mostly accurate. If this is true of resemblance in visible figure, there will be relatively little slippage between those marks actually preserving visible figure and those experienced as doing so. More or less, then, only those marks preserving visible figure will count as depicting the table. The challenge to the view is to make room for a wider range of marks, counting as depictions of the table.

Showing that the resemblance view can meet this challenge is a complex matter. Here I can do no more than sketch some of the ingredients in a full reply. In this section I make three points. All three embody the basic observation that marks depicting the table need not match any further in content than that.

The first point is that not all marks depicting the table need depict it accurately. Some, that is, might depict the table as having properties it does not actually enjoy. It is obvious that, in general, pictorial misrepresentation is possible. A caricature of Tony Blair need not show his nose as being the shape it is and may indeed distort his features quite drastically, while still depicting him. So there is no reason for every picture that depicts our table to show it as the shape or color it really is or as having the appropriate number of legs. Such misrepresentations differ in content from each other and from accurate depictions (save, of course, that at least one element is common to the content of all: the table). Now, with respect to such groups of pictures, the resemblance view, far from precluding differences in the marks composing them, actually expects such. Like any account of depiction, it seeks to say what it is for a picture to have its pictorial content. For instance, it will say that for something to be a picture of the table as having six legs, a round top, and so forth, is for it to be experienced as resembling in visible figure the table with six legs, a round top, and so on; but that to depict the table as round topped, and so forth, but with seven legs, the marks must be experienced as resembling the table with seven legs, a round top, and so on. The view does not say how the surfaces must be marked to sustain these experiences. But given the rather limited slippage between actual resemblance and experience of it, it will at least be comfortable with the idea that different experiences of resemblance will be sustained by differently marked surfaces. Here then is one simple way in which marks depicting the table, from the specified angle, may differ from one another, so that not all of them preserve the table's actual visible figure.

The thoughts underlying this move are central to the second point, too, so it is worth spelling them out. Pictures need not be of particular things: a painting can depict a horse without their being any answer to the question of which horse it represents. But let us for the moment stick to pictures that do depict particulars. In effect, I have said that for these pictures the view makes central, not experienced resemblance to the picture's object as it actually is, but experienced resemblance to that item with whatever properties it is depicted as having. As I have noted, it is in a way obvious that this is how things should be. For only thus can the view perform its main job, of stating what it is for a picture to have a given pictorial content. For because the content of a picture is always richer than just the representation of some particular, and because there is no need for the properties filling out that content to be limited to ones the particular actually enjoys, the view must say that what matters is that resemblance to the object be experienced with whatever properties the picture ascribes.

However, despite this obviousness, discussions of resemblance views have always overlooked this point. There are several reasons for this. Some are good reasons, although there is no space here to argue that they do not justify rejecting the claims of the last paragraph.[7] But others are very poor. Among the poor reasons is a fixation on the idea of perspectival systems as ways of projecting particular objects onto plane surfaces. Thinking that this is what perspectival systems do, and thereby thinking of nonperspectival picturing as another way, or set of ways, of achieving the same result, makes it especially hard to grasp the thought that the test of the resulting marks is experienced resemblance to whatever the picture depicts and not experienced resemblance to the original projected object. Yet in fact the notion of a perspectival system, at least in its full generality, has nothing to do with the projection of real things. As I noted at the start, rather than conceiving of perspective in this historical way, it is better to think of it as a set of conditions that completed pictures may or may not meet. So conceived, perspective can apply, or fail to apply, to pictures whether they are of particular objects represented accurately, of particular objects with properties they do not in fact enjoy, or not of any particular object at all. If we do not conceive of perspectival picturing in this way, it will seem less interesting than it really is. For, as noted, pictures in general are not limited to representing particulars nor to representing any particulars they do depict as having the properties they actually do. So picturing in perspective, if it is conceived as a way of projecting particular objects onto surfaces, does not, whatever its other benefits and limitations, offer the same range of possible contents, in terms of fundamental logical kinds, as picturing in general does.

This first point begins the process of broadening the range of pictures the view can countenance. But it only gets us so far. For misrepresenting pictures too might either be in perspective or not. We have seen how very different marks might all depict our table, by ascribing different properties to it. But nothing said so far shows how those pictures might be other than perspectival. So let me turn to the second point. This is to identify a second way in which pictures of the table might differ in content: rather than being inaccurate, their content might be imprecise. One might represent the table's shape very precisely, while another represents it as merely roughly round. For pictorial content to be imprecise is for there to be no answer, beyond a certain level of detail, as to which of two distinct properties the picture ascribes to its object.[8]

It is clear that pictures can have imprecise content. A quick sketch might represent nothing more than a figure's rough shape and posture. It should be equally clear that the resemblance view can allow for this feature of depiction. As we saw, what matters is experienced resemblance to the object as depicted. There is no reason why marks should not be experienced as resembling something with fairly indeterminate properties. But it will help meet the challenge to spell out just what such an experience does and does not involve.

What is not required is that the subject misperceive the marks, or only perceive them with some rather limited level of precision. I can see a child's drawing as resembling in visible figure our table, with the properties the picture ascribes, even if I see the wobbly lines that make up the drawing with perfect clarity. Nor is it required that I experience those marks as only resembling the (relatively indeterminately characterized) table *to a certain degree*. In the preceding text I made no mention of degrees of resemblance in explaining how the view accommodates misrepresentation, because there is no need to appeal to that notion. For all I said was that we experience pictures as resembling their objects, as depicted, *perfectly*, even when the objects as they actually are do not share the marks' visible figure. And the same holds here. I may experience the child's wobbly lines as perfectly resembling a table in visible figure, provided the table in question is only roughly characterized, for example, as more or less cuboid, rather longer than it is wide, and so forth. What is required for such experiences is that although I may see the detailed features of the marks, only certain aspects of them are salient in my experience of resemblance. It is the rough shape of the line, not its meandering edges, that is prominent for me in seeing the resemblance to the table, indeterminately characterized.

How exactly do these observations about imprecise pictorial content help the resemblance view respond to the challenge? Different pictures of our table might, without misrepresenting it, differ in content from the perspectival representation, by depicting less determinate properties. Again, where there is a difference in content our view will predict, rather than preclude, that there at least may be a difference in the marks having that content. For, again, if two sets of marks are to be experienced as resembling different things, one way to achieve this is for them to differ from one another.[9] One might think that these nonperspectival pictures succeed in depicting the table only insofar as they approximate to the perspectival depiction. But that is quite wrong. They are experienced as resembling a table somewhat indeterminately characterized, but there is no sense in which the actual table, with its real properties, provides some privileged way of filling in the indeterminacies. If one of them depicts the table as roughly cuboid, it matters not what the precise shape of the real table is. That is no more relevant to our characterization of the experience of resemblance than any other way of filling in the gaps. So there is no sense in which the perspectival picture preserves perfectly the visible figure that the other pictures merely roughly preserve. And, as noted, there is no room for the thought that the nonperspectival pictures are experienced as resembling their objects to some weaker degree than the picture in perspective. So the claim of nonperspectival pictures with relatively indeterminate content to depict the table is not in any way parasitic on, or less secure than, the claim of the perspectival picture to do so. Also, given that in different pictures with imprecise content different aspects of the marks composing them may be salient, it seems that appeal to such imprecision widens considerably the range of marks that count as depictions of the table.

The third point develops the theme of imprecision. Thus far I have assumed that where pictorial content is imprecise, so will be the experience determining that content. That is, if pictures ascribe relatively indeterminate properties to their objects, that is because they are seen as resembling objects with indeterminate properties. But there is another means by which pictorial content can be imprecise. Remember that depiction is not merely a matter of experienced resemblance to some item. It also requires that some standard of correctness renders it right to see the marks as resembling that thing (section 7.2). It is possible for these two elements in the view to come apart. In general, this merely prevents depiction from occurring, as when patterns in the frost on a window pane fail, despite being seen as resembling a figure of some kind, to depict that figure, or anything else, because nothing makes it right to see them as resembling something (Wollheim 1987). But in certain cases a mismatch between the experience of resemblance and the standard of correctness can merely serve to modify pictorial content. This occurs when what the standard makes it right to see the picture as resembling is less determinate than what the picture is seen to resemble. An example is provided by stick figure pictures. We see these as resembling very thin people, with swollen heads. But, although they depict people, they do not depict them as oddly shaped. For, although the drawer's intentions make it right to see the resemblance to people, it is not intended that resemblance to emaciated figures be experienced. The drawings depict people, but it is simply indeterminate, within certain broad limits, what shape they are. Here, then, pictorial content is imprecise in ways in which the content of the experience of resemblance is not.

A relevant instance of indeterminacy attained by these means may be pictures in oriental perspective. These preserve their objects' visible figure but only that visible figure formed at a point very distant from, and standardly some distance above, the depicted scene (Hagen 1986). Thus there is no trouble understanding how these pictures can be seen as resembling their objects in visible figure, despite the fact that they do not deploy classical Western perspective. It seems to me an open question whether they depict their scenes from the high, distant, viewpoint described. But even if they do not, the resemblance view can easily accommodate this difference. The content of the picture is less precise, with respect to viewpoint, than is what is seen in it, because what is seen in these marks and what it is right to see therein comes apart in the way I have described.

There is more to be said about this alternate method for generating imprecise content. In particular, we need to know how those who see the pictures work out just what is depicted, that is, which aspects of their experience to rely upon in interpreting the pictures and which to set aside. I will not go into these matters here (but see Hopkins 1998, chap. 6). My point now is that provided these questions can be answered, this second route to indeterminacy further widens the tolerance of the resemblance view. As the case of stick figures illustrates, marks very different from those required by perspectival systems can depict, given this latest refinement to the view.

I said at the start of this section that my three points would all exploit the possibility that different pictures of our table might differ in content. This is true, but the second and third in particular also allow us to see how rather different marks might nonetheless exactly match in pictorial content. They can do so if only certain aspects of them are salient in determining what the marks are seen as resembling. Or they can do so by supporting experiences of resemblance to things with different properties, provided only the common aspects of those resembled items are underwritten by standards of correctness and thus retained in the content of the pictures.

7.5   COMPROMISING WITH THE CONVENTIONALIST

The points of the last section go a good way toward meeting the challenge to the resemblance view. Marks very different from those preserving our table's visible figure might nonetheless depict it, from the right angle, provided they either misrepresent it or represent its properties only imprecisely, or, of course, do both. But I promised to do more than merely deflect objections. I promised some form of compromise with those who take depiction itself, and perspectival picturing in particular, to be either properly conventional or a nonconventional consequence of conventions. How does the view yield that compromise?

We can see room for compromise by getting clear about the view's ambitions. It seeks to analyze depiction in terms of the experience to which it gives rise, seeing-in. To do that, it needs to tell us what that experience is. It is the experience of resemblance in visible figure. But characterizing an experience is not the same thing as describing its causes. So far our view has not said much about how the world must be for a given surface to bring a given spectator to see a given thing in it. It is not entirely without implications for this question. If seeing something in a set of marks is a matter of experiencing them as resembling that thing in visible figure, then, given some basic facts of optics and psychology, the only marks that will do, except in exceptional circumstances, are ones at least approximating to the object's visible figure. And although the last section argued that there is no need for the approximation to be very exact, it does not follow that it need not hold at all.[10] But the causal condition thus stated is at best necessary. Many other factors will come into play in dictating whether a given experience of resemblance in fact occurs. Saying what these factors are is no part of the brief of our position. Its goal is to analyze seeing-in, and thereby pictorial representation, not to describe the empirical facts about when that experience is engendered. However, the view can at least *acknowledge* these facts. It is here that the seeds of compromise can be found. For the view can allow that many of the factors empirically determining a given experience of resemblance are precisely those which the skeptic about perspective wished to emphasize. I offer three examples.

The first factor is the nature of the spectator's general perceptual environment. We can see that this environment must play a role in determining what folk see in surfaces, by better understanding why that cannot be determined by preservation of visible figure alone. The problem is that a given visible figure is compatible with an infinite range of 3-D shapes.[11] The attraction of placing visible figure at the core of an account of picturing is precisely that objects of different shape, and in particular pictures and what they depict, might share visible figure. They need only be arranged differently, that is, at different distances, along the same set of directions from a given point. But by the same token any other arrangement differing from these two only in respect of depth will likewise share that visible figure. So the fact that a picture preserves the visible figure of a particular 3-D shape cannot alone determine what is seen in it. For we might equally see therein one of the many other shapes the visible figure of which is thus preserved.

What, then, *does* determine which of the infinitely many compatible 3-D shapes we experience a given set of marks as resembling in visible figure? In part, the answer is surely our general perceptual environment. We see cubes in pictures of them, rather than irregular trapezohedrons, because our world contains far more of the former than the latter. Such examples may seem to offer little comfort to the skeptical, conventionalist, cast of mind. For these folk want to stress the variation across cultures in the reception and use of perspective; whereas many of the environmental features whose role we are now describing will be common to all cultures. But the structure of the issue here is more general. A lot of people look more or less alike, some very much so. What determines that people see some of these look-alikes rather than others in their portraits and holiday snaps? It is not resemblance in visible figure, because what so resembles one look-alike will equally resemble all. So the answer must lie in past perceptual experience: a person has seen one look-alike but had no contact with the other. Here there is variation across different groups of people of just the sort the skeptic seeks to highlight. The resemblance view can acknowledge the role of that variation not by offering a conventionalist account of depiction but by allowing the variation a role in the causal determinants of seeing-in.

The second factor I want to discuss is closer to the skeptic's heart. This is the spectator's pictorial education. It is a matter of the sorts of pictures to which a person has been exposed and the ways in which those have affected that individual's perceptual sensitivities. Although few have realized this, the resemblance view is easily able to acknowledge the role such factors play. As Reid noted, visible figure is "fugitive," that is, it is hard to perceive with precision and accuracy. The less sharp one's perceptual grasp of it, the less sensitive one will be to a picture's failure to preserve it. In consequence, many nonperspectival pictures may well have been experienced as resembling their objects in visible figure perfectly well, for all that they don't in fact resemble them more than approximately. For they may have been intended for, and enjoyed by, viewers whose perception of visible figure was less than ideally acute. And one result of the rediscovery of perspective may have been to sharpen viewers' ability to perceive visible figure, thereby altering which marks will be experienced as resembling things in that respect.

Here the compromise with the skeptic is considerable. Our view allows that picturing essentially involves something independent of conventions, the generation of a particular experience, but the view also allows that certain pictures may themselves alter which pictures are experienced in that way. The suggestion is that perspectival pictures may be one such case, altering viewers' general perceptual propensities in order to bolster their own position as the marked surfaces most likely to elicit the required experiential response. The point can be illustrated by tackling an argument of Nelson Goodman's, one intended precisely as an objection to perspective's special status.

One of Goodman's points against perspective was, in effect, that not even pictures in Albertian perspective preserve visible figure (1969, chap. 1). The Albertian system requires receding horizontal parallels to be represented by converging lines but not so parallels receding in the vertical plane. As Goodman observed, this is not true to the geometry. The difference between the directions of opposing points on the parallels narrows just as rapidly with recession in the vertical plane as in the horizontal. What Goodman overlooked, however, is that this discrepancy may reflect an aspect of our *experience* of visible figure. Setting aside pictures for a moment, consider our face-to-face experience with things. Suppose that in such experience we are more sensitive to this shift in the direction of points on receding parallels when the recession is horizontal, as along railway tracks, than when it is vertical, as with the sides of a building viewed from the street. Then we would expect pictures that are experienced as preserving visible figure to exhibit precisely the discrepancy noted. Systematic discrepancies in our face-to-face experience of visible figure will dictate analogous discrepancies in our depictive practices. This provides a response to Goodman's objection, but it also suggests another point more relevant to present purposes. For it may be that our differing sensitivities to vertical and horizontal recession is as much effect as cause of the Albertian system. Perhaps the prevalence of picturing in Albertian perspective has sharpened our perception of one of these aspects of visible figure over the other.

Of course, it is only a supposition that there are the systematic discrepancies in experience just described. And it is only a hypothesis that any such discrepancies might be fed by, as much as support, the pictorial systems we have adopted. These claims need testing empirically. But they can serve my purposes prior to such investigation. For the supposition alone is enough to neutralize Goodman's objection to perspective's privileged status, pending further investigation. And the hypothesis serves to illustrate that to the extent that the skeptic is right to think that acculturation affects which pictures look natural or right to us, the truth in such claims is consistent with the resemblance view. For the hypothesis, produced within the framework of that view, is that a perspectival system has altered our perceptions in such a way as to ensure its own entrenchment as a way of generating pictures that look right. Suspicion that perspective's success is down to such bootstrapping is surely one of the motors of skepticism about it.

The third factor determining experiences of resemblance is another one that might vary across cultures: the way we view pictures. Once again, we can approach the point via a potential objection to perspectival picturing's special status.

In Raphael's *The School of Athens,* 1510/1511, a figure on the far right holds a sphere, resting on the fingertips of his upturned hand. The sphere is depicted by a circular mark. However, classical perspectival systems suggest that thanks to its oblique position away from the vanishing point of the picture, the sphere should be represented by an *elliptical* patch of paint. This preserves the visible figure a sphere would have at the single, highly precise, point in depicted space from which the entire scene might be viewed and from which Raphael depicts the scene. In the nineteenth century, Jules de La Gournerie tried substituting, on an engraving of *The School,* an ellipse for Raphael's circle. However, the effect looked quite wrong, whereas Raphael's circle looks exactly right. The reason is, once again, that actual resemblance in visible figure is no guarantee of experienced resemblance therein. What determines the discrepancy here? The answer is that the way we view pictures affects which marks we see as resembling others in visible figure. Were we to view the Raphael from the point, in front of the marked surface, at which it exactly matches the visible figure, at the pictorial point of view, of the depicted scene, and were we to view it from there with one eye, then the elliptical patch would look right. That is, it would be seen as resembling an off-center sphere in visible figure. But we don't normally look at pictures in that way. We move about, positioning ourselves at different distances from the marked surface and at different points along its length. We use both eyes. We let our impressions build over time. All these factors dictate that the circular patch is the one we see as resembling a spherical, off-center ball; and thus that such a patch is what depicts the ball. Things would be different were we the sort of viewers, with different habits of attending to pictures, La Gournerie's unduly rigid application of perspective supposed us to be. Then an elliptical patch would carry the content of our circular one.[12]

7.6   WHAT IS SPECIAL ABOUT PERSPECTIVE?

The last section tried to show that the resemblance view can accommodate some of the factors that have impressed those skeptical about perspective's special status. Section 7.4 argued that the view is in no way obliged to restrict depiction to picturing in perspective. This leaves one issue outstanding. We need to say what is special about perspectival picturing, according to the resemblance view. If it's not the only picturing there is, and if the truth about both depiction in general and perspectival depiction in particular leaves room for at least some of the culturally relative factors the skeptic emphasizes, then how should we answer the question with which we began this chapter? Is perspectival picturing conventional or a consequence of conventions? And if it is not conventional, what is the problem that it solves better than any rivals?

Perspectival picturing is not a consequence of conventions, for picturing itself is not conventional. Pictorial representation essentially involves the generation of a certain experience, one of resemblance in visible figure. Generating this experience, in such a way as to effect communication, is the problem that methods of picturing have to solve. More precisely, in any particular case the problem is so to mark a surface such that it can be seen as resembling, in visible figure, a certain thing or scene, with certain properties, from a certain angle. Given our account of convention (section

7.1), picturing will be conventional just if there are two or more equally good solutions to each such problem, the choice between them being made on the basis that others have also chosen likewise, it also being common knowledge that this is what is going on. There are three reasons why this condition is not met.

First, the range of possible marks in which the target content can be seen is narrowly constrained. For despite all the concessions made above, it remains the case that in general a causally necessary condition is that the marks preserve, at least roughly, the relevant visible figure (section 7.5). This excludes most of the possible ways of marking the surface from being solutions to the problem in hand.

Now, those concessions were real. I allowed that other factors do play a role in determining experiences of resemblance, factors other than the marks' actually reproducing the visible figure of the target scene. Nonetheless, none of these factors plays the role convention would require. For— the second reason—they are not in general factors under the control of a given group of picture makers or consumers. This is clearly true for the general nature of the perceptual environment. We can control the nature of what others or ourselves are in perceptual contact with but only under special circumstances (e.g., persuading someone to take part in a psychological experiment) and over very limited portions of space and time. The limited context over which we thus exercise control plays a highly restricted role in conditioning pictorial perception, compared with the subject's perceptual life history. The point also holds for pictorial acculturation. No doubt for any pictorial education a viewer has had, there is a different one that person might have undergone. But it does not follow that either the viewer, or any picture maker currently attempting to communicate with that viewer, could have chosen to give him the one rather than the other. It is a matter of the history of the viewer's culture and own exposure, over many years, to various images. And something similar is at least in part true of our habits of viewing pictures. One can, by prescription or by constricting the viewer's movement, in exceptional circumstances limit the ways in which the picture is viewed. But even here many of the key factors, such as the tendency to deploy eye or head movement, reflect engrained perceptual habits and even basic facts about visual physiology, which cannot be swept aside, however determined we are to find a new way of doing things.

Perhaps these considerations do not exclude every relevant possibility. Perhaps they leave some room at the margins, by manipulating the factors discussed, for alternative means to the same experiential end. But, and this is my third reason that the aforementioned condition on conventionality is not met, even if it is true that alternative means exist, it is not common knowledge that it is. Different viewing habits, for instance, may affect what people see a set of marks as resembling, but those people are not aware that this is so. This will prevent them from knowing that what they are responding to is one of two equally good solutions to a given pictorial problem. And thus, insofar as the factors of section 7.5 meet the control condition for conventionality, they do not meet the common knowledge condition. Picturing, it seems, is not conventional.

Nor is it the case that perspectival picturing is conventional. It might seem that my attempt to defuse the objection that the resemblance view is hopelessly narrow forces just this result. For if perspectival picturing is not the only sort there is, and if the problem solved by all pictorial systems is just that of generating experiences of resemblance to certain things, it may seem that there is nothing left for perspective systems to do better than their rivals. If not, we would have in place at least part of what is required for their adoption to be a matter of convention. But this line is mistaken. There is something perspective systems do that others do not: they are not the only pictures, but they constitute the only way to depict a certain kind of thing. For only pictures in perspective depict detailed spatial content. Or so at least I will argue. I cannot derive this conclusion from the resemblance view alone. However, the only extra support needed is a little theoretical reflection and some plausible psychological speculation. Given these foundations, although nonperspectival pictures might depict spatial detail, it seems that they do not in fact do so. Moreover, a lot would have to change before they would.

The theoretical reflection is this. Consider properties that admit of ordered variation. Colors are one example—there are many shades between pure green and pure blue. Spatial properties are another—my hand can occupy many positions between my two feet. One can represent such properties, of course, in more or less precise ways—merely by specifying rough hues or locations, or by specifying more determinate ones. Now, some forms of representation allow one to represent instances of these properties in a highy precise but piecemeal way. One could, for instance, have a word for a particular shade of blue, without having words for any but the roughest categories of the other colors. But depiction is not a form of representation that allows for this possibility. If you can *depict* an instance of some color, at a certain level of precision, your representational resources must also allow you to depict other colors, with equal precision. And likewise for spatial properties.[13]

Coupled with the resemblance view, this thought promises to ensure that only pictures in perspective can depict precise spatial properties. For suppose we consider a competing system—so-called inverse perspective. In pictures drawn on these principles, receding parallel lines in pictorial space are represented by lines on the canvas that *diverge,* in sharp contrast to perspectival systems, in which such lines converge. Thus, because perspectival systems preserve visible figure, inverse perspective cannot do so. Now, despite that, there is no reason to deny that inverse perspective yields *depictions.* For an inverse perspective drawing of an oblong table may indeed be seen as resembling, in visible figure, an oblong table. But this is only obviously possible if the object the picture is experienced as resembling is reasonably indeterminate—a table that is roughly oblong, no more. So let us consider under what conditions, if any, such a system would yield depictions of precise shape and other spatial features. They must be conditions allowing for the depiction of any of a wide variety of such shapes and arrays, or so our theoretical reflection suggests. So the rules of inverse perspective will have to allow for projecting a wide variety of such shapes and arrays onto surfaces. But if we are to appreciate the detailed content of the pictures thus created, it seems we must be sensitive to small differences between the way a given canvas is marked and the ways in which it might have been. Now, those differences are precisely between marks that do not preserve the visible figure of what they represent, and their not doing so is important to their representing, according to the rules of inverse perspective, what they do. So an appropriate sensitivity to the relevant details of the surface markings cannot, in all psychological plausibility, accompany experiencing the marks as resembling, in visible figure, something with the precise spatial features in question. Thus, although the marks may depict something, and although they may systematically represent spatial detail, they do not *depict* that detail. The only conditions under which they would do so would be ones in which our psychology were quite different from how it in fact is.

Of course, inverse perspective fails in a radical way to preserve visible figure. However, any other way of marking surfaces that fails less spectacularly will also confront the basic problem here. So the resemblance view, coupled with our theoretical constraint on depiction and our sense of what is psychologically possible for us, does seem to preclude any depiction of spatial detail that is not depiction in perspective. If this conclusion seems outrageous, remember that it is restricted to a certain, highly special, form of pictorial content. Once one focuses that thought clearly, I think the conclusion loses its air of reductio and starts to seem plausible. At least it allows us to say what is special about drawing in perspective. The Renaissance did not invent depiction, but it did discover a way to expand our depictive powers. For only with the articulation of perspectival drawing systems did we acquire the ability to depict space with precision.[14]

One issue remains. Which systems are the perspectival ones? I am not sure what to say about this. If the speculations just offered are correct, we could pick them out as those systems permitting depiction of spatial detail. The cost of doing this, however, would be to trivialize my claim that perspective is not a matter of convention. For I made good that claim by saying that no rivals can solve the problem of depicting spatial detail, an assertion the proposed characterization would empty of content. What is needed, therefore, is a way of picking out the perspectival systems that renders my speculation plausible without trivializing it. I am not sure what, other than a list of particular systems, would do this. But I am also not sure that this is particularly a problem for the position articulated here. I suspect that everyone who wants to talk clearly about whether perspectival systems have a special status will have to define which systems they mean, and to say, in independent terms, which problem those systems are intended to solve. Although this chapter has not managed the first of those tasks, it has at least made an attempt at the second.

Notes

1. This is a drastically simplified version of David Lewis's much admired account (1969).

2. Logic leaves room for another position, on which picturing is not conventional but picturing in perspective is so. Although intriguing, this view is not adopted by any writer known to me and is not discussed here.

3. Visible figure is what I have elsewhere (Hopkins 1998) called "outline shape."

4. Do not be misled by Reid's term. It is not part of the notion of visible figure that it is the only spatial property, or "figure," that vision represents. My view is that others, including 3-D shape, are also seen. Although Reid disagreed (see Hopkins, 2002), this claim is a further, and optional, element in his position.

5. This last is an empirical speculation but a plausible one. If right, it allows us to dismiss an incipient worry. This is that because we see with two eyes, we cannot see from a single point of view and hence that something is amiss in my claims about the perception of visible figure.

6. Given this, I need not at this point address the issue, set aside in section 4.1, of which systems are the perspectival ones.

7. These reasons are (1) it is assumed the resemblance view is designed to do a job it should not, in fact, attempt to do, namely, explaining what it is about the picture that leads people to experience it as they do (see section 7.5); (2) it is correctly assumed that the resemblance view will want to give *some* role to how the depicted item actually is, the appropriate role then being misunderstood; and (3) the worry that if what matters is resemblance to the depicted object as depicted, the view takes for granted part of what it is supposed to explain, thereby guaranteeing that its analysis cannot be sufficient. For discussion of these objections, see Hopkins (1998).

8. As I will say, the content is *imprecise,* and it is *indeterminate* how things are in the depicted realm.

9. This is only one way in which this might be achieved, because given the point about salience, matching marks might, under the right conditions, differ in content in virtue of different aspects of each being salient in the experience of resemblance. Hence the view predicts, not that the perspectival and nonperspectival pictures will differ but that they might.

10. In section 7.4 I said that the view makes no appeal to (experienced) degrees of resemblance in characterizing seeing-in. Indeed, the notion of degrees of resemblance does not figure in any of the claims that constitute the view. It is quite consistent with this that the view, coupled with some basic optics and physiology, has implications involving (actual) degrees of resemblance.

11. Strictly, the relevant range is of different pairings of 3-D shape and orientation.

12. For La Gournerie's experiment, see Pirenne (1970, p. 122). His engraving seems certain to have been far smaller than Raphael's original. This complicates the relationship between the story and the moral I want to draw from it. However, I think it obvious that the outcome would have been the same had La Gournerie tampered with the Raphael itself, so I ignore this complication here.

13. This thought is really the offspring of Goodman's account of depiction (1969). It ignores some of his view's difficulties by restricting itself to certain sorts of properties and by resisting the temptation to insist on infinitely precise representation. But the most significant difference is that I do not offer it as a definition of depiction, more as a test for it. For another use of a similar thought, see Lopes (1996).

14. John Hyman (1992) has reached somewhat similar conclusions independently. It might be fairer to consider the Renaissance achievement one of rediscovery. See, for instance, White (1987).

Plate 1
Edouard Manet, *Portrait of Emilie Ambre as Carmen*, c. 1879. Oil on canvas, 36 3/8" × 28 15/16".
Philadelphia Museum of Art: Gift of Edgar Scott. See chapter 1.

Plate 2
Pieter Jansz Saenredam, *Interior of the Saint Jacob Church in Utrecht*, 1642. Bayerische Staatsgemäldesammlungen, Alte Pinakothek, Munich. See chapter 2.

Plate 3

Paul Klee, *Mit grünen Strümpfen (With Green Stockings)*, 1939, watercolor and blotting paper, 34.9 cm × 21.10 cm. (13 3/4" × 8 1/4"). Felix Klee Collection, Berne. ©2001 Artists Rights Society (ARS), New York/VG Bild-Kunst, Bonn.

Plate 4
The pleasure of René Magritte's *The Listening Room/La chambre d'écoute* is in the uncertainty of its reality through the ambiguity of perceived size. Oil on canvas, 45 cm × 54.7 cm. 1952. Private collection. ©A.D.A.P.G. Paris. ©2002 C. Herscovici, Brussels/Artists Rights Society (ARS), New York. See chapter 13.

Plate 5
From Theodor De Bry's *Collectiones peregrinatorum in Indiam Orientalem et Indiam Occidentalem (1590–1634)* (1990, p. 27). See chapter 15.

Chapter 8

Resemblance Reconceived

Klaus Sachs-Hombach

As the existence of different types and schemata of pictures demonstrates, pictorial forms of representation are subject to historical and cultural influences. This can be seen as supporting a "convention theory" of pictorial meaning but does not exclude a resemblance theory. This chapter defends the latter view on the basis of an internalized resemblance criterion.

8.1 INTRODUCTION

Imagine you are shown a passport photograph of an unknown person. A short time later you recognize someone on the road as the person in the photograph. This phenomenon of pictorial reference is common but puzzling. Many interesting empirical findings, from, for instance, psychological and neurological research, cast light on it. In contrast to such empirical approaches, philosophical analysis aims, first of all, to clarify what is meant by "pictorial reference." This requires us to give an account of what pictures are, that is, to formulate a criterion allowing us to classify certain things as pictures, or, at least, certain signs as pictorial signs.

There are currently two fundamentally different lines of thought within philosophical analysis that claim to be able to give such an account.[1] One holds that, like linguistic expressions, pictorial reference is conventionally determined (so that the nature of pictures cannot be defined by their semantics); the other assumes a genuine relation between the picture and its subject (so that the internal structure of the picture allows us to determine at least partially what the picture depicts). Consequently, theories of the first group maintain that a picture could have looked quite different while still fulfilling its purpose; a variety of forms is available to depict something, and the choice depends on cultural influences. Theories of the second group insist that a picture, in order to be considered to depict a certain object or event, must have some essential properties in common with the object or event depicted; so that at least all objects devoid of these properties are eliminated as referents. A prominent theory from the first group is Nelsm Goodman's symbol theory.[2] Resemblance theory belongs to the second group.[3]

For some time now, the usefulness of resemblance theory has been questioned. Certainly, the issue of resemblance criteria is highly problematic and requires further explication.[4] It is Goodman's merit to have pointed out these difficulties. However, the conventionalist view (particularly when applied to our example) seems to me extremely implausible. I would, therefore, rather defend the resemblance criterion, at least with respect to clear cases of figurative pictures. The passport photograph is a particularly strong example of this kind of picture, because it has intuitive appeal. In section 8.2, I discuss the intuition addressed by this example in more detail. In section 8.3, I present my own proposal, which attempts to reconcile the two previously cited approaches. In my view, pictures are perception-based signs.[5] In a final section, section 8.4, I take a brief look at the problem of pictorial reference and certain puzzling cases.

8.2   A FIRST INTUITION

The example of the passport photograph is meant to elicit a strong intuition in favor of resemblance theory. With it, one points out that our use of pictures is bound to a particular competence, which is different from the competence one needs in verbal communication. We are, it seems, able to understand the passport photograph immediately, without having learned whom it stands for. If we do not have to learn its individual referent, we presumably make use of a fundamental competence with which we are already endowed, principally that of perceiving objects. The example is, then, meant to refute the conventionalist view in favor of a perceptualist view. On this perceptualist view, in order to know what is special about pictures, we have to know what is special about the competence we employ when treating something as a picture.

Let's take a closer look at the example. We may assume in general that we can identify an individual entity as individual only if we already know something about it. If, for example, we want to apply a proper name correctly, we must either have already become acquainted with the corresponding person or have obtained some knowledge of him or her from other sources—for instance, via description.[6] However, this does not apply to a passport photograph. Unlike the proper name, the picture gives us the clues necessary to determine the person that the photograph refers to. The clues come from the picture and only from the picture. We do not need any additional information, nor do we need to know the person.[7] In this regard, the mechanisms by which a photograph and a proper name function are basically different, although they may be used similarly in certain situations. (The case of twins is a special case I will discuss later on.)

If we accept the assumption that we get the information necessary to correctly interpret a passport photograph exclusively from the physical basis of the picture—the "sign vehicle" so to speak—we must also assume that there is a nonconventional relationship between the picture and the object depicted. This relation has the following form: in order to be the referent of a picture, an object must have some relevant properties in common with the sign vehicle.[8] Naturally, this relation can be thought of as a resemblance relation. No other relation so clearly suggests itself. The resemblance theorist thus wishes to use this example to elicit an intuition: that resemblance is the only plausible relationship allowing us to describe the identification. On this basis, the resemblance relationship could be regarded as a necessary property of figurative pictures. Of course, the resemblance theorist does not need to defend such a strong version. The theorist might take the resemblance criterion merely as a sufficient condition for distinguishing pictorial signs from linguistic ones. This weaker version of the theory is the one I shall argue for in what follows. The interpretation of pictures does not necessarily make use of this resemblance criterion. There might be some pictures (or some aspects of pictures) that we interpret differently. But whenever we employ the resemblance criterion, the sign thus interpreted should be classified as a picture. This allows the resemblance theorist to speak of a core area of depiction. My explication is meant to be applicable at least to that area.

8.3   PICTURE THEORY AND RESEMBLANCE

My explication of the term "picture" consists mainly in introducing the resemblance criterion in a rational way. "To introduce a criterion in a rational way" means to argue step by step what this criterion is supposed to do and why it should be adopted. This will at the very least provide us with a better understanding of why and at what point the resemblance criterion fails to do its job.

Before starting my explication, I would like to make a few method-ological remarks. Although I assume that one can arrive at a full under-standing of how pictures function only if one combines the findings of different sciences, particularly of psychology and philosophy, these aspects are on different methodical levels and should be kept apart. The philo-sophical explication of the term "picture" formulates criteria that allow us to classify something as a picture. This should be distinguished from the question under what conditions an individual can apply such criteria. I consider that question only briefly in section 8.4.

As I have already noted, I will proceed from a narrow concept of pictures. As pictures in this sense, I will address only such entities that are two-dimensional (and thus visually perceptible), artificial, and at least semipermanent. The first criterion excludes mental and three-dimensional pictures. The second criterion excludes so-called natural pictures, for example reflected images. The last criterion excludes transient phenomena such as clouds, in which we might see a landscape.

Pictures in this narrow sense are therefore paintings, drawings, or pho-tographs. The broader phenomenon, which would include most of what I have just excluded, might be termed "iconicity." Given this specificity (to which I should add the further restriction "figurative pictures"), I do not intend to claim that we should use the term "picture" only in this narrow sense. Instead, I restrict my explication to a core area in order to have a solid starting point. In respect to this area, I shall introduce the resem-blance criterion as a sufficient condition that should allow us to classify certain signs as pictures. Here is a first draft version of the explication I am going to set out and amend step by step:

(S1) An object is a picture if it is used as a sign and if it resembles what it refers to.

This explication is of course in need of further explanation. The term "sign" and the term "resemblance" are, as yet, undefined. Concerning the term "sign" I consider a rather short explanation sufficient:

(S2) An object is a sign if we take it to stand for something else, that is, if we assign a content to it, which, in many cases, allows us to determine a referent.

Statement (S2) is not supposed to answer the question of what a picture is. It only offers some distinctions that I take to be unproblematic within semiotics. According to the semiotic triangle, (S2) proposes to distinguish between the sign vehicle, the sign content, and the sign referent. In connection with (S1), the statement suggests that such a distinction also makes sense for pictures. So pictures should be considered as normally having a vehicle, a content, and a referent. The vehicle is a physical object with properties, such as the visual ones of shape and color. The referent of a picture is what the picture is taken to refer to: this can include all kinds of objects and events—for example, the person we recognized on the road after seeing the passport photograph. Finally, the content consists in those properties that we consider to be relevant for representation and that we relate to an object or an event. Thus the content normally provides us with a procedure by which to determine the referent of the picture. The content can also be characterized as an intentional object, which—so to speak— we can see *in* the surface of the picture vehicle.[9] A somewhat different but, I think, equivalent formulation would be to say that the content is what we see the relevant properties of the picture vehicle *as*. For example, we might see a certain line on a canvas as the silhouette of mountains. The process that constitutes a content should be termed "interpretation."

As far as the distinction of vehicle, content, and referent is presupposed in the following, pictures are signs by stipulation. Because this is the meaning of the term "picture," I would find it difficult to understand what was meant if someone denied that pictures were signs. But one might also say that in the following I am going to deal with pictures only insofar as they are signs. Thus the question I want to answer is What criterion allows us to distinguish pictorial from other kinds of signs, particularly linguistic signs? I would like to argue that the resemblance criterion will perform this function. In order to argue this, I am now going to introduce the notion of resemblance, in a form initially independent of the picture notion.

(S3) Objects resemble each other if they have, in relevant respects, essential properties in common.

Putting it this way, the term "resemblance" remains vague, because there is nothing said about the meaning of "relevant" and "essential." But this reflects the way we use this term. Normally, we take resemblance to be a gradual relation that applies to different objects only with regard to a certain respect. Which *respect* should count as *relevant* depends on our intentions and on the context. Compared to tables, quite different chairs resemble each other, but compared to a variety of other chairs they might not, because now size, color, or height are relevant. Also, what *property* should be taken as *essential* depends, of course, on what respect is relevant. Furthermore, it depends on how our perception works. We take, for example, certain shapes to be typical as shapes of dogs or cats. An essential property is, therefore, a property typical of visual appearance that normally helps us to classify something when we have seen it. How this mechanism really works is an interesting empirical question. It might be subject to cultural and historical influences. However, in order to be more precise about what is taken as essential, one would need to have greater empirical knowledge about how we classify different appearances. Because I am not pursuing a psychological account, I will not go into this problem. Within the framework of my philosophical explication, it is sufficient to point out that such a psychological variable should be taken into account. Whatever its outcome, it strongly suggests internalization of the resemblance criterion. I have formulated this suggestion in the following sentence:

(S4) Objects have essential properties in common if the perception of the corresponding properties under a certain perspective is identical.

In adopting this internalized resemblance criterion, I abstain from the possibility of explicating resemblance as a mathematically explicable relation between two sets.[10] Instead of this (but without intending to criticize it), I would like to take an intuitive notion of resemblance as a starting point. According to this intuition, things are considered similar when they *seem* so to us. Regarding the resemblance criterion as internalized this way does, of course, not answer the question about which are the essential properties, but it does suggest that one should discuss it on the perceptual level. Thus (S4) emphasizes the perceptual conditions under which we experience something as similar, namely, when the perception of the corresponding essential properties is identical. I think that this move allows us to account for the variety of different styles more effectively. Furthermore, it suggests why making something look realistic is not the same as depicting something correctly from the geometrical point of view. For example, in relation to a house, the front door should be painted larger than it is, if it is to appear correctly.

Note that it is not required that the entire perception be identical. This may apply to the special case of perceiving twins or illusionistic paintings (trompe l'oeil). But, normally, we have no difficulty in distinguishing the two things or events we consider similar. According to my explication, the reason for this is that we refer only to the essential properties when we experience something as similar to something else, whereas the simultaneous perception of the other properties enables us to be aware of their differences. It is of course difficult to separate the two components of our perception, but that does not falsify my explication. Having internalized the resemblance criterion in this way, we can now apply it to the sign relation. I will do this in two steps.

(S5) A sign resembles some other object if the sign vehicle and the other object have, in relevant respects, essential properties in common.

Statement (S5) is directly linked to (S3). It simply says that the resemblance criterion also applies to objects used as sign vehicles, independently of the sign relation. Statement (S5) does not really follow from (S3), because, strictly speaking, only the sign vehicle resembles some other object, whereas the notion of a sign includes at least a content. But I take (S5) to reflect our normal way of talking and I propose that we actually refer to the sign vehicle when we say that a sign resembles some other object. I find this argument unproblematic insofar as signs necessarily have a sign vehicle and can be considered as objects in this respect. But putting it this way does not, of course, tell us very much. More important is the second step, which is intended to characterize pictorial signs.

(S6) A sign is a picture if the sign vehicle and some other object have, in relevant respects, essential properties in common (i.e., if they resemble each other) and if these properties are constitutive for the interpretation of the sign.

In order to use resemblance as a criterion to distinguish pictorial from other kinds of signs, (S6) adds a restriction to the resemblance criterion. It excludes in its second part those properties that other objects may also have but which do not contribute to the content of the sign, that is, which are irrelevant to its interpretation. Regarding something as a picture makes irrelevant how heavy it is or what its back looks like. Therefore, in order to be taken as a pictorial sign, it is not enough that the sign vehicle has essential properties in common with some other object. These properties must also be regarded as relevant for the representational function of the sign.

One could leave out the second part if one understood the expression "in relevant respects" in (S6) as saying "in respects relevant for representation." But because I have already suggested in (S3) that objects resemble each other in principle in relevant respects only, for example, in respect of color, the notion of relevance is already introduced in a broad sense. I therefore prefer (S6) the way it is. It is more explicit about the need to assume two different levels within resemblance theory. First, one determines relevant respects while comparing two objects and takes them to resemble each other. Second, one determines the respects that are also relevant for representation, that is, constitutive for interpretation. Thus, "to take an object as a picture" means that we, sometimes automatically, delimit the respects relevant for resemblance to the respects that are also relevant for representation.

Compared to (S5), (S6) points out that there might be signs that are similar to other objects without being pictures of these objects, because some similarities are not relevant for depiction. Ruling out such cases, for example, self-referential linguistic expressions, reference to the process of interpretation implies that our classification of different kinds of signs depends on how we use the signs. This implication seems acceptable, because, depending on the context, we actually classify some objects as pictures or as texts. In both cases we have to take the object as standing for something else, that is, we have to assume a content and, if possible, a referent, but the respects we consider relevant—and which partially determine the content—are not the same for pictures and text. In the case of linguistic expressions, we do not, for example, consider color relevant. In determining the properties that are relevant for representing something, we therefore also determine what kind of sign we take this to be. In some cases, mainly perspectival pictures that conform to Albertian principles, this happens immediately and involuntarily. According to my explication, this is exactly what one would expect, because resemblance is a gradual relation: the greater the number of essential properties a picture has in common with an other object, the more easily we recognize this object *in* the picture. Often this also implies that more respects are relevant for representation. Thus, perceiving the picture becomes more and more like perceiving the object depicted itself. This case might be described more adequately by (S7), which simply combines (S4) and (S6):

(S7) A sign is a picture if the perception of the essential properties that the sign vehicle has in relevant respects is identical to the perception one would have of the corresponding properties of some other object under a certain perspective and if this perception is constitutive for the interpretation of the sign.

Determining which properties we take to be relevant for representing something is also helpful in distinguishing kinds of pictures. In a diagram, for example, it is not important to know how thick a line is, whereas this is normally relevant in a painting. Goodman has named this aspect "repleteness." In my explication, it is linked to the resemblance view. Because the resemblance criterion is vague, that is, being determined in regards to certain respects only, it allows us to accommodate quite different phenomena, which I have summarized under the heading of "iconicity." In photography, we regard most respects as relevant that are also relevant in perceiving objects, whereas in diagrams we leave aside many respects. "To leave respects aside" means that the picture is taken to resemble some object only relative to the remaining respects. A diagram does not tell us anything about what an object looks like.

But the more we abstract entire respects, the more we need to know about the pictorial subsystem in order to be able to understand a picture adequately. This leaves room for cultural influences. Here I am in agreement with Ernst Gombrich's position. According to Gombrich, the different pictorial schemata in art history have been developed in respect of particular functions the pictures were supposed to perform. Such a development is only possible because the picture vehicle does not in itself determine which properties are relevant for the depiction, so it remains possible to establish different respects as dominant. The pictures still resemble their objects but only in regards to particular respects.

8.4   CONTENT AND REFERENCE

If my explication is consistent, it also indicates how we should understand the relation between pictorial content and pictorial reference mentioned in the example of the passport photograph. I now add some brief remarks regarding this problem. According to the internalized resemblance criterion, pictorial content is related to visual experience. It is therefore an intentional phenomenon and certainly not identical with the pictorial referent. It consists in the perceived properties we consider essential to the object depicted and which provide us with a criterion for determining the referent. According to this criterion, the referent must be such that if perceived, it would cause a perception of its essential properties identical to the perception of the corresponding properties of the picture. This applies, too, if you consider Goodman's example of a photograph of a black horse showing only a pale speck in the distance. Could this possibly be a picture of a horse? Normally, of course, we would not take it to be a horse picture, but because we perceive horses in the far distance only as dots, this example does not contradict the assumption that the pictorial content partially determines the referent.

Pictorial content therefore provides us with a necessary condition for determining the reference of a picture. But actually there are several impediments to the determination of a referent, and this shows that pictorial content cannot supply us with a sufficient condition. Pictorial content always comprises a whole set of elements, without indicating which element is referential. This effect is not confined to cases in which the pictorial content is ambiguous, where, for example, we see in certain lines either a rabbit or a duck. In principle, we never know just from looking at the picture vehicle which object is being referred to. This is no less true of a passport photograph, because the subject of the photograph might have an identical twin. In addition to pictorial content, the underlying causal chain is here required for us to finally determine which twin is meant. Reference is never, therefore, decided at the level of pictorial content alone; but the content always gives us a set of elements. If we want to know which particular element is referential, we normally need also to know the context in which the picture is used.[11]

Another interesting case is the problem of different photographic prints. We do not consider successive prints as pictures of each other. But would this not follow from (S1), as the prints are signs and very similar to the other prints? The answer is as follows: in principle, a print can be a picture of another print, but normally we do not use prints in this way, because no visual properties are emphasized that we consider essential for prints. Consequently, we have no problem in accepting photorealist paintings as pictures of photographs, because here precisely properties are emphasized that are essential for photographs. If such hints are missing, we just take those respects to be relevant that are also relevant in ordinary perception.

Now the basic notions related to the concept of a picture have all been introduced. According to these notions, pictures are perception-based signs. This means not only that we must perceive pictures as signs (all signs must be perceived as such) but that their interpretation is in a systematic manner bound to our perceptual competences. This allows us to specify when someone is able to use an object as a picture. It presupposes a minimal understanding of how signs function and a rather complex perceptual competence. "To take an object to be a picture," then, means that we perceive it as though we simultaneously perceived the object itself in relevant respects. Normally, we remain aware that we perceive the picture and not the object depicted, because the perception is identical to the corresponding perception of the object only in relevant respects.

Does this explication tell us much? Is it helpful in understanding a painting? I think one should not expect too much from conceptual analysis. To understand a particular painting is surely not equivalent to recognizing the subject depicted. Using a picture is a communicative act that includes very different levels of meaning. We might use a picture to visualize something, but we can also use it to express our feelings. Often pictures symbolize abstract concepts, such as justice. Resemblance theory thus reveals little or nothing about the meaning and value of famous paintings. Nevertheless, what my explication shows is that our understanding of pictures is grounded in perceptual competences. This helps to account for our customary attitude toward pictures, for example, that we use them to illustrate what things look like. Pictures call upon perceptual competences that we normally employ without questioning their reliability. Because this intermediation is very basic, our use of pictures cannot be understood adequately without a grounding of the resemblance-theory type.

Notes

1. See Lopes (1996, p. 11).

2. See Goodman (1968).

3. This view is sometimes ascribed to Gombrich (see Gombrich 1960 and 1982), but the ascription is only partially correct. See Lopes (1992). A refined version of the resemblance view can be found in Peacocke (1987).

4. For critical comments, see Scholz (1991).

5. My proposal is oriented toward the view Gombrich holds. See also Sachs-Hombach (1999).

6. There is, of course, much more to be said about proper names. In order to contrast them with our intuitive resemblance theory, however, it is sufficient to point to their conventional nature.

7. The claim I am considering here is termed "natural generativity" by Flint Schier (see 1986, p. 43). See also the comments on this feature by Hopkins (1998, p. 31 f.).

8. Having some properties in common with the sign vehicle is not, however, a sufficient condition for being the referent of a picture. Particularly in photography, we also regard the underlying causal relation between object and picture as essential. I will discuss this problem later.

9. For a deeper discussion of "seeing-in," see Wollheim (1980) and Hopkins (1998, p. 15 f.).

10. For such an explication, see Rehkämper (1995).

11. Pictures should thus be seen as analogous to general terms, not to proper names. See Sachs-Hombach and Rekämper (1998, p. 124).

Chapter 9

What You See Is What You Get: The Problems of Linear Perspective

Klaus Rehkämper

9.1 INTRODUCTION

The two leading questions of this paper are, Is there just one way to see the world? and, closely connected to that, Is there a correct way to represent the world pictorially? The plain and simple answer to both questions is, Yes, there is! Perspectival pictures represent the world correctly, because the underlying theory describes correctly the way human beings see the world as well as the making of correct pictorial representations. The theory of perspective connects picture making and human vision. Several arguments against this view, which is sketched very briefly, have been formulated over the years. The three most prominent will be discussed in following: the curvilinearity argument, the immobile eye argument, and the argument that a picture drawn according to the rules of linear perspective would not be accepted as natural. A closer examination of these arguments shows that all three are not convincing and that they also fail to show that the use of linear perspective in pictorial representations is merely a convention.

9.2 THE THEORY OF LINEAR PERSPECTIVE AND ITS CRITICS

Let me start with a few remarks about the different answers different scientists have given over the years to the aforementioned questions. Euclid was the first to describe the process of vision geometrically; he defended the rectilinear propagation of light (a fact that no one has doubted and it holds as long as we are talking about things happening on earth; here we live in a Euclidean space). And Euclid also introduced the cone of vision. During the Renaissance the rules of linear perspective—a system of representing spatial relations—were discovered and described by Filippo

Brunelleschi, Alberti, and Leonardo da Vinci, to name just a few. A picture drawn in linear perspective—so the argument goes—is correct because human vision is correctly described by these rules. A representational painting is like a window onto the real world, and the picture is the window pane. All questions concerning the way in which to represent space seemed to be solved; linear perspective was *the* answer. But at the end of the nineteenth century, some new ideas arose. Linear perspective taught that every straight line has to be represented by a straight line (or in some extreme cases by a single point). Because the human retina is not a plane (as pictures usually are) but a part of a sphere, straight lines—the new dogma said—ought to be represented as curved lines. So it seemed that linear perspective was not the correct and natural way of representing things; it was just one and not even the best way. The question of whether there is a natural way of representing space or not was again open for discussion.

Before I go any further in describing the history and the content of linear perspective and its rivals, I will try to clear up the different alternatives, with the help of a quotation from a paper by Maurice Pirenne: "We must decide between two main propositions: either (A) there is a natural system of perspective corresponding to the way we see; or (B) there is no such system, a number of different artificial systems being perhaps all equally valid, or invalid. Further, if (A) is true, then either (Aa) Renaissance perspective is the natural system of perspective, or (Ab) the natural system differs from Renaissance perspective" (Pirenne 1952/1953, p. 170).

This is a very good description of the existing alternatives. If there is a natural way of representing things, it is either linear or another kind of perspective, perhaps one that is not yet known; or it is all a matter of convention. Convention means that every pictorial symbol system has to be learned, and such a system can be chosen almost at random. There is no inherent connection between the pictorial symbols we use and the things represented.

Nelson Goodman in his book *Languages of Art* (Goodman 1968/1976) attempts to defend this latter alternative, (B). In trying to represent spatial relations he states, "The behavior of light sanctions neither our usual nor any other way of rendering space; and perspective provides no absolute or independent standard of fidelity" (ibid., p. 19).

Before I probe deeper into Goodman's arguments, I shall quote another source, the psychologist James J. Gibson: "From what I know of the perceptual process, it does not seem reasonable to assert the use of perspective in paintings is merely a convention, to be used or discarded by the painter as he chooses. Nor is it possible that new laws of geometrical perspective will be discovered, to overthrow the old ones.... There are no differences among people in the basic way of seeing—that is by means of light, and by the way of the rectilinear propagation of light. When the artist transcribes what he sees upon a two-dimensional surface, he uses perspective geometry, of necessity" (Gibson 1960, p. 227).

These quotations should be sufficient to prove that both alternatives (A) and (B) can be found in the discussion about linear perspective. But what are the arguments against the thesis that linear perspective gives the correct way of representing the things in the world? There are mainly two arguments: (1) the curvilinearity argument, and (2) the immobile eye argument. But Nelson Goodman adds a third one: the argument that a picture drawn according to the rules of linear perspective would not be accepted as natural.

9.3   THE CURVILINEARITY ARGUMENT

I have mentioned argument 1 very briefly at the beginning of this chapter. The retina is not a plane but a part of a sphere, and therefore it is vaulted. Hence, straight lines are not seen straight but curved. And consequently an artist, who wishes to represent what he or she sees, has to paint straight lines curved. This argument was at first brought up by the German mathematician Guido Hauck at the end of the nineteenth century, but it became well known through the art historian Erwin Panofsky's famous article "Perspective as 'symbolic' form," published in 1927. Panofsky denies that the rules of Renaissance perspective hold either for vision or for naturally representing spatial relations in a picture: "Finally, perspectival construction ignores the crucial circumstance that this retinal image—entirely apart from its subsequent psychological 'interpretation,' and apart from the fact that the eyes move—is a projection not on a flat but on a curved surface. Thus already on this lowest, still prepsychological level of facts there is a fundamental discrepancy between 'reality' and its construction. This is also true, of course, for the entirely analogous operation of the camera" (Panofsky 1927/1991, p. 31).

And he continues arguing that "correct" representations of straight lines have to be curved: "[F]or while perspective projects straight lines as straight lines, our eye perceives them (from the center of projection) as convex curves. A normal checkerboard pattern appears at close range to swell out in the form of a shield; an objectively curved checkerboard, by the same token, will straighten itself out. The orthogonals of a building, which in normal perspectival construction appear straight, would, if they were to correspond to the factual retinal image, have to be drawn as curves" (ibid., p. 32 f.). So the curvilinerarist will drop alternative (Aa) from Pirenne's description, but he has not to decide whether (Ab) or (B) is true.

I postpone the discussion of this argument for when I try to rescue the theory of linear perspective. But let me just ask two questions: Do artists really to reproduce their retinal images in order to produce a correct and natural representation? Should artists really draw the world as it appears to them?

9.4 GOODMAN'S ARGUMENTS

Arguments 2 and 3 (from the end of section 9.2) can be found in Goodman. At first he gives a correct summary of the basic assumptions of linear perspective: a picture drawn in correct perspective will, under specified conditions, deliver to the eye a bundle of light rays matching that which would be delivered by the object itself. This matching is a purely objective matter, measurable by instruments. And such matching constitutes fidelity of representation; for because light rays are all the eye can receive from either picture or object, identity in pattern of light rays must constitute identity of appearance (Goodman 1968/1976, p. 11). Gibson would agree with this summary; in his 1960 paper he states: "It is the light to the eye that counts.... [O]ther things being equal, two identical instances of stimulation must arouse the same percept" (Gibson 1960, pp. 219, 222).

Goodman takes his descripton as a basis for his arguments against the theory of linear perspective. In the first of the two arguments, he tries to show that the "specified conditions" required are too artificial and impossible to achieve, an argument that already can be found in Panofsky's article. A picture drawn in linear perspective has to be looked at with a single unmoving eye from a certain well defined-distance. Usually this is done by looking through a peephole. The represented object itself must be viewed through a peephole but not necessarily from the same distance and under the same angle. First of all, according to Goodman, if the eye is not allowed to move it becomes blind. Even if one allows the eye to move, "the specified conditions of observation are grossly abnormal" (Goodman 1968/1976, p. 13). Under circumstances that are no more artificial than an immobile eye—e.g., using suitably contrived lenses—one can wring out of nearly every picture (i.e., pictures not drawn according to the rules of perspective) a pattern of light rays that matches. And so, he continues, even if the patterns of stimulation are identical, "the same stimulus gives rise to different visual experiences under different circumstances" (ibid., p. 14)—A red light might mean "Stop" on the highway and "Port" at the sea. Furthermore, we usually do not view pictures motionless through a peephole but in a gallery, where we are free to walk around. So, the artist's task in representing an object is to decide what light rays, under gallery conditions, will succeed in rendering what he sees. This is not a matter of copying but of conveying (ibid., p. 14). And Goodman closes this argument by saying that "pictures in perspective, like any other pictures, have to be read; and the ability to read has to be aquired" (ibid., p. 14).

For the sake of the first argument, Goodman has accepted the rules of perspective, but in his second argument—argument 3 in section 9.2—he attacks these rules. The main point now is handling the representation of parallel lines. Goodman is not a curvilinearist, but he claims that pictures that are accepted as natural do not obey the rules of perspective; in fact, they disregard them. One of these rules, which he quotes, states that every two parallel lines, which should be represented in a picture, have to be drawn converging. This seems to conform with a statement of Panofsky's, about the rules of linear perspective: "[A]ll parallels, in whatever direction they lie, have a common vanishing point" (Panofsky 1927/1991, p. 28).

But as a matter of fact, not all those lines are drawn in this correct way; some stay parallel in perspectival pictures. And this is so only because of convention, so the argument goes. Telephone poles bordering a street and vanishing in the distance usually do not converge when represented in a photograph but the street does; railroad tracks are another example of this effect, as they are also drawn converging. But the edges of a facade running upward from the eye are usually not represented as converging. We use cameras with tilting backs and elevating lens-boards to avoid such converging; we try to make vertical parallels come out parallel in a picture. And so Goodman concludes: "The rules of pictorial perspective no more follow from the laws of optics than would rules calling for drawing the tracks parallel and the poles converging. In diametric contradiction to what Gibson says, the artist who wants to produce a spatial representation that the present day western eye will accept as faithful must defy the 'laws of geometry'" (Goodman 1968/1976, p. 16).

It is clear from this short description of Goodman's standpoint that he argues for alternative (B). There is no natural system of representing space: all such systems are based on convention and they have to be learned. Cubist or oriental paintings seem to be strange and unnatural to us not because they are not drawn according to the rules of perspective but because we are not used to them—we have not learned to read them properly.

9.5   SOME REMARKS FOR RESCUE OF LINEAR PERSPECTIVE

Are these arguments convincing? In the following text, I will make some remarks for rescue of linear perspective. The position I try to defend is alternative (Aa): there is a natural system of representing spatial relations, and this system is that of linear perspective. But this does not mean that everything said against linear perspective is unreasonable, even if it is not entirely right, if right means that linear perspective is shown to be wrong by these arguments.

Let me give a short introduction to the theory of perspective. With this, I will differentiate between two relations: (1) the relation of a picture drawn according to the rules of perspective to the object depicted, and (2) the relation that holds between such a picture and the beholder of that picture. Relation 1 is a matter of mathematics, or to be more precise a matter of projective geometry; relation 2 is where interpretation and therefore psychology come into play. Unfortunately these two very different relations are often mixed up in the discussion about linear perspective.

What you need to produce a two-dimensional representation of a three-dimensional scene in perspective is an object or an arrangment of objects, G, a center of projection (often called the eyepoint), O, a cone or pyramid of vision having its apex in O and its base at G, and a surface, B, intersecting the cone of vision. Now imagine (light) rays connecting the object and the eyepoint. These rays are also intersected by the surface, and the intersection points make up the two-dimensional representation of that three-dimensional object relative to the eyepoint. It is important to note that the surface intersecting the cone of vision need not be flat. It might also be curved as in GB (figure 9.1). And you can also extend the cone of vision beyond the center of projection into another cone (figure 9.2).

Intersecting the cone of vision not between G and O but behind O you get a representation in perspective that is turned upside down and left-right reversed (B2 or GB2). That is the way a camera obscura works. Having a curved surface, for example, part of a sphere instead of a flat plane, you get a picture that is similar to a retinal image. But as you can

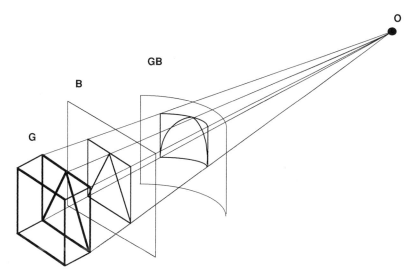

Figure 9.1
The cone of vision with a flat and curved picture plane.

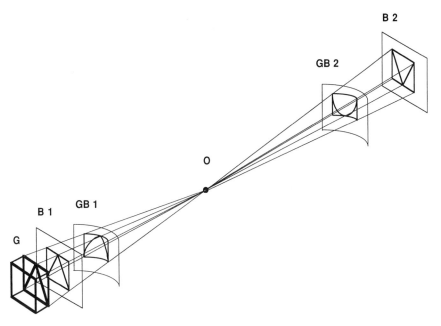

Figure 9.2
The cone of vision extended beyond the center of projection.

see in figure 9.2, instead of having an object G to produce the pattern on B2 or GB2, you can also use a picture in perspective of G such as B1 or GB1. The results will be identical.

It all seems to be very simple. But I will give you an example of the unholy mixture, not to differentiate between relations 1 and 2 I just mentioned. Although Panofsky in his aforementioned article correctly draws the distinction between the "psychologically conditioned 'visual image'" and the "mechanically conditioned 'retinal image'" (Panofsky 1927/1991, p. 31), the latter of which is a correct picture in perspective, he is completely wrong in assuming "that the planar cross section of the visual pyramid can pass for an adequate reproduction of our visual image" (ibid., p. 29).[1] And this assumption of Panofsky's that a picture in perspective is an adequate reproduction of our visual image is shared by *no* theorist of perspective.

Let me now return to the three arguments against the view that linear perspective gives a correct and natural representation of spatial layouts. I will start with the argument of curvilinearity. It is true, that the representation of a straight line on the retina is a curve, but this does not matter. We do not see our retinal images. What we see is the real world, and pictures are a part of this world. The task of the artist, while producing a representation of the world, is not to paint her retinal image but to produce a pattern of light on a two-dimensional surface that is identical to the pattern emitted by the object viewed from a specific point. It is not the artist's subjective visual appearance that has to be represented. The theory of linear perspective describes the relation of a picture to the world and not the effect the picture has on an observer. If you draw a straight line curved on the picture plane, you do not produce the same pattern of light. This can easily be shown: a curved line on a window pane does not cover completely a straight line in the world, so the patterns are not indistinguishable. There are of course occasions when a straight line is represented by a curved one, but only if the picture plane is also a curved surface, for example, the ceiling of the sistine chapel or the movie screen in a "Cinerama." And these occasions agree completely with the theory of perspective; the picture plane need not be flat.

The second argument—the argument from the immobile eye—is not in itself convincing. It is true that the theory of perspective holds just for one eye and the head has to be kept immobile, but the eye is allowed to move. Picture and object are both entities of the world, and the eye can observe the object in the same way it can observe the picture.

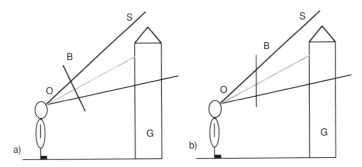

Figure 9.3
Different picture planes. *O*, eyepoint; *B*, picture plane; *S*, cone of vision; *G*, object.

The next point of discussion involves the different distances and angles under which both object and picture have to be seen. As explained earlier, what you need is an eye point, an object, a cone of vision having its apex at the eye point and its base at the object, and—last but not least—a plane intersecting the cone of vision usually somewhere between object and eye. As mentioned before this plane need not be flat and it also need not be vertical. All that counts is that the cone of vision is intersected by the plane. From this, I think, it is clear that the distance from the eye point to the object is usually greater than the distance from the eye point to picture. And the angle under which the object is seen may differ from the angle of eye point to picture. Suppose you a looking at the top of a tower, then the main axis of your cone of vision meets the facade of the tower at an angle less than 45°, but the picture plane may intersect the cone of vision at an angle less than 90°.

That does not contradict the theory of perspective. But—and this leads me to argument 3—Goodman is not right in assuming that all parallels of the world always have to be drawn in a picture as converging. The parallel edges of the facade are drawn converging in figure 9.3a but parallel in figure 9.3b. This holds only for those parallels that are not parallel to the picture plane; the others remain parallel. Or to rescue Panofsky, they have a vanishing point in infinity. And if we use cameras with tilting backs, we obey the rules of perspective. The only thing we are doing is changing the angle under which the picture plane intersects the cone of vision and make it parallel to the facade. And using lenses also does not defy these rules; it is all in the range of physical optics.

I fully agree with Goodman that a stimulus can give rise to different visual experiences under different circumstances. But this does not affect

Figure 9.4
Floor or facade? (After Paul Klee.)

the theory of perspective, which holds for relation 1 described at the beginning of this section. His argument belongs to the second relation, the interpretation of the picture by someone who looks at it.

And while I am at it, Goodman also quotes the famous painter Paul Klee to support his argument. Showing a drawing of Klee's (imitated in figure 9.4), he states: "As Klee remarks, the drawing looks quite normal if taken as representing a floor but awry as representing a facade, even though in the two cases parallels in the object represented recede equally from the eye" (Goodman 1968/1976, p. 16 Fn. 16). But if one has a closer look at Klee's own description of the problem, it becomes obvious that he is not supporting Goodman's view.

Why is figure 9.4 wrong as a picture of a vertical facade? "It is not logically wrong, because the lower windows are closer to the eye than the upper windows, which in terms of perspective means 'larger.' As a representation of a floor this perspective drawing would be at once accepted. This picture is not *logically wrong*, but *psychologically wrong*. Because, in the interests of maintaining its balance the animal wishes to see as vertical all that is in reality vertical" (Klee 1925/1981, p. 31).[2] Here again Goodman but not Klee mixes up the two different relations. Arguing against an interpretation, which is based on a psychological attitude, does not affect the picture-object relation. Therefore it cannot show that perspective is merely a convention.

The last point I would like to mention is the problem that pictures are usually looked at with two eyes and that pictures hang on walls. But this does also not effect the theory of linear perspective. The theory of linear perspective describes the relation between a picture and the scene depicted under specified circumstances. Under these conditions the theory obeys the laws of optics. And to borrow a phrase from Ernst Gombrich: "Having achieved this aim, [the theory of perspective] makes its bows and retires" (Gombrich 1960/1993, p. 217). The observer's problem of how to read a picture while it hangs on the wall is not a problem of the theory here under discussion. The conditions specified by the theory are not fullfilled in this scenario. And if we leave the specified conditions behind, then other problems crop up. In these cases we have to learn to read the pictures. But in the case of perspectival pictures this is not like learning a language, the symbols of which are chosen by convention. These pictures have as a core the natural system of linear perspective— a system that also describes correctly the way the human visual system works—and that is why representational pictures of this kind are much easier to read under "normal" conditions than any language is.

Notes

1. In the English edition Wood translates *Sehbild* as "visual image" in the first quotation I have cited and "optical image" in the second. In doing this, he tones down the contradiction but introduces a new, third term, which is, I believe, not intended by Panofsky.

2. The original formulation used by Klee is "Warum ist Fig. 44 als Bild einer senkrechten Hauswand falsch? Es ist nicht logisch falsch, denn die unteren Fensterebreiten sind dem Auge näher als die oberen Fensterbreiten, was perspektivisch "größer" bedeutet. Als Darstellung eines Bodens würde diese Perspektive glatt akzeptiert. Dieses Bild ist also *nicht logisch falsch*, sondern *psychologisch falsch*. Weil das Animal im Interesse seines Gleichgewichtes sämtliche Senkrechten der Wirklichkeit auch als Senkrechte sehen will" (Klee 1925/1981, p. 31).

Chapter 10
Pictures of Perspective: Theory or Therapy?

Patrick Maynard

> Dear Theo:
> In my last letter you will have found a little sketch of that perspective frame I mentioned. I just came back from the blacksmith, who made iron points for the sticks and iron corners for the frame. It consists of two long stakes; the frame can be attached to them either way with strong wooden pegs. So on the shore or in the meadows or in the fields, one can look through it *like a window*. The vertical lines and the horizontal lines of the frame and the diagonal lines and the intersection, or else the division into squares, certainly give a few fundamental pointers which help one make a solid drawing and which indicate the main lines and proportions—at least for those who have some instinct for perspective and some understanding of why and how the perspective causes an apparent change of direction in the lines and change of size in the planes and in the whole mass. Without this, the instrument is of little or no use, and looking through it makes one *dizzy*. I think you can imagine how delightful it is to turn this "spy-hole" frame on the sea, on the green meadows, or on the snowy fields in winter, or on the fantastic network of thin and thick branches and trunks in autumn or on a stormy sky. Long and continuous practice with it enables one to draw quick as lightning—and, once the drawing is done firmly, to paint quick as lightning, too.... The perspective frame is really a fine piece of workmanship. (van Gogh 1959, pp. 432–434)

Revealing shop talk about a technical device made for a stated practical purpose, to be deployed by someone who knows how to use it: how different from what we are used to in the theoretical literature of perspective, which as often as not can make one "dizzy." For now we must put aside the most interesting aspect of Vincent's typically articulate and engaging report: "pictorial space" in the sense of the *composition* of pictures, especially pictures of nature—including fantastic networks of branches and the lie of the land and the clouds—so far removed from the cubes, crated spheres and cylinders, checkerboard *pavimenti* of most theoretical presentations. In this brief space we will stay with our project's most simple,

practical aims: that of identifying and addressing the bases of a culturally, generally confused state of ideas regarding pictorial perspective,
beginning with simple fallacies and concluding with more difficult matters.

10.1   REAL PERSPECTIVE: PERSPECTIVE USES

Luckily, our problems about linear perspective are not so bad, as they
exist more in the realm of theory than of practice. Let us begin with some
brief reminders about general practice, before considering the conceptual
problems.

As described by Vincent, his viewing frame was a device, a simple bit
of engineering. I suggest that what he used it for be thought of techno-
logically, also; indeed, that in our considerations of "pictorial space" we
recognize linear perspective itself as a kind of *technology*. What is a technology but an amplifier of our powers to do certain things?[1] Looking at it
that way encourages us to be specific about perspective, to ask, do what
things? For his part, Vincent was clear: to make convincingly laid-out
depictive pictures from nature, whether drawings or paintings. How does
linear perspective allow this? Like any technology, by exploiting preex-
isting natural structures or forces. In this case the tapping into natural
powers is rather direct: linear perspective gathers overlap/occlusion and
foreshortening (which it shares with other projective systems) together
with its distinctive diminution with distance according to a simple relationship, all into one correlated system in which foreshortening is affected
by diminution and by other factors—that is, into a "space"—then feeds
the result into a visual system that is *naturally* tuned to using such information. Zoom. Like most successful technologies, linear perspective developed from a variety of related dodges or practices, got consolidated and
then greatly elaborated at historical points, was diffused, and then—
again, like most successful technologies, such as the wheel, plow, water-
mill, printing press, automobile, computer—created its own markets and
rather changed the ends for which it was the means. This change of ends
is partly due to the fact that every technological amplifier is also a filter—
indeed a suppressor: get one form of power, lose another (which normally
we soon come to disvalue, even forget).

Perspective, like other technologies, has usually been mixed in with
its alleged rivals. Rather as we might call a Degas "a pastel," despite the
other things it is in (and the underlying monotype), we usually call pic-

tures "perspective" when they are partly in perspective while also produced through other shape- and space-rendering techniques. In this respect, perspective's history is like that of a close pictorial relative, namely shade and shadow techniques, which were also consolidated, systematized, theorized, closely controlled, passed from specialized refinement to mixed use. My next observation is that the listed components of linear perspective— including foreshortening, overlap, diminution as a function of distance, unified space—are frequently disassembled and stuck in with other systems. In general, it is good to approach linear perspective that way, in terms of its components and their relations, rather than as monolith. As we look around, we find what one might call "perspective patois," even "pidgin perspective," in much of its familiar use in mass printing of images today. Indeed I think that you will often find mainly oblique techniques predominating there (with some orthogonal), though often inflected with a bit of diminution—sometimes convergence of parallels—for effect: and *effect* is, after all, the whole point of "pictures on a page." What about the photography which pervades these media? Is not linear perspective, as we often hear, simply built into camera optics? Again, when we actually look, I think we find similar mixes in commercial photography, notably in advertising: the use of long lenses and closing up of backgrounds (often stressing L-, fork, and arrow junctions), as the parallel systems, oblique and orthogonal, predominate, with emphasis on object shape and texture (so well rendered by photographs), with a residue of diminution. The sense of a space, in terms of coordinated common vanishing points, is rather rare in such work, perhaps because that would draw attention from the surfaces that are being marketed to just space, which is not. Of course one does see there, as in cinema and TV work, much strong perspective, though again shapes on a page—including print and other graphics— rather than "pictorial space" are the goal.

10.2 PERSPECTIVE SOPHISTRIES

Thus, very briefly, use. Now, what of conception, theory? I said that "we call pictures perspective," but who are *we?* Most people, including those who ought to know better, seem rather vague about what perspective and its main features actually are, typically conflating perspective with a number of other projective techniques. For example, MoMA's director of painting describes an isometric cityscape as done by "perspectival plotting" and oblique sun-cast shadows rendered in an orthogonal projection as showing "perspectival deformations" (Varnedoe 1990, pp. 234, 238). A harmlessly loose usage, perhaps, unless it exemplifies pervasive vagueness about that variety of projective drawing systems that guide the most important drawings of the modern world: indeed those design drawings that made a modern world possible. But the effects of this carelessness get worse, fast. Consider that book on perspective said to be "the most critically-acclaimed work of art history to have been published in France through the second half of the twentieth century" (Carani 1998, p. 309), elsewhere admired as of "vast learning," and find, among its more than 400 pages, evidence that its author does not distinguish foreshortening from diminution, does not remember that a picture can have other vanishing points besides the orthogonal, indeed cannot tell if a Renaissance demonstration picture features an orthogonal vanishing point or not.[2] The rave notices, from architecture as well as art faculty, are representative of those fields of higher learning. So what should we expect when we turn to the more literary commentators?

Attitude follows ignorance. No one can be well versed in everything; all of us go—one hopes corrigibly—on general impressions, dependent on our own experiences to a point but also very much on general, nontechnical treatments of the subject. This is where widely read, popular accounts have influence, providing us glosses by which we think and talk about a variety of matters. And on the subject of perspective of late, we all know what that entails. Most people are probably unmotivated to know about linear perspective. Perspective's way into general discourse has therefore not been via the sort of knowledge of those crucial drawing systems just mentioned. Rather, linear perspective is usually introduced through "art," a conception that carries in our time a sense of great importance tinged with unease. But regarding *art*, there was first perspective's criticism as a stultifying standard of the teachable part of an art education practice now disdained; there was its alleged rejection by modern artists, beginning with the Expressionists (though that situation is rather complex); there were its alleged illusionistic tendencies, denying the materiality of the support. Most recently have come charges of Western perceptual imperialism: "the hegemony of the eye," "visual-ization," and "the ideology of the visible linked to the Western tradition of systems centered on a single point."[3] As one observer has recently remarked, "postmodernism has grown out of a neo-romantic tradition steeped in subjectivity and a general hostility to the objectivity of perspective construction" (Topper 2000, p. 115).

Therefore these remarks belong to only the most recent version of what Panofsky long ago called "the ultra-modern criticism of art," in words still worth citing:

It is now clear that the perspective view of space (not merely perspective construction) could be attacked from two quite different sides: if Plato condemned it in its modest beginnings because it distorts the "true sizes" of things and puts subjective appearance and caprice in the place of reality and law, the ultra-modern criticism of art makes exactly the opposite charge that it is the product of a narrow and narrowing rationalism. The ancient East, classical antiquity, the Middle Ages, and every archaistic art, such as Botticelli's, have—more or less completely—rejected perspective because it seemed to bring into a world that goes *beyond* or *above* the subjective something individualistic and casual; expressionism (for recently there has been another swing of the pendulum) shunned it for just the opposite reason: perspective confirms and preserves the remnant of objectivity that even impressionism had still had to remove from the power of the individual will toward form, that is, three-dimensional real space as such. But at bottom this polarity is the two-fold aspect of one and the same thing and those objections aim at one and the same point. (Panofsky 1924/1925, p. 18)

It may seem paradoxical that the common strategy of the more recent "ultra-moderns" has been to attribute to perspective, among all drawing systems, the most extreme form of subjectivity. Thus a very influential popular book for nearly three decades states that "the convention of perspective, which is unique to Europe ... centres everything on the eye of the beholder." "Every drawing or painting that used perspective," it continues, "proposed to the spectator that he was the unique centre of the world" (Berger 1972, pp. 16, 18). Such opinions produced in cinema theory ideas about what has been called "the ideology of the visible," with remarks such as the following: "[P]erspective-system images bind the spectator in place, the suturing central position that is the sense of the image, that sets its place (in place, the spectator completes that image as its subject)" and "[T]he installation of the viewer as subject depends on reserving for him or her, the reciprocal in front of the image of the vanishing point 'behind' it.... To launch an assault at the window [as depicted in Alfred Hitchcock's *The Birds*] is, in turn, to assault the place of the viewer [of it]; it is an act of aggression against the eye of the beholder and the 'I' of the self-as-subject."[4]

10.3   PERSPECTIVE FALLACIES, I: THE STANDARD HEURISTIC

Thus I remind you of muddles in much of what is taught and written about perspective in our time. Practical remedy might include two steps.

First, understanding of the rudiments of perspective and other projective systems should be required of people getting graduate degrees in art history, cognitive psychology and related fields, and basic competence about such matters should be required of literary people writing about the subject or people refereeing their manuscripts; also information about the actual *uses* of these systems should be part of the curriculum. It is, after all, not difficult to understand these systems in outline, and though it takes a bit more time to learn about the facts of actual usage, most students should find that "hands-on" study very interesting. Second, something has to be done about a penchant for overgeneralization regarding perspective. In quoting those lines about viewers of Alfred Hitchcock's film *The Birds*, for example, I do not mean to reject the idea that a film—even that cinema—might use perspective to make viewers experience their viewing positions in such a way as to work some further effects on them. Rather, I am criticizing the apriorism that attributes this effect to the mere presence of perspective: that "perspective-system images bind the spectator in place," "suture" them to their seats, and so on.

What is the source of these excesses? My impression is that the underlying fallacies of perspective pervade the thought, writing, and teaching of the actual curriculum I just endorsed: so much so that they have seriously compromised our theoretical conceptions of pictorial depiction and other kinds of graphic representation. The situation is so bad that we may have somewhat to excuse the views I just quoted, as the responses of those who, rightly perceiving danger, attempt in inarticulate rhetoric to reply. Do I exaggerate? Let us begin by considering an admittedly extreme position—and rather than picking old or easy targets, a sample from a contemporary scientist of the human mind (from a source that, again, is selling very well): "The picture exploits projection, the optical law that makes perception such a hard problem.... Now, a *picture* is nothing but a more convenient way of arranging matter so that it projects a pattern identical to real objects" (Pinker 1997, pp. 215 f.). If we agree with that, it is game over for "reconceiving pictorial space." For if what a pictorial depiction essentially *is,* is a perspective projection onto a surface (or the inept, abbreviated or degenerate state of one), and also if what perspective projection in depictions mainly is, is a way of representing space there, there is no question of whether, when it comes to depicting space in a picture, perspective has first place.

However, pictures are not essentially in perspective or any other kind of projections. Consider the converse: surface projections (perspective or otherwise) as depictions. Although there exist in the universe perspective and other kinds of projections—indeed uncountable real, physical projections: that is, wherever some kind of radiation gets partly blocked before it hits a surface—a vanishingly small number of these are pictures or any other kind of graphic representation. Turning that around again: there has existed on this planet a much smaller but still uncountable number of depictions and other kinds of graphic representations that are not even partly perspectival, or even projective, not even in any inchoate or degenerate way. Although over the last demimillennium we have engineered interesting intersection of these two huge classes (one of literally astronomical proportions), there is not much more excuse for confusing that intersection with the one class than for confusing it with the other. That there is a persistent tendency to do so is something that calls for explanation. What happened?

Following our technological approach, we can say that a very successful technological means for (partly) producing images has been mistaken for its end, depiction. Theoretically, having a well-systematized account of perspective (along with other projective systems) but not even the beginnings of an account of depiction, cognitive inquirers, abhorring that vacuum, have stuffed the former in for the latter. This shows up generally, as in the lines just quoted, or piecemeal, when findings about particular successful perspectival effects in pictures are taken to show these to be *constitutive* of depiction itself. Therefore I doubt that we will correctly conceive, or reconceive, pictorial space until we correctly conceive depiction itself. Short of offering a theory of depiction, we might at least keep in mind some simple, familiar facts. We need to recall that even where perspective is used to make depictions, it does not follow that the space *defined* by the projection is the kind *depicted* in the picture. For example, when a movie or TV camera produces, as it must, a perspective projection of part of what is in front of it—that is, a series of props, including models, back projections, and so on—the resulting *depicted* space is usually quite *different* from the space relations that are projected: that is much the point of using props and backgrounds. And we have all seen enough movie dream sequences to know that the depicted space can even be nonperspectival. Means is not the same as end: all this should seem as unsurprising as the fact that it is possible to draw or to photograph plywood, cloth, and styrofoam in order to depict stone, flesh, and metal.[5] Why should anyone have thought differently about the devices of linear perspective?

Therapeutically, we can trace the fallacy through a series of equivocations, which are conveniently gathered, it so happens, in the book that coined the expression "linear perspective": Brook Taylor's *Perspective,*

New Principles of Linear Perspective, whose first definition repeats its subtitle as follows: "Linear perspective is the Art of describing exactly, on a Plane Surface, the Representations of any given Objects," which gets parsed immediately as follows: "let the Reader consider, that a Picture drawn in the utmost degree of Perfection, and placed in proper Position, ought so to appear to the Spectator, that he should not be able to distinguish what is there represented, from the real original Objects actually placed where they are represented to be" (Taylor 1719, p. 2; see also Anderson 1992). Stop there and notice the equivocation on the very general term "representation." Taylor began by talking about a way of projecting 3-D patterns onto 2-D, called such projection "representation," then substituted the word "picture" (because pictures are often called "representations"): voilà, a projection *is* a depictive picture. This equivocal slide is now the slicker for being so well worn, as projections in cameras and in eyes have long been loosely termed "pictures."[6] But, as just stated, no mere projection onto a surface, whether actual or—as in the case of nearly all expositions—fantastic and merely imagined, is either necessary (not Taylor's assumption) *or* sufficient (Taylor's assumption) for pictorial depiction of anything: a fortiori not for objects actually or just notionally projected.

Compare a closely related possible equivocation: cast shadows are very like pictures; also pictures can be made very effectively by *use* of cast shadows—there are important technologies for this, such as X rays and "magic shadows." Therefore, why not call *all* pictures—or at least ones made from shadows—"shadows," or at least try to understand how we see pictures by how we see shadows, or try to explain the pictures that are not made by shadows as *derivatives* from the ones that are? This is clearly fallacious: of course projections and shadows become pictorial only when they are *used* in certain ways, in ways notably connected with visual perception and imagining, as with hand shadows. The word "used" should immediately put an end to a priori assumptions. Yet one of the most basic, amazing, fallacies of most theorizing about perspective is the neglect of difference between a tool (perspective) by which a picture might be made, actually or theoretically, and the spatial characteristics that the picture depicts or represents.

To be fair, Taylor and his descendants in viewpoint typically do indicate one perceptual use, even include perceptual constraints. But that narrow, artificial use is usually, as Taylor wrote, perceptual indistinguishability: you do a picture like that in order to produce a situation that

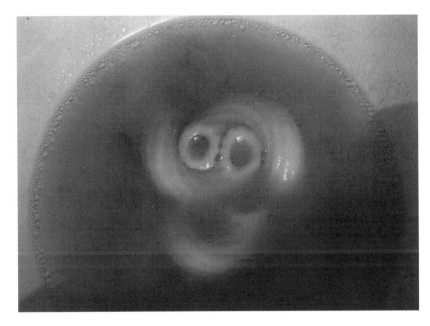

Figure 10.1
Faces in strange places: memento mori soup.

is visually indistinguishable from what another situation would be. Not a promising description of depictive use, but one that has wide appeal—even driving recent image technologies. As for the *constraints,* whereas the old ones took account of what Taylor called "proper Position," we find contemporary accounts needing to append "post-Ames" remarks about what "the brain is biased to recognize" (Pinker 1997, p. 215), or what "excite neural circuits that would be excited by" entities that mattered in the course of evolution (Shepard 1990, pp. 187, 198)—given that even geometric projection is radically nondeterminative of depiction. (I am grateful to Jan Koenderink for his ingenious subversion of the famous Taylor diagram.) Such recent constraint qualifications turn out to be rather *more* than qualifications. Indeed, anything such as a brain bias or "neural circuit" approach to depiction dooms the projective paradigm for depiction, by letting in facial, gestalt, movement, textural, and tactual factors—a mass of other nonprojective inciters to visual imagining (figures 10.1, 10.2, and 10.3).

Therapy for theory would not be complete without noting another pervasive fallacy expressed by Taylor's account: a reciprocal one. Just as

Figure 10.2
Faces in strange places: birch eyes.

theoretical conceptions of pictorial depiction have been confused by standard presentations of linear perspective, conceptions of perspective have
in turn been muddled by their pictorial applications. The theoretical meeting of perspective and depiction has thus been a road accident of ideas in
which all parties' heads have been banged. As a method of algebraic or
geometrical projection, perspective has nothing to say about vision. Also
it does not mention light. Nevertheless, in its standard heuristic presentations, when we are getting ready to think about its pictorial uses, it is usually explained in terms of highly theoretical, not real, light rays (typically
imagined to go clean through the wall or whatever surface the picture is

Figure 10.3
Natasha toothbrush.

to be drawn on). Next, crucially: further anticipating the model—that is, application to pictures—the projective-point variable for these rays is usually decorated by a picture of an *eye,* as in Taylor. Obviously, this eye has nothing to do with the projection, considered geometrically or even light-ray fantastically. Yet the problem of decorating the diagram with such images is not simply one of what is called "chart junk"; the problem is what has perhaps proved the worst source of confusion so far. And that is the fallacy that (as we saw early on) linear perspective, as used in pictures, automatically, inevitably, introduces *subjectivity.* That fallacy deserves special treatment.

I have already suggested what misunderstanding of linear perspective has done to the understanding of, and attitudes about, perspective among those who are unclear about what linear perspective is. Following is a recent report from someone who has read more of this material: "Mistrust and indignation before the crass theatrics, the arrogance, the pedantry and scientism of the so-called legitimately constructed perspectival picture have become the norm among a wide range of theorists and historians. Perspective is treated not merely as a severe distortion of the actual fact of seeing. . . . Today perspective is treated as a complete abstraction . . . [even as something] irrevocably 'bourgeois' or 'ideological'" (Wood 1995, p. 680). I also offered evidence that although, as our source reports, there are other grounds for this resentment, much of it is owing to the alleged egocentricism of perspective, as presupposing, or imposing, a subjective viewing eye, so that, as one of our influential sources puts it, "the visible world is arranged for the spectator as the universe was once thought to be arranged for God" (Berger 1972, p. 18).

Confident rhetoric—or a cry for help? Once again, perhaps we should not (much) blame the sources for these reactions, when even the experts on the subject standardly present perspective constructions in pictures as indeed made for a single privileged viewpoint, and as intelligible only by reference to that viewpoint. Consider, for example, yet another influential expert's overgeneralization: "[An occluded]-surface perspective view—whether photographed, hand-constructed, or computed—implies an eye-witness. It suggests that there was an observer at the station point, and it puts us precisely in the shoes of that invisible observer. . . . We are confronted with the paradox of disembodied viewing—a paradox that every photograph and every consistently constructed perspective contains" (Mitchell 1992, p. 134). "Every photograph"—like those on packages, such as cereal boxes? To be sure, this is again an extreme expression—

though, after all, by a computer graphics specialist. Still, what many perspective theorists normally say is not far off that. No point to a parade of quotations here: we know that the standard heuristic exposition of linear perspective is simply, without argument, to identify the perspective construction point as the picture's viewer's point and to take that quite literally. This is sometimes even expressed (again by one of our quoted experts) as "the viewing position of the artist" or "the artist's unique vantage point" (Shepard 1990, pp. 191, 196 f.), sometimes as "where the artist stood"—as though perhaps Masaccio had stood before the Trinity, or Raphael behind Saint Paul preaching in Athens—or at least behind an actor on a set, and so on! Part of the pity of this amazingly careless way of speaking, thinking, is that—just as viewer position in cinema *is* sometimes part of the content of the experience—in some cases it *does* matter that the artist was at that point, just as it sometimes *does* matter for the content of a picture that we understand there to have been a viewer at a more-or-less precise point, just as it sometimes *does* matter that we view the picture from near the construction point. Sometimes these concerns matter, but, in the overgeneralized, a priori fog round the topic, such "finer" points of picture meaning are soon lost.[7]

10.4   PERSPECTIVE FALLACIES, II: VIEWS

Although I have tried to indicate the wide influence of the positions reviewed here so far, it might be objected that, from Taylor on, they have been extreme or carelessly stated. And, given that linear perspective is, surely, through its exploitation of natural resources, a highly successful technology for spatial rendering—thus rejecting the accounts of some extreme current relativisms—that must have something to do with linear perspective's pictorial matchup to the light geometry of environmental vision. This being true, the question is what to make of it, and the first thing to do is to put our topic itself into useful "perspective." So, as our next reminder, consider the most loose, general meaning of the word "perspective" as "point of view." Dictionaries tell us that "perspective" means *prospètto,* so, not "seeing through," as Albrecht Dürer thought, but "prospect," or "view."[8] This suggests seeing from a distance, which has two general connotations. First, we have perspective on matters when we are not too close to them but, by standing back, can better understand them in context. Second, we realize how things may appear different from different perspectives or standpoints. In short, unless we are radical

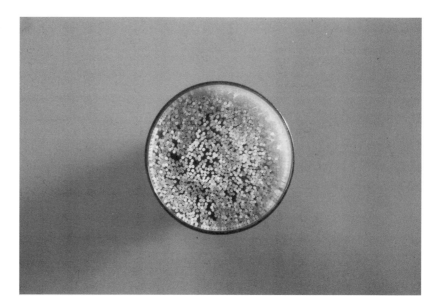

Figure 10.4

relativists, we will hold that some perspectives (in the second sense) afford better perspectives (in the first sense) than do others—although, if we are reasonable, we will also be willing to consider things from others' faulty perspectives. But what has this to do with pictorial perspective, except as the agency that brought these usages into modern languages? One appeal of a perspective paradigm for all depictions may have been that linear perspective renders what are considered *views,* and visually effective pictures of any kind usually show views of things.[9] That this is a constraint on effective pictures is hardly surprising, because we often recognize things by perspectival contours. Indeed, the famous word *eidos,* developed by Greek philosophers and reworked by Latin as "form," meant—and this root meaning persisted through the theoretical elaborations—that about the look, notably of the shape, of a thing that allows us visually to recognize it. Consider, for example, a clear photograph that does *not* present such a view (figure 10.4). When pictorial perspective does provide effective views, there is nothing peculiar to it, and a "peephole" need no more be involved in linear perspective than in any other method.[10] Not only are most depictive drawing systems designed to exploit such views, perspective has weaknesses as well as strengths in that regard. Such are the systems' trade-offs, or "trades"—one motive for that practical use of mixed devices discussed at the outset.

To consider this point more closely, we need to consider views more closely. So far we have been considering views of things (such as spaghetti noodles in a plastic container), but people observe views in a literally broader sense, which includes groups of objects. They get a room with a view, admire the view. They find the view's been spoiled by developers or a volcano, or is not so good as if you'd just climb a few more steps; they turn off the highway at posted scenic viewpoints. Indeed, there was once a market for paintings (for example by Canaletto), called *vedute*—usually in perspective—of views; and today tourism, whole economies, depend on views. Such views are of course relative—perspectively relative, even relative to humans—but they are not subjective, nor do they imply any viewer. "The view from there is terrific" is on a par with "the water's fine" (that is, for normal swimmers), which evokes no ghostly bather or privileged epidermis. With views of scenes, as with views of objects, it needs to be emphasized that, contrary to popular claims, there are long traditions, in literature as well as visual art—such as that of China—of vividly capturing precisely such views, as views, innocent of any perspective conception of the job.

Recalling our technological context, when systematized linear perspective *did* come along, it joined an old family of view-depictions—to be sure, with considerable jostling—bringing specially big advantages regarding views, in both the object and the broader sense of "view." But it also brought disadvantages; such are the trades: every technological amplifier being also a filter. Although perspective somewhat changed the pictorial end, as people learned how to work it, and to see with it, it has joined the general bag of depictive tricks. Most people are rather *vague,* looking at perspective pictures—including their own photographs—about the locations for the views, even when they look at such pictures *as* views, which is far from normally the case. Just as well: in most *real* cases (particularly away from carpentered subject matter), it is impossible to retrieve the construction points. In this regard people tend to treat perspective pictures so like any others that, once again, the cases in which they do *not* so treat them have special meanings.

Thus perspective "view," as what is shown *in* pictures. But, oddly, much of the controversy about picture perspective has to do with another topic: our views *of* pictures. In other words, there is much recent interest in perspective views *of* perspective pictures themselves, that is, in how they work when we see them (as we normally do) at a variety of slants and distances. This interest is usually based on an assumption—call it "the coincidence assumption"—that, in order to work, perspective pictures would need to be seen from their construction points. (Because such theorists usually count parallel systems such as the engineers' and architects' orthogonal, oblique, and axonometric as limiting cases of perspective, they should also wonder why we would not prefer looking at such drawings at such remote distances that we need binoculars.) The coincidence assumption, which has a long history, is of course well refuted by normal practice, from which we might draw the following analogy. Previous to the 1870s, when articulate utterances were heard, one could assume that they were heard from a position fairly close to the source, in time and in space; such were our physical limitations. Technology changed that, for phonographs and telephones freed us of those limits: thus "his master's voice." Previous to the 1440s, when anyone had the experience of seeing a thing or view in perspective, one could assume that this was from a position at the optical construction point. Technology of course changed that, too, for linear perspective technology (as used in pictures, as well as in stage settings, architecture, gardens, etc.) freed us of that restriction, as well. That it turns out that perspectives still work when viewed away from their construction points does not mean that they work the same way or even as well, but the same can be said about telephone, voice recording, and so on. Nevertheless, they all do work, and it is, after all, typical of technologies to loosen natural restrictions.

Frankie, looking at her snapshots of Johnny and herself, has no notion that, given the lens on her 35 mm point-and-shoot, the projection point for these $4'' \times 6''$s would be along a solid perpendicular to its middle, at exactly the length of the ballpoint pen with which she just wrote on the back—a viewing distance strictly for the nearsighted. But (our next reminder), Frankie, like everybody else, tends to look at *all* pictures from around the middle, roughly on a perpendicular—that is, when she can. Although like everyone else, she usually settles for somewhat angled views, close enough that she can see it all. Frankie also does this with the newspaper (even when Johnny is reading it), with train timetables (despite slow-reading backpackers planted in the middle), and with the titles and printed credits on cinema and TV screens, when she is seated off to one side. I recall a young woman intently viewing the Rijksmuseum "Golden Age" show from a wheelchair, the pictures well above her head, in gallery after gallery, twenty-one in all. Theorists may wonder how she could have done this with all those *perspective* pictures, but the same issue arose if she went to the Kurt Schwitters show down the street at the Stedelijk. Leave it to those so gripped by the a priori projection-point heuristic that they have invented a special research project for perspective. Some favor deft trigonometric extrapolation of the projection point. But, as illustrated by Frankie and the photo, not only will people not know what we are talking about here, it is implausible to suppose that their visual systems have much motive, or means, to do so. As we watch movies, flip magazine pages, and encounter a fast flux of camera positions and focal lengths—in magazines, of cropping formats—we show scant tendency to adjust our viewing distances. The sense of close-up and long-shot certainly do register, but that so-called close-up may have been taken some distance off with a telephoto lens, to keep the background blurred, whereas the wide-angle lens that *was* used close in mainly distorts features so as to make faces look ugly or menacing.

The argument is not that it is vain for perceptual theory to investigate generally how we reckon shapes on or of surfaces. After all, most of the surfaces we work on or walk on meet vision at acute angles. Getting the three blocks from the Rijksmuseum to the Stedelijk along Paulus Potterstraat to see the Schwitters would involve a lot of estimating in that regard—probably harder at a child's or wheelchair's lower perspective. My worry is, again, about what is behind the assumption, without argument, that optical inclination poses a particular problem regarding perspective pictures. Perspective is capable of winning its way empirically as a method of producing pictorial space (and other things) and has no need for the standard stacked decks—or opening, a priori, sleights of hand.

10.5   ANOTHER SLANT ON PICTURES

By now, real treatment of our cultural picture-perspective perplexity may be on the way: not through words like these, but where we began, through actual practice. Everyday experience with shifting small cameras and now camcorders may be doing it. If the old geometric heuristic has been so badly misleading, is it too much to hope that, as algebraic computer drawing takes over, the old heuristic may lose its theoretical grip? Could it be that alternative wireframe algorithms, computer translations, back and forth, between $x, y,$ and z coordinate-triples and x, y projection-pairs will spread graphic literacy, as the division of the x and y coordinates by the $z,$ which characterizes perspective, may be understood as one effective option, without having to imagine fictive light rays, an intermediate projection plane, and so on?

I stress "back and forth" because I perceive another problem with that heuristic beyond what I have indicated. It has continually—unwittingly, to be sure, but influentially—imbued thinking with the prejudice that drawing perspectively, or in any way projectively, has not only the connotation of passive, mechanical skills of projecting ("a machine could do it") but something deeper, which seems never articulated: the *derivative* connotation that underpins that heuristic, that the 3-D subject is somehow given, whereas the drawing is gotten *from* it. Thus the standard talk about a "real world" or "real object" (mostly fictional) and "its" picture-projection. If this connotation did not actively depress projective drawing, it did little to help such drawing in its recent times of trouble. Ironically, what actually happens is often the reverse; as remarked, most of the real things that define the modern world (that is, all the artifacts in it) are made *from* projective drawings, rather than the other way around.

I doubt that one will achieve a satisfactory account of the depiction of space in pictures unless one has a good general account of depiction itself. Not having attempted that, I close with two critical remarks in that direction, which are more radical than what I have argued so far. First, briefly, insofar as the depictive challenge is spatial, why assume that this is necessarily a matter of going between 2-D and 3-D, when 0-D, 1-D, 2-D, and 3-D are all involved, even in visual depiction? As visual depiction of space is by no means confined to pictures, I suggest questioning the focus on pictures that has dominated discussion—in isolation from reliefs, masks, carving, sculpture, and so forth—even when talking narrowly about perspective. (Remember the meaning of three old words, *arti del disegno*.)[11]

Second, the idea "insofar as depiction is spatial" has been assumed, but must it be? Far more radically, I suggest that we are unlikely to gain an adequate conception of any kind of depiction so long as we think of it even as an essentially spatial affair—less so, as long as we accept the standard idea that "the basic trick of pictures" (to quote one outstanding art historian of our time) is that of "marking a flat plane to suggest the three-dimensional" (Baxandall 1985, p. 106). Here is not the place to challenge a dominant space-based conception of vision that reinforces the dominant space-emphasizing approaches to visual depiction, which has less to say about substance, process, movement.[12] Still, as a "simple" example, the earlier physiognomic examples should have already suggested what this wonderful, eidos-capturing, 3,000-year-old, double-necked pot painting shows: that not only are pictures not essentially flat or even plane, but that we need to think whether the *basic* challenge of pictorial depiction has to

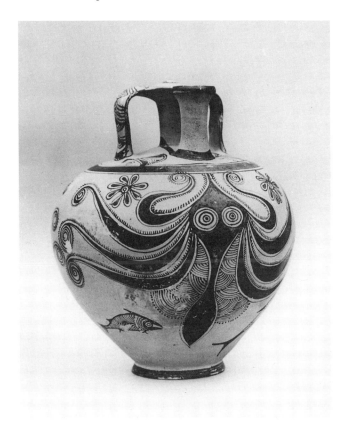

Figure 10.5
Stirrup jar: Octopi and fish. Mycenean, terracotta, c. 1200–1125 B.C., h. $10\frac{1}{4}$ inches.
The Metropolitan Museum of Modern Art, Louisa Eldridge McBurney Gift Fund,
1953. (53.11.6)

be dimensional—even spatial at all (figure 10.5). I point to a couple of
features of this example, regarding the theme of "pictorial space."

Not only is the surface not flat; the painting uses the (double) curvature
of the pot to swell out the form of the cephalopod: indeed, its eyes big, the
startled animal seems to swell out at *us*. I mean swelling (a process), for
note how the vertical curvature changes, as the arms bend back in space,
slowly coiling in sequential rhythm. We also sense it settling again, for this
"still" picture is always in motion. And there is something else to notice:
how the image pays the pot back, for it *decorates* the pot it is painted on.
Its swelling enhances our experience of the convexity of the pot, as its

motion out and up emphasizes our sense of the pot rising and expanding through belly to shoulder, then closing through handles and lips, as the fish spring up from the foot.

That such decorative depiction forms a central kind of depiction seems rather lost on modern theorists, misled by a few centuries' dominance of technologies of "unlocated" depictions—that is, of images put on surfaces made for just that purpose and devoid of intrinsic interest—such as we find in cinema and TV screens. Technologies of photo reproduction convey the impression that such is the historical norm. And those who take decorative depiction as marginal to issues of pictorial space might recall that a favorite example of those drawn to the topic, Andrea Pozzo's painted ceiling for the nave of the Chiesa di Sant' Ignazio in Rome (1688–1694), is essentially—not coincidentally—a decorative depiction. That ceiling was not just a convenient ground on which Pozzo could place his images. As we began with technological uses of perspective, let us recall that here linear perspective's primary function is to promote our imagining, of the very nave in which we stand, that its walls rise much higher above us and are occupied by diverse figures in motion, that its roof is open to the clouds, that the saint is visible above us, carried up by angels. As decorative, the image is more than what Maurice Pirenne calls Pozzo's "imaginary structure" (Pirenne 1970, p. 79), for (and this happens, too, with some restaurant decor) its practical purpose is to have us imagine things *of* that actual architecture—and thereby of ourselves, as well. Through attention to such cases of perspective and other methods in actual use we should find improved bases for an understanding of visual depiction, which can guide our research into pictorial space.

Notes

1. I have taken this approach to photography, for example in Maynard (1997a, 1997b), and to perspective in Maynard (1994).

2. See Damisch (1994, pp. 63, 107, 158, etc.). I make further comment in review of the book in Maynard (1997b, pp. 84–85). The quotations are from editorial reviews available on booksellers' Websites.

3. This citation is from Noël Carroll (1988, p. 128). For more careful argument of the material in sections 10.2 and 10.3, see Maynard (1996, pp. 23–40).

4. These citations are also from Carroll (1988, pp. 128 f.).

5. It is even a fallacy to go from "x is a depictively essential constituent of (picture) P" to "P depicts something as x," because that fails for such values of "x" as being a painting, being monochrome, and so forth.

6. This does not necessarily commit the fallacy we began with, that of claiming that all pictures are essentially projections. Notice how Henry Talbot could only invent photography, a more recent source of the projection/picture mix-up, by fighting off that very tendency: "The picture [sic]" from his camera, he wrote, "divested of the ideas which accompany it, and considered only in its ultimate nature, is but a succession or variety of stronger lights thrown upon one part of the paper, and deeper shadows on another" (Talbot, 1844–1846/1969). If Talbot meant his camera lucida, where the image is virtual, there would not have been lights upon the paper.

7. These careless, common phrases might be revealing of something: maybe drafters' often assuming their pictures' construction points when doing observational drawings, in order to "eyeball" the perspective, has encouraged the idea that viewers need to do the same. An odd inference, in any case: it is like saying that because roofers have to go on the roof to shingle it, you have to go up there, too, to see the roof.

8. Erwin Panofsky noted Dürer's error here in Panofsky (1924/1925): "[D]ies 'lateinisch Wort,' das schon bei Boethius vorkommt, ursprünglich einen so prägnanten Sinn gar nicht besessen zu haben scheint" (p. 258).

9. For an account of "effective pictures" and "views," see Willats (1997, pp. 22 f., 207, 219).

10. As is claimed in Shepard: "[E]ach picture of a three-dimensional scene carries its own peephole" (1990, p. 122, repeated on p. 196). The photograph shows the top of a spaghetti tube.

11. As Vasari's phrase *arti del disegno* indicates, sharp distinctions among painting and sculpture, architecture, and relief are recent. To call pictures 2-D media is somewhat misleading, as there, with 0-D, 1-D, and 2-D marks, we depict not just 3-D but also 0-, 1-, and 2-D situations. In 3-D sculpture and architecture we depict the same, using 0-D junctions, 1-D contours, 2-D shapes and expanses, and so on. It is also possible to depict in 1-D media.

12. In Maynard (2001), I hazard remarks about biological and technological vision as aimed more at process and motion than at objects and spatial forms. Ernst Gombrich is one leading theorist of depiction who has confessed an overemphasis on space at the expense of representation of transparency and life (Gombrich 1987, p. 16).

PART III

THE NATURE AND STRUCTURE OF RECONCEIVED PICTORIAL SPACE

Chapter 11

Reconceiving Perceptual Space

James E. Cutting

11.1 INTRODUCTION

How do we perceive the space in pictures? In answering this question theorists typically consider standard photographs and other representational images, such as architectural drawings, engravings, and paintings in linear perspective. Adding motion augments this domain, including cinema and computer-graphic sequences. But cartoons, caricatures, and much of twentieth-century art and photography are seldom overtly considered. This, I think, is a mistake; without a broader perspective on pictures one is lulled into thinking too metrically, about pictures and about the real world as well.

Certain philosophers and psychologists have spilled a lot of ink discussing pictures and the space depicted within them; other philosophers and typically other psychologists have done the same about perceived space in the world around us. What I propose is that our perception of these spaces is done in pretty much the same way, that neither are guaranteed Euclidean but that they are built upon available information. In essence my chapter is on the promise of a constructive and cooperative measurement-theoretic approach to all perceived space. The more information, the more constraints, the more any perceived space will incrementally approach a Euclidean ideal.

A Précis of Measurement Theory

After his broadscale survey of how scientists measure their subject matters, S. S. Stevens (1951) reported that we measure the world in four ways—using nominal, ordinal, interval, and ratio (or metric) scales (see also Luce and Krumhansl 1988). Nominal scales name, or simply categorize, differences. Such categorization is always the beginning of science, and taxonomies (which are nested nominal scales) remains critically important in biology today. Ordinal scales categorize *and* order, but they say nothing about distances between what is ordered. The division of U.S. college students into freshmen, sophomores, juniors, and seniors is an example, for this only gives a rough idea of their "distance" from graduation requirements. Interval scales categorize, order, *and* provide true distances, but there is no true zero on such a scale. Thus, one can say that the distance between 5°C and 10°C is the same as that between 10°C and 15°C, but one cannot say that 10°C is twice as warm as 5°C. Finally, ratio scales categorize, order, provide true distances, and have a true zero. Thus, one can say that 1 m is half as long as 2 m. In doing psychophysics, for example, one often manipulates a physical variable along a ratio scale, and records some psychological variable that is almost surely only ordinal.

Stevens's (1951) classification system of the four scales is itself ordinal. That is, one cannot really know the "distance" between nominal and ordinal scales, for example, as compared to interval and ratio. However true this is logically, one can nonetheless state psychologically that through various considerations one may find that ordinal information can be used to approximate a metric scale (Shepard 1980). And this is the crux of what I have to say. I will claim that all perceived spaces are really ordinal. However, sometimes these spaces can be said to converge on a metric space.

Framing the Problem(s)

What I have to say is framed by the title of the conference "Reconceiving Pictorial Space," on which this volume is based, and on three questions that seem to underlie its motivation. Each query comes in sequence as a slight refinement of the previous.

11.2   IS PERCEIVING A PICTURE LIKE PERCEIVING THE WORLD?

Yes—and for some pictures to a large extent. This is one reason nonprofessional, candid photographs work so well; the cinema can act as such a culturally important surrogate for the everyday world; and precious little experience, if any, is needed to appreciate the content of pictures (Hochberg and Brooks 1962) or film (Messaris 1994). Nevertheless, almost all theorists who bother to address this question—and few actually do—answer largely in the negative, choosing to focus instead on differences between pictures and the world, regardless of how they define pictures or they might define "the world." Consider views from the humanities and then from psychology.

Among artists and art historians, statements about the similarity of pictures and the world are not prevalent. To be sure, few would deny the impressiveness of certain trompe l'oeil (e.g., Cadiou and Gilou 1989; Kubovy 1986) as having the power to be mistaken for a certain type of reality, but equally few would claim this is other than a relatively small genre, and it does not legitimately extend even to photographs. Moreover, the effectiveness of trompe l'oeil is predicated, in part, on a tightly constrained range of depicted distances from the observer, or simply depths.

Rather than concentrating on similarity or verisimilitude of images and their naturalistic counterparts, many in the humanities have focused on viewer response. Responses to images are often indistinguishable from responses to real objects, and this was an important problem in the development of the Protestant Church in the sixteenth century and in the Catholic Counter Reformation. Worship *with* images could not always be separated from the worship *of* images, a violation of the Old Testament's First Commandment (Michalski 1993). This flirtation probably contributed to the prohibition of images in Judaic and Islamic worship as well. Over a broader cultural sweep, Freedberg offered powerful analyses of how pictorial objects evoke the responses in people as real objects, but he never claimed that pictures are mistaken for reality. To be sure, "people are sexually aroused by pictures …; they break pictures …; they kiss them, cry before them, and go on journeys to them" (1989, p. 1), but they don't actually mistake them for the real objects they represent. Instead, images (and sculptures) stand in reference to the objects they represent, attaining an equal status with them, to be loved, scorned, appreciated, or decried in full value.

More generally, there are simply the difficulties of generating mimicry. Ernst Gombrich, for example, suggested that "the demand that the painter should stick to appearances to the extent of trying to forget what he merely 'knew' proved to be in flagrant conflict with actual practice.… The phenomenal world eluded the painter's grasp and he turned to other pursuits" (1974, p. 163). Indeed, with the invention of photography there was even a strong sentiment that, as Rodin suggested, "it is the artist who is truthful and it is the photograph which lies.… [H]is [the artist's] work is certainly much less conventional than the scientific image" (Scharf 1968, p. 226).

Within psychology, James J. Gibson used the picture versus real world difference as a fulcrum to make a distinction between direct and indirect (or mediated) perception. He is often quoted: "Direct perception is what one gets from seeing Niagara Falls, say, as distinguished from seeing a picture of it. The latter kind of perception is *mediated*" (1979, p. 147). Although the nature and the wider ramifications of this distinction have been much debated (e.g., see Cutting 1986a, 1998, for overviews), it is clear throughout all discussions that picture perception and real-world perception are conceived as different.[1] Although few other psychological theorists use pictures to discuss a direct/indirect distinction (but see Sedgwick 2001), Alan Costall (1990), Margaret Hagen (1986), Julian Hochberg (1962, 1978), John Kennedy (1974), Michael Kubovy (1986), Sheena Rogers (1995), and John Willats (1997) all emphasize differences between the world and pictures of it. Indeed, for William Ittelson (1996) there are few, if any, similarities between the perception of pictures and the everyday perception of reality.

In most psychological discussions of pictures versus reality, the essential element centers on the truism that pictures are two-dimensional surfaces and that the world around us is arrayed in three dimensions. At their photographic best, pictures are frozen cross sections of optical arrays whose elements do not change their adjacent positions when the viewer moves. In particular, what is left of a given object seen in a picture from a given position is always left of that object; what is right, always right; and so forth.[2] This is not always true in the natural environment. As one moves forward, to the side, or up or down, objects in the world cross over one another, changing their relative positions. In the world the projective arrangement of objects is not frozen.

To be sure, there are other differences between pictures and the world than the 2-D versus 3-D difference and the lack of motion in pictures. At a comfortable viewing distance, the sizes of objects as projected to the eye are generally smaller in pictures than in real life; pictures typically have a compressed range of luminance values (and often of color) compared to the real world; and there are lens effects that compress or dilate space. I will focus on lens effects later, but let's first consider a second question.

11.3   IS PERCEIVING PHOTOGRAPHIC SPACE LIKE PERCEIVING ENVIRONMENTAL SPACE?

Again, yes—more or less—and, I claim, certainly more so than less so. However, to answer this question, one must begin with an understanding of the perceived space in the world around us. Variously, I will call this environmental space, physical space, and even reality. My intent in this multiplicity (other than to avoid semantic satiation) is to emphasize the assumption that I consider all of these identical.

Two interrelated facts about the perception of physical space must be considered. First, perceived space is anisotropic (Luneburg 1947; Indow 1991). In particular, perceived distances are somewhat foreshortened as compared to physical space, particularly as physical distances increase. This fact has been noted in various ways by many researchers (e.g., Gogel 1993; Loomis and Philbeck 1999; and Wagner 1985; see Sedgwick 1986, for a review), although some methods of judging distance yield quite different results from others (Da Silva 1985; Loomis et al. 1996).

Second, this compression is likely due to the decrease in information available. Such decreases in available information have been shown experimentally by Teodor Künnapas (1968) in the near range (<4 m) of physical environments. They have also been demonstrated for near space in computer-generated ones (Bruno and Cutting 1988). I contend that the dearth of information about depth is responsible for compressions throughout the visual range, particularly at extreme distances.

The Shape of Perceived Environmental Space

We don't notice that our perception of space is not veridical. Where it is compressed most, it is sufficiently far away that it has no consequence for our everyday behavior; any "errors" in distance judgment would not usually matter.[3] The amount of compression throughout perceived space is often said to be well captured psychophysically by an exponent. That is, perceived distance (ψ) is a function of physical distance (ϕ) with an exponent less than 1.0, $\psi = f(\phi^{<1})$. To my knowledge, all previous investigations have assumed that the exponent is constant throughout perceived space, and I think this is incorrect. Instead, it seems that exponents near the observer are near 1.0, then generally decrease with the distance range investigated. Shown in the top panel of figure 11.1 are plots for eleven studies done in naturalistic environments and including distances beyond 20 m (see Da Silva 1985, for a more complete review). The horizontal lines indicate the range of egocentric distances investigated (in meters); their height in the figure corresponds to the value of the exponent best fitting the data. Notice that exponents are generally from near 1.0 to .65 for studies investigating ranges out to about 300 meters but nearer to .40 for the only naturalistic study I know done beyond 1 km (Flückiger 1991).[4]

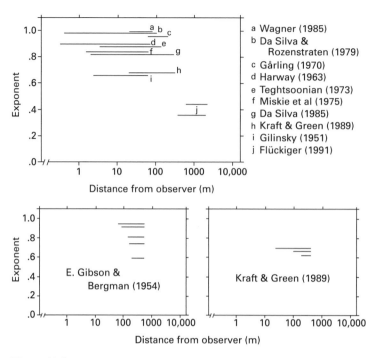

Figure 11.1
The top panel shows the exponents of perceived distance functions plotted by the range of egocentric distances investigated in eleven studies. Notice the general decline with increasing distance. This suggests an accelerated foreshortening of space, from near to far. All studies chosen were done in naturalistic environments. Those included, listed by order of decreasing exponents are Da Silva and Rozenstraten (1979, reported in Da Silva, 1985), method of fractionation; Gårling (1970), magnitude estimation; Harway (1963), method of partitioning; Teghtsoonian (1973), magnitude estimation; Miskie et al. (1975), magnitude estimation; Da Silva (1985), magnitude estimation; Kraft and Green (1989), verbal reports from photographs; Gilinsky (1951), method of fractionation; Flückiger (1991, two studies), method of reproduction. The bottom panels select the data of naive viewers from Gibson and Bergman (1954) and the data of Kraft and Green for special analysis. That is, data are shown first with exponents and full egocentric depth range but then with ranges incrementally truncated in the near range. This truncation systematically lowers the exponents. This means that the shape of perceived space beyond about 50 to 100 m compresses faster than is captured by exponential analysis. Exponents for the studies of Flückiger (1991), Gibson and Bergman (1954), and Kraft and Green (1989) were calculated from the published data for this analysis; others are available in Da Silva (1985).

With the addition of the data of Michelangelo Flückiger, the pattern in the top panel of figure 11.1 looks as if there is a trend: as the range moves outward from the observer, the exponent decreases. But is this just an anomaly of an outlier study? A cleaner analysis of this effect can be seen in the lower panels. Here, the data sets of Eleanor Gibson and Richard Bergman (1954, for their naive subjects) and of Robert Kraft and Jeffrey Green (1989) are considered. First, the complete published data sets were fit with a series of exponents and a best-fitting exponent found. Next, the data points nearest to the observer were omitted from the data sets and the procedure for finding best exponents repeated. Truncation and refitting procedures were repeated again until the data became unstable or too sparse for further analysis.[5] Notice that in both cases the truncation of near data caused the best-fitting exponent to diminish. This can only happen if perceptual space compresses faster than is captured by a single exponent. Consider next the information available in the real world as the beginnings of an explanation for such compression.

Information in Environmental Space

Peter Vishton and I (Cutting and Vishton 1995), among many others (Landy et al. 1995; Luo and Kay 1992; Massaro and Cohen 1993; Terzopoulos 1986), suggested that many sources of information about the layout of the world around us are combined in complex ways. Cutting and Vishton (1995) provided a list of nine different sources of information used—occlusion, relative size, relative density, height in the visual field, aerial perspective, binocular disparities, motion parallax, convergence, and accommodation—although similar lists are stated or implied in works from Euclid (Burton 1945) to Hermann von Helmholtz (1911/1925) and continuously to the present day.[6]

These sources of information often measure the world in different ways. For example, occlusion offers only ordinal information (what is in front of what but not by how much); relative size has the potential of offering ratio-scaled information (if two objects are identical in physical size and one subtends half the visual extent of the other, then it is twice the distance from the observer); and stereopsis and motion perspective may yield absolute distance information (e.g., Landy, Maloney, and Young 1991). Because it is not possible to compare the efficacy of measurement on different scales, we employed *scale convergence* (Birnbaum 1983). That is, we reduced the measures of information for each source to their weakest shared scale—ordinal depth. We next located threshold measures for ordinal depth in the literature and then used them to make suprathreshold comparisons (Cutting and Vishton 1995). The results are shown in the top panel of figure 11.2.

In the panel, threshold functions for pairwise ordinal distance judgments are shown for nine sources of information known to contribute to the perception of layout and depth. They are based on various assumptions and data and applied to a pedestrian. Inspired by and elaborated from Shojiro Nagata (1991), the data are plotted as a function of the mean distance of two objects from the observer (log transformed) and of their *depth contrast*. Depth contrast is defined as the metric difference in the distance of two objects from the observer divided by the mean of their two depths. This measure is similar to that of Michelson contrast in the domain of spatial frequency analysis.

Notice that, plotted in this manner, some sources are equally efficacious everywhere. In particular, I claim that potency of occlusion (the most powerful source of information), relative size, and relative density do not attenuate with the log of distance. Depth contrasts of 0.1%, 3%, and 10%, respectively, between two objects at any mean distance are sufficient for observers to judge which of the two is in front. However, other sources are differentially efficacious. Most—accommodation, convergence, binocular disparities, motion perspective, and height in the visual field—decline with the log of distance. One, aerial perspective, actually increases with the log of distance (it is constant with linear distance), but this source of information, I claim, is used generally to support luminance contrast information for occlusion. Notice further that, integrated across all sources, the "amount" and even the "quality" of information generally declines with the log of distance. This seems the likely cause of compressed perceived distances.

The general shapes of the functions in figure 11.2, plus a few practical considerations, encouraged us to parse egocentric space into three regions (see also Grüsser and Landis 1991). *Personal space,* that which extends a little beyond arm's reach, is supported by many sources of information and is perceived almost metrically (Loomis et al. 1996), that is, with an exponent of 1.0. This means that observers can generally match a lateral distance of, say, 40 cm with a 40 cm distance extended in depth. After 2 m or so, height in the visual field becomes an important source (a normal adult pedestrian cannot use this information until objects are at least 1.5 m distant), and motion perspective for a pedestrian is no longer a blur; but accommodation and convergence cease to be effective.

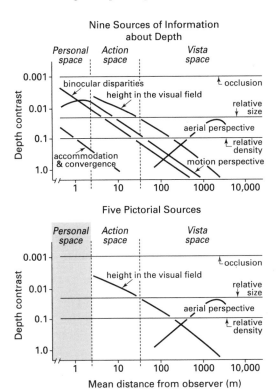

Figure 11.2
The upper panel shows the ordinal depth thresholds for nine sources of information (panel modified from Cutting and Vishton 1995). Egocentric depth (the abscissa) is logarithmically represented. Depth contrast (the ordinate) is measured in a manner similar to Michelson contrast in the spatial frequency domain. That is, the difference in the metric depths of two objects under consideration $(d_1 - d_2)$ is divided by the mean egocentric distance of those objects from an observer $[(d_1 + d_2)/2]$. Egocentric space is also segmented into three general regions, which grade into one another. Personal space, out to about 2 m, is perceived as Euclidean (exponent of 1.0); action space, from about 2 to about 30 m, demonstrates some foreshortening (exponents near 1.0); and vista space, beyond about 30 m, often demonstrates considerable foreshortening (exponents declining to .40 or so, as suggested in figure 11.1). Different sources of information seem to work differentially in the different regions. An assumption made is that threshold measurements, shown in the panel, are good indicators of suprathreshold potency. The lower panel shows those thresholds isolated for pictorial sources of information, with personal space excluded because few pictures (before the twentieth century) depict space within 2 m of the viewer.

We suggested that at this distance (at about 1.5–2 m) there is a boundary, and it marks the beginning of *action space*. This new space extends out to about 30 m or so. Using 10% depth contrast as a general threshold of utility, both disparities and motion perspective cease to be useful at this distance. Most practically, an average individual can throw something reasonably accurately to a distance of 30 m. But perhaps most interestingly, 30 m is about the height of the Andrea Pozzo ceiling in the Chiesa di Sant'Ignazio in Rome (1694), where pillars and architectural ornaments are painted on a vaulted ceiling so that real pillars and painted pillars are indistinguishable when observed from a designated viewpoint (see Pirenne 1970). Action space is perceived near-metrically; its exponents are often only slightly less than 1.0.

Finally, there is *vista space,* everything beyond about 30 m. Here only the traditional pictorial sources of information are efficacious, and vista space becomes increasingly compressed with distance. Exponents in the near vista may be near 1.0, but those near the horizon become distinctively less.

Two caveats: First, although the boundaries between the spaces as we have drawn them are not arbitrary, neither are they well demarcated. Anywhere between 1 and 3 m could serve as the personal/action boundary and anywhere between 20 and 40 m could serve as the action/vista boundary. Training, stature, and a variety of other variables could also influence these boundaries. Most emphatically, one space should be expected to grade gracefully into the next.

Second, some functions can change (Cutting and Vishton 1995). If, for example, one places an observer in a British sports car driving through the countryside, then the function for height in the visual field would move a bit to the right. This is due to adjusting to the reduction in eye-height to about 1 m and because motion perspective would move considerably to the right (adjusting to an order of magnitude change in optical velocity). Some other functions change with the environment—height in the visual field as plotted is for vision standing on a plane (hills introduce changes in slant, altering the function, and occluded regions that create discontinuities in the function); aerial perspective is plotted for a clear day (humidity, mist, and fog would move the function considerably to the right). Still other functions may not prove useful in a given setting—there may be no objects on which to compare relative sizes. Finally, some functions change with characteristics of the observer: some people are stereoweak, others stereoblind, and sometimes this can occur after only a few hours of stereo deprivation (Wallach, Moore, and Davidson 1963); many people over the age of forty can no longer accommodate; and, of course, adults are of different sizes and youngsters crawl and toddle, further changing the function for height in the visual field. All of these factors contribute, I claim, to the lability of perceived distances across people and environments.

Information in Pictorial Space

Most relevant to the purposes of this volume, I will claim that parts of this scheme can be applied directly to the perception of most photographs and to some art (particularly that using linear perspective). Again, such an application is suggested in the lower panel of figure 11.2, where pictorial sources of information—occlusion, relative size, relative density, height in the visual field, and aerial perspective—are shown. The first four comprise what was traditionally called artistic perspective (and with the addition of receding parallels, linear perspective; Kubovy 1986), with the fifth being added by Leonardo da Vinci (Richter 1883). In addition, at least with respect to art before the twentieth century, few paintings depict anything within personal space. Portraiture and still life—certainly the most proximal of artistic genres—typically portray their objects from just beyond arm's length, if not a greater distance. Moreover, this generally remained so even after the invention of photography. Thus, in the lower panel of figure 11.2, personal space is omitted.

Of course, there is additional information in pictures—information specifying that there is no depth (see discussion of flatness in Rogers, chapter 13 in this volume; Sedgwick, chapter 3 in this volume). When holding a photograph, the status of our accommodation and convergence, and the lack of binocular disparities and of motion perspective, all tell us that we are not really looking into the distance. Thus, pictures are endemic situations of information conflict. I think we fairly readily discount such conflict, although there may be residual influences. Reducing such potential conflict is one reason cinema is typically viewed from a distance, often 20 m or so, where accommodation and convergence are inactive and binocular disparities not salient.

A Case Study with Different Lenses

Representations of space often have manifold consequences; they even cause a perceptual elasticity. This changeableness can be demonstrated in at least two ways—in the effects of lenses (e.g., Farber and Rosinski 1978; Lumsden 1980; Pirenne 1970), and in the effects of viewing pictures from noncanonical viewpoints of pictures, such as to the side (Cutting 1986b, 1987). Only the former will be discussed here.

Consider how camera lenses transform information for depth. Figure 11.3 shows two images from Charles Swedlund (1981) with the same content but taken with different lenses—a 35 mm lens (a somewhat short lens for 35 mm film) and a 200 mm lens (a telephoto). These images have been cropped, their sizes have been adjusted, and they were *not* taken from the same viewpoint. Instead, Swedlund normalized the relative sizes of the sign at the right of both images so that the sign takes up roughly the same proportion of the image space. To do this Swedlund was about four times farther away from the sign in the lower image, as noted in the plan view in the right panel of the figure. But look at the basketball backboards to the left in the background. These have grown enormously in size in the lower image, and their difference in relative size has diminished. The latter is due to the compressive effect of telephoto lenses. Ordinarily, a 200 mm lens blows up space 5.7 times compared to a 35 mm lens. With the 5.7-fold increase in image size, there should be a 5.7-fold decrease in apparent image depth. This is not quite true in the Swedlund (1981) images, the deviation due to cropping and sizing.

How exactly does a telephoto lens compress depth? Telephoto lenses enlarge the image for the observer. All enlargements compress depth—those created by longer lenses and those created by moving the observer forward toward the image from the original station point (the point of composition, or the point from which, when looking at the image, the optics are reconstructed most perfectly). How compression occurs is schematically suggested in figure 11.4. Because the points on the image do not change, and because the lines of sight from the observer to these points can be extended into "pictorial space," they find their end points at different pictorial depths. The closer the observer moves toward an image, the more compression in depth there should be; the farther he or she moves away from the image, the more dilation there should be. Sometimes these effects are demonstrable in experiments, but sometimes they are not. One point I would like to emphasize is that our perception of spaces is somewhat elastic; sometimes we pick up on information, sometimes not.

But what information is changed with a long lens? This is a bit more difficult to explain. Enlargements play with familiar size. A person 10 m away would ordinarily be in action space; a person 100 m away is ordinarily in vista space. Seen through a 500 mm lens, however, the latter

Swedlund (1981)

35-mm lens, cropped to 24°

200-mm lens, cropped to 6° , size adjusted

Figure 11.3
The two images on the left are from Swedlund (1981), reprinted with permission of Holt, Rinehart, and Winston. These images show the changes in pictorial space due to changes between a short and a long lens. The point from which the bottom image was photographed was about four times the distance of that for the top image, and both were cropped and sizes adjusted to make the appearance of the sign in the foreground the same. The diagram to the right is a plan view of the layout of the sign, the two backboards, and the two camera positions. It was reconstructed knowing that backboards are usually about 25 m apart and from the measurements of their heights (in pixels) in the digitized images. (Photographs from *Photography: A handbook of history, materials, and processes,* 2nd edition by Charles Swedlund and Elizabeth U. Swedlund, copyright © 1981 by Holt, Rinehart and Winston, reproduced by permission of the publisher.)

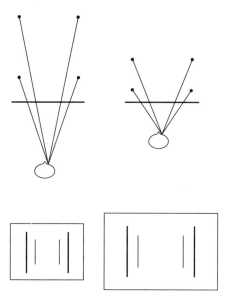

Figure 11.4
An affine reconstruction of pictorial space. The left panels show slices through
untransformed pictorial space as seen from the composition point and the image
seen by the observer; the other panels show transformations and views due to
changes in observer position away from the composition point. Top panels show
the affine transform in horizontal planes; the bottom-right panel shows a similarity transform (enlargement). After Cutting (1986b).

person has the same image size as the former seen through a 50 mm
lens. Thus, familiarity with sizes of objects in the environment shifts, in
this case, the whole of the environment shifts one log unit toward the
observer; familiarity with what one can do with those objects move distant
ones into what appears to be action space. (In telephoto images, as in regular images, there typically is no content in personal space.) Thus, what
passes for action space now really extends out to perhaps 300 m.

   If we carry with us a set of expectations about objects and the efficacy
of information in real space to what we see in the telephoto image, perceptual anomalies will occur (Cutting 1997). Compared to the perception
of environmental and normal pictorial spaces, relative size differences and
relative density differences are reduced. Consider size. Basketball backboards are normally about 25 m apart. In the Swedlund images in figure
11.3 the ratio of sizes (linear extent) of the two backboards is 1.5:1 in the
top image but only 1.24:1 in the bottom image. The perceived distance

difference in the top image could rather easily be 25 m; that in the lower image could not. In near space, we expect smaller relative size differences for similar objects closer together. In addition, height in the visual field also changes; the difference in height between the base of the poles for the two backboards is three times greater in the telephoto image. We expect larger height-in-the-visual-field differences for nearer objects.

The Shapes of Perceived Photographic Space

Consider next the data set of Kraft and Green (1989), already considered earlier as if it represented judgments about depth in the real world. Although gathered for different purposes,[7] these data are a definitive example of lens compression and dilation effects. Kraft and Green presented many photographs to observers. These were taken with a 35 mm camera and five different lenses: 17, 28, 48, 80, and 135 mm (where the first is called a *short* lens and the last a *telephoto* lens). With such lenses the horizontal field of view subtends about 105, 60, 45, 32, and 20°, respectively. Because a 48 mm lens is essentially a standard lens for a 35 mm camera (35 mm is the measure along the longer edge of the film frame; about 50 mm is the measure along its diagonal, and the functional diameter of the image circle; see, for example, Swedlund 1981), the layout of objects and their depth should appear relatively normal. Moreover, since the time of Leonardo, recommendations have been made to keep the larger, usually horizontal, subtense of a picture within 45°–60° to avoid distortions (Carlbom and Paciorek 1978). In two different outdoor environments, Kraft and Green (1989) planted poles at distances of 20, 40, 80, 160, and 320 m from a fixed camera. Viewing different arrangements of fifty slides, observers made judgments of the distance of each pole from the camera. Mean results are shown in the left panel of figure 11.5. This fan-shaped pattern provides grist for further analyses.

Notice first that perceived distances are generally quite a bit less than real distances, even for those stimuli shot with the standard lens. Ideally this should not occur.[8] To assess this general effects of foreshortening due to the experimental manipulation (the photographic lenses) and the experimental situation, I regressed the mean perceived distances in the left panel of figure 11.5 against a parameter cluster: $\phi \cdot (50/L)$. This is the physical distance of the posts from the camera multiplied by 50 (the standard lens length) over the lens length used. The second half of this composite variable is the extent to which perceived space ought to be compressed ($50/L < 1$) or dilated ($50/L > 1$; Cutting 1988; Lumsden 1980).

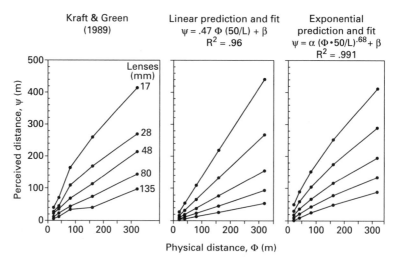

Figure 11.5
The data of Kraft and Green (1989) are presented in the left panel, showing perceived distances of posts as functions of their physical distance from a camera and its lens. The middle panel shows a model prediction based on the combination of physical distance and lens length; and the right panel shows a prediction based on this parameter and an exponent of .68. The fit shown in the left panel is statistically superior to that in the middle panel, revealing compression in perceived depth.

Thus, for example, a 135 mm lens should compress depth by a factor of about 2.8 (multiplying depth values by 0.37); a 17 mm lens should compress it by a 0.35 (actually dilating perceived space, multiplying values by 2.85).

This analysis accounted for 96% of the variance in the data ($R^2 = .96$, $F(1, 23) = 595$, $p < .0001$), fitting the pattern of data extremely well. The weight (a) given the parameter $\varphi \cdot 50/L$ in the equation was .47, about half what might have been expected. Perceived half-depth could be a compromise between full depth (carried by height in the visual field, relative size, relative density) and zero depth (enforced by no disparities and no motion perspective). Regardless, the schematized data, however, can serve as post hoc "predictions" for (i.e., model fits to) the real data. These are shown in the middle panel of figure 11.5. The match between them is quite good but not quite good enough.

Notice that there are some distinguishing characteristics in the shape of the predicted functions that are not generally wanted. Most salient is that at large physical distances (φ) there is insufficient foreshortening in the perceived distances (ψ) when compared to the Kraft and Green data. This means that beyond general compression, there is general change in compression rates in the data, suggesting exponents less than 1.0. I reran the regression analysis with various exponents to determine the value of the best fit. A *single* exponent of .68 captured the most variance, increasing that accounted for to 99.1% ($F(1, 23) = 2660, p < .0001$), a reliable improvement ($\chi^2 = 7.2$, $p < .01$) over the exponentless prediction. The model fits with the exponent are seen in the right panel of figure 11.5. (Remember, truncating the data at the near end decreases the exponent, as shown in the lower panels of figure 11.1.)

Of course, it may be simply a coincidence that judgments of distance in photographs (Kraft and Green 1989) and judgments in the real world (e.g., Da Silva 1985; Wagner 1985) are so similar, as shown in the top panel of figure 11.1. In may also be that the similarity in the decline in exponents found by truncating the near-distance data is similar in both photographic data (Kraft and Green 1989) and in real-world data (Gibson and Bergman 1954), shown in the lower panels of figure 11.1, is also a coincidence. But I think not. Most pleasantly, there are some elegant data gathered at ZiF (Center for Interdisciplinary Research), the site of the conference on which this volume is based. These show similar effects in the real world and in photographs of it (Hecht, van Doorn, and Koenderink 1999).[9] These data, if not the reanalyses that I have presented here, ought to be sufficiently convincing of the strong similarity—indeed functional identity—between photographic and real-world spaces.

11.4   IS PERCEIVING THE LAYOUT IN OTHER PICTURES LIKE PERCEIVING THAT IN ENVIRONMENTAL SPACE?

Yes—at least in terms of principles if more than the end result. Earlier I had suggested that psychologists and others interested in pictorial space have spent perhaps too much time with photographs and linear perspective paintings, drawings, and etchings. These are among the more recent of pictures that human beings have crafted. Manfredo Massironi and I (Cutting and Massironi 1998) suggested one might equally start at the other end of time, at least from the perspective of human culture. Cave paintings—some of which are at least 30,000 years old—as well as cartoons, caricatures, and doodles are made up of *lines*. These pictures are not copies of any optical array, and yet as images they depict objects well.

Many of these compositions can be read to represent animals in depth, often by occlusion of one by another.

How do line drawings work? What kind of space do they build? Cutting and Massironi (1998) suggested that there are four basic types of lines and that these ordinally parse the regions on either side of the line or parse themselves from those regions. The four types are shown in figure 11.6. *Edge lines* separate a figure from background, where one side belongs to the figure and is closer to the viewer and the other side belongs to the background. We notate this type of configuration [aAb] or [bAa], where letter order denotes ordinal position in depth, [a] in front of [b]; and uppercase [A] denotes the line, lowercase [a] one of the two regions on either side of the line. A second kind is an *object line,* where the line stands for an entire object in front of the background [bAb]. Its inverse is the *crack line* [aBa], where the line invites the viewer to imagine the interior space hidden from view. Finally, there are *texture lines,* which subdivide again. Texture lines can represent small edges, small objects, or small cracks; and they can also represent shading, color, or what the traditional pedagogical literature on drawing calls *mass* (Speed 1913).

Consider an example from the oldest known works of paleolithic art. Shown in figure 11.7 are several rhinoceroses from La Grotte Chauvet in the south of France (see also Bahn and Vertut 1997; Chauvet, Brunel Deschamps, and Hillaire 1995; Clottes 2001). As part of this figure one can see edge lines (outlining a rhinoceros), object lines (its horns), crack lines (its mouth), as well as texture lines (the coloring of the flank). The antiquity of this image, and the fact that it has the complete set of line primitives outlined by Cutting and Massironi (1998), suggests that line primitives are not culturally limited or even culturally determined. The fourfold use of lines seems deeply embedded in our genome.

I claim that each line serves to carve up a small bit of pictorial space; each contributes a local bit of ordinality. Nothing is needed in this case but a segregation of two different depth planes—one of the animal and one of the background against which it stands. As images get richer in information, depth can become richer as well. Consider another example from La Grotte Chauvet in figure 11.8.

Here a few well-crafted lines represent four horses. There is great controversy about whether or not these horses should be read as occupying the same space, each occluding another that is higher up in the pictorial place. Nonetheless, I think depth is inescapable. In the paleolithic corpus of images, one often finds the superimposition of lines from different

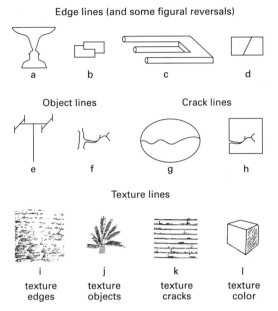

Figure 11.6

A taxonomy of lines. Edge lines separate the regions on either side and assign different ordinal depth. Four figures that play with this relationship are shown: (a) the faces/goblet illusion, after Rubin (1915); (b) an ambiguous occlusion figure, after Ratoosh (1949); (c) the devil's pitchfork, after Schuster (1964); and (d) a rectangle/window, after Koffka (1935). Next are shown some object lines: (e) is a mid-twentieth-century version of a television antenna; and (f) shows the twigs at the end of a tree branch. Third are figures with crack lines: (g) is the mouth of a clam, after Kennedy (1974); and (h) is a crack in a block. Note that (f) and (h) are exact reciprocals—switching from object line to crack line. Finally, four texture line types are shown: (i) texture edges of occlusion in cobblestones, after de Margerie (1994); (j) texture objects as palm fronds, after Steinberg (1966); (k) texture cracks as mortar between bricks, after Brodatz (1966); and (l) texture color, indicating shadow. (Adapted from Cutting and Massironi, 1998)

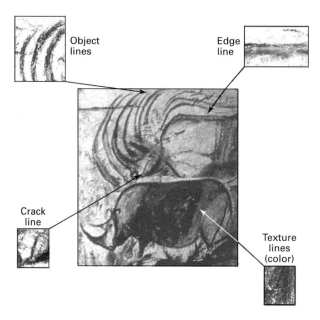

Figure 11.7
A thresholded detail from a painting in La Grotte Chauvet demonstrating the use of four types of lines—edges, objects, cracks, and textures. Because this image is at least 30,000 years old, it would appear that this typology of lines is not culturally relative but possibly biologically engrained. (Image reprinted from Clottes, 2001, with the kind permission of Jean Clottes, Ministère de la Culture)

animals in different orientations, lines crossing, suggesting that they were composed without respect for one other. Here, however, we find what appear to be true occlusions of horses each in the same orientation. Each edge line can be interpreted locally to generate depth, and local depth assignments can be written [bAa]. However, taken as an ensemble, several relations have to be rewritten, pushing some regions and lines farther into depth. Thus, the occluding edge of the second horse becomes [cBb], the third [dCc], and the fourth [eDd]. In this manner global coherence can be built up from local depth assignments, and multiple, ordered depth planes can be built up as well. I suggest this is done in a manner not much different than seen in cooperative stereo algorithms (Julesz 1971; Marr and Poggio 1976), although in pictorial cases it is much simpler. Depth is incrementally built up, in more difficult cases perhaps with many passes through the data. Moreover, there can be great play in this. Figure 11.6a–6d are examples from the psychological literature, but of course

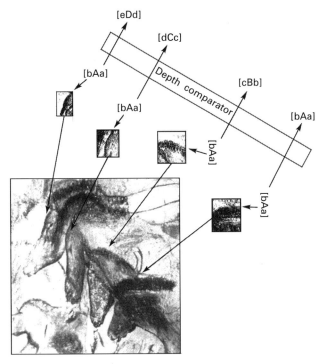

Figure 11.8
From pairwise ordinal depth relations to five ordinal depth planes. A thresholded detail from perhaps the most famous and controversial image in La Grotte Chauvet. Many claim it should not be read as four horses in depth, although I disagree. If it is read in depth, one can follow the assignments of occlusions, using edge lines [bAa]. Each of four pairs has this assignment. If this information is fed into a comparator that knows that objects can occlude, the end result is five ordinal pictorial depths, [a]–[e]. (Image reprinted from Clottes, 2001, with the kind permission of Jean Clottes, Ministère de la Culture)

much of the corpus of M. C. Escher (Bool et al. 1981) can be construed this way.

Assignments of edge lines [aAb] and [bAa] are often judgments of occlusion. Assignments of many lines (and all line types), however, could also be made on the basis of height in the visual field; assignments of similarly shaped objects (made up of lines) could also be made on the basis of relative size; and so forth. Thus, bringing knowledge to bear on a graphic situation, one can assign depth order to many elements, The five pictorial sources of information—occlusion, height in the visual field, relative size, relative density, and aerial perspective—can constrain one another quite well so that a reasonably rich, affine space is established. Moreover, an approximation to a metric space can also be achieved, particularly with the application of linear perspective.

How might this be done? The analogy I wish to make is with respect to nonmetric multidimensional scaling (Kruskal 1964; Shepard 1980), and it is a deep lesson in measurement theory. By considering only pairwise ordinal relations among all (or even only most) members of a set of data, one can assemble a nearly metric space of that set. Metric distances, even ratios, are not needed. Yacov Hel-Or and Shimon Edelman (1994) demonstrated the logical efficacy of this approach to qualitative stereo, and Cutting and Vishton (1995) suggested it should work considering depth in general. Thus, one can think of perceived space—even at its articulated, near-Euclidean best—as built up incrementally from constraints of ordinality. These constraints, when sufficiently rich, converge on a near-Euclidean framework.

In summary, I claim that perceiving depth in pictures and perceiving depth in the real world are cut from the same informational cloth. Thus, if we misunderstand perceived pictorial space (as might be suggested by the title of the conference on which this volume was based), then it follows that we misunderstand perceived environmental space as well. I claim further that when ordinal depth information is sparse, perceived depth is also crude, confined to a few depth planes. When ordinal information is richer, perceived space becomes more articulated, allowing first for many depth planes (and an essentially affine representation). When that information is extremely rich, as with the addition of binocular disparities and motion perspective in cluttered environments and in daylight, ordinal constraints can become sufficiently tight to approach a metric representation. Thus, the concatenation of ideas from measurement theory and from the computational practice of multidimensional scaling allows promise of considering the perception of space in pictures and in the world as proceeding from the same principles.

ACKNOWLEDGMENT

I thank Claudia Lazzaro for many fruitful discussions and for her patience in listening to many ill-formed ideas, Robert Kraft for sharing methodological information about this study of pictorial depth, and Patrick Maynard for some insightful comments.

Notes

1. Earlier in his career, however, Gibson was less sure: "It is theoretically possible to construct a dense sheaf of light rays to a certain point in a gallery or a laboratory, one identical in all respects to another dense sheaf of light rays to a unique station point thousands of miles away" (1960, p. 223), although he denied it was obtainable in practice.

2. This is an axiom from Euclid's optics (Burton 1945). Euclid's axioms and his proofs deal with both stationary and moving observers.

3. This is not to say that people cannot be trained to perceive vista space more veridically; clearly they can, and the data of E. Gibson and Bergman (1954) and Galanter and Galanter (1973) show this. The focus of this chapter, however, is on what normal adults, without specific distance training, will perceive and judge.

4. Flückiger (1991) had observers judge the distance of boats floating on Lake Leman, looking from near Geneva toward Montreux. Only relative size and height in the visual field would provide firm information, perhaps with the addition of aerial perspective and relative densities of waves. Experimental results for judgments between 0.2 km and 2.0 km and between 0.75 km and 2.25 km were quite tidy; whereas those between 2.8 km and 5.6 km were not. Flückiger did not fit exponents to his data, but this is easily done. Mean exponents for the first complete data sets were .36 and .44, respectively. In addition, I have omitted the data of Galanter and Galanter (1973) here. Their observers were highly trained and, although they viewed objects up to 10 km into the distance, they viewed them from airplanes at altitudes of about 60 m. This raises the function of height in the visual field by a factor of 40, as discussed in the next section.

5. Exponents become unstable when a first pair exhibits overconstancy (more perceived distance between them than physically present). When this occurs, exponents tend toward zero. This also happened in the analysis of the data of Flückiger (1991).

6. Linear perspective, often cited as a single source of information, is really a concomitance of occlusion, relative size, relative density, and height in the visual field, using the technology of parallel straight lines and their recession.

7. Kraft and Green (1989) believed that the foreshortening of space seen in photographs due to the use of lenses of different lengths is caused by the truncation of the foreground. Although this is a possibility, the purist form of the argument is that the foreground is truncated but the remainder of space remains the same. Their own data (Kraft and Green, 1989, experiment 1) are not consistent with this idea; they show a fan effect rather than parallel lines.

8. The Kraft and Green article did not give full details of the presentation of the stimuli. Thus, I contacted Robert Kraft and he kindly provided additional experimental details (Kraft, personal communication, May 24, 2000). First, the length of the lens used to project the images was 100 mm. This means that the images are half as large than they would be with a 50 mm projector lens from the distance of

the projector. Ideally, when seen from the projector, such diminution should dilate depth by a factor of about 2.0 (multiplying distances by about 2.0; see Cutting, 1988, for a similar analysis). However, the distance of the projector to the screen was at 6 m, twice the mean distance of the observers (3 m). This latter effect enlarges the image by a factor of 2, compressing depth (multiplied by 0.5). These two effects are linear and should cancel. Theoretically one would expect perceived distances to be compressed by a factor of $0.5 \cdot 2.0$ (multiplied by a factor of 1.0). This also means that the images seen in the experimental situations subtended the same angle as the corresponding images in the real world.

9. The most convincing comparisons in the data of Hecht, van Doorn, and Koenderink (1999) are for angular judgments of the intersections of wall of buildings at ZiF, which has few right angles.

Chapter 12

Pictorial Space

Jan J. Koenderink and Andrea J. van Doorn

12.1   WHAT IS "PICTORIAL RELIEF"?

When you are handed a "straight" photograph of, say, a statue you can either

- look *at* it and see a flat piece of paper covered with pigments in a certain simultaneous order, or
- you can look *into* it and see an object ("the statue") in "pictorial space."

The former perception is of a "physical object" that has an objective existence in the usual sense; the latter is a purely "mental entity."

Pictorial space has no objective existence in the usual sense. It has nothing per se to do with the fact that the photograph might have a certain history. For suppose that it—the physical object—turned out after all to be a piece of paper covered with darkish fungus growth, such that you, erroneously as it turned out, had mistaken it for a photograph. Such facts would be quite irrelevant with respect to the pictorial space. Indeed, it is well known that people often see pictorial spaces in clouds or dirty old walls (Leonardo da Vinci 1989). Thus "pictorial space" is a somewhat mysterious entity; small wonder that little objective knowledge concerning its properties has become established so far.

The phenomenology of pictorial space is familiar enough to people from cultured societies. You experience the visual field—a two-dimensional simultaneous presence—augmented with a "depth" dimension. The depth is like a "flow away from you" (Hildebrand 1893/1945) that may be checked or stopped by more or less "opaque objects." When we say opaque objects, we mean that you don't see "through" them. This has nothing to do with optics proper of course. We are outside the realm of physics.

Opaque objects manifest themselves through their "boundary," a "surface," often called pictorial relief. A definitive reference on this is by the German sculptor Adolf Hildebrand (1893/1945). As a sculptor Hildebrand was mainly interested in *actual* objects, that is to say, artfully formed chunks of marble, and not so much *pictures* of objects. Here we meet with an unexpected twist, though, for Hildebrand essentially didn't distinguish between pictorial space and the optical perception of physical space in front of the observer! When "motion-related perceptions" are excluded "optical space," that is, what you see in front of you in a real environment, and pictorial space are phenomenologically similar indeed. Examples of motion-related perceptions are those associated with eye movements (vergence), accommodation, binocular disparity, motion parallax, and so forth. The ontologies of optical space and pictorial space may be taken to be quite dissimilar or rather similar depending upon your point of view.

What inhabits pictorial space is usually described in terms of geometrical or physical properties, or both, that refer to the generic structure of the observer's biotope. In fact, observers don't seem to have any other option. Thus you describe the face you see in a cloud in terms of properties of actual human facial structures with which you are familiar, although you know perfectly well that clouds are differently structured from faces and you are convinced that there isn't any face in the cloud from the perspective of the meteorologist, that is to say, that the face is a mere "illusion." By illusion, you mean a mental thing without objective reference. This applies equally to pictorial and to optical space. A pair of hills may look like "female breasts" (such as in the movie *King Solomon's Mines*) and the rippled water on a lake in the moonshine "silvery," although there are no giant women nor precious metals in the real landscape in front of you or in the picture of the landscape that you may happen to behold. Nor need you believe there are. Of course the real landscape looks real enough to you, whereas the picture looks like a (real) picture of a possible landscape to you.

A valid way to describe pictorial space in different terms is the way of the artist. Artistic renderings can be absolutely compelling in many or a few respects, although you are never "fooled," because you know quite well that you are looking at a certain rendering of a scene, not at a real scene. Artistic statements are different in (objective) structure from straight photographs, though. So far science has not been able to exploit the uncanny ability of artists to produce such responses in human observers. Although this matter is highly interesting, also from a fundamental scientific perspective, we won't pursue it here.

Observers bring expectations of a similar kind to both optical and pictorial space. Thus you may notice spontaneously that painted grapes look "glassy" (or vitreous) and thus somehow not "right." They don't look to you like real grapes "should" in either optical or pictorial space. Yet the "grapes" in pictorial space may look like perfectly good *pictures of grapes,* in a particular painterly style say. Glassy-looking grapes in optical space don't look right in *any* sense, and you may well suspect to be confronted with hard to swallow (fake) specimens.

The scientific studies of optical and pictorial space may largely coincide or be totally distinct according to whether you study the relation of perceptions to the distal objects or study relations *intrinsic* to optical or pictorial space. In this chapter, the emphasis will be almost singularly on the latter approach.

Issues of "Information"

Here is a remarkable fact: *When you look at the scene in front of you you pretty much see the scene in front of you.* We mean this in the sense that you find no problem in making judgments of either a geometrical or a physical nature that you know are likely to be corroborated by various explorations you might make were you to walk up to the scene and explore it in various ways. Examples of geometrical attributes would be sizes, distances, and spatial orientations; examples of physical attributes would be such properties as being rough, smooth, metallic, wooden, or wet.

Although you know that your judgments are unlikely to be correct in every detail, you are convinced that they are *good enough* for most interactions with your trusty environment. When you get out of your generic biotope, things may turn out to be different than expected, though, and you have to be more careful; that is, you have to reckon with various forms of erroneous—in the sense of leading you to unsuccessful action—judgments. For instance, you are likely to seriously misjudge distances and shapes when transferred to the submarine environment (Lythgoe 1979), and you will probably misinterpret X-ray pictures.

Because your only physical interaction with the scene is of an optical nature, it must be the case that you interpret the "radiance" at the location of your eye in terms of "information" relating to the geometry and physical properties of the scene. For the moment we consider only monocular vision.

The radiance is a function of position and direction that for each position and direction specifies the photon spectral number density per unit solid angle, unit area, unit time, and unit photon energy interval. It is subject to few constraints. Photon number density is nonnegative throughout, and, at least in empty space, the radiance at different locations in the direction of their connecting line must be the same. Otherwise, the radiance is quite arbitrary. The best intuitive way to think of radiance is as an infinite storage cabinet containing all possible photographs, taken from any conceivable viewpoint, field of view, view direction, spectral filter, and so forth. Its structure is extremely complicated in the sense that when you increase the resolution you obtain more and more variation. You would see all the hairs on the body, the tiny organisms that live in the crevices of the skin, all the tiny articulations of these, and so forth. In that sense the radiance is not a simple function (i.e., it is not continuous and differentiable) at all, but what mathematicians call a "distribution."

From the perspective of physics the radiance is due to the scattering of photons emanating from certain "primary sources," for example, the sun, by the scene to your eye. Multiple scattering is the rule. A photon that arrives at your eye is likely to have been scattered many times by the atmosphere and various objects in the scene. All photons of a given energy are the same; they don't carry an imprint of their history. It is only the radiance as a whole that may be interpreted in terms of a history of scattering events in the scene (Born and Wolf 1959).

Your eye transducts the radiance at the position of the cornea into a simultaneous-successive order of action potentials in the optic nerve. The retina doesn't distinguish between the energies of photons once they have been absorbed (see the "Law of Univariance"; as described by Wyszecki and Stiles 1967), and many different patterns of photon absorptions lead to identical optic nerve patterns. The structure of the "input to the brain" reflects—in an extraordinarily complex way—the structure of the scene in front of you (Zeki 1993). Some correlations between certain aspects of this structure and certain aspects of the structure of the scene are understood, or even well understood, but much still awaits discovery. That is one reason, though not the most important one, why we deem it prudent to distinguish between "structure" and "information."

Structure simply refers to aspects of spatiotemporal order. It implies a topology (adjacency in space-time) but has nothing to do with any reference to the scene. Information is structure referred to a real or imaginary scene by an observer. Thus the concept of information implies an observer with experience with generic scenes who posits a particular scene and takes the available structure as referring to that scene. This is Franz von Brentano's "intentionality" (*Intentionalität*), which turns structure into information in the sense of "meaning" (Brentano 1874). To take structure for information in this way is an act of faith on the part of the observer. Structure is not *intrinsically* information in any way, although most textbooks are designed to mislead you on the issue. That is why information can be wrong, even information concerning the (real!) scene in front of you. Structure is never wrong, nor is it ever true; it simply exists. Of course the act of faith on the part of the observer need not be a conscious one. It typically is not. Organisms simply have to stick their necks out or they won't survive.

Classically (Berkeley 1709/1975) optical information is discussed in terms of "cues." The meaning of cue is differently construed by various authors. Here we take it to refer to structure interpreted by an observer in terms of knowledge of "ecological optics" (Gibson 1950). "Knowledge" is understood in the sense of "know-how," or capability. Such knowledge is of two kinds, generic and particular. Knowledge of generic ecological optics coincides with the laws of physics as they apply to perception. An example would be that large and small images of similar things indicate near and far distances of these things. Generic knowledge holds good in virtually all biotopes. In contradistinction, particular knowledge applies to particular biotopes and may easily fail in the wrong setting. An example would be that strong and otherwise unaccountable contrasts ("glitter") indicate wet or metallic surfaces. This won't work in an art gallery where chrome objects are rendered in paint on canvas. Notice that the knowledge, be it generic or particular, is almost never overt. It may even be anatomically implemented (Riedl 1988; Vollmer 1990). It always derives from *uncontradicted experience* though, whether phylogenetically or ontogenetically.

Because generic ecological optics (Gibson 1950) coincides with a subset of physics, it is the same for all observers (species) and can be formally understood via an analysis of the pertinent physics. Much of our present knowledge derives from applied physics and computer vision. Whether a given observer or species actually *exploits* such knowledge is of course up to behavioral verification. Empirically we find that many generic facts of ecological optics are reflected in the behavior of very different species, though the precise implementations may differ widely. After all, flies are constructed differently from man, though both orient and navigate partly via "optical flow." This indicates, by the way, that a mindless reductionism is not going to get one very far in understanding such feats of living organisms.

Types of "Pictures"

There exists a bewildering variety of artifacts that are commonly referred to as "pictures." In this chapter, we reserve the term "images" for perceptions and use "pictures" for such things as photographs, paintings, and drawings. Although pictures are simply physical objects, they are pictures *to an observer*. That is to say, an observer *has to take them* as a picture. A footprint in the sand is a picture to human observers, whereas a photograph is merely a piece of paper to your dog. Images are in the mind, whereas pictures may be handled. Here we are mainly interested in pictures "of" something, either of actually existing things, such as a horse or a cow, or imaginary things that still fit into some observer's realm of expertise in ecological optics. Think of unicorns or dragons, for instance.

For our purposes it is of minor interest whether a picture has been produced by some mechanical means such as footprints on the beach, photographs, or computer graphics, or whether it came about through an act of artistic rendering. Indeed, it is impossible to decide on the basis of the picture as object alone. What will be important is the particular bouquet of cues that the picture offers the observer. For instance, a silhouette, a cartoon (line) drawing, a painting in flat tones, a pointillist (realistic) painting, and a straight photograph offer quite different bouquets of cues (see figures 12.1 and 12.2). Remember that cues are bits of information and exist only in relation to certain observers.

Because cues can be, and often are, *qualitatively* different chunks of information, different pictures offer not simply different *amounts* of information but qualitatively different informational contents. Thus different renderings of a *single* "fiducial object" may well specify *distinct* pictorial objects to an observer (see figure 12.2). The fiducial object may be a real (or physical) object in the case of photographs, or a concept in the head of an artist (a unicorn, say) that may materialize as a painting, drawing, and so forth.

In many cases it may not be very useful to speak of a fiducial object at all, because artists often aim at a concrete result, such as a painting, rather than (or in addition to) the expression of an idea. Whereas many ideas can be drawn, painted, or described in words, this need not be universally the case. For instance, painted unicorns cannot be drawn, for the simple

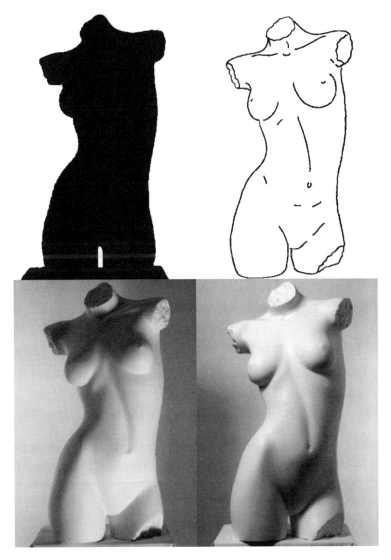

Figure 12.1
Four pictures with identical geometry but different rendering.

Subject CC

Silhouette

Cartoon

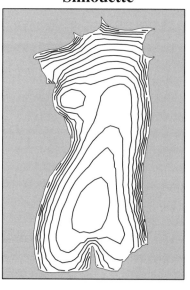
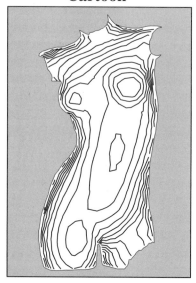

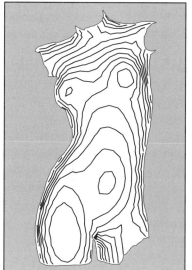
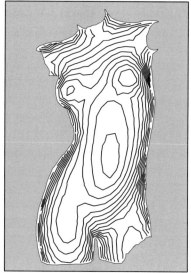

Illumination
from lower right

Illumination
from upper left

reason that drawings are not paintings. In such cases, like in the case of a face seen in a cloud, the picture is all there is.

Modes of Seeing

Pictorial spaces are mental entities and depend upon the observer just as well as upon the picture. Without observers there are no images and pictures remain forever "planar objects covered with pigments in certain simultaneous orders"; to echo Maurice Denis: "Remember that a picture—before being a battle horse, a nude woman, or some anecdote—is essentially a plane surface covered with colors assembled in a certain order" (Denis 1890/1976, p. 380). There are many different modes of seeing: a face may be seen in a cloud, a person may be seen frontally (facing you) in a painting viewed obliquely, a photograph may be seen as a flat object *and* you may see a pictorial space in it simultaneously, and so forth.

Of particular interest are cases in which the observer assumes a certain viewing mode with the express purpose to influence the structure of pictorial space. Such viewing methods are often practiced by artists (Leonardo da Vinci 1989) to either flatten optical space for purposes of drawing, or deepen pictorial relief for purposes of monitoring the effectiveness of rendering. Optical space is flattened through such devices as monocular viewing, "screwing up the eyes," viewing through a wireframe, using a Claude glass (tinted mirror) or camera obscura, and so forth (Dubery and Willats 1972). (See figure 12.3.) Pictorial space is deepened through monocular viewing, deemphasis of the frame, a frontoparallel vantage point, and so forth.

The case of deepening the relief in pictorial space is interesting, because the structure relating to the pictorial relief that is sampled by the eye(s) is obviously the same whether you view the picture monocularly or binocularly. Yet the "information" is different because the structure relating to the actual scene—you holding the photograph and looking *at* it—is different. With two eyes open, there are strong indications that you are looking at a flat object. Apparently this cue "conflicts" with the pictorial cues proper. More on that later. This conflict is an indication that a clean

Figure 12.2
Pictorial relief for the four pictures shown in figure 12.1 with identical geometry but different rendering. The lines are loci of constant depth. The pictures represent different pictorial objects to the observer CC. In the case of the silhouette you may guess the object is a torso, but it is ambiguous whether you see the front or back of it. This observer apparently split the difference.

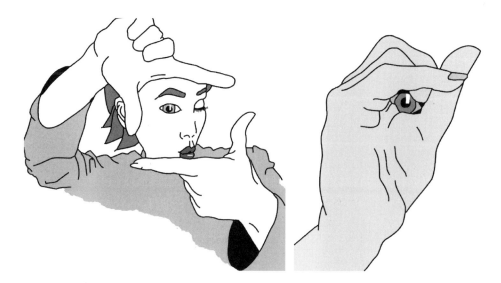

Figure 12.3
(*Left*) "framing" the scene in front of you and looking at and through the frame with one eye is a time-honored method to "flatten" a scene. Optical space starts to look as a picture. (*Right*) cutting out context is an excellent way to remove depth and relief in order to be able to focus on textural properties and color.

segregation between "pictorial space," that is, the space in which the pictorial content unfolds, and "physical space," that is, the space that contains the picture, is not necessarily made by a given observer.

The Issue of "Veridicality"

The issue of "veridicality" need not come up when you see a dragon in pictorial space or a face in a cloud, that is, when you are convinced you are experiencing an "illusion," but it seems natural enough in the context of optical space or the pictorial space related to a straight photograph. Yet the issue is a particularly vexing one, even in those cases. It is also an important issue and is generally ignored or misunderstood.

The problem is that a photograph by no means specifies a scene, although most people seem confident that it does. There exists a many-to-one relation between scenes and photographs (see figure 12.4). In fact, a given photograph could have been due to *infinities* of different scenes. One particular example is the actual scene in front of the photographer at the time of exposure. Let's agree to call it the "fiducial scene." Another is the photograph itself in front of a camera, at the right distance and so

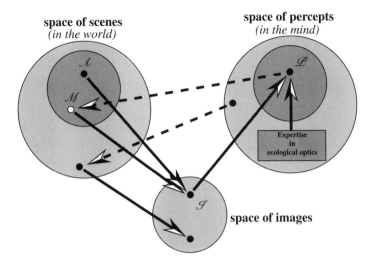

Figure 12.4
The actual scene *A* gives rise to an actual image *I*, which again gives rise to a veridical perception *P*. A "nonveridical" perception would indicate a scene that would lead to a different picture. All scenes (like *M*) that lead to the picture *I* are "metameric" to the actual scene and would be equally veridical perceptions. All such metameric scenes are related by a group of ambiguity transformations.

forth. But many *really* different possibilities exist. It is perhaps sufficient to remember that Hollywood movie producers rarely go to the trouble to build castles or Martian landscapes. These are "faked," though we all know that the movie scenes can look only too real to us. It is easy enough to think of the weirdest examples. For instance, consider a stellar constellation that happens—by an incredible cosmic coincidence—to excite your retina in the same way as when you look at Leonardo's *Gioconda* at the Louvre from a particular vantage point. The "pixels" are stars at essentially random distances (many light years away). Though perhaps somewhat unlikely, this is clearly *possible,* and it vividly illustrates that things need not at all be what they seem. George Berkeley (1709/1975) was quite right that vision is impossible in principle! Helmholtz (1896) was right that we see what is (for us) the most likely explanation of our present retinal activity. The fact that we can write this shows that the odds are perhaps slightly in our favor. Although vision is indeed impossible in principle, it generally works fine for us.

Clearly observers "have to bring something" with them in order to even stand a chance to look at a picture and see a pictorial space. This something is an intuitive understanding of the causal nexus of laws of ecological optics (in a way "vision" is a process that embodies this understanding) and a generic knowledge of frequently encountered objects and scenes. In the top left of figure 12.2 we see that the observer "fills in the blanks" and because there is nothing in the picture except a global reference, the filled-in structure has to come from the observer's memory. Notice that any additional information is used to override the idiosyncratic content, though. When we correlate the psychophysical response reliefs of different observers we find that they correlate low on the silhouette rendering, higher on the cartoon rendering, and very high on the fully shaded renderings. This shows that the idiosyncratic content diminishes when information is added and that it is overridden by objectively specified structure. The being overridden is the same for all observers because it is due to structure that is in the picture and not in the head so to speak.

When the reader pages forward, it will appear that we often use human torsos as objects in our experiments. We do this because these are suitably "generic smooth" objects as opposed to the cuboids, cylinders, and ellipsoids that seem to dominate the literature. The latter are ill suited for the study of pictorial relief because they are highly nongeneric and degenerate. Many algorithms from ecological optics will not work or malfunction on such degenerate objects, whereas they work fine on generic ones. (For instance, the contours of ellipsoids are planar curves, so are the isophotes of shading. This is highly nongeneric.) When we present our work, there is invariably someone who will object that "we know what humans look like." This is true to some extent (of course we also know what cylinders and so forth look like). However, this "knowledge" seems to be mostly limited to the ability to name parts (limbs, major bones, and muscles). As anyone who ever attended a figure-drawing class knows, beginning students have surprisingly scant understanding of the human form. Anyhow, when we vary cues (for instance, shading) slightly, we notice changes in the pictorial relief. Apparently observers easily let pictorial cues override their superior knowledge of the human body. A study with computer-rendered random shapes (potato-like blobs with various bulges and cavities) confirms that the use of these torsos should give no cause for concern.

Because the fiducial scene is by no means singled out among the infinite set of scenes that could have led to the photograph, the issue of "veridicality" is really a nonissue. This is equally true for optical space, because there is hardly a difference between looking at pictures or at real scenes at the level of the radiance. Veridicality in perception becomes an interesting issue in the setting of perception and action—perhaps potential action—where the issue becomes one of the success or failure of optically guided, actual or potential, behavior. We strongly believe that the topic of veridicality can be safely ignored when the intrinsic structure of pictorial space is discussed. However, the reader be warned that we have been severely criticized for this offbeat standpoint.

Recent progress in the analysis of optical information ("cues") has revealed the structure of the set of scenes that correspond to certain cues (Belhumeur, Kriegman, and Yuille 1999; Faugeras 1993; Koenderink and van Doorn 1997). Such analyses are only available for a small number of cues and rather strong assumptions to constrain the problem and make it tractable. We find that the "solutions" are mutually related by certain "ambiguity transformations" that change the scene but leave the photograph (the bouquet of cues) invariant. Such transformed scenes are obviously equally "valid" interpretations of the photograph. These ambiguities are not (indeed, by their very definition) specified by the photograph, but the observer has perfect freedom to select one and thus arrive at a unique interpretation of the photograph. Such selection is by its nature fully idiosyncratic. We will refer to it (as in Gombrich 1959) as the "beholder's share."

12.2   METHODS TO OPERATIONALIZE PICTORIAL RELIEF

The first problem we have to face in the study of "pictorial relief" is how to "measure it." The way we phrase it here perhaps *sounds* reasonable but actually puts you on the wrong foot. The problem is that in order to measure something that "something" has to exist independently of the act of measuring. If the something is operationally defined (by the measurement) you don't measure it, but rather the measurement *creates* "it."

It is a priori evident that methods of measuring physical quantities will not be applicable to the case of pictorial space, because pictorial space is a mental entity. Likewise, physiological methods (electrophysiology, functional brain imaging, etc.) are by their nature unable to address the problem. Pictorial relief is a mental entity and thus can only be probed via mental operations. An example would be to have an observer describe the pictorial space verbally or in terms of an artistic statement. Although such methods certainly have their advantages, they are hardly suited to arrive at a body of quantitative, parametric data.

At the next level we may ask the observer for magnitude estimates of "depth" or "surface attitude" (slant and tilt) and so forth of pictorial points or surface elements. Such (verbal) estimates are judged to be extremely difficult by typical observers and, what is worse, they yield very variable responses (Mingolla and Todd 1986). Much easier are judgments of relative magnitudes, such as "nearer" or "more distant" (Koenderink, van Doorn, and Kappers 1996). Here we may establish fairly well-defined discrimination thresholds under various, parametrically varied, conditions. Such methods helped to make up most of the classical corpus of scientific data on the topic, and they remain important to this day.

A problem with these classical methods that is hardly recognized in the literature is that (discrimination) thresholds don't yield any handle on what the observers actually *experience*. Another problem is that it is prohibitive to collect the really rich data sets we desire, say the equivalent of an elaborate description, such as a fairly fine triangulation, of pictorial relief. These data are indeed desirable because they would enable us to perform calculations of a differential geometric nature and thus relate apparently disparate data sets. For instance, you might want to predict curvature data from attitude data through differentiation. But the operation of differentiation requires a fine-grained description. There is preciously little one can *do* with sparse data. In figures 12.5 and 12.6 we show an example of what we mean by a "rich data set." Here the response is essentially a *surface*.

What is needed are methods that go beyond thresholds, yet avoid the problems that bedevil absolute magnitude estimates, and that are *fast,* that is, enable us to collect hundreds or thousands of data points within a reasonable time span, such as an hour. Indeed, a picture may be roughly characterized through at least 10 by 10 (100) to a 100 by a 100 (10,000) samples, and a single experimental session cannot last for more than roughly an hour (that is less than 10,000 seconds). Thus we need methods that allow us to collect a data point at least every few seconds for periods up to not much more than an hour. This evidently eliminates both magnitude judgments, where observers say, "hmm, . . . , well, . . ." for a minute per data point, and threshold measurements, which require a full psychometric curve—at least a 100 yes/no judgments—per data point. It cannot be stressed enough that powerful methods to address pictorial relief have to be based on methods that yield rich data, essentially "fields of estimates." For instance, a dense field of depth estimates can be considered a "surface," that is, a true geometrical entity, whereas a mere handful of

Figure 12.5
(*Left*) a stimulus with two superimposed gauge figures. Notice that the white one "fits," and the black one doesn't. (*Right*) Result of one-half hour's work: a dense field of gauge figure settings.

depth values is nothing but a (geometrically) meaningless bunch of numbers. But—mirabile dictu—the literature doesn't acknowledge this basic fact.

Suitable methods are methods of reproduction, methods of adjustment, and methods of fit. In a "method of adjustment" the observer is asked to adjust some pointer such as to indicate a direction, curvature, and so on, of pictorial relief (see figure 12.7, left). The pointer may be superimposed on the picture at the location of the sample. For instance, an arrow at a certain location may be rotated so as to indicate the direction of the depth gradient of pictorial relief at the position in pictorial space corresponding to the location of the arrow in the picture.

In a "method of reproduction" the observer has to "reproduce" some pictorial entity in terms of another entity, perhaps in a different pictorial space. For example, the observer may be asked to reproduce a depth difference as a stretch in the frontoparallel plane or to reproduce a section of a pictorial surface with a plane that extends purely in depth in the frontoparallel plane (Koenderink et al. 2000b). (See figure 12.7, center.)

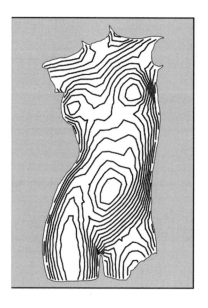
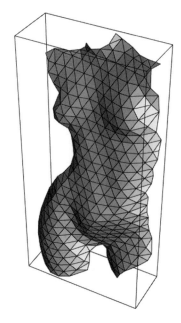

Figure 12.6
The result from the attitude sampling can be integrated to a depth field (*left*) or a
"pictorial relief" (surface in three-dimensional space) (*right*).

Notice that the slider bar might as well have been plotted outside the
picture frame proper.

In a "method of fit" an observer is asked to change the appearance of a
"gauge figure" in such a way that it "fits" the pictorial relief (see figure
12.7, right).

The method of fit is especially interesting because the judgment of fit
applies to *pictorial space* proper and to nothing external to it. This is not
true for the other methods, which introduce alien elements (markers,
pointers, etc.) that don't properly belong to pictorial space but are graphi-
cal elements superimposed upon the picture that may (like the punctate markers or the arrow) or may not (like the slider bar) relate to the
graphics sustaining pictorial space.

An instance of the method of fit that we have exploited frequently
(the method of fit is much more generally applicable, though) is the measurement of surface attitude (Koenderink, van Doorn, and Kappers 1992).
(See figures 12.7, right, and figure 12.8.) We superimpose a gauge figure
that is under control of the observer, who is supposed to adjust it in such

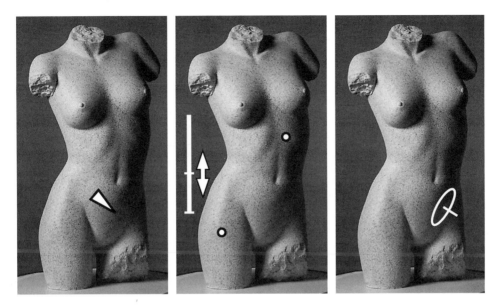

Figure 12.7
(*Left*) example of a method of adjustment. Notice that the arrow exists in the picture plane, not in pictorial space. (*Center*) example of a method of reproduction. Although the punctate markers seem to lie on the pictorial surface, the slider bar is in the picture plane and seems fully unrelated to pictorial space. (*Right*) example of a method of fit. The "gauge figure" belongs to pictorial space and relates to pictorial objects.

a way that it "clings to the pictorial surface." From the setting we derive numerical values of slant and tilt, but at no time the observer is required to estimate or even distinguish between slant and tilt. The task is simply to establish a fit in pictorial space. Observers find this an easy (almost trivial) task, whereas they are hard put to estimate slant and tilt values when asked to do so.

We belabor this point because it is so often misconstrued. It is not that the observer has to estimate the attitude of the pictorial surface and of the gauge figure *separately* and somehow make them become equal. The task is simply to produce a *fit,* and the slant and tilt never enter into this. The fit can be judged cheerfully within a small fraction of a second, whereas observers take up to a minute to estimate slant and tilt explicitly—and bitterly complain about that task. What is important here is that the method of fit requires only judgments that are intrinsic to pictorial space. This important fact is generally misunderstood. For instance, people have

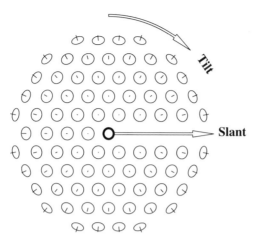

Figure 12.8
Gauge figures used to probe spatial attitude of pictorial surface elements. Parameters are the slant and tilt angles. The array shows a "natural" planar interface: a polar diagram with slant as radius and tilt as orientation.

studied the judgment of slant and tilt of a gauge figure in isolation and used the result to "correct" the results of the fit method. It is entirely unclear that such a procedure is at all reasonable unless one is ready to take very strong and—to our mind—unlikely prior assumptions for granted. It seems much more reasonable to take the results of the method of fit as an "operational definition" of pictorial relief and to take the work on gauge figures in isolation as (perhaps interesting) essentially *un-related* data. In order to relate such initially unrelated data, one stands in need of some theory. The theory itself is subject to empirical verification of course.

Local and Global

An important distinction to be made is that between judgments of properties that exist at a single location of pictorial space, we call these "local" properties, and judgments that require the comparison of properties that simultaneously exist at two or more disparate locations, we will refer to these as "global" properties. The difference is important for the practical reason that observers tend to have little problems with local tasks but find global tasks extremely difficult to perform. It is also important because of conceptual reasons. It is not at all clear that freedom to compare properties at different locations in pictorial space should exist at all. This is up

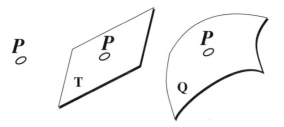

Figure 12.9
The relief in the neighborhood of a point *P* in the zeroth-order (leftmost, only location), first-order (center, tangent plane *T* added), and second-order (rightmost, "osculating quadric" *Q* added) approximation.

to empirical verification. After all "pictorial space" is virgin territory and it is quite unknown whether objects can be moved about and brought into close vicinity of each other for the sake of easy comparison, with the mad abandon they can in Euclidian space. We certainly should avoid far-reaching prior assumptions here. Otherwise the conclusions aren't worth more than the assumptions.

Orders of Differentiation

When "pictorial relief" is a more or less smooth surface, like the surface of a polished marble sculpture, then it should be possible to speak sensibly of various "orders of approximation" to the surface (Koenderink 1990). (See figure 12.9.) In the "zeroth order" we merely indicate the location of a point on the surface. Thus we know where the surface is, but we don't know its attitude, let alone its curvature, and so forth. In the "first-order" approximation we also know the attitude of the tangent plane at the point. Then we know both the location and the orientation of the surface, but not its curvature, and so forth. In the "second-order" approximation we know in addition the "osculating quadric" of the surface. Then we know the location, attitude, and (local) shape of the surface. The local shape is defined via the directions of principal curvature and these principal curvatures themselves, and so forth, for the still higher orders.

When we indicate a point in the picture (two degrees of freedom, e.g., Cartesian coordinates), the zeroth order gives another degree of freedom (the depth, a third Cartesian coordinate), the first order adds two degrees of freedom (e.g., the slant and tilt angles of the surface), and the second order adds another three degrees of freedom (the direction of the maximum curvature and the two principal curvatures, e.g.).

Figure 12.10
"Integratability constraints." On the left, the "deck of cards" example. Second from the left, a case where a field of tangent planes can easily be integrated to a closed ribbon. For the case second from the right, this doesn't work (the planar elements at the endpoints are at different depths). The case on the right is different: the planar facets at the endpoints have different spatial attitudes. In order to obtain a "fit," the field of planar elements has to be quite special.

Of course the observer might also be sensitive to a higher-order (say, curvature) and insensitive to lower order(s) (for instance, depth and slant). This is up to empirical verification. When such would turn out to be the case, there should be little reason for surprise. After all, the human observer is exquisitely sensitive to luminance contrast but rather insensitive to the absolute luminance level. Cases like these are frequent in human perception.

Reference to the order of approximation is very practical, because most methods yield estimates of properties of only a certain order. Estimates of depth sample only the zeroth order, the method of fit described earlier samples the first order, and so forth. Notice that the order of approximation applies only to purely local methods.

By *differentiation* of a field of local estimates, you obtain a prediction for the next *higher* order (thus depth estimates allow a prediction of surface slant and tilt). By *integration* of a field of estimates, you obtain the next *lower* order up to indeterminate additive constants. Thus surface attitude estimates allow the prediction of a depth field up to some unknown depth shift. In the latter case there is a little, but important, twist in that it is not necessarily possible to perform the integration at all, unless the initial estimates satisfy some constraint (Spivak 1975). For instance, the playing cards in a deck are "local attitude estimates" (see figure 12.10, left) but clearly don't allow of an integral surface. In this case it means that you gain a check on "surface consistency" (see figure 12.10).

Differentiation takes you from global to local, whereas integration takes you from local to global. Thus there exist a great many possibilities of comparison of apparently qualitatively different results. The important condition is that you need rich enough data, that is to say, "fields" of estimates, rather than mere point samples. This is the main reason the classical results have remained essentially barren. There is simply no way to compare results of different experiments in interesting ways. Of course the literature doesn't acknowledge this fundamental fact, because it is not concerned with rich data sets in the first place.

Cognition versus Perception

"Perception"—visual perception, that is—is best defined as "optically guided potential behavior." Notice that a well-known definition in biology "optically guided behavior" will not do for us, because it admits pure reflex action as "vision" and has no place for consciousness, which is why our definition was framed as it is of course. Because pictorial space is a mental entity, we cannot talk about it except in the context of consciousness. Our definition manages to catch that, yet remains squarely in the realm of objective science.

Potential behavior can be probed through variation of the observer's goals. When the behavior correlates with the optical structure over arbitrary goal variations, we may say that the observer behaves in a certain way because he or she has certain goals and because he or she knew certain facts due to optical interaction ("saw something"). Notice that this is simply the commonsense definition. When you hear the public address system at an airport make some announcement and see people do various things that may differ according to their goals in response to the sound, you know they both heard and *understood* the announcement and did not react reflexively, as they might have in response to the sound of a sudden explosion. Reflex actions are stereotypical, whereas actualized potential actions can be virtually *anything,* depending on the present goals. It might seem a drawback of the definition that it applies only to observers for whom you can influence the goals, for example, by promising payment in return for their efforts. Thus you can't probe visual perception of Martians or mollusks, although these may well display optically guided behavior. Indeed, psychophysics, as opposed to physiology, implies a certain degree of "empathy."

Though observers may show indications of visual perception, they need not necessarily be able to verbalize their percepts, nor need they be able to use the percepts in overt reasoning. For example, cats and dogs clearly perceive yet are not capable of such cognitive acts. In fact, the result of overt reasoning is not a perception in the proper sense. This is an important point because some methods require overt reasoning or verbalization (e.g., "call out slant and tilt in degrees for yonder surface patch") whereas others don't (e.g., "make that gauge figure fit that surface"). Moreover, some observers may be rather immediately "optically guided," whereas others seem to reason out what to do. For instance, in the gauge figure fitting task they might actually make overt estimates in degrees, reason out the shape of the gauge figure for those estimates, then change the gauge figure to that form.

We find (purely empirically) that observers typically fall into two distinct classes. Observers from one class take a second or so for a gauge figure setting, the others at least 10 to a 100 times as long. Practice doesn't change this, the "fast" ones don't need any practice at all, and the "slow" ones never "learn" anyway. This observation strongly suggests that *such observers function quite differently*. Moreover, some implementations of certain tasks almost *force* observers to switch from perceptual to cognitive strategies. For instance, when you interface the attitude gauge figure in such a way that the observer has to set slant/tilt in Cartesian coordinates instead of the more natural polar way (Pollick et al. 1992), the task becomes an almost impossible one and requires much careful thinking. Ever try to write your name with an *XY*-movement device? Though such details may seem irrelevant, indeed often go unmentioned in publications, they are really crucial.

In our work we carefully optimize the interfaces and we select observers (simply by ignoring the—very small—group that takes at least an order of magnitude longer at the task than most others will) to ensure that we address perceptual, rather than cognitive, issues. As a rule of thumb a setting shouldn't take more than a few seconds at most and should feel "natural" so that the observer almost effortlessly keeps at the task for a half hour at a stretch. In such cases as when settings take longer than a few seconds at most and observers complain that something is seriously awry, we would hesitate to accept the results as very informative.

It makes sense to check for such things in the method sections of papers, though the issue is rarely addressed. Yet any reasoning on the part of the observer may introduce spurious elements (see later discussion). This consideration, although rarely mentioned, is far more important than the number of observers, whether they are naive, and so on, factors based on which reviewers of research papers conventionally rate the scientific merit of manuscripts.

The Meaning of a "Measurement"

When you have to measure the temperature in a bucket of water you are for once in good shape. For physics has developed a theory of many types of potential thermometers and—even more important—you may rest assured that "the temperature" *exists* even if you don't measure it and that various methods to measure will lead to the same result for that very reason. Things can work out quite differently in other fields. For instance, the measurement of cosmological distances is difficult because the concept of "distance" may be different on scales we're not accustomed to and because the various methods sometimes lead to different results. If so, which one is right? Is any of them right? Does "being right" have a meaning at all?

The measurement of properties of pictorial space are in yet another category. It is by no means a priori clear that "surface attitude," say, exists before the act of measurement. The act of measurement creates a novel state of affairs for the observer that yields a certain result, for instance, a number. Thus different methods to measure it need not refer to the same property, at least not in principle; this is up to empirical verification. The numbers you obtain should be labeled with the method by which they were obtained, for they are only operationally defined.

Failure to grasp this basic point has led to numerous misunderstandings in the literature where things are typically labeled with familiar terms ("depth," "slant," etc.) without any further indexing by method. But there may exist *numerous* "depths" and there is no a priori reason they should correspond. To think that they "should" is to assume that pictorial space exists in the same way that a bucket of water does. That is clearly preposterous, at least to us. Many experts in the field think differently though, the reader be warned.

Notice that this argument indicates that we should not look for any single "best" method to measure pictorial relief. For best has no meaning here. Instead, it seems most appropriate to work with as extensive a battery of methods as possible and to look upon the comparison of different methods to measure "the same" entity as a valuable research tool by itself.

Rather similar problems arise when measurements of *different* properties are compared. For instance, although you can indeed obtain surface attitude by differentiation of a depth field in *Euclidian space,* the same operation may turn out to be baseless in pictorial space. Again, these are empirical issues. Pictorial space is an entity to be explored, and we should be wary of attributing properties to it (most probably similar to those of our trusty Euclidian space) without explicit empirical evidence. Again, ignoring this basic point has led to numerous unfortunate misunderstandings in the literature. This is also one reason observers in the "cognitive mode" may yield results that differ from those from observers in the "perceptual" mode. The former observers typically apply (perhaps unknowingly) knowledge of Euclidian relations to change the task into "equivalent" tasks that they find easier to perform. For instance, they may assume that two angles of an isosceles triangle have to be equal, although there is no a priori reason this should be the case in the visual field.

That we seem to be consciously aware of globally consistent pictorial surfaces when we look into a straight photograph of a piece of sculpture is a feeling that need not necessarily be corroborated empirically. It may well be the case that various, mutually incompatible, representations are simultaneously present in our subconscious; that our awareness merely glosses over this, not resolving ambiguity when the task doesn't call for it; and that our awareness simply selects an appropriate representation for the task at hand. Then the inconsistencies would not necessarily be noticed, and results obtained by different methods may well turn out to be mutually inconsistent. If such possibilities exist, and indeed, neurophysiological findings seem to indicate that this is most likely, then the result of a measurement need not exist in the mind before the very act of measurement. We are at far remove indeed from the measurement of the temperature of a bucket of water.

12.3   PRELIMINARY EMPIRICAL FINDINGS

A simple method to operationalize pictorial relief is by way of surface attitude measurements (see figures 12.5 and 12.6). Observers can easily produce 1,000 samples per hour with the gauge figure fitting method. In practice we perform measurements at the barycenters of a regular triangulation. The triangulation remains hidden to the observer. Measurements are done in random order, one at a time. This produces the attitude or depth gradient of the faces of the triangulation. We then assign depth values to the vertices in such a triangulation in order to "explain" the depth gradients of the faces in the best possible way. These depth values are only determined up to an arbitrary common constant. The residual difference between the depth gradients explained by the depths at the vertices and the actual measurements may be due to either of two factors. One is the intrinsic uncertainty in the measurements, which can easily be

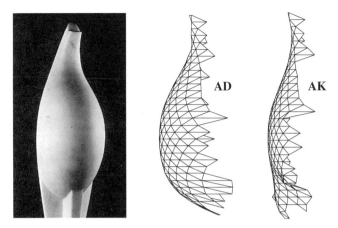

Figure 12.11
On the left, the stimulus; on the right, two pictorial reliefs from different observers. Depth runs to the right. Notice that the reliefs are different and differ mainly by a depth stretch.

estimated from the scatter in repeated trials. The other is a possible "inconsistency." The empirical depth gradients may actually turn out to be incompatible with *any* surface. We have found that the residuals can be explained from the scatter in repeated trials. Thus (most remarkably) the local attitude samples are invariably compatible with a surface. This "pictorial relief" thus explains the results from local attitude samples.

We may consider the pictorial relief to be the "psychophysical response" to the stimulus, that is, the picture. Two pictorial reliefs may be compared in many different ways. A way that is often useful is to simply look at a scatter plot of all the depth values at corresponding points in the picture. When the correlation is high, the slope is a relevant entity; it specifies a depth magnification between the two reliefs. We find that when we test the same observer repeatedly over a long period, the coefficients of determination ("R-squares") are in the 99% ballpark and slopes vary unpredictably by factors of up to 15%. When different observers are compared, the coefficients of determination are also quite high (R-squares typically over 95%), but the slopes may differ by a factor of two or more. What this means is that observers typically generate the same pictorial relief modulo an idiosyncratic depth stretch (figure 12.11). With respect to the notion of veridicality, we conclude that the responses of at least one (but probably both) observers cannot be veridical in the naive sense.

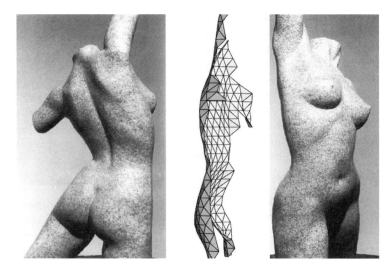

Figure 12.12
On the left, the stimulus, and in the center, a pictorial relief with depth increasing
toward the right. On the right, a picture of the actual scene taken at right angles
with respect to the viewing direction for the stimulus. "Naive veridicality" would
imply identity of the outlines of the relief (*center*) and picture of the rotated object
(*right*). Clearly it does not pertain.

As expected, the pictorial reliefs we find are superficially similar to the
actual object at the time of exposure of the photograph but (often very)
significantly different in detail (figure 12.12). Notice that we cannot draw
any conclusions as to veridicality from this, because there is no easy way
to find out whether the pictorial reliefs generated by the observers indicate
objects that might have yielded the photograph. In a trivial way they
always might; that is, when you allow the object to be painted ad libitum,
then a trompe l'oeil painting would fit the bill. Thus the problem has to be
suitably constrained in order to have it make sense at all. We consider the
issue of veridicality irrelevant in this context.

Viewing Modes

When a method such as the one discussed yields a pictorial relief as psychophysical response to a photograph (the stimulus), we may study the
stimulus-response relation over a large number of parametric variations
of both the stimulus and the viewing conditions. In this section we consider the variation of viewing conditions.

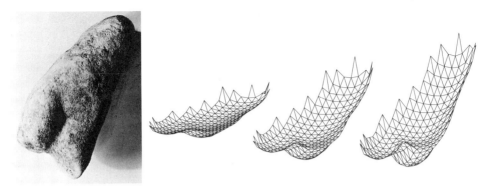

Figure 12.13
Stimulus and three pictorial reliefs, from left to right, with binocular, monocular, and synoptical (see figure 12.14) viewing. In these pictures the depth dimension is vertically upward. Notice the differences in total depth range and qualitative similarity of shape.

When only the viewing conditions are changed, the photograph is invariant and so are all cues that relate to pictorial space. It is only the cues that relate to the photograph as an object in optical space that are varied. In conventional language we may speak of a "cue conflict" situation. Because the observers are always simultaneously aware of both the optical space that contains the photograph as a physical object and the pictorial space that exists as a completely disparate entity, cue conflict is perhaps an unfortunate term, as it suggests that different cues are in conflict with respect to the resolution of a single entity. However that may be, it is evident that a change of viewing conditions, such as viewing monocularly versus binocularly, looking straight at the photograph versus viewing it at an oblique angle, and so forth, affects the cues that relate to the photograph as a flat object in optical space. They do not affect the cues that relate to pictorial space.

We find that such changes in viewing conditions have a strong influence on pictorial relief (see figures 12.13 and 12.14). As perhaps expected, the relief remains qualitatively the same—after all, the pictorial cues are identical. What happens is that pictorial space suffers a "depth stretch," whose amount is immediately correlated with the viewing condition. We find that the depth of pictorial relief is expanded by factors up to two when the observer changes from binocular to monocular vision by closing one eye, assuming normal binocular stereopsis. Similarly, we find that depth of

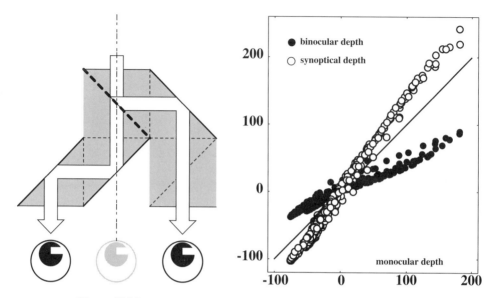

Figure 12.14
(*Left*) the principle of the "Synopter." Left and right eyes are optically super-imposed into a single "cyclopean eye." (*Right*) Scatter plot of depths at corresponding points of the reliefs shown in figure 12.13. Notice the nice, clean linear correlation. The differences are a mere depth dilation or contraction.

pictorial relief increases by factors up to two depending upon the obliquity when the observer moves from an oblique vantage point to a normal one.

When we allow the observer to look with both eyes but introduce an optical mechanism that removes the disparity by superimposing the centers of rotation of the eyes optically, depth of relief increases by factors up to two over that obtained with monocular viewing. With such "synoptic viewing," we have found increases of up to a factor of five over binocular viewing (Koenderink, van Doorn, and Kappers 1994). (See figures 12.13 and 12.14.) Indeed, the change in pictorial relief brought about by such a "synopter" is a striking one and has been commented on before (Carl Zeiss Jena 1907).

Cue Variation

When we fix viewing conditions, for example, monocular viewing, and vary the photograph we expect qualitative changes of the pictorial relief. If such changes do not occur, or are only minor, we may well use conventional terminology and speak of "constancy."

A particularly interesting class of experiments is that in which the geometry of the scene is kept fixed. We use photographs of an object with fixed pose and fixed camera position. Changes in the resulting photograph, then, are brought about through changes in lighting, background, or surface properties of the object. In such cases the changes in pictorial relief can easily be correlated with changes in the scene.

In one particular study (figures 12.15 through 12.17) we change the direction of the main light source in the scene. The resulting photographs look greatly different, though geometrically identical. We find that the pictorial reliefs are very similar despite the differences in appearance, thus revealing a remarkable "shape constancy" with respect to large variations in shading. However, closer analysis reveals that—superimposed over the constancy—there remain minor but clearly significant variations in the relief that are correlated with the changes in illumination direction. These residuals are *qualitative changes* of the relief, rather than mere variations of the depth of relief. An intuitive way to describe the nature of these changes is to say that protrusions of the relief tend to point in the direction of the light source.

As a general point of methodology, we find that such parametric variation of a single cue as one component of a full bouquet of cues, and subsequent correlation of the response with the parametric variation, is a much better way to study the importance of particular cues than the traditional reductionist method of cue isolation. Many cues cannot be studied properly in isolation at all, because they only contain useful information in a setting that includes other cues. An instance is the shading cue just referred to, which is essentially inoperative in the absence of contours (Erens, Kappers, and Koenderink 1991, 1993). The nature of a specific cue is most properly studied when the "set point," to borrow a term from systems engineering, is a natural one. This is an important consideration because most of the literature on cues either uses the method of reduction, that is, to bring cues in isolation, or cue conflict, that is, to "pit cues against each other." Neither method allows one to confront the observer with pictures that would ever be considered anything close to "normal" by naive people. Common sense suggests that it may be prudent to prefer the more "natural" stimuli.

Local versus Global

The pictorial relief as operationalized via the gauge figure set method is an example of a global geometrical entity, a surface in a three-dimensional

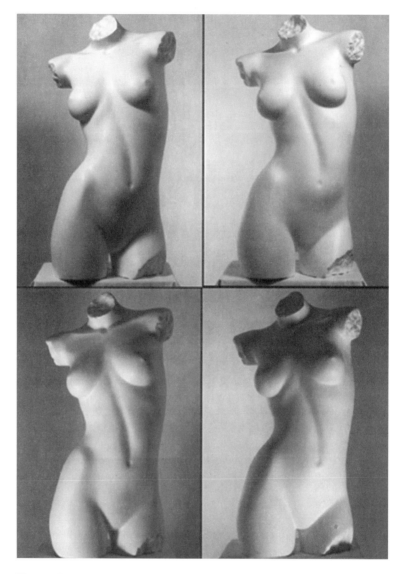

Figure 12.15
Four stimuli with identical geometry but different chiaroscuro. The illumination is from top left in the top left figure; in the top right figure it is from the top right; in the bottom left figure it is from bottom left; and the bottom right figure is illuminated from the bottom right.

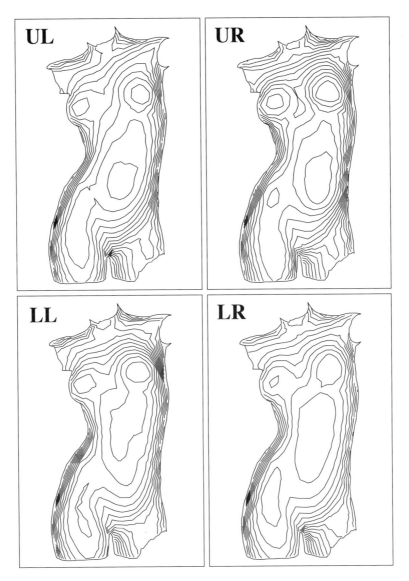

Figure 12.16
The pictorial reliefs obtained from the stimuli shown in figure 12.15 for a single observer. The curves are loci of constant pictorial depth.

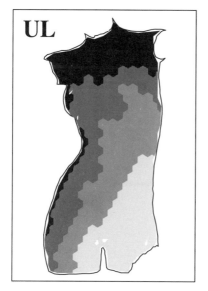
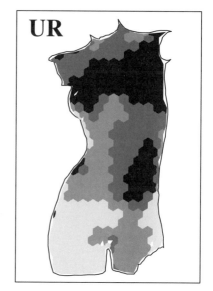
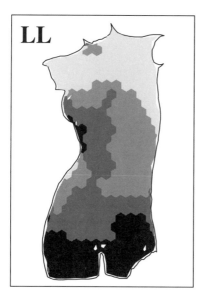
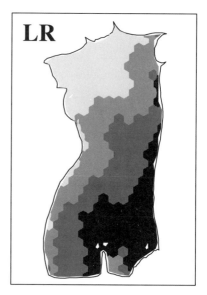

Figure 12.17
The residuals for the pictorial reliefs of a single observer (shown in figure 12.16) obtained with the stimuli shown in figure 12.15. Notice that the distribution is systematic, rather than random. The pattern of deviations from the mean of the four reliefs depends systematically upon the direction of illumination of the scene.

space, that has been obtained via the integration of many (a field of) local samples of surface attitudes. The local settings are the immediate result of the observer's efforts; the integration is done only after all settings are completed, via a mechanical process of numerical integration. Remember that the settings are obtained in random order, quite independently of each other. It is an empirical question whether the surface as a global entity is available to the observer, in the sense of being a causal factor in the successful completion of some task, or not. A priori this availability is not necessary to the observer's success, even though all the necessary data to determine the global surface (the individual settings) are evidently available to the observer in the sense that they are produced when the observer is asked to perform the gauge figure fitting task.

In order to establish whether the observer has access to the global surface as an integral entity, we need a task of a global nature. A possibility that we have explored (Koenderink and van Doorn 1995) is to put two punctate marks on the photograph and let the observer decide which of the marks appears nearer in depth. The marks are on the photograph, but they are seen in pictorial space and they appear to be *located on the pictorial surface*. They don't appear to hover in front of the pictorial surface, for instance. Thus the task is accepted as a natural one by all observers. When we fix one mark and vary the location of the other mark, we can explore the probability of the observer's judging the mark "nearer" in a two-alternative forced choice task ("nearer/farther"). When the observer has access to the integral surface, we expect the result to be almost binary. For the mark should be closer with 100% probability if the mark on the global surface is nearer than the fiducial mark, and it should be closer with 0% probability in case it is farther away. Only on the curve on the surface that is the locus of points all equal in depth to the fiducial mark do we expect probabilities of intermediate values. The task should be a trivial one. Here is how to do it: simply threshold the integral surface at the depth of the fiducial mark.

But this is not at all what we find (see figures 12.18 and 12.19). We find that the depth order of any two marks can be established with some degree of certainty *only* in cases where the points can be joined by a path that either goes into depth or toward the observer, but not when such paths don't exist and there is a hill or valley that separates the points (see figure 12.19). It is as if the observers can only check whether the direction of the gradient at nearby points matches up. Thus the pictorial relief as a global geometrical entity is not available to the observers, even

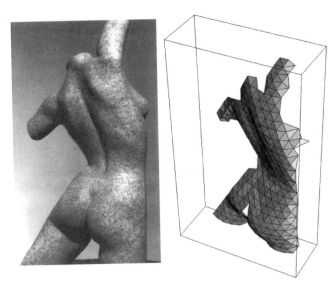

Figure 12.18
(*Left*) A stimulus. (*Right*) The pictorial relief as measured via gauge figure fits.

though a field of local data that is sufficient to determine the global entity was obtained psychophysically and is thus *in principle* available to the observers.

This is a very important and perhaps somewhat surprising finding. There is much information (or structure?) in the brain that is not available to our consciousness. What enters the brain need not enter the mind.

Task Variation

When the task is varied for the same picture and viewing conditions, we have a case in which the "freedom" of the observer is constrained by the picture, that is to say, the bouquet of cues. Though we may expect different results from different tasks, all these results should be compatible with the cues. We have found a particularly surprising example (Koenderink et al. 2000b) of a pair of similar tasks that turn out to yield spectacularly different results (see below). We use a method of reproduction that requires the observer to produce a (global) "normal section" of a pictorial object. A normal section is defined as the intersection of the pictorial object with a plane that contains the visual direction. In the picture, such a plane can be represented through a straight line. In the paradigm we simply draw such a line over the picture and let the observer produce the shape of the

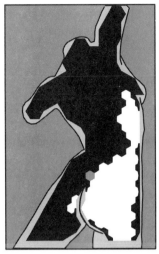

Figure 12.19
(*Left*) Prediction of the probability for any point to be closer than the fiducial point (gray hexagonal dot) arrived at by thresholding the pictorial relief obtained from a gauge figure fitting method. (*Center*) Prediction on the basis of depth gradient following. (*Right*) The actual probabilities obtained empirically. Notice that the result is perhaps closer to the latter than the former prediction, although the observer can do the global task to *some* extent.

intersection in a drawing (another picture) that represents the plane of the section. Thus we have a paradigm where the response to a stimulus (a picture) is another picture, one that contains a curved line (the curve of intersection). The whole procedure is suitably constrained in order to enforce reproducible results.

The lines in the stimulus picture may have any orientation. The difference in the two tasks lies in the orientation of the drawing. Notice that the picture plane can be represented by a straight line in the drawing. In one variation of the task, this line is always parallel to the line that represents the cut in the picture. Here we mean parallelism in the visual field, which contains both the stimulus picture and the drawing in a single plane. In another variation of the task, the line that represents the picture plane in the drawing is always horizontal (see figure 12.20).

We find, perhaps surprisingly, that a straight scatter plot of pictorial depths at corresponding points obtained with these two tasks reveals no significant correlation (see figure 12.21, left). Thus the pictorial reliefs obtained with the two tasks are not related by a depth stretch. When we

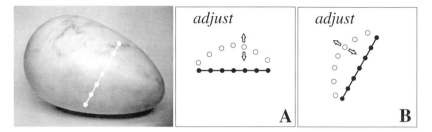

Figure 12.20
The method of reproduction of normal sections. The observers have to drag points in an auxiliary (A or B) orthogonally to the line.

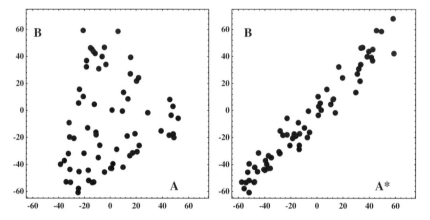

Figure 12.21
(*Left*) A straight scatter plot of the depths at corresponding points obtained with methods A and B. (*Right*) Result of a multiple regression including the picture plane coordinates.

perform a multivariate regression on the pictorial depths *and the Cartesian picture plane coordinates,* we find very significant correlations with coefficients of determination of over 95% (see figure 12.21, right). This shows that the pictorial reliefs may be different but also that the difference is of a special kind. There exists an affine transformation such that the reliefs are actually *identical modulo the affinity* (see figure 12.22).

In another example (figures 12.23 and 12.24) we show that the affinity may be far removed from the identity, in this example a shear of more than 60°! Thus the frontoparallel plane may be slanted by tens of degrees by such an affinity. This is a most remarkable finding. It means that

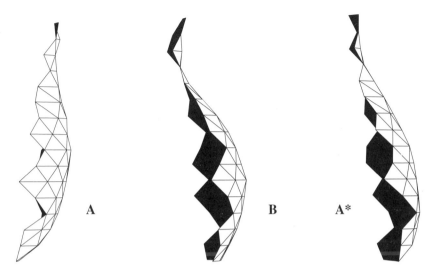

Figure 12.22
(*Left*) Pictorial relief (depth in the horizontal direction) obtained with method A. (*Center*) Pictorial relief for the same stimulus, obtained with method B. These reliefs produce the scatter plot shown in figure 12.21, left. (*Right*) The pictorial relief shown on the left after an affine transformation obtained via multiple regression including the picture plane coordinates (figure 12.21, right). Now the reliefs obtained with the two methods are nearly equal. Notice that the transformation looks much like a rotation (although it is a depth shear).

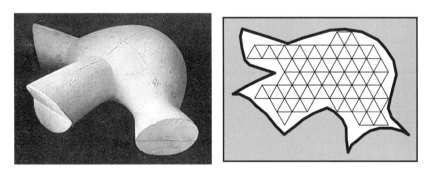

Figure 12.23
On the left the stimulus, a "turtle" by Constantin Brancusi; on the right, the (rather coarse) triangulation used in the study.

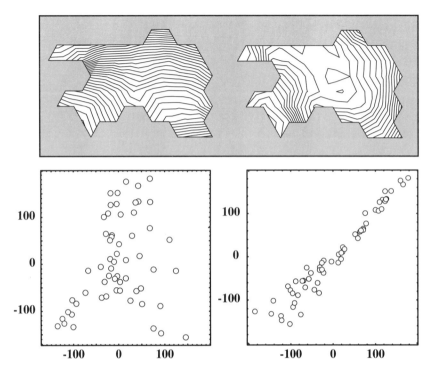

Figure 12.24
The pictorial reliefs (curves of constant pictorial depth, top row) for the picture shown in figure 12.23, left, and a single observer. Here the results are due to an apparently minor variation of the cross-section task. Notice that the frontoparallel points are completely different. In the bottom row we show a straight scatter plot of depth (*left*) and one with an affine correction. The affinity has the effect of raising the correlation from not significant to highly significant indeed.

even such a (at first blush well-defined and simple) geometrical property as "frontoparallelity" need not be well defined, and indeed may be extremely volatile with respect to minor task variations, in pictorial space. Such a result should be shocking when you have been led to believe that pictorial spaces due to photographs roughly resemble (in an Euclidean way) the physical scenes in front of the camera at the moment of exposure. They don't, at least not in any naive sense.

We have found such transformations even in the case of single task results. In such cases we sometimes find low correlations between observers. Scatter plots often reveal high correlations in certain areas of the picture. Apparently different transformations apply to different parts. An

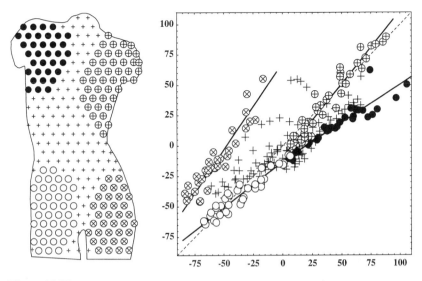

Figure 12.25
A comparison of pictorial reliefs for two observers (same task, same picture). The precise nature of the task is not important here; we find similar results with any task. In the scatter plot of depths (on the right) we detect discrete branches. On further analysis these correspond to contiguous regions ("parts") in the picture (figure at the left).

example is shown in figure 12.25. This observation indicates that things do not necessarily go on in a global, but rather in a piecewise, fashion, the pieces corresponding to "natural parts." We have reason to believe that observers use different "mental viewpoints" (see later discussion) for the different parts. This strategy is reminiscent of certain drawings by Picasso (Bouret 1950), where this artist combines various perspectives in a single drawing.

The Beholder's Share

The "beholder's share" is often an important factor in pictorial relief. We distinguish three essentially different classes of pictorial relief in which the beholder's share plays a decisive or at least quantitatively significant role:

1. In illusions of the "faces in the clouds" variety, the beholder's share is decisive. It may be called "creative imagination," perhaps somewhat checked by structures in the picture.

2. In cases of pictures that lack certain pieces of vital information, the observer's share must "fill in the blanks" (see figures 12.1 and 12.2). This

is also creative imagination, though much more thoroughly constrained by the picture. An example would be a silhouette of a human body. Although the picture may be clear enough in the sense that you see a human body in it, it remains essentially indeterminate whether the picture depicts a ventral or a dorsal view of a figure. Observers typically "perceive" the one or the other, though, not some kind of entity that is simultaneously a ventral and a dorsal view.

3. In straight photographs that would generally be considered "true" and "complete" pictures, the beholder's share has much less freedom. It is still the case that a picture is compatible with infinitely many physical scenes, though, and the beholder's share has certainly the freedom to roam through this huge space of equivalent interpretations of the picture and to select one as the present percept.

In the third case we may draw on the formal analysis of optical cues in order to predict the freedom left to the beholder's share.

12.4   THE STRUCTURE OF "PICTORIAL SPACE"

Does pictorial space have a similar structure to the space we move in? The latter will be taken as the conventional three-dimensional Euclidian space. Consider Euclidean space first. Euclidean space is infinitely extended and looks essentially the same anywhere. Any line can be extended indefinitely in either of its two directions and admits of an aperiodic, linear metric. In contradistinction, the angular metric of the Euclidean plane is periodic; the angles are confined to a finite range. In Euclidian space you can make a *full turn* and end up in the same orientation. The difference between the length and angle metrics precludes full duality between points and planes. Although three distinct points determine a unique plane, three different planes need not specify a unique point, because two of them may turn out to be parallel. Although there exist parallel lines and planes, you have no parallel *points* in Euclidian space, because *any* two points can be joined with a line. Thus Euclidian space is much less symmetric than for instance projective space. The group of orientation-preserving isometries (also known as congruences, or motions) of Euclidian space contains rotations and translations. "Euclidean shapes" are invariants under congruences. By definition, two objects have "the same shape" when they can be brought into superposition through a suitably chosen motion.

It is a priori evident that pictorial space is *not at all* like Euclidian space. For instance, the "visual rays" are different in character from lines in frontoparallel planes. The length metric cannot be the same for these lines.

You cannot make a full turn in pictorial space, for it will be forever impossible to obtain a dorsal view of a person (as pictorial object) when the picture is a photograph in a ventral view. Thus the angle metric must be aperiodic, like the length metric is. When we define pictorial lines as straight, one-dimensional entities that correspond to straight lines in the picture, then there exist "parallel points," namely, points that cannot be connected by any straight line. Such points coincide in the picture and thus fail to define a line in the picture. They lie on a single visual ray. But notice that the visual rays fail to count as proper pictorial lines because they do not correspond to any line in the picture.

Thus pictorial space is quite different from Euclidian space, and it becomes of much interest to establish its geometry in formal terms. The next few sections are devoted to this issue.

Hildebrand's Contribution

Hildebrand has to be considered the first person to establish a formal framework for pictorial space. He noticed that observers often fail to distinguish between flat relief and sculpture in the round. Thus he concluded that arbitrary depth dilations and contractions have to be considered either *congruences* or *similarities* of pictorial space.

This idea has immediate consequences for the formal analysis of "shapes" and "features" of pictorial objects. These must be invariants under arbitrary depth scalings. We have studied these invariants previously: they are the "depth flow" (Hildebrand's term, it means essentially the congruence of curves of fastest depth descent on pictorial surfaces), the near and far points (which are points on the pictorial relief where the local tangent planes are frontoparallel), the ridges (like "divides" of the flow) and ruts (the "courses" of the flow) (Koenderink and van Doorn 1995, 1998). Such features as ridges and ruts are indeed important features that have evidently been deployed by many sculptors. We can easily compute them for the pictorial reliefs we obtain empirically (see figure 12.26).

The Group of Congruences

Although Hildebrand evidently identified an important group of congruences or similarities, we don't think it is *complete,* and hence it is insufficient to fully define the structure of pictorial space. Indeed, although we have found numerous examples of the Hilbebrand type of ambiguities, we have found impressive evidence of a much larger group of such congruences, namely, the affinities mentioned earlier. It seems somewhat surprising to us that Hildebrand failed to mention these, because relief

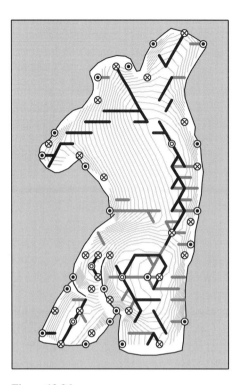

Figure 12.26
The Hildebrand invariants of pictorial relief in a particular case. Shown are near
points (circles with an open center dot), far points (circles with a filled center
dot), and saddle points (circles with a cross), as well as ridges (dark lines) and ruts
(gray lines). Near, far, and saddle points that don't appear on the boundary are
frontoparallel points.

sculpture involving such affinities is not particularly hard to find in Western art (Wittkower 1977).

A general argument that strongly suggests that the special group of
affinities mentioned earlier, which includes Hildebrand's depth scalings,
exhausts the pictorial congruences is the following. We use the fact that all
cues define shape only up to some group of ambiguities (see figure 12.27).
For convenience we assume orthographic projection throughout.

The key observation is that almost all cues allow the observer to distinguish planar from nonplanar surfaces. A typical example is "shape from
shading." In the usual setting, typically involving illumination with a
single parallel, collimated beam illuminating Lambertian surfaces, planes
give rise to uniform patches in the picture (Horn and Brooks 1989). Any

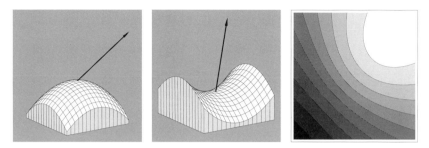

Figure 12.27
An example of the ambiguities associated with "shape from shading." The convex
and the saddle-shaped surface patch can be illuminated in such ways (the illumination direction is indicated by the arrows) that a picture (taken vertically downward) turns out to be identical for both of them (the figure on the right).

Figure 12.28
The patches on the left and center are uniform. The shape from shading inference
is that they are planar, though their spatial attitudes are indeterminate. The patch
on the right reveals some nonuniformity; thus it cannot be planar.

nonplanarity induces nonuniformity, such as a shadow, highlight, or a
combination of these, and can thus easily be detected (see figure 12.28).
We may conclude that planes should be conserved as a family by congruences and similarities, though not necessarily on an individual basis. Of
course the congruences have to respect the structure of the picture as a
planar surface too; thus the "pixels" or "visual rays" have to be conserved
on an individual basis (see figure 12.29). It is remarkable that these generic constraints fully determine the group of congruences. No additional
arguments are required. When $\{x, y\}$ denotes the picture plane Cartesian
coordinates, and z the depth, then the similarities are

$$x' = e^{\mu}(\cos \phi x - \sin \phi y) + \tau_x,$$

$$y' = e^{\mu}(\sin \phi x + \cos \phi y) + \tau_y,$$

$$z' = \sigma_x x + \sigma_y y + e^{\gamma} z + \delta,$$

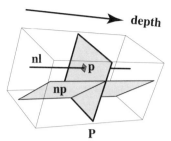

Figure 12.29
"Normal lines" (denoted *nl,* these correspond to the pixels, e.g., *p* in the picture plane *P*) and "normal planes" (denoted *np,* these are straight lines in the picture plane *P*) are invariants of pictorial space.

where we have included arbitrary Euclidian similarities of the picture plane for convenience. The Euclidian similarities of the picture plane are a homothety of magnification $\exp(\mu)$, a rotation over an angle ϕ, and a translation by τ_x in the x and τ_y in the y directions. This Euclidean similarity (or Euclidean motion in the case $\mu = 0$) is augmented by a number of true pictorial space transformations. These are a shift δ in depth (which is really irrelevant because it can't be addressed empirically), a depth magnification of the Hildebrand type $\exp(\gamma)$, and a shear about a plane containing the visual direction (σ_x, σ_y).

Notice that you obtain the identity transform when you set all parameters to zero. The concatenation of any two of these transformations is equivalent to a third of the same. For any of these transformations, you can find another one that "undoes" it. Thus these transformations constitute a group.

This is an eight-parameter group. For $\mu = \gamma = 0$ we obtain a six-parameter group of motions or "congruences." When we ignore the Euclidian similarities in the picture plane ($\mu = \phi = \tau_x = \tau_y = 0$), we obtain a four-dimensional group of essential pictorial similarities. This is the group that should replace the one suggested by Hildebrand. You easily verify the group properties in all cases.

Notice that the coefficient γ describes the Hildebrand-type depth scalings, whereas the coefficients σ_x, σ_y describe the affinities we described earlier (figure 12.30). These are of quite different types, the former being a similarity, the latter a congruence.

In figure 12.31 we illustrate some congruent objects in pictorial space. Notice that the shears ("rotations" in pictorial space, shears in the Euclid-

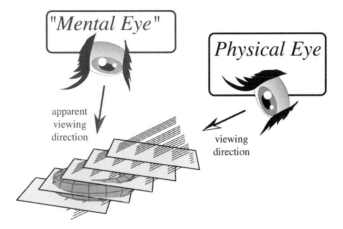

Figure 12.30
The group of congruences in pictorial space allows the observer to adjust the "direction of view of the mental eye" ad libitum. Any patch of pictorial relief can be made to appear frontoparallel.

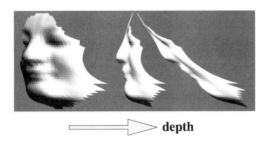

Figure 12.31
Illustration of pictorial congruences.

ian sense) have effects that are in many respects reminiscent of the trusty rotations from Euclidean space. They are indeed very similar when small but appear vastly different when large.

Features as Invariants under Congruency

The group of congruences (the equations listed in the previous section) defines the geometry of pictorial space in the sense of Felix Klein's famous "Erlanger Programm" (Klein 1893). In fact, it turns out that the geometry of pictorial space is exactly one of the twenty-seven three-dimensional Cayley-Klein geometries (Yaglom 1988).

The relation between two points $\{x_1, y_1, z_1\}$ and $\{x_2, y_2, z_2\}$ that is conserved by the congruences is $\sqrt{(x_1 - x_2)^2 + (y_1 - y_2)^2}$, that is, simply the Euclidian distance in the picture plane. One says that pictorial space has a "degenerate metric" because the metric "forgets" the depth dimension. When two points coincide in the picture plane they can still be *different* because they may differ in depth. For such points the depth difference $z_1 - z_2$ is conserved, and it can be used as a "special distance." For a pair of generic points the depth difference is typically *not* conserved. Thus we need two types of distances in pictorial space (Strubecker 1956). One is the distance in the picture plane: it applies to any pair of points seen in different directions. The other is the depth difference: it applies *(only)* to points seen in the same direction. Both distances are conserved under arbitrary pictorial congruences.

The congruences (by design) conserve a family of parallel directions (the direction of the z-axis, or "visual direction"). This conservation has the immediate consequence that you can't make a full turn in pictorial space, except about a visual axis. These latter rotations are trivially the rotations in the picture plane. If we define proper lines as any lines other than a visual direction, and proper planes as any planes not containing a visual direction, then any (proper) plane or line can be brought into correspondence with any other (proper) plane or line through a suitable congruence.

When you consider a point in the picture plane that does not lie on the (projection of) the line of intersection of two planes, the point in the picture plane corresponds to a point on each plane in pictorial space. The distance between these points is their special distance. When you divide it by the distance of either point to the line of intersection of the planes, you obtain an invariant. This invariant relation between intersecting planes may be taken as the "angle" between the planes (Strubecker 1956). This angle is aperiodic. There exist proper planes that fail to subtend an angle in the generic sense because they are parallel. Such planes have a well-defined depth difference, though, which can be taken as a special angle.

There exists a full metric duality between planes and points, angles and distances in pictorial space. Thus we speak of "parallel points" when their distance, but not their special distance, is zero. This makes the space in many respects simpler, though in many respects richer, than Euclidian space. Because of the aperiodic and identical nature of the metrics, we have two distinct types of similarities in pictorial space. One type ($\mu \neq 0$, $\gamma = 0$) scales distances and conserves angles; the other type ($\mu = 0$, $\gamma \neq 0$)

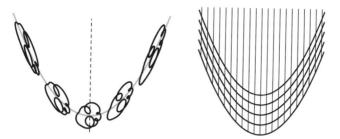

Figure 12.32
A cyclical rotation in a normal plane (*left*). Compare the rotated copies of the scribble: it doesn't "turn around," yet the elements of the scribble change orientation. On the right a "wagon wheel" in the normal plane. The "spokes" are normal lines and thus invariant. (The "hub" is at infinity.) The parabolas are "circles" in this geometry; a rotation shifts them inside themselves, like the rim of a wagon wheel. The "circles" drawn here are concentric, though they may look "shifted" to your Euclidian eye.

scales angles and conserves distances. The latter type is exactly the group identified by Hildebrand. A "general" similarity (neither $\mu = 0$, nor $\gamma = 0$) is characterized through a *pair* of magnifications, one for the lengths and one for the angles (Yaglom 1979).

Notice that the "depth shears" (the σ parameters) take over the place of rotations in the normal planes (figures 12.32 through 12.34). They supplement the Euclidian rotations in the frontoparallel planes. With such a shear you may turn any proper plane into a frontoparallel attitude. Yet the angle between any pair of proper planes is conserved by these shears; they thus appear indeed as "rigid rotations." Although you can rotate any proper plane into any attitude, the rotations don't let you make a full turn. Thus you can't turn the pictorial object that corresponds to the picture of a person in a ventral view such as to obtain a dorsal view. Full turns can only be made about a visual ray, that is, in frontoparallel planes. Such rotations appear as rotations of the picture plane in itself and are thus trivial with respect to pictorial space.

The differential geometry of curves and surfaces in pictorial space is much simpler (though certainly not less rich) than that in Euclidian space (Sachs 1990). We can define curvature in such a way that it is conserved by arbitrary motions in pictorial space. We can again introduce principle directions of curvature, curvedness and shape index, ridges, and so forth. Although such features have rather similar properties as their Euclidian counterparts, they are not the *same* as these.

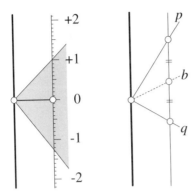

Figure 12.33
A "protractor" (*left*) in a normal plane. The shaded sector subtends an angle of
2.25 (simply read the scale). For easier reading you may "turn" the protractor to
bring the bottom line of the sector in a horizontal position (figure 12.34, left,
shows you how). On the right we show the construction of a bisectrix (*b* bisects the
angle subtended by *p* and *q*).

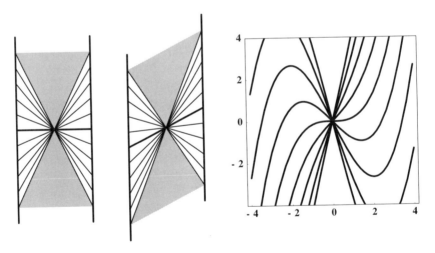

Figure 12.34
On the left, we show the effect of "rotating a protractor." On the right, a family of
congruent curves. These curves can be transformed into each other via rotations.

The differential geometric properties of pictorial objects are much more relevant for perception than their Euclidian counterparts. The latter only play a role when veridicality is an issue, but as we have seen a great many important questions can be approached without ever worrying about the veridicality issue at all, which is a can of worms to begin with and better left alone when at all possible. Thus the relevant differential geometric properties of pictorial objects are the "new" ones. This opens up a whole novel area of investigation in the study of pictorial shape. Such properties as "curvature" finally acquire a meaning outside the straightjacket of veridicality. The present theory leads to numerous predictions that await empirical study.

Multiple Pictures

The police would never record the scene of a crime via a *single* photograph. It is well known that multiple photographs, taken from different vantage points, are necessary to produce a reasonably "complete coverage" of a scene. This is what most people have done when they bring home their holiday snapshots. In the limit you would have many pictures in an almost continuous sequence, that is to say, a movie sequence. The lower limit is a mere *pair* of pictures (Koenderink et al. 1997).

It is easily possible to study the type of information in a pair of photographs that is not available from a single one. We have devised the "method of corresponding points" to do exactly that. The paradigm is a most simple one. We present two pictures next to each other and put a mark on one of them. An observer is asked to put a mark on the other picture such as to indicate the point in *pictorial space* that corresponds to the first mark (see figures 12.35 and 12.36).

The paradigm is perhaps deceptively simple. Notice that the task requires that the observer has to be simultaneously aware of *two distinct pictorial spaces,* one for each photograph. The task cannot possibly be done on the basis of mere (two-dimensional) image structure (see figure 12.36), unless there are small local landmarks that show up in both pictures. In our examples, such landmarks are virtually absent though. The image structures in the neighborhoods of corresponding points may indeed be completely different. This task cannot be done by any algorithm as available today, because it requires the construction of two three-dimensional interpretations each based on a single image. Successful three-dimensional interpretion in computer vision is still based on multiple image correspondences, though (Faugeras 1993).

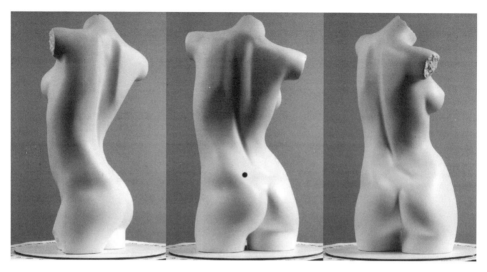

Figure 12.35
Three pictures depicting the same object in the same light field, photographed from the same vantage point but rotated about the vertical between exposures (by 45° either way). Can the reader find the corresponding points for the black mark in the center figure on the figures left and right?

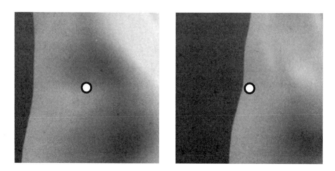

Figure 12.36
Two local environments of corresponding points. Notice that the relation to the contour, the contour itself, and the shading patterns are quite different. It is unlikely that the task would be possible at all if you only had such a local neighborhood. Observers no doubt use global information as context.

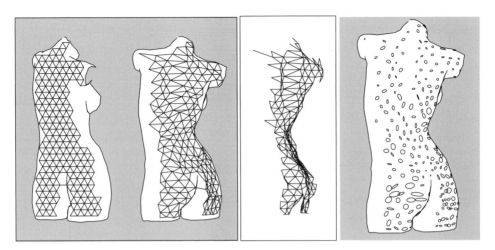

Figure 12.37
(*Left*) Result of a correspondences session. (*Center*) Profile view of a correspondences result. (*Right*) Covariance ellipses indicating scatter in correspondences.

We find that human observers don't complain at all when confronted with such a task but are able to establish correspondences easily (many hundreds within an hour). From the results we can again construct the pictorial relief (using standard techniques established in computer vision— once the correspondences have been established, all the rest is simple), this time as it pertains to multiple pictures (see figures 12.37 and 12.38). From two pictures plus a known rotation, we can find the relief. Likewise, from three or more pictures we can find both the rotation angles and the relief.

The "precision" by which observers are able to do the task depends on the difference (mutual attitude difference of the objects in the scene) between the pictures as well as on the nature of the local structure of the pictorial relief. In figure 12.39 we show an example of the scatter. Notice that it is as large in the vertical as in the horizontal directions, though the rotation of the objects was about the vertical. Apparently observers don't use such knowledge (obvious from cursory examination of the two pictures) at all. They don't go by two dimensional cues but perform the task in the pictorial domains.

Human observers apparently succeed in this intrinsically very difficult task because they are able to compare the local pictorial shapes of two pictorial reliefs. From our other experiences with pictorial space, we have to assume that both pictorial reliefs are only determined up to some

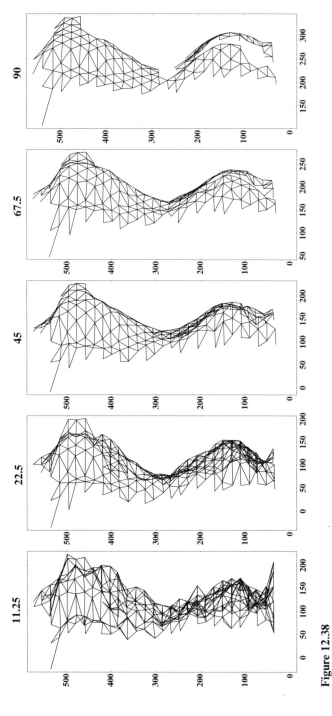

Figure 12.38
Profiles of pictorial reliefs obtained from correspondence settings for various rotations between the two images. For the sake of reference: the rotation due to ocular disparity (vergence angle) would only be a few degrees in this case.

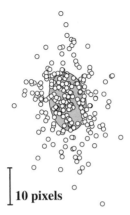

10 pixels

Figure 12.39
Scatter in correspondence settings. Notice that all disparities are *actually* limited to the horizontal direction, but the scatter is roughly isotropic. Observers search for correspondences in the pictorial spaces, both in the horizontal and vertical directions.

arbitrary pictorial congruence, most likely different for each. Thus the correspondences must be due to a comparison of local pictorial shape, where "shape" is defined as invariants under pictorial congruence.

This use of comparison was studied in a setting where we had three photographs of a scene containing a mannequin (figure 12.40). The difference between the three photographs was that the mannequin was rotated by 30° about the vertical between exposures. Because the viewing and lighting geometries remain unchanged, both the perspective and the chiaroscuro of the mannequin in the pictures changed. In this study we did both correspondence settings on pairs of pictures and gauge figure settings on the individual pictures. We can define relief both from the correspondences and from the gauge figure settings. We find excellent agreement in the sense that the reliefs are very similar up to a 30° (Euclidian!) rotation about the vertical if we first apply certain pictorial congruences (non-Euclidian!) to the individual reliefs (van Doorn, Koenderink, and de Ridder, in 2001). (See figure 12.41.) These results show that the observers apparently establish the correspondences on the basis of the pictorial shapes.

12.5   THE EYES KEEP STARING AT YOU

It is a familiar phenomenon—often enough remarked upon spontaneously by naive observers—that the eyes of the person in a portrait painted *en*

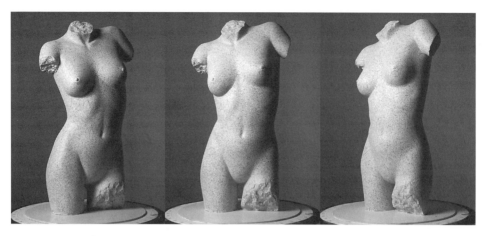

Figure 12.40
For the pictures on the left and right of the center the object was rotated by 30°
(either way) about the vertical. Notice that the light field in the scene was the same;
thus shading and geometry are different for these three stimuli.

face appear to "follow you around the room" (Busey, Brady, and Cutting
1990; Sedgewick 1991; Gombrich 1959). This is typical of *pictorial* relief,
for the effect fails to occur for a marble bust, for example. The same effect
occurs for people and some objects "pointing out of the picture" (see
figures 12.42 and 12.43).

Here we have a very complicated situation in which at least three distinct spatial entities play a key role, to wit:

1. The physical space contains both the observer and the picture.
2. The picture frame exists (as a physical object) in physical space, as a
visual object in optical space, and as a pictorial object in pictorial space,
all simultaneously.
3. The person depicted in the picture exists in pictorial space.

Although physical, optical, and pictorial space are distinct, (only) the
picture frame exists in all of them. It tends to appear as a frontoparallel
layer in pictorial space, but "mental eye movements" may freely skew it.
Thus the observer has the freedom to skew the frame in pictorial space
such that it "coincides" with the picture frame in optical space, thereby
removing possibly awkward ambiguities. Notice that this has the effect
of effectively *connecting* pictorial and optical space in the observer's consciousness. In such a case the frame would establish a kind of "wormhole"

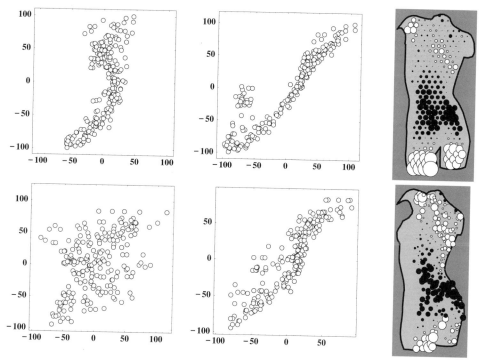

Figure 12.41
Comparison of pictorial reliefs from attitude samples and correspondences. The two rows illustrate opposite rotations of 30° about the vertical. In the left column, we show a straight scatter plot; in the middle, scatter plots corrected for the best shear. Clearly the shear component is appreciable here. On the right we show the residuals after taking rotation and shear into account. Apparently the deviations are systematic, indicating a piecewise transformation.

between the distinct spaces. What actually happens is of course an empirical issue.

In a recent experiment we used several methods to measure the pictorial relief of the picture of a mannequin in a dorsal pose, as well as the attitude of the picture frame in optical space and the apparent frontoparallel points of the mannequin. We used the picture shown in figure 12.42. We also prepared a number of projectively deformed copies of this picture. All pictures were presented on a CRT (cathode-ray tube) screen and were viewed either frontally or obliquely (at a 45° angle). The retinal image could correspond to either that in the case of the original picture (figure 12.42) viewed frontally or viewed obliquely (figure 12.43). However, due

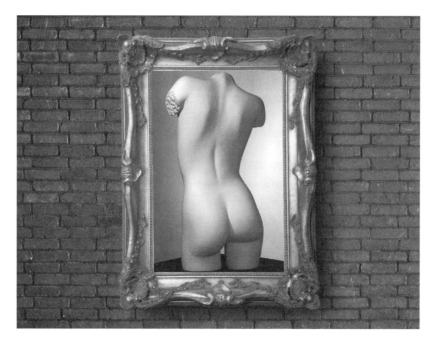

Figure 12.42
A framed picture hung on a wall.

to projective deformation the "oblique" case could also be obtained with
actual frontal viewing and vice versa; thus we decoupled the geometry of
the retinal image from the viewing geometry. Moreover, in using the
gauge figure task the gauge figure could also be projectively deformed (for
instance, in order to counteract the foreshortening effect of oblique viewing). We investigated a number of a priori interesting combinations. In
figure 12.44 we show the pictorial reliefs for the cases of frontal and
oblique viewing. Due to the 45° viewing angle in the oblique case, the
width of the relief is severely foreshortened (by a factor of $\sqrt{2}/2$) in the latter case. Otherwise the two reliefs are very similar indeed ("same shape").
Clearly the same features point toward the observer in either case. This is
especially clear from figure 12.45, where we present a scatter plot of the
depths. Any shear component is vanishingly small. There is only a minor
depth contraction. (Depth measured in units of the width, thus corrected
for foreshortening.)

We corroborated this result with an independent method. The observer
had to indicate frontoparallel points (either "near" or "far" points) on

Figure 12.43
An oblique view of the framed picture hung on a wall (figure 12.42). Notice that the same features in both pictures appear frontoparallel. This is the same effect as that of the portrait with "eyes following you."

Figure 12.44
Pictorial reliefs obtained with frontally (*left*) and obliquely (*right*) viewed stimuli. Due to foreshortening, the right relief is only $\sqrt{2}/2$ the width of the left one.

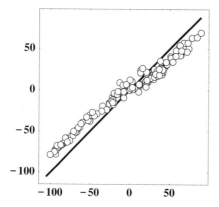

Figure 12.45
Scatter plot of pictorial depths at corresponding positions for the reliefs shown in figure 12.44. Although there is a depth contraction (of about 15%), the shear is not significant.

horizontal levels in the picture. These settings were done in random order. In figure 12.46 they are seen to line up nicely as ruts and ridges of the relief. These features are almost identical for frontal and oblique viewing.

The connection of optical and pictorial space is such that (mirabile dictu) the visual direction may be oblique in physical and optical space (the wall being seen slanted) and *simultaneously* in the "straight ahead" direction in pictorial space (see figure 12.47). Thus the effect of the "eyes following you around the room" is resolved due to the different angular metrics in the various spaces (and geometries) involved in the situation. In retrospect the effect is nothing special.

12.6   PICTORIAL SPACE: WHAT NEXT?

In this chapter we could only scratch the surface of a topic as intricate as pictorial space. Indeed, much research will be needed in order to arrive at a somewhat coherent view of the matter. We simply list a few (to our mind important) topics here.

It is of paramount importance to add to the repertoire of possible operationalizations and to gain experiences with these. "Good" methods will feel natural in the sense that the task is immediately obvious and requires no cogitation to speak of. They yield results very fast, that is to say, at least a sample of some relevant geometrical quantity every few seconds for sessions lasting up to an hour. The most useful results are huge data

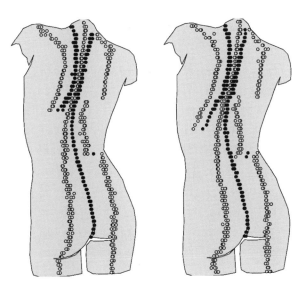

Figure 12.46
Frontoparallel points on horizontal scan lines for the reliefs shown in figure 12.44.
Notice that the points line up neatly to form "ruts" and "ridges." Notice also that
the ruts and ridges are virtually identical for these two reliefs.

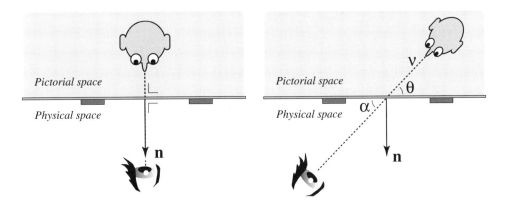

Figure 12.47
An observer views a portrait hung on a wall seen frontally (*left*) and at an oblique
angle (*right*). The vector **n** is the normal to the picture plane. In the right-hand picture the angle *a* equals 45° (oblique viewing), but the angle *θ* is a right angle! This
is because the line *v* is the viewing direction, and thus normal to the picture plane.

sets, of the order of 100 to 10,000 (more is better) samples in some geometrical skeleton framework. Methods are needed that address all the various aspects of geometry.

It is important to relate the results from as many different operationalizations as possible to each other. This is the only way to get to grips with the structure of pictorial space in the generic, abstract sense, detached from any *specific* method. Any claims to general conclusions on the basis of any single method (by no means rare in the literature) should be regarded with the highest suspicion.

We are still a long way from understanding the nature and efficacy and—especially—the interrelations of the various cues. The conventional methods, almost invariably based on stimulus or response reduction, are highly questionable. We need results in realistic settings (many computer-graphics-generated stimuli are not above suspicion, because it is rare to see the relevant physics being taken into account). From experience with computer vision, we know how difficult and vulnerable interpretations on the basis of monocular cues really are. The existing algorithms are not at all robust against small variations on the (typically extremely "ideal" and thus unlikely) prior assumptions. Thus one should be very wary of confronting the observer with "cues" that are quite unlike (or even a little different from) those from the observer's generic biotope.

We are still a long way from a quantitative theoretical understanding. This is partly due to the extreme scarcity of empirical data. Most of the classical data is hardly of the type that could successfully be confronted with quantitative theories of the type that would enable you to predict the geometrical properties of pictorial space or objects. It is also due to the fact that the available data are very hard to detach from the—often implicit—prior assumptions. In our opinion most of the available knowledge is a hindrance rather than a help in gaining an understanding, exactly because it is so intricately wrapped up in unfounded prior assumptions. What is sorely needed is a fresh approach, not based on the tangle of unfortunate terminology that is taken for granted by even most professionals. This is hard, because who doesn't like to trade essential uncertainty for the certainty of a word sanctified by silent concensus? For example, we all nod in understanding when someone mentions "depth," yet there may be a dozen (or more) meanings of the term that we do not know how to relate to one another. Many discussions going on in the literature are effectively void because one uses the same words for different entities.

Pictorial space is quite unlike Euclidian space. We don't understand it very well but enough to know that reasoning based on Euclidian precepts is (at best) unlikely to get us far or—more likely—to lead us into error. This means that *any* transformation or operation involved in the comparison of data or the prediction of phenomena on the basis of observed phenomena stands in need of empirical validation. Our Euclidian intuitions simply cannot be relied upon. This opens up a large field of empirical inquiry. It is important that such expertise be gained, for further progress critically depends on it. At this moment we are still at the very beginning.

Chapter 13
Truth and Meaning in Pictorial Space

Sheena Rogers

Pictures of all kinds fill our world. They hold records of past events, promises of the future and now, simulations of an alternative present. Some pictures are still, some move, and some surround us, interacting with us in a virtual reality. All seem to present some truth about the world. Indeed, perspective pictures, photographs, and movies seem to be fragments of reality itself, like insects in amber, caught in some medium merely to ensure their longevity. Seeing the picture and understanding what is depicted there seem simple. We do not pause to ponder the picture's success. Young children follow a story in a picture book before they can read. Wordless narratives depict biblical events in hundreds of medieval churches. We are reassured daily of the truthfulness of pictures by their constant presence in our lives. The pictures we encounter seem to be as simple to see as the real world on which they present a window.

Photographic pictures seem to capture reality in an especially immediate way. The medium is transparent. We see through the picture to the world beyond it (Walton 1984). It has even been argued that "the photographic image *is* the object itself" (Bazin 1967, p. 14, emphasis added). So, when I look at a photograph I literally see my daughter, or a London bus, the ocean, a chair. "Viewers of photographs are in perceptual contact with the *world*" according to Kendall Walton (1984, emphasis added). On this view, the photographed world is the world itself and so our perception of the three-dimensional spaces and objects in both must proceed in the same way. It is a seductive argument, and many writers on picture perception have fallen for it (see, for example, Walton 1984).

Yet pictures pose a special challenge to theories of perception. Representational pictures are flat, yet they depict a world with solidity and form. Still pictures present frozen moments, torn from the comfortable supporting arms of the spatial and temporal context of real life and held up for our inspection, isolated and alone. Even moving pictures, where action and observation unfold over time, fix the viewer in space, attached to the camera, a couch potato unable to step up and engage in the life of the depicted world (see Rogers in press for more on the perception of movies). Discrepancies between the location of the observer's eye and the location of the original camera or center of projection generate changes in the virtual layout of the picture or movie (Rogers 1995). These differences between pictures and real scenes are important. The possibility of realism under these conditions must be explained. If there is meaning in pictures, it does not come easily.

Unquestionably, much of the credit for the success of pictures in carrying meaning must go to the artists. The nature of their contribution should be examined carefully, however. The devices and designs that picture makers employ to show a three-dimensional world in frozen frames have suggested to some that pictures communicate by means of a language, an agreed-upon system of signs (e.g., Kepes 1944). Pictorial signs may "short-circuit" their route to meaning through their visual similarity to the objects depicted (see Metz 1974), but meaning is nevertheless obtained through a process of decoding. On this view, the image is never equivalent to the object itself. Realism is an illusion. Although a picture may tell about reality, it can never be a surrogate for it.

I have presented two extreme views and hinted at decades of argument about the fundamental nature of pictorial representation. There are, of course, many variants of these views and many subtleties I have not expressed. Instead of pursuing these arguments and weighing their relative merits, I propose that the debate be shifted to empirical grounds. What exactly do pictures and natural scenes have in common, and can we obtain experimental evidence of similarities and differences in their perception?

Drawing on the ecological approach to the psychology of perception, I have argued elsewhere that the perspective structure of pictures can present geometrical structures to the eye of the observer that, under certain constraints, are identical to those available in nature (Rogers 2000). I have selected one of these structures, the horizon ratio, for empirical investigation, and will describe it here as a test case in our search for truth and meaning in pictorial space. The results of the experiments I will describe here show that although the same geometric structure is available, it is not always perceived in the same way. Under certain conditions, observers responded to a pictorial scene exactly as they did to the real scene, and the picture acted as a reasonable surrogate for reality. The availability of

equivalent structures does not guarantee perceptual equivalence, however. Distortions of the perceived space did occur. We will see that there
are limits to the ability of pictures to substitute for real scenes, but under the
right conditions, and in at least some respects, surrogacy can be achieved.

13.1   THE ECOLOGICAL APPROACH TO PERCEPTION

The principal claim of the ecological approach to perception is that there
is meaningful structure in the light reflected from the surfaces of the world
(Gibson 1966, 1979). The available geometric structures carry *information*
about the nature of events, the properties of objects, and the layout of the
surfaces that make up our world. If an observer can detect these informative structures, then the world can be known. For pictures to provide the
same kinds of information about the world, light reflected from them must
carry at least some of the same structures. For a picture to be perceptually equivalent to the corresponding real scene, the same structures must
not only be available; they must be shown to be detected in the same way
and to result in the same perception.

To qualify as informative, in this technical sense, a structure must fulfill several conditions. First, it must uniquely and unambiguously specify
some state of affairs in the world under some identifiable set of constraints. Second, it must be relevant to some possible action by the perceiver. Third, information "points two ways" (Gibson 1979, p. 141). It
allows us to see ourselves in the world (ibid., p. 225), and in this way it can
guide our actions: "Information to specify the utilities of the environment
is accompanied by information to specify the observer himself ... to perceive the world is to co-perceive oneself.... The awareness of the world
and of one's complementary relations to the world are not separable"
(ibid., p. 141).

13.2   THE HORIZON RATIO AS INFORMATION FOR SIZE IN REAL
SCENES AND IN PICTURES

The horizon ratio seems to me to exemplify an informative structure. The
optical horizon is implied in the perspective structure of the scene, it is
visible as the origin of optical flow vectors, and it is approximated by the
earth's horizon. It allows you to see your place in the world because the
horizon itself is always at eye level. As you climb up on a step, or kneel
down, you can see the horizon move up and down in relation to the

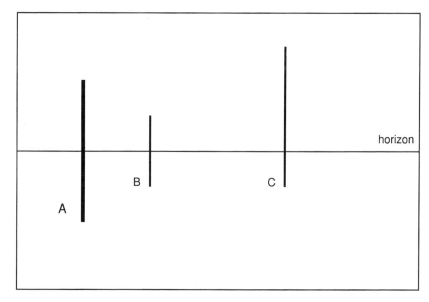

Figure 13.1
The horizon ratio specifies the size of objects standing on the ground. Objects A and B each have a horizon ratio of two and are twice eye-height. Object C has a horizon ratio of four and is four times eye-height. Object C is twice as tall as objects A and B.

objects standing on the ground around you. The horizon ratio relates your eye-height to the height of these objects. It specifies precisely the sizes of the objects relative to your eye-height. In figure 13.1, for example, objects A and B are each twice eye-height, and object C is four times eye-height.

The horizon ratio is given as the relation between two visual angles, though it can also be described as a relation of two extents on the picture plane (Sedgwick 1973, 1980, 1986). In figure 13.2, the angle O subtended by the whole object o from base to top is divided by the angle H subtended by the distance from the base of the object to the horizon h. The general version of the ratio is $(\tan Y + \tan H)/\tan H$, but the angles O and H themselves approximate the tangents of the angles when they are small, so $o/h \approx O/H$ (Sedgwick 1973, 1986).

Objects A and B in figure 13.1 each have a horizon ratio of two ($O/H = 2$). If eye-height is known in some metric, such as feet and inches, then the absolute sizes of objects in the scene can be labeled in that metric. In addition to information about absolute size based on eye-height, the sizes of objects in the scene relative to each other are also given by the

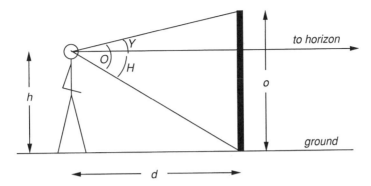

Figure 13.2
The horizon relations are given in terms of visual angle. The horizon ratio is $(\tan Y + \tan H)/\tan H$. The horizon distance relation is $d = h \operatorname{ctn} H$.

horizon ratio. Object C, for example, has a horizon ratio of four and so it is twice the height of objects A and B. (In the case of both absolute and relative size, the constraint that objects are standing on the ground plane must be met. The sizes of objects floating in space, like the classical stimuli of early psychology experiments, are not specified by horizon-based information, e.g., Holway and Boring 1941.)

For our purposes, the horizon ratio is especially interesting. The structure is present both in real scenes and in all perspective pictures: paintings, photographs, television, movies, and virtual reality representations. The optical horizon is always implied in the perspective structure of the picture, and it may even be visible as a physical line or edge. Indeed, in the construction of a perspective picture, the horizon may be the first line laid down on the paper, canvas, or wall. A short stretch of it is often seen in the background of Renaissance paintings. The horizon defines the limit to the ground, and in so doing, creates the skeletal structure of a 3-D world. Although, to my knowledge, horizon ratios have never been used to lay out the objects in a perspective picture, they could be. Perspective manuals usually recommend the construction of vanishing points for parallel lines lying on the ground plane as the next step (e.g., Ware 1900). Horizon ratios fall naturally out of perspective structure, however. This is most easily seen in a picture of a row of objects of the same size receding into the distance. A perspective line connecting the tops of the objects will meet a perspective line connecting their bases at a vanishing point on the horizon. The objects, being of the same real size, will be intersected in the same proportion by the horizon (see figure 13.3).

Figure 13.3
The horizon ratio is a component of perspective structure.

The relative sizes of objects (that is the sizes of objects compared to each other) in the pictured scene are fully specified by the horizon ratio, as we saw earlier. In pictures, however, an additional constraint is required to guarantee this information. For the pictorial horizon ratios to match precisely the horizon ratios from the real scene, the observer's eyes must be located in the horizontal plane that extends out of the picture from the horizon. If the observer's eyes are lower or higher than this, the ratio changes. Despite this constraint, the horizon ratio is robust in most ordinary picture-viewing situations. Ratios of visual angles are preserved as we adopt a viewpoint to the side of the picture, as we walk past it, and as we approach the picture or step back from it. Whereas some aspects of pictorial space will deform during these maneuvers, the information for the relative sizes of depicted objects does not (see Rogers 1995).

A demonstration of the existence of a potentially informative structure in pictures is not, of course, a demonstration that perception is based on that structure. Together with my students, I performed a series of experiments designed to investigate the effectiveness of horizon-based information for relative size, relative distance, absolute size, and absolute distance in natural outdoor scenes, and in pictures, movies, and virtual reality. I will review the findings of this research program before returning to the question of truth and meaning in pictorial space and to the possibility that a picture might act as a surrogate for reality.

13.3   PERCEPTION OF RELATIVE SIZE IN REAL SCENES AND IN PICTURES

As we have seen, relative size is fully, and precisely, specified in pictures by the horizon ratio. Using a variety of tasks, participants in my studies have demonstrated quite accurate perception of relative size in pictures. In one task participants were shown a simple picture containing only a horizon, a vertical sticklike object standing on the ground plane, and a small cross. Starting at the cross, participants drew a line upward until this second comparison object appeared to have the same real size as the standard. In experiments using some version of this task (Rogers 1996; Rogers and Costall 1983) many participants were able to make same-real-size matches very accurately. There were some limits however—performance was best when the objects were tall enough to be intersected by the horizon and when it was clear, from additional information, that the horizon line was the distant limit of the ground plane.

We have also examined the accuracy of relative size perception in more elaborate pictures. In two experiments, these are simulations of ground, sky, and a field of poles generated on a computer in desktop virtual reality (Rogers and Watson 1996a and 1996b). In three other experiments we used photographs of natural outdoor scenes of a similar field of poles and compared picture perception to performance in the real scene itself (Rogers and Pollard 1998; Rogers and Fichandler 2000). In these experiments a set of vertical poles ranging in size from 1 ft. to 22 ft. was arrayed at distances of 25 ft. to 300 ft. from the observation point. On each trial, observers made a comparison of the size of two of the poles. They were told that one pole was ten units tall and asked to make an estimate of the relative size of the target in the same arbitrary units (a magnitude estimation task). In all studies, whether estimates were made when looking at a drawing, a photograph, a movie, a drawn scene in interactive desktop virtual reality, or a real scene, relative size perception was quite accurate. In general, relative size was slightly underestimated at between 95% and 99% of the size predicted by the horizon ratio. Again there were limits to the structure's effectiveness. Accuracy fell when objects were very small, very large, or when the difference in size between a pair of objects was extreme.

I conclude that the optic array from both pictures and real scenes contains information for relative size, that this information is based on horizon (or eye-height) relations, and that the information is equally effective in pictures and in real scenes. The perception of relative size appears to be achieved in the same way in pictures and real scenes.

13.4   PERCEPTION OF RELATIVE DISTANCE IN REAL SCENES AND IN PICTURES

Another visual angle relation based on the horizon specifies distance along the ground to the base of the object by relating the angle of gaze elevation to eye-height. In figure 13.2, this distance, d, is equal to h ctn H, where h is the height of the point of observation and H is the visual angle subtended by the extent from the base of the object to the horizon (Sedgwick 1973, 1986). (H is the angle through which one's gaze would travel if one were to look at the base of the object and then raise one's eyes to the horizon.) The angle H becomes smaller the farther the object is from the observer and the closer it is to the horizon (and regardless of the size of the object). Observers could estimate the relative distances of two objects by comparing the angle H for each object. (The angles themselves approximate the cotangent of the angles when the distances are large relative to eye-height, as they were in my displays.)

We asked observers to make estimates of the relative distance of many pairs of poles using the magnitude estimation procedure described. In desktop virtual reality (Rogers and Watson 1996a), in photographs, and in real outdoor scenes (Rogers and Pollard 1998) estimates of relative distance were quite accurate. Estimates were between 95% and 100% of the relative distance predicted by the horizon distance relation.

I conclude that in addition to information for relative size, the optic array from both pictures and real scenes contains information for relative distance, this information is also based on horizon (or eye-height) relations, and the information is equally effective in pictures and in real scenes. As we found for the perception of relative size, the perception of relative distance appears to be achieved in the same way in pictures as it is in real scenes.

13.5   PERCEPTION OF THE ABSOLUTE DIMENSIONS OF PICTORIAL SPACE

To say that we have perceived the absolute dimensions of a scene is to say that we know how big or how far something is in some metric. In sharp contrast to the discussion of the perception of relative dimensions, the perception of absolute size and absolute distance in pictures is problematic. Recall that absolute size is given by the horizon ratio in units of eye-height (as is absolute distance). This fact is still true in pictures, only now, the eye-height unit refers to the height of the original center of projection (the station point or spectator point for a perspective painting, the location of the camera for a photographic image), which is not known. The observer's own eye-height has become detached from the optical horizon in the pictorial space. Thus the absolute dimensions of pictorial space are not given. Absolute size and absolute distance are theoretically indeterminate in pictures.

How are picture viewers to understand the scale of a scene shown in a picture? Are there any circumstances under which a picture could act as a surrogate for a real scene? There are three possible options: (1) Picture viewers could scale the pictorial space according to their own eye-height, even though they cannot know whether their eye-height matches the height of the picture's station point. So, for example, if their standing eye-height is 5 ft. from the ground, by the horizon ratio, objects A and B in figure 13.1 will each appear 10 ft. tall. If they are sitting at an eye-height of 3 ft., the objects instead will appear 6 ft. tall. Considerable instability in pictorial space would result if observers adopted this strategy. However, if observers could be anchored at the appropriate eye-height, the pictorial space should look a lot like the real one it depicts. This artistic (as opposed to perceptual) strategy is the basis of the stunning 3-D illusions that are possible in some forms of trompe l'oeil paintings (see Leeman, Elffers, and Schuyt 1976, for many examples). (2) Picture viewers could use a default value for eye-height, perhaps their own or a typical standing eye-height. Margaret Hagen and Robert Giorgi (1993) in fact found that when observers were asked to locate the position of the camera in a photograph of a room, they tended to estimate a camera height of about 5 ft. Sitting or standing, picture viewers would perceive our example objects to be 10 ft. tall. Of course, the observer still cannot know whether this eye-height matches the height of the station point, and if it doesn't, distortions in the scale of the scene will result. (This is not all bad, as any filmmaker will attest. A miniature model can stand in for an enormous space ship if it is filmed from a correspondingly low vantage point. See figure 13.4 for a related example.) (3) Picture viewers could perceive absolute size as indeterminate. The detachment of the pictorial horizon from the optical horizon is visible whenever the observer moves her head because there is

Figure 13.4
When we relate our own standing eye-height to the horizon ratio in a photograph
with an unusual camera location, distortions of perceived size occur.

no consequent optical flow within the array from the picture. Instead, it
becomes immediately apparent that the pictorial horizon is not coincident with one's own optical horizon. When we do not know the size of the
eye-height unit in the picture, the scale of the space is unknown. Artists
can take advantage of this ambiguity of course. René Magritte, in *The
Listening Room* (1952), fills a room with an apple. The horizon is clearly
halfway up the apple and halfway up the room, so both have a horizon
ratio of two. We don't know if we see a large apple in a normal room
(from a standing eye-height) or if we see a normal apple in a dollhouse
room (while laying on the ground). The pleasure of the picture is in the
perceptual uncertainty (see figure 13.5 and plate 4).

The foregoing options are not exclusive. Any one may apply in some
particular circumstance, and it may be possible to create particular perceptual effects by forcing perceivers to adopt one option over another.
Fortunately, the question of how perceivers understand the scale of pictorial space is open to empirical testing. We can assess the similarity between
perception of absolute size and distance in real scenes and in photographs, and we can explore the perceptual options described through care-

Figure 13.5
The pleasure of Rene Magritte's *The listening room/La chambre d'écoute*, 1952, is
in the uncertainty of its reality through the ambiguity of perceived size. Oil on canvas, 45 cm × 54.7 cm, private collection, © A.D.A.P.G. Paris. © 2002 C. Hersovici,
Brussels / Artists Rights Society (ARS), New York. See plate 4 for color version.

ful manipulation of observers' eye-height, camera elevation, and viewing
conditions.

13.6   PERCEPTION OF ABSOLUTE SIZE IN REAL SCENES AND IN PHOTOGRAPHS

Observers in one of the open field and pictorial space studies described
earlier were also asked to estimate the absolute sizes and distances, in feet,
of the poles in the field (Rogers and Pollard 1998). In the real outdoor
scenes, absolute size estimates of 4 to 12 ft. poles, positioned at distances
from 100 to 300 ft., were extremely accurate (close to 100% of the actual
sizes). Observers viewed photographs of the scene on a large-screen computer display with the horizon at the observer's standing eye-height, and
all visual angles matched to the real scene. Under these conditions estimates of absolute size were near perfect at distances below 200 ft., and
slightly overestimated at distances beyond this.

Information for absolute size seems to have been available both in pictures and in real scenes for the observers in our study. The experience of

looking at the large-screen display felt something like looking through a window at the scene beyond. If our observers were relating the real scene to their the eye-height in the outdoor study, the conditions we created for picture viewing probably encouraged the same perceptual strategy they would use outside in the real world to be used with the pictures.

Corroborating evidence for this suggestion can be found in the same study. We asked participants in our study for their height in feet and inches. If one's own eye-height is involved in the perception of absolute size as option 1 from the previous section suggests, then there should be a distinct difference between perception of this property in a real scene compared to its perception in a picture taken from a fixed eye-height. In the real scene, the horizon will intersect the poles at the observer's own eye-height. The resulting ratio will be different for a tall person than for a small person, but the perceived size of the object should be about the same for both because the ratio is scaled with correspondingly different eye-height values. In a photograph, however, the horizon ratio is set by the height of the camera at the time the photograph was taken. A short person seeing this picture and scaling the horizon ratio with a smaller eye-height value should perceive the objects to be shorter than would a tall person scaling the same horizon ratio with a larger eye-height value. (For a simple example, an object with a horizon ratio of two in the photograph should appear to be 8 ft. tall to a person with a 4 ft. eye-height but would appear 12 ft. tall to a person with a 6 ft. eye-height.) And, indeed, in our experiment, we found a significant tendency for pictured objects to appear taller to tall observers and shorter to short observers in the photographs but not in the real scenes. The pattern was not completely clear and there was considerable variability between observers, but the finding is consistent with the idea that absolute size is perceived in units of eye-height. In contrast, there was no relationship between the height of the observer and relative size perception. This suggests that the observer's eye-height is not related by the perceiver to the horizon relations that specify relative size. For this scene property, horizon relations seem to be utilized extrinsically.

I conclude from these findings that the optic array from both pictures and real scenes provides information for absolute size, that this information is based on intrinsic eye-height scaling of horizon relations, and that the information can be equally effective in pictures and in real scenes. Perception of absolute size can be achieved in the same way, by the same perceptual process, in pictures as in real scenes. That is not to say that absolute size in pictures is always perceived this way, as we will see after a summary of our findings for perceived absolute distance.

13.7   PERCEPTION OF ABSOLUTE DISTANCE IN REAL SCENES AND IN PHOTOGRAPHS

It has long been known that distance is often substantially underestimated, as you can observe for yourself by setting out to walk to an unfamiliar distant landmark. It has also been reported that distance in pictures is usually compressed (see Rogers 1995 for a review). Few studies have made a direct comparison between perceived absolute distance in real scenes and in pictures, however. In our study (Rogers and Pollard 1998) observers looked at a photograph of the real scene displayed on a large-screen monitor from the pictorial station point; thus the two conditions are geometrically equivalent. In the real scene, observers underestimated the distance to the poles quite substantially: at all distances from 100 ft. to 300 ft. they reported that distances were only about 40% of the actual distance. In the photographs, distance was compressed to only half this. Thus a pole actually 200 ft. away appeared to be about 80 ft. away in the real scene and only about 40 ft. away in the photograph. Here is one scene property that is not well captured in a picture, even one presented under conditions that led to accurate real-scene-like size perception.

Distance compression in pictures might be expected under ordinary viewing conditions. We have two eyes open and can move our heads and so binocular disparity and motion parallax reveal the smooth flatness of the picture surface. These sources of information for flatness conflict with distance information from within the picture itself. Removing them through peephole viewing has been shown to "undo" the compression and produce excellent illusions of 3-D space (see Rogers 1995 for reviews). You can roll up a piece of paper and inspect a nearby photograph through the tube to re-create the effect for yourself. You don't even need to be at the picture's station point for the illusion to work.

I conclude from this finding that although the optic array from both pictures and real scenes can potentially provide information for absolute distance based on horizon relations, this scene property is not accurately perceived in either case. The truth might be told in the visual angle relations of the optic array, but we do not seem able to hear it. In this one respect, pictures are deprived of meaning by conflicting flatness cues and so picture perception is even less truthful than perception of the real scene. This is an important difference between pictures and life, one that should be expected in all ordinary picture-viewing situations.

13.8   INDEPENDENCE OF PERCEIVED SIZE AND PERCEIVED DISTANCE

In the analysis presented here, size and distance are specified independently by related but distinct horizon relations. Traditional accounts of size perception, on the other hand, have always held that perceived size is dependent on perceived distance (the so-called size-distance invariance hypothesis, e.g., Ittleson 1960). Size, it is claimed, cannot be perceived directly but is instead obtained indirectly by scaling the single visual angle subtended by the object with its perceived distance. Thus the causal chain of perception builds one percept upon another (called percept-percept coupling; see Epstein 1982). The results of the experiments I have described indicate that size and distance are, indeed, perceived independently, in line with the hypothesis that perception of these properties is based on horizon relations. This finding supports the idea that perception of size is achieved directly (see Epstein and Rogers, in press, for discussion of other apparently coupled percepts). We found, for example, that despite tremendous compression in perceived pictorial distance, perceived size remained stable and was not affected by this distortion. In addition, in the analysis of individual observers' data, the accuracy of their size estimates was only weakly related, if at all, to the accuracy of their distance estimates.

13.9   WHEN IS SEEING A PICTURE LIKE SEEING THE WORLD?

The evidence presented so far strongly suggests that perception of size and distance is achieved through detection of horizon relations (with the possible exception of absolute distance). These relations are available in pictures, and the experiments demonstrate that the perception of pictorial space is governed by the information they provide. Pictures do seem able to reveal the truth about the spaces they depict (again, with the exception of absolute distance). We saw, however, that in at least one important respect, pictures are not reality: the pictorial horizon is not yoked to the observer's optical horizon, and therein resides the possibility for pictures to lie. The height of the point of observation for the picture is not known, and observers must use one of the solutions described earlier to make sense of the pictured space. We have seen some tendency among observers to use their own eye-height to understand the scale of a pictured scene. If the location of the original station point (or camera location) for the pictured scene was similar to the picture viewer's current vantage point, no harm will be done and the picture will be a truthful depiction of the scene. But what happens when this constraint is not met? Do we continue to see ourselves "in" the pictured scene—to see the pictorial space as coextensive with our own? Can we resist the pull to scale the pictorial world in eye-height units? Are there some conditions under which seeing the picture is like seeing the world, and some where it is not?

The pictures used in my experiments so far have all been presented on a large-screen computer display, with the observers at the station point, their eye level and optical horizon coincident with the pictorial horizon. These conditions may have enhanced the observers' sense of immersion in the scene through information that the pictured ground plane was co-extensive with the real one. Observing the photographs this way was like looking through a window to another place but one still very much a part of the world we are in, whose ground continued outside the picture to pass under our own feet. But what of a picture made on paper and hanging on the wall? And what of a picture made from an unusual spectator point? Is the perception of these pictures like the perception of the world?

In another experiment, a student and I (Rogers and Fichandler 2000) manipulated this connection between the observer and the pictorial world. We compared perception of size and distance in a real scene, with a paper photograph and with a trompe l'oeil presentation of the photograph in a peephole viewing box. In addition, we introduced two manipulations designed to reveal the extent to which observers see themselves to be connected to the pictorial space and so perceive the pictorial space as if it were reality.

We set up a field of poles as before, on a field next to the ocean with an unobstructed horizon line. We photographed this scene from four different camera elevations: the photographer lay on the ground, sat on a box, stood on the ground, and stood elevated on the box. We prepared two sets of these four views as $8'' \times 10''$ photographs. One set we mounted on the wall of the laboratory, the other we mounted in a viewing box with a peephole positioned so that the visual angles of the picture matched those of the real scene. The box was then hung on a structure erected outside in the actual ocean-side field. The peephole could be positioned at each of the original observation points for the photographs. Thus, when the pictures were mounted at the correct elevation, they fit smoothly into the ambient optic array from the real scene. The observer was anchored at the station point, and the viewing box minimized binocular and motion-based information for the picture's flat surface, creating a trompe l'oeil effect. Under these conditions, the picture came as close to a reality surrogate as it could. Removing the photograph and flipping open the back wall of the viewing box gave us the real scene comparison condition, which was viewed with one eye through the peephole.

The four camera elevations generated four different sets of horizon ratios for the same scene. If observers use a default value of eye-height, perhaps their own standing eye-height, as suggested earlier in option 2, the different horizon ratios in the picture should lead to differences in the perceived sizes of the poles. Objects photographed from low viewpoints will have larger horizon ratios and should appear larger than objects photographed from higher viewpoints.

We examined the possibility that as perceivers we relate our current eye-height, which varies as we move about the world, to the horizon relations (option 1), rather than a fixed, default value (option 2). Observers viewed the pictures from each of the four positions, lying down, sitting, standing, and standing on a box. If they were to ignore their current eye-height and use the default value, their viewing position should have no effect on perceived absolute size. If, however, the observer's current eye-height is the unit by which horizon relations are understood, then for a given horizon ratio, changes in eye-height elevation should lead to changes in perceived absolute size. Lower observer viewpoints should lead to the perception of shorter objects, and higher viewpoints should lead to the perception of taller objects.

Observers viewed the four pictures from the one congruent viewing position for each picture (e.g., sitting photographer with sitting observer) and from each of the three incongruent ones (in this example, sitting photographer with lying, standing, and raised observer). If picture viewers relate their own current eye-height to the horizon ratio (option 1), absolute size should be accurately perceived in all congruent conditions, but distortions of perceived size should occur in the incongruent conditions. For example, the raised observer viewing a picture photographed from a sitting position should overestimate the size of the object.

The most compelling finding of this study was a difference between the perception of the trompe l'oeil presentation and the paper photographs. Observers did not relate their current eye-height to the absolute size of the poles in the paper photographs. Estimates of absolute size were very close to the actual pole sizes and did not vary with viewing position, suggesting that a default eye-height value was used (option 2). In the trompe l'oeil condition, however, estimates of absolute size did vary with viewing position. When in the lower viewing positions, observers perceived the poles as slightly shorter than they did when they were at higher viewing positions. Under- and overestimates of pole size were not as large as would be predicted by entering the actual value of eye-height into the horizon ratio, but the difference in the pattern of responding for these two conditions was clear, and it was statistically significant. I take this difference between perception of the paper photographs and the trompe l'oeil presentations to indicate that the observer's current eye-height can influence perceived size in pictures (option 1) but only when the observers are forced to treat the picture as if it were part of their reality. In effect, the trompe l'oeil condition prevents observers from noticing that the pictorial horizon is not in fact their own. In other words, picture viewers do not necessarily perceive pictorial space to be coextensive with the space they occupy in the real world, although under special conditions they can. If they do not, then there is no reason to scale the pictorial space in units determined by their actions in the real world.

That is not to say that they do not necessarily bring the same psychological process to bear on picture perception that they use in everyday perception of the world. Instead of using the changing eye-height value generated during movement, picture viewers could still use a default value of their own standing eye-height (option 2) to extract meaning from horizon relations. Indeed, there is evidence that this is what picture viewers were doing in our study. Raising the camera made objects appear smaller, lowering it made objects appear larger, as option 2 predicts. Although current actions and body position were not relevant to picture perception, observers did in some sense see themselves in the pictorial space and see the pictorial space as part of their world. Once more the observers' own body size mattered. Our taller participants saw the poles as taller than they were, and our shorter participants saw them as shorter than they were. These two effects occurred in both the paper photographs and in the trompe l'oeil presentations, implying that the strategy of scaling horizon ratios with our normal standing eye-height is a general one and not one specific to picture perception.

I conclude from this last study that picture perception is very like the perception of real scenes, though there are differences. Horizon relations are the basis of perceived absolute size, relative size, and relative distance in real scenes and in pictures. (Absolute distance is inaccurately perceived in real scenes and worse in pictures. It is possible that this scene property is not governed by available horizon-based information.) Horizon relations can be exploited extrinsically, that is, without reference to our own bodies, and this seems to be what we do when we perceive relative size and distance in both real scenes and pictures. Horizon relations can also be related, intrinsically, to our bodies. We can use our own eye-height as the unit for understanding absolute size when it is visible in the optic array. The evidence of this last study is that at least in picture perception, eye-height is understood as our usual standing eye-height. We are not tempted to use a changing eye-height value that results from interacting with the world (kneeling, climbing, etc.) with ordinary pictures. I would argue that this is not a "decision" to adopt a picture-specific perceptual strategy but a behavior guided by optical information. In ordinary picture viewing there is optical evidence that the pictorial horizon is not linked to our eye-height. Horizon relations do not change as we approach the picture and adopt one of the four viewing positions. When they do, as they would in a real scene or in virtual reality, they reveal our place in the world, and our momentary eye-height may well become the unit that scales the dimensions of the pictorial space. When there is no information that the pictorial horizon is not linked to our bodies (in the trompe l'oeil condition), we proceed as if it were and relate to the picture as if it were a real scene. In this case, perceptual judgments are influenced by the position of our body and our momentary eye-height, even in pictures.

13.10   TRUTH AND MEANING IN PICTORIAL SPACE

We must return now to the question behind our opening discussion. Do pictures tell the truth about the world? Do they convey meaning in the same way as the real scenes they represent? The answer to both questions is that they can, but they need not.

Pictures can make available to the observer some of the same informative optical structures that are found in natural optical arrays. However, a picture can lie in a way that the natural world cannot. When we look at a picture, we see the picture itself as well as what it depicts. But the picture is not a layer of glass between a three-dimensional reality and us. We do not see through a window to another world beyond, though the artist may try to convince us that we do. If we are allowed to move our heads, the optical flow patterns reveal the true nature of the picture as a marked surface. The illusory world will deform and rotate as we move (see Rogers 1995). We cannot always trust the picture to tell us the truth about distance, or about the sizes of objects depicted.

How, then, are pictures so successful? Why are André Bazin, Kendall Walton, and others convinced that pictures put them in contact with reality? I claim that it is the very success of most pictures that blinds us to their origins. Hand your camera to a three-year-old and show her the shutter release. The randomly frozen optical moments that result in the images will convince you that meaning is not so easily captured. The absence of spatial and temporal context, and the absence of artistic control, can strip meaning from images. To present the illusion of a window on reality, pictures must first capture available informative structures and then support the meaning in those structures through the satisfaction of the constraints that underwrite them. Specifically, the horizon relations provide meaning only when the objects in the scene are on the ground. If the scene is in a picture, additional constraints apply. For the original horizon relations to be preserved, the observer must view the picture from within a horizontal plane extending out of the picture from the horizon. If these horizon relations are to tell the truth about the dimensions of the scene, the camera or center of projection must be at a reasonable standing eye-height. Too high or too low and the picture will lie. Further, if there is any risk that the picture viewers will not realize they are looking at a picture, they must observe it from a location that matches their eye-height to the height of the camera. Too high or too low and the picture will lie.

The potential for distortions and ambiguities in pictorial space have given fright to many who have pursued a geometrical account of picture perception like this one (for expanded treatment of this problem, see Kubovy 1986; Rogers 1995; and Rogers 1997). This potential is handled here, not by the hypothesis of a shared set of signs that code for distance, size, and 3-D shape in a picture, or by a cognitive juggling act on the part of the beholder that fixes any problems, but by the recognition of the important role of the artist in making pictures meaningful. The careful deployment of conventional practices (not signs) on the part of the picture maker can ensure that distortion and ambiguity are minimized, that the loss of temporal context is compensated for, and that the constraints under which certain geometrical structures provide meaning are satisfied.

The perception of a meaningful and truthful three-dimensional space from the picture by means of these structures can then proceed in the same manner as the perception of the three-dimensional world from which the picture arose. When the constraints are not satisfied, errors in perception should be expected. The pictured world will not be the same as the real world it represents. If pictures seem natural it is because they are exceptional artifacts. Thus the question of truth and meaning in pictures properly concerns not *if* but *when* they can be found.

Chapter 14

Line and Borders of Surfaces: Grouping and Foreshortening

John M. Kennedy, Igor Juricevic, and Juan Bai

Like an astronomer, a perceiver has the job of using incoming information to become aware of what sent the information in the first place. The universe zooms in on the astronomer, and our homely environment projects information toward us. Then we humble perceivers invert the projection. This is especially obvious with photographs, because these are flat objects but we ask what three-dimensional world might have given rise to them.

It is a mystery why a few lines in a brief outline sketch let us readily perceive figures, faces, and so on. Outlines provide us with precious little material for constructing a 3-D scene, but we do it anyway. They copy a few borders and leave the spaces between entirely blank. Their success tells us boundaries in the scene are vital for much of perception. But, truth to tell, they are little understood, and the accounts that have been proposed are often quite controversial. That's why we are investigating borders here. In a nutshell, much of the story we will tell is that lines (even dotted lines with prominent gaps between the dots) picture the continuous borders of 3-D surfaces. In like vein, vivid continuous surface borders appear in motion and stereo perception, stimulated by elements with gaps between them. In our account, picture perception, though like real-world perception, gets remarkable, distinctive work out of its ability to make groupings, cross gaps, and cause the outlined borders that result to trigger special geometries of 3-D that are cousins of real-world polar perspective.

All vision ever receives is gradual changes (gradients) in between abrupt changes (borders). Inverse projection of gradients and borders involves options, which are useful to outline perception. In a nutshell, inverse projection of outline provides impressions of surface borders, not all borders, and continuous borders, even when there is no complete line. This perceived continuity across empty space is the basis for outline depiction.

The perceived continuity used by outline is shared by surface borders. It is facilitated by evenly distributed elements in close proximity. Outline

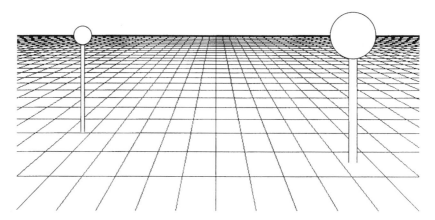

Figure 14.1
Piazza with columns.

uses perspective foreshortening but fails to give us shape-from-shadow perception. For examples of impressions marshalled by outline, gradients, and foreshortening consider figures 14.1, 14.2, and 14.3.

Figure 14.1 is a tiled gradient, like a piazza, stretching into the distance. Two vast and footless columns stand on the piazza, at different distances, one on the second row of tiles and one on the fourth. The verticals in the picture that stand for columns bear outline circles, one to our left and one to our right. The piazza's rectangular tiles are radically foreshortened by perspective. The result is we see a level ground (Gibson 1979). Interestingly, we readily take the circles as outlining spheres, and not just flat circles, but the perspective projections of spheres to left and right of us would be elliptical (Pirenne 1970; Kubovy 1986). Evidently, impressions given by inverse projection do not follow the laws of incoming projected light precisely.

Figure 14.2 is a picture of a 3-D cube. Its bright bars are induced by gaps between hatched lines in the 2-D picture. We take this to be a picture of a 3-D cube made of continuous bars. It gives us an impression that the borders of the hatchmarks are due to continuous edges of bright foreground bars cutting across the hatchmarks.

Further, where four white lines on the page come together to form a "+," we can readily see complete horizontal bars in front of partially hidden vertical bars. Also, the order of the bars in depth can reverse, so the vertical bar appears in front. Interestingly, the bar in front can seem to have complete contours. In the center of the "+," where the horizontal

Figure 14.2
Cube bars from discontinuous lines.

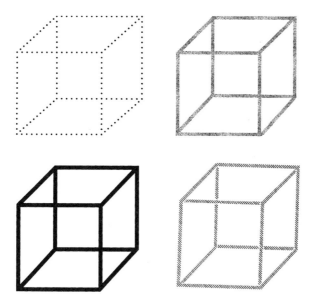

Figure 14.3
Dotted lines can outline a cube, and a cube's bars can be shown by solid lines, dotted strips, and hatched lines.

and vertical arms come together, the frontal bar can seem to be flanked by a pair of contours, running across empty space. The pair is horizontal when the horizontal bar is in front and vertical when the bars reverse in perception.

Figure 14.3 contains a dotted-line picture of a cube. It also reverses in depth. The dotted lines function as outlines, suggesting continuous bars, corners, and obliques oriented in depth. The dots belong together in lines even though no continuous contour joins them on the page, or in our percept (Arnheim 1974). The dot at the center of the "+" where four lines come together can be seen as belonging to the foreground bar.

Figure 14.3 also includes a picture of a cube with dotted strips forming lines, a black line picture of a cube, and a hatched-line picture. Despite their varied constituents, the cubes appear to have the same proportions. The obliques recede in depth and are all foreshortened equally.

The dotted strips forming "+" shapes can be grouped as horizontal bars in front of vertical bars, or the reverse. The central dots of each "+" belong with the bar in front, in these percepts. They belong to the frontal bar even with no continuous flanking contour in the percept, much as lines of dots can group without needing continuous contours.

The black-line cube can seem to have contours crossing the empty space at the centre of the "+" intersections, much as in figure 14.2's white cube. In the hatched figure, some hatches are omitted to distinguish the front and back bars. The hatches of the front bars are grouped together as a long continuous row. The line of hatch marks has a discontinuous border on the page, but the bars being depicted, we have the impression, have continuous edges.

14.1   OUTLINE AND INDUCTION

Of course, a continuous edge can also be depicted by a continuous border. Figure 14.4 is a picture of a house, a road, and hills. This little landscape was drawn by a blind girl of twelve, Gaia. Blind since birth, Gaia had some peripheral sensitivity to light for her first six–seven years. She never had enough vision to see the lines she uses in drawing. She likes to draw, using a raised-line drawing kit (Kennedy and Merkas 2000). She has drawn since she was about three years old. Much like other twelve-year-olds, she draws novel pictures, making up scenes, buildings, people in intriguing clothing, and so forth. Gaia can feel a line with a fingertip, one small section at a time, and take it as a long continuous line showing

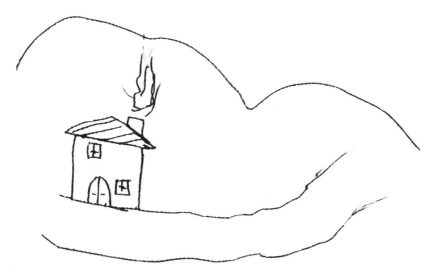

Figure 14.4
Copy of a raised-line drawing by Gaia. (From Kennedy, in press, with permission from Prion Press)

a continuous edge, much as sighted people see small sections of line such as hatch marks and group them as if they had continuous borders.

Gaia's drawing uses lines for borders of tangible surfaces. The surfaces of her house are flat, and so their borders are the occluding edges of flat surfaces. Her hills have brows, that is, occluding boundaries of rounded surfaces. All surfaces are either flat or curved, so Gaia has deployed lines to show the borders of the only kinds of surfaces there are.

The skillful use of line in Gaia's picture invites us to explore the possible use of outline in pictures. Lines have affinities for tangible borders, in touch as well as vision, Gaia's picture suggests (Kennedy 1993). What kinds of borders can we perceive, besides occluding surfaces, and which suit outline, and why?

Perceptual borders arise from features in the environment, like Gaia's surface edges. The inverse projection problem is to decide which feature. In the light coming to our eye there may be a "contrast" border between dark and light. But what was its origin? A flat surface's occluding edge, such as the roofline of Gaia's house? Or a rounded surface's occluding boundary like the brow of a hill? Or what?

Perception takes in a limited sample of the light projected to it, and, in inverse projection, gives us awareness of its possible cause. In this respect, perception is like the person who notes a few blackbirds in a field on Monday, Tuesday, and Wednesday mornings and leaps to the conclusion that there are always blackbirds in the field in the morning. This leap is subject to the problem of induction.

An inductive leap is fallible. An infinite number of possible generalizations fit a set of observations. The blackbirds may be there only on weekdays. Or only on days people go past the field. Or only until Fall. Or the birds may actually be light-colored birds, but the fields are covered with highly reflective snow.

If the borders in light always had hallmarks indicating what environmental feature projected them, inverse projection would be fail safe. Perception could lock on to the distinctive hallmark and register the environmental feature. For example, shadows are darker than their illuminated surrounds. But there are few hallmarks as reliable as the darkness of shadows at borders. As a result, perception has options at borders. Generally, perception takes in the border and its setting and uses many features of the setting as indicators of the origin of the border. If only a few features are available, in a sketch for example, several options are open. Because lines in pictures have borders, they can offer these options, and the more schematic the picture the more options perception can exercise. This ability to exercise options, we hypothesize, explains our capacity for outline representation. But to understand just what options outlines have, we need to consider the induction problem further.

14.2   INDUCTION

Alas, poor observer, finite data fit an infinite number of curves. Any finite perceptible pattern can be projected by an infinite number of origins. So what are we to do?

One drastic error in the study of perception was to argue vision only has brightness and color as its core because we only have luminance and spectral values to work with. In fact there is nothing to stop us having impressions of any kind whatsoever from stimulation X. We see purple, which is not in the spectrum, when certain combinations of spectral values come to us. We see continuity where there is only a group of separate marks. We get spheres wrong in inverse projection. So it may not be entirely surprising that borders have affinities with some features of an environment but not with all.

One cannot predict a priori which elements allow which percepts. The problem of induction at borders has to be given an empirical solution, for there is no single solution logically. Psychology has the task of uncovering the empirical solution, and although the variables used for inverse projection generally make good sense, as they reflect projective geometry, they contain many quirks important in picture perception.

Reacting to a problem that is logically insoluble, George Berkeley thought God must help us to perceive in practice. Denis Diderot thought we must use independent knowledge of the state of affairs. Hermann von Helmholtz said we must use inferences (using just another word for inductions). These solutions all accept the problem at face value. Immanuel Kant realized there must be a set of prior conditions (Cazeaux 2002). James J. Gibson (1979) offered some prior conditions, but the ones he advanced were simply to do with the environment. But, it is important, in doing so he rejected the way the problem was framed. He asserted there must be a lawful environment in which perceptual data are obtained, not one with no restrictions. He also contended we could successfully differentiate and integrate our percepts from a given starting point as children, toward a better fit with the environment. Alas, there are an infinite number of possible differentiations and integrations, for these are just inductions by another name.

We need another insight besides Gibson's. Just as the world must be governed by finite rules, we the observers must have a working beginning to guide us.

By way of analogy, consider induction of units in words. Words are made of phonemes. Young children find the relevant phonemes for their native language in the sounds they hear. But there are an infinite number of ways of cutting up sounds. For example, all the sounds you hear when you first wake up might be one phoneme. All the sounds you hear at lunch might be another phoneme. No one uses those kinds of divisions, of course. But the probability of any two children, unaided, picking up the same phonemes from a corpus of sounds is zero. Hence children are aided. What they must do is have a limited set of possible phonemes, and then the corpus must match some of that set.

The issue then is arriving at a working beginning in vision, as phonemes are in hearing. One extremely useful starting point is the border. There is a closed set of perceptible borders, and a fixed set of origins for these borders, rendering induction's problem manageable. Once these sets are appreciated, other factors can be understood—first, elements that group as borders; second, foreshortening at some orientations; and third, failure to show shadows.

	Luminance Differences		Spectral Differences	
	Static	Moving	Static	Moving
Monocular	b/w drawings	b/w movies	color paintings	color movies
Binocular	b/w stereo illustrations	b/w stereo movies	color stereo illustrations	color stereo movies

Figure 14.5
Kinds of borders and pictures using them.

14.3 KINDS OF BORDERS IN VISION

The light that comes to our eyes has luminance borders, between high intensity and low intensity. Likewise, between what we informally call two "colors," it has what we may call a spectral border. (The luminance borders are generally more effective in perception.) Figure 14.5 classifies borders into luminance and spectral, moving and static, monocular and binocular. It gives examples of pictures that fit these types.

Luminance and spectral borders can be arranged to form dots, lines, and textures. The elements (dots or lines or other units) in a texture are arranged with some regularity over a region. Vision groups the elements in a region as a unit (a gradient like that in figure 14.1 or a simple form or gestalt-like lines or squares in figure 14.2), despite the units' being spatially separate. Trees on a snow-covered hillside define its continuous slope in vision even if each tree is quite separate. Dots, lines, and continuous borders are evident in monocular vision, with our eye in one vantage point and a static incoming array.

Motion in an array can also provide a monocular border, much like the border between two regions. If we were standing looking at two distant Celtic hills covered by yellow gorse bushes and purple heather, and the hills partially overlapped each other from our vantage point, they might look like a single slope. But if we move to one side, we will reveal new bushes on the more distant hill. The occluding brow of the foreground hill would become evident. The visible brow would be defined by new heather and gorse texture being added or "accreted" optically. If we move back to where we started, the texture will be "deleted," but this too will reveal the brow of the hill. The motion-defined border given by accretion and deletion of a few distinct bushes against uniform backgrounds can appear as continuous as a line of dots, and on occasion it can appear as continuous as a luminance or spectral border.

Binocular vision can provide borders too—stereo borders. These rely on relations between the luminance or spectral borders in two eyes, as motion borders are based on two moments in time. With one eye a grass-covered lawn may seem like a smooth expanse. Binocular vision may make out a small ridge ahead in the lawn. If we move, the ridge will give a stereo border and a motion border in correspondence.

Binocular vision can produce an impression of a continuous border, given a few spatially separate inducers, just as motion can. This purely stereo border can appear as continuous as a monocular line of dots, and it can appear as continuous as a luminance or spectral border.

(We could have several motion-defined borders in one eye and a slightly different set of motion-defined borders in the other eye. The difference between the two eyes can provide a stereo border, invisible to either eye alone, rather like the one in the lawn. This is a purely motion-defined binocular border. Presumably, we could have many of these borders, too, say defining small squares or small circles. The shapes may fall into two regions, with a border between a square-texture region and a circle-texture region. Indeed, these borders could define further shapes, say diamonds and ellipses, each in their own superregions. We could define many such regions, and "superborders" between them. And superborders could form regions with "superduper" borders, and so on. Perhaps some of these motion and stereo borders can appear continuous.)

In sum, visual borders can be luminance or spectral, monocular or binocular, and static or motion defined. The borders can be physically continuous, and appear so, but also they can be matters of grouping, appearing as a continuous gestalt even though they are based on elements that are spatially separate. Often all the kinds of borders coincide in vision, for color, brightness, stereo, and motion can all tell us about a cliff edge, simultaneously. But they need not. Markings on the hide of an Alpine cow have luminance and spectral borders but no stereo or motion ones.

Each source of a visual border indicates borders independently of other sources to some degree (Cabe, Abele, and Kennedy 1999). Presumably this is why static monocular vision can suggest borders of three-dimensional bars, when we look at a picture like figure 14.2, whereas motion and stereo vision do not (see also Sedgwick, chapter 3 in this volume): they record the 2-D flatness of the page. The bars look complete, but we also see gaps between marks. Because each kind of border in vision can be independent of the others, vision accepts two kinds of contradictions readily—3-D versus 2-D and continuous versus full of gaps.

If borders carried distinctive hallmarks, as shadows do, then perception would find them unambiguous. But in fact many apparent borders use the same inputs. Does a luminance border always coincide with the figure-ground edge of a foreground object? The Alpine cowhide tells us no (Kennedy 1974, 1993; Peterson 1999), a lesson we should now explore.

Kinds of Visible Borders

The flanks of a zebra can have different shades or surface colors. Its back may be silhouetted against a ground such as a sandy-colored hillside. It can cast a shadow onto the ground, and a shiny wet hoof may reflect an arc of light on the sand. On the zebra's belly may be attached shadows, from the sun overhead. The result is reflectance borders (lightness and color), shadow borders (cast and attached), and illumination borders on the sand.

Also, as Gaia's picture showed, the surfaces in a visible scene can be curved, like hills, or flat, like a roof. They can be occluding, in which case there is a foreground and a background (or figure-ground). Or they can form corners, as in figure 14.6, such as concave and convex corners

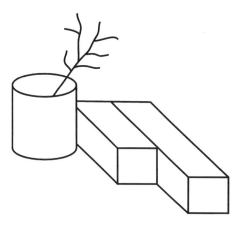

Figure 14.6
The outline depicts occlusions, corners, cracks, and wires.

(two foreground surfaces meeting, or figure-figure). Two coplanar surfaces meet with an elongated crack between them, as in two blocks nestling together in figure 14.6 (also figure-figure). If a single surface is elongated and very thin it makes a wire or stick (with background on either side, or ground-ground), as in the twig in figure 14.6 (Cutting and Massironi 1998).

Surface, reflectance, and shadow borders are the worldly origins for the borders in light. This much is helpful in providing an answer to induction's problem. There are two limited sets—the optical borders and worldly origins of these borders.

The correspondence between the two sets is not a simple one-to-one matter. Rather it is many to one. The origin of a luminance border could be any of the worldly borders. It could arise from a reflectance border on cowhide, a cast shadow border on the ground, or an attached shadow border on a belly. Also, it could be from a corner or an occluding edge. For example, the luminance border could be from a light foreground object silhouetted against a dark wall.

Because some perceptual borders could be inversely projected as any of several kinds of environmental features, there are several options for a line in an outline drawing. But the line may have restricted affinities, that is, only a few actors, albeit ones influenced by instructions in various settings (texture, gradients, binocular differences, and accretion-deletion).

Information or Affinity

What normally removes ambiguity at a border? One factor is what lies between borders. The region between borders is textured. Indeed, the surfaces we find in our environs are generally textured. That is, color, luminance, and texture boundaries usually coincide. Recognizing the presence of textured surfaces may help us understand the function of perceiving continuity where the elements are separate. Surfaces have continuous reflectance and continuous borders but separate texture elements.

Helpfully, the separate texture units on a continuous surface are usually uniform. On a breezy day, lake surfaces have waves (texture units) very different from the rocky or grassy margins of the lake. Little wonder vision has the useful ability to see a continuous region with a continuous border when the input is separate texture units.

The texture gradients (figure 14.1) in a region help us see a single surface stretching away from our vantage point. Perspective governs the change in angle subtended by each unit as its distance increases (Sedgwick

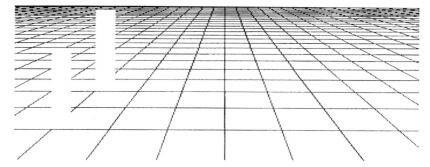

Figure 14.7
The heights and depths of ghostly columns are shown by the scene's meridians.

1986; Kubovy 1986). Vision detects how the variations fit with perspective. Also, it can readily detect the number of texture units between us and the foot of an object until foreshortening reaches limits set by our acuity. The result is good perception of depth up to the distance where foreshortening crushes texture units to the degree where they are indistinct (twenty or so units in a flat piazza such as that in figure 14.1).

Figure 14.7 is a version of figure 14.1 with two ghostly columns. The grid of converging lines tells us the upper column is larger than the lower one. Both columns stand on one of the converging lines, but the tops are aligned with quite different lines in the grid. The upper column projects three converging lines above the line grazed by the top of the lower column. Where the line grazed by the lower column meets the upper column indicates the relative heights of the two. The converging meridians of the sides of the tiles in the scene indicate height as well as the parallel meridians of the fronts of the tiles indicate depth. Much of inverse projection involves applying these informative meridian rules to texture units in visual scenes.

However, outline omits texture, and the uniform texture between the lines tells us the picture is simply flat. Is perspective irrelevant to outline as a result? It does not offer large expanses of darkness, unlike shadows. Is shading irrelevant, as a result? Shortly we will show just how aspects of perspective and shadows do and do not matter to drawing in outline. Here we wish to note simply this: an outline drawing omits perspective gradients of texture, and shading, and offers static flat surfaces. Its binocular inspection and accretion-deletion simply indicate it is flat. This suggests, intriguingly, outline operates despite countervailing information. Outline's ability to show a surface edge may therefore be independent of information for depth, slant, and occlusion. Rather than information of this kind, inverse projection of an outline may rely on an affinity between lines and edges of surfaces. The affinity could be due to common features of lines and surface edges. The general principle here is that perception sidelines information and may home in on something in common between what we use to see our normal surroundings and what we use when we depict the same scene. If so, theory of pictures must reveal the "common features" and what factors in perception govern their use.

For clarity's sake, let us note here that people use two forms of representation. One form involves fiat or conventions and the other uses common features.

Words represent by convention mostly. A hedgehog is smaller than a pig, even though the word "hedgehog" has more letters than "pig." Words sometimes use onomatopeia. The word rivulet nicely stands for a little stream. A babbling brook is onomatopeic for its referent. When words stray like crooners into sounding like their subject, they offer a glimpse of the world of representation by common features.

We have probably only the barest understanding of representation by common features (Cazeaux 2002). John Searle (1993) once wrote that when we say "Jill is icy" and mean she is unemotional, the connection between emotion and being chilled is hard to explain. Being unemotional just is, somehow, being cold. We detect something in common between the two. But what? Those of us who have a gift for synesthesia will sympathize with Searle's puzzlement over common features we cannot make explicit, ties that cannot speak their name. Astonishingly, George Lakoff and Mark Johnson (1999) have argued that much of our thought resides in implicit connections like synesthesia. The connections are said to be metaphoric, like John Searle's metaphor for cool Jill, or Shakespeare's warmer metaphor "Juliet is the sun."

Juliet is as pleasant, comforting, attractive, and essential as a summer's day. We do not have to go far to find common features to use in a literal sentence akin to Romeo's, though our list of features may not have his flair. Also, most if not all of Lakoff and Johnson's metaphors can be shown to have a literal base. But the search for relevant common features in matters of representation is by no means easy.

The fact that there are common features for two objects does not mean that one readily stands for another. Think of two objects. They have in common that you have just thought of them. But the fact that you thought of them does not mean one stands for the other. Look at two objects. The fact that you looked at them together does not make one

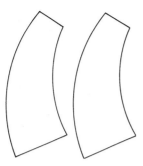

Figure 14.8
Two C-shapes facing to the right, with the illusion that the right-hand C looks
bigger than the left-hand one. If each of the two is flipped in place, without
exchanging places, the left-hand C will look bigger. Subjects then report they are
the same size.

stand for another. Consider two objects that are nearly identical: two cars
off a Rover plant in England. They may be almost indistinguishable, but
that does not make one stand for another, Nelson Goodman (1968) noted.

Context shifts the relevance of features. All objects have many common
features. We have to find some common features and then select the one
pertinent at the time. "Man is a wolf" can shift "hunter" to "killer," for
example. At a dance, we might say, "he is a wolf," meaning predatory, and
we might be gossiping about some glamorous and assertive patroller of
the dance floor. In war, we might say he is a "wolf" and mean a vicious
killer.

The problem here, at heart, is the induction problem once again. All
objects have an infinite set of properties in common. Unaided, picking the
proper one has a probability of zero. Hence there have to be guides or
restrictions to our choice.

When we consider pictorial representation, we must ask about relevant
matching features. We can ask what the possible set could be and what
factors influence them. This should be a limited set. Out of the limited set,
only some should provide the relevant match.

Pictorial representation has limits that are not open to change. The referent of a word is arbitrary, but a picture must look like its referent to
some extent (Wollheim 1973).

It may be helpful to distinguish here the perceptual looks of things from
information gained by watching things alter. Two equal C-shapes placed
side by side, like "((", both facing the same way, look unequal (figure
14.8).

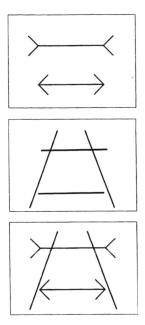

Figure 14.9
Illusions add effects: Müller-Lyer (*top*), Ponzo (*middle*), and combined figure
(*bottom*).

But if each of the two shapes is turned in place, to face the opposite way,
like)), the apparent inequality will reverse. Observers exclaim, "Oh, they
are equal!" The appearance remains unequal, but the information gained
from the alteration is "they are equal." Pictures are about providing
appearances, not about the information gained from perceptible transformations. In a phrase inspired by Heinz Wimmer and Josef Perner (1983),
pictures are about what allows false belief: viewing with restrictions. They
are about what arises when static conditions are provided and what then
induces appearance and illusion.

Helpfully, figure 14.9 shows a distinctive feature of inducers of appearance. The top panel is the Müller-Lyer illusion. The upper horizontal line
looks longer than its twin, just below it. In the middle panel, the Ponzo
illusion also makes the upper line look longer than its twin, the lower line.
In the bottom panel, the two illusions are combined. Remarkably, the
effect is additive (Kennedy and Miyoshi 1995).

Appearances are additive. In this respect, appearances are quite different from information. Information does not add; it confirms. Each of the
meridians in figure 14.7 confirms what the others tell us about the size and

distance of the ghostly columns. If five bits of information tell us one line is twice another, the five tell us "twice" five times. They do not add to tell us "ten times bigger." (We should note that if the Ponzo causes a 5% illusion and the Müller-Lyer 10%, their combined effect may be 14%, because of common factors. If the first illusion is due to factors a, b, and c, and the second to factors c, d, and e, their combination offers a, b, c, d, and e, with c as a common factor only appearing once, not twice. The process is additive, but the sum is an imperfect addition.)

Pictures govern appearance, straying at times into illusion and additive effects. In particular they offer lines giving the appearance of edges, influenced by perceptual factors given by the patterns of the lines.

Pictures are unlike words, because words, despite onomatopoeia, are not essentially about looks. Also, phonemes, the components of words, do not mean things, but the looks of pictorial borders may rely on common features with other borders. So let us ask about the features in pictures such as Gaia's line drawing.

14.4   NUMBER OF BORDERS

One simple theory is that for each border in the depicted world there is one in the picture, and no more. This is hardly true for outline, a moment's thought reveals. An abrupt border on a surface we can call a contour, an abrupt border in the light to the eye we can call a contrast, and an abrupt change in depth at the border of a flat surface we can call an edge. Interestingly, pictures such as Gaia's have lines formed of two contours close together, forming a line in an outline picture. Although the outline in the picture has two contours projecting two contrasts, it generally is taken to stand for one edge—a single edge of a single surface (Kennedy 1997). That is, the referent of two contours is one edge of a surface. The affinity of line for edges is independent of number of borders.

14.5   CURVED AND STRAIGHT LINES AND CURVED AND STRAIGHT SURFACES

The second explanation we might consider is one I owe to Nelson Goodman (personal communication, 1972). I pointed out to him that lines can show edges of flat objects and boundaries of curved objects. He wondered if the reason was lines are straight and curved, and their referents are straight and curved. The common property is shape.

This theory explains too little (as Goodman's Project Zero colleague David Perkins pointed out at the time). Certainly common shape properties are important. But there is more. Edges of flat-surfaced objects such as cubes are indeed depicted by straight lines. But the boundaries of cylinders and water glasses are too, and these are curved. We see the straight lines stand for boundaries of surfaces curving away from us. The affinity of lines for edges does not depend on matching straight for straight and curved for curved (Willats 1997). If a close match of shape were vital, young children could not draw in outline.

14.6   JUNCTIONS OF LINES MATCH VERTICES OF OBJECTS

A third explanation to consider is based on the vertices or junctions of lines. These form shapes such as L-junctions, T-junctions, Y-junctions, and X-junctions, and at ends of lines there are simply termini (abrupt or fading). When we draw a cube, we draw vertices as well as straight lines. Junctions have common shapes with vertices of cubes. Does that explain the success of the outline drawing? Gibson (1979) thought so.

This explanation also falls short. The explanation emphasizes junctions, which do indeed look like vertices of cubes, but it neglects the lines joining the junctions. The lines between the vertices look like edges. At the least, the junctions have to extend an influence to the adjoining lines. In addition, proportions of regions between junctions are important. At one extreme, using a kind of connectionist topology, the argument could be that the set of vertices are arranged in a certain order and that is all that is important. But if only topology mattered, squishy puddles of orderly vertices would be identified as cubes. In fact, we need more. There are definite effects of proportions.

14.7   CONCENTRATION OF ELEMENTS

A variant on the explanation emphasizing vertices is a theory speculating that perceptual information is concentrated at vertices and other points of rapid change (Attneave 1954; Biederman 1985; Kennedy and Domander 1985). Alas, experiments testing this theory were confounded. In one condition, only regions between vertices were removed. In another, only vertices were removed, supposedly, but in fact vertices and regions between vertices were both removed. If the parts are removed in the same fashion, there is little difference between the two sets of pictures (figure 14.10), and

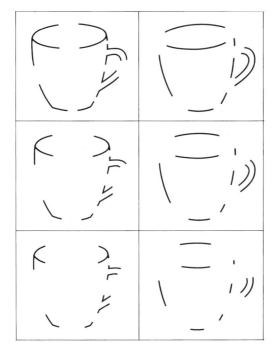

Figure 14.10
Cups with partial deletion of outline. Omitting sections between vertices (*left*) creates the same problems for perception of the cups as omitting sections with vertices (*right*).

some parts of the figure with vertices removed, such as handles, are easier to perceive. Further, five evenly distributed dots on each line in a picture of a box suggest the overall figure more readily than dots concentrated midway between vertices, and least effective is one with dots concentrated at vertices (figure 14.11). If the figure has curved lines, like a bird does, one with dashes evenly distributed suggests the overall form much more effectively than one with dashes concentrated at changes of direction (figure 14.12, from my Toronto student Ramona Domander). A figure with many indentations, such as a hand, also tells the story. The hand with evenly distributed dots is easier to see than one with dots concentrated at points of change (figure 14.13, from my Salzburg student Christoph Obermair).

Figure 14.13 includes two hands made by joining the dots with straight lines. Instructively, the one made from the concentrated-dots figure looks more like a hand. Evidently, when we look at the even-dot figure we do

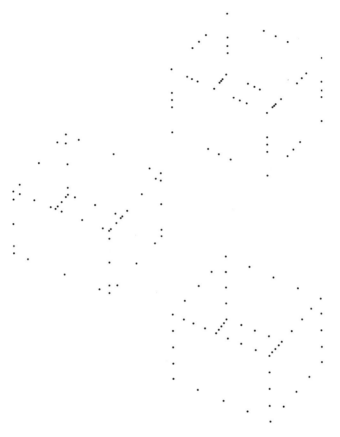

Figure 14.11
Boxes and dotted lines. The box shown by lines with evenly spaced dots (*bottom right*) is easier to see than the box with dots concentrated at midlines (*top right*), and the poorest figure is the one with dots concentrated at vertices (*center left*).

not just join the dots with straight lines. We fit curves. Joining the concentrated-dot figure with straight lines succeeds because then its dense dot regions approximate curves.

Even distribution is hardly the sole factor grouping elements in lines. Density matters. Like the bird pictures, the hands use the same number of elements, distributing them over two perimeters with the same length. Overall density is constant, and even distribution is shown to be significant. However, we group figure 14.14 (from my Toronto student Rizvana Chishty) as five straight columns of diamonds with irregular spacing. We

Figure 14.12
The bird figure with lines evenly spaced is easier to see than the bird figure with lines concentrated where contour changes direction.

cannot readily see figure 14.14's seven rows of perfectly evenly (horizontally) spaced diamonds, orthogonal to the five irregular columns. Vision favors the five columns with irregular but denser spacing.

14.8   FORESHORTENING OBLIQUE LINES

The distribution of elements between vertices influences vision. The proportion of these parts is important in outline shape perception. But how? Children are said to draw what they know, not what they see. In this popular theory, outline drawings of cubes by children are not based on perception and inverse projection, using foreshortening, but rather on drawing lines in the same proportions as the edges of the object.

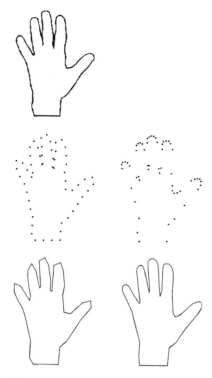

Figure 14.13
The hand with dots evenly spaced is easier to see than the hand with dots concentrated where contour changes direction. But if the dots are connected with straight
lines the one based on concentrated dots is more like a hand.

Consider lines on the page that are oblique, horizontal, or vertical in
figure 14.2. Andrea Nicholls and Kennedy (1995) asked adult subjects
about drawings of blocks, like those in figure 14.2, with short and long
obliques. The subjects were asked which obliques suggested receding lines
equal in length to the square's lines. Subjects selected oblique lines that
were about 65% of the length of the square's lines. Further, figure 14.15
shows that blocks drawn using frontal squares and obliques of the same
length are taken as having obliques much longer than the lines in the
squares. The angle of the oblique varies from 25° to 65°, with no change
in this apparent proportion as observed by subjects. Subjects also judge
the obliques on the page to be about one-third longer than their true proportions, when judging obliques 1.5 to 5 times longer than the square's
side.

Figure 14.14
Columns of irregularly spaced diamonds are seen, not regularly spaced rows with
less density.

In another study, Nicholls and I changed the frontal square into a trapezium (figure 14.16). This has four equal-length obliques and no right
angles. Now the oblique misjudgments should apply to both the front face
and the long obliques, when subjects assess their length on the page, and
they should be compared more fairly. Indeed they are. At 1 (front trapezium) to 1.5 (long oblique) they were judged veridically. Further, given an
oblique of 5 times the front trapezium the judged ratio was 1.1 times the
true ratio.

If the front face of a brick is depicted by a trapezium, the brick appears
to recede at an acute angle to the picture surface. If the front face is a
square, the brick recedes as if orthogonal to the picture surface. The result
is more foreshortening for the square-fronted drawing. Obliques of length

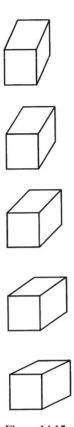

Figure 14.15
The obliques are seen as longer than the horizontals and verticals of the bricks.

Figure 14.16
Trapezium fronts invoke less foreshortening of obliques than do squares.

1.5 appear longer in the square-fronted drawing than in the trapezium-fronted one.

Why should oblique lines be judged longer than verticals and horizontals? The answer surely is that foreshortening applies to obliques showing edges receding from the frontal-parallel picture plane. Why subjects use 65% as the best ratio to perceive 1:1 length is as yet unexplained. (The actual length on a picture surface of the oblique attached to a square showing the frontal side of a cube ranges from zero to infinity, in polar projection. It is zero for a cube in front of the center of projection, small for a cube slightly to one side, and infinite for a cube far to the side; Kubovy 1986). We do not know what the preferred ratio is for many of these cubes. And we do not know what the ratios are for cube drawings subtending various angles at the eye. The 65% ratio here is just a helpful starting point for investigation.)

Drawing and Foreshortening

An outline showing a cube stimulates perceptual impressions, not just preference judgments. Its obliques give misleading impressions of size, because of foreshortening. However, the theory that children draw what they know and not what they see predicts that children drawing cubes will make all lines equal on the page. They know all the sides are equal in the cube, so they will make all the lines equal. To put this idea to rest we need to measure what line lengths children do in fact use. And indeed, children of nine and ten use foreshortening in their drawings of cubes (Nicholls and Kennedy 1992, 1995). They do not use a 1:1 ratios of frontal square to oblique. Rather they use 60%–70% ratios, foreshortening in a fashion that fits the foreshortening ratios used by vision.

Foreshortening is inverse projection. It influences perception in many ways, though its effects cannot be predicted a priori. Indeed, if we set out to draw pictures like figure 14.1, we often fall into very sizable error. We are often dramatically wrong when we try to estimate the foreshortening of objects at different distances, if they are not optically adjacent (Kennedy and Juricevic 1999). This is why painters hold up pencils to compare relative visual sizes of distant objects.

We can demonstrate the painter's problem as follows: bend your left arm. Also, put it halfway between straight ahead and directly to the left. Then pose your left hand close to vertical. Now stretch your right arm far to the right. Pose your right hand close to vertical. Your arms should be 135° apart. One hand should be twice the distance of the other from your eyes. Now try to estimate the relative visual angles of the two hands (their vertical extent). Most people say the right one looks about 90% the visual angle of the left. Now swing both arms to straight ahead, being sure to keep one bent and the other straight. Now the right hand's visual angle looks to be about 70% of the left's. Now close one eye. Be sure the hands are optically adjacent, but the right is still twice the distance of the other. Now the right's visual angle looks close to 50% of the left's. Evidently, visual angle ratios of the hands are judged to be close to their ratio in length (in centimeters) when the two hands are set widely apart in angle, and we view binocularly (getting good length information). Igor Juricevic and I found these effects in studies with real objects set on a tabletop, and studies with pictures of objects like that in figure 14.1. Judgments of visual angle ratios vary from 100% veridical when objects are aligned (optically adjacent) to judgments that are increasingly like length ratios as angular separation increases. The judgments move steadily toward length ratios, and come close to 100% of length ratios when objects are set 180° apart (one to our extreme left and one to our extreme right).

Little wonder we have trouble drawing in perspective! The relative visual angles of nearby objects are misperceived quite massively. Photographs arrange patches on a picture surface to match visual angle ratios of objects in the 3-D world. To draw with photographic realism, we need to judge relative visual angle ratios of the 3-D target objects. We cannot do this accurately without aligning objects optically. That is why artists hold up pencils optically alongside target objects.

Consider using a pencil like an artist when drawing two identical electricity pylons, one near and the other far, one to our left and one to our extreme right. The ratio of the nearby pylon's visual angle and the pencil's are judged correctly: say 0.6 to 1. Then a second pylon is assessed against the pencil: Say 0.3 to 1. This tells us the ratio of the two targets' visual angles is 2 to 1. If we had not used the pencil we might have judged the visual angle ratio of the pylons as say 1.2 to 1, close to the height ratio.

The effects of foreshortening are related more and more to length and height information as target objects separate in angle. Thus vision is not predictable just from the laws of perspective. We should use foreshortening, because it is everpresent, but some impressions we get from it are not predictable from laws of perspective alone. Pictorial impressions are to do with these effects, which are dramatic and little understood. The effects require empirical investigation, not just a priori geometrical considerations.

14.9   YOUNG CHILDREN USE OUTLINE

Outline invokes impressions, we have argued. However, in the earliest years of using lines, say from ages two to five, Constance Milbrath (1998) has argued, children are not using line to stand for perceived edges of surfaces and do not make any use of the observer's vantage point. This theory may underestimate the child. First use of outline for the visible borders of a person or an animal occurs at about age two or three. Similarity of shape is evident in drawings of children of about three (Kennedy, Nicholls, and Desrochers 1995). These early and rough outlines show borders of objects. Notably, they show the occluding boundaries of rounded objects. Hence, they imply a vantage point (Hopkins 2000; Lopes 1997; Willats 1997).

In a remarkable discussion, Milbrath argued that outline is something only talented children use especially effectively at young ages: "talented children quickly caught on to the idea that a line should stand for an edge and a plane for a surface" (p. 357). This much is surely harmless, and follows from her observations of two-year-olds and kindergartners. But Milbrath went on to claim most children do not catch on easily to using outline effectively (pp. 181–182), and by adolescence many of the "less talented children" have not done so (p. 357). But surely viewer-centered features, implicating the observer's vantage point, are what any child draws when using outline at any age. Outline readily shows occluding edges of surfaces, and these edges of surfaces are surely available early in the development of perception.

14.10   LINES AND DISCONTINUITIES

In Gaia's picture, lines clearly depict surface edges. But should we generalize and suggest lines can stand for any discontinuity? Let us consider two theories, one arguing that any discontinuity suits outline, the other arguing that lines show surface edges but not purely visual margins such as those of a shadow's.

A line has two contours. A black line on a white page is a thin black region with white surrounds on both sides. The luminance border that relies on black giving way to white is the shadow border.

Lines can match the shapes of any spatial discontinuity, including a border of a shadow (Kennedy 1974). But what can they look like? Interestingly, they cannot look like shadows, or objects bearing shadows.

Figure 14.17
Shape-from-shadow fails in outline because it provides a negative contour along-side the shadow.

A face in strongly directional illumination can have many shadows, cast on the cheek by the brows and nose for example, or attached to the side of the nose. High-contrast pictures of faces with cast and attached shadows work quite well in perception (figure 14.17, leftmost panel, solid black figure, and rightmost panel, solid gray figure). They trigger a "shape-from-shadow analysis" that allows us to see the face, its 3-D configuration, and its expression. Such pictures have two tones, one bright for illuminated regions and one dark for shadow regions, in a "positive." (A "negative" reverses the positions of the bright and dark, so the bright region in the picture stands for what was in shadow in the original.) The grouping of dark patches in the picture reveals well-defined areas on a continuous surface with several slopes, showing the face surface rising and falling over forehead, nose and cheeks.

If outline depicted any spatial discontinuity, and hence any source of contrast patterns, it should be able to stand in for shadow patterns. We should be able to use a line in place of the discontinuity between shadowed and illuminated regions. The outline should allow perceptual analysis to provide a percept of the face, its configuration in depth, and its expression. The grouping of the patches surrounded by lines should seem ordered, and firmly grouped, and not like independent puddles or islands.

In fact, outline cannot readily stand in for the borders of shadow patterns (see figure 14.17, outline figure, second from left). It does not trigger shape-from-shadow analysis (Kennedy 1993, 1997; Kennedy and Bai 2000; Cavanagh and Kennedy 2000). Likewise other purely visual borders such as color borders cannot be replaced by outline with any degree of success. Just as we do not see outlined shadow patterns look dark, we do not see familiar color forms look colored when shown purely in outline. Hence the discontinuity theory is too general.

14.11   OUTLINE MATCHES ONE CONTOUR

Could the explanation of outline be that a line uses one of its black-white borders to match the referent's border? That is, some borders, such as shadow borders, are "polarized" so that they are darker on one side. A shadow is darker than the illuminated region neighboring it, a factor that plays an important role in shadow perception (Cavanagh and Leclerc 1989). Does outline work if it matches a polarized border?

A theorist might contend that an outline will work like a shadow if it had a contour with the shadow's polarization. This hypothesis fails, alas, because one of the black outline's two contours in figure 14.17 has precisely this pattern of polarization—the contour alongside the white, illuminated region.

Another explanation of the failure of outline to trigger shape-from-shadow is that outline has two contours, and a shadow border has one. Alas, a shape-from-shadow figure with two borders succeeds, provided both are polarized in the correct direction (figure 14.17, second panel from right). That figure has a black area for shadow, a grey area for a line, and a white area for illuminated regions. Indeed, in studies with Juan Bai, I have found that more than two borders can be provided and if they are all polarized like a positive, shape-from-shadow succeeds. A successful explanation of the failure of outline with shadow borders is that one of the line's contours offers incorrect polarity at the border of the shadowed region. Hence the failure of a figure with a gray region for shadow and a black outline (figure 14.17, third from left). The figure has gray for shadow, a black line, and a white area for illuminated regions in the referent. The line's contour alongside the illuminated region has the correct polarity. The line is dark and the illuminated area bright. But the contour it provides to the shadowed region is polarized like a negative. It is gray on the shadow side and darker on the line's side.

14.12   OUTLINE AND GROUPING

Up to this point, the list of theories of outline has treated outline as using continuous contours. But outlines with gaps work well too. We can draw a cube with lines of dots. If outline can be served by lines with gaps, then it is the grouping of the elements that is at work. The axis of the grouping is crucial. This has a location and a direction from us, but no color or brightness. Hence it does not matter to outline whether the marks on the page are black or white dots, or dashes or continuous lines, as figures 14.2 and 3 reveal. (I should note that Willats [1997] disagrees with this conclusion.)

What do lines with continuous and discontinuous borders share with their referents? The referents are surface borders, that is, corners and occlusions. Any given outline is therefore ambiguous. The pattern in which it is found helps it take on a referent in perception, but inverse projection of outline works with vague sketches with no decisive features. The key therefore is some common feature of a dotted line, with gaps, and a continuous surface border. But what feature?

Surfaces can be textured sparsely or densely. The contrasts telling us about borders of surfaces are sometimes continuous optically, but sometimes they are full of gaps. Likewise, random-dot stereograms have regions with no continuous contour in the stimulus display, but binocularly they give us an impression of a continuous border. The border has no brightness polarity, just like dotted outline. Similarly, kinetic random textures use accretion and deletion of elements, with discontinuous stretches where grouping of elements occurs across gaps, to push us into percepts of sharp borders. Again, these borders are not brightness-polarized.

In sum, the optical patterns that specify borders of surfaces have features that match the patterns operating as outline. Both kinds of patterns can provide continuous stretches of luminance or spectral contour, but often they offer gaps that need to be bridged. The physical factors that permit grouping and apparent continuity, without polarization, can be triggered by both outline and information for surface edges.

14.13 AMBIGUITY OF CONTOUR AND OPTICAL EDGE INFORMATION

Outline is ambiguous about its referent in the absence of context. So too is a continuous luminance or spectral contour. It might, however, be thought that accretion and deletion borders (Gibson 1979) are distinct from outline in that they are far from ambiguous. Accretion and deletion might be thought to specify occluding edges without recourse to context. If this were so, the similarity of outline and accretion-deletion boundaries

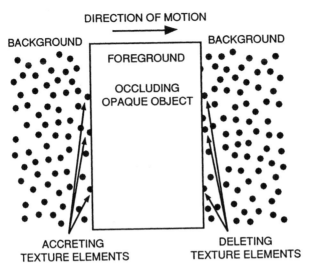

Figure 14.18
Accretion and deletion occurring with moving opaque foreground objects, in uniform illumination, with no shadows.

would be threatened. Only outline would need context. However, accretion-deletion contours are ambiguous about the role of occlusion, both physically and perceptually.

One well-known physical condition creating accretion and deletion is an opaque object passing in front of a textured background. The leading edge of the opaque object deletes background texture and at the trailing edge background texture accretes. Texture that is accreted and deleted indicates background (figure 14.18).

However consider the case of snow falling from a white sky against a dark background (such as distant hills, trees, or windows in white buildings) and then falling further against a white background (like a snow-covered field or a white wall of a building). Often, the snow is only visible against the dark background. The snow accretes at an upper edge of a dark patch in the background and deletes at a lower edge. The same is true for rain. The accreting and deleting elements are in the foreground. The accretion and deletion does not cause us to see dark trees as holes into a world beyond.

Similar effects occur for smoke rising, or leaves whirling upward, or insects swarming. Often they are only visible against a light background. Also, the wind can create a whorled pattern across a field of wheat, or a

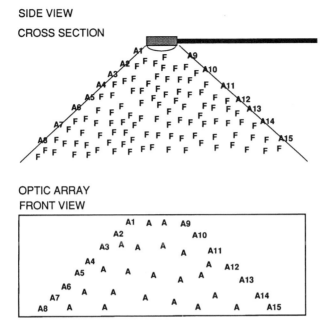

Figure 14.19
Accretion and deletion occurs for snow accreting in a beam from a light. The *A* elements are accreting, and *F* elements are falling. A cross section of the beam has accretion for elements at the left and right borders. A frontal view also has accretion in the center regions between the left and right borders.

water surface. At the leading edge, optical units accrete, and at the trailing edge units delete, and we see a single continuous surface. The elements accreting and deleting are on the surface of water and the top layer of wheat.

Related effects occur at night with directional illumination. As an obstacle moves between us and a light source, its shadow sweeps through the falling snow. Deletion occurs at the leading edge of the shadow and accretion at its trailing edge. Snow can fall into a light beam, from a dark sky, and accrete in the optic array. In figure 14.19, the *A* units are accreting and the *F* units are falling. Snow can fall through the horizontal light beam from a car headlight, deleting optically at the lower edge of the beam. The particles seen in a street lamp's light can be seen falling until their background is the snow-covered sidewalk. The continuing dance downward, visible when passing in front of a dark wall, is no longer visible against the white sidewalk. The snowflakes accreting and deleting are in

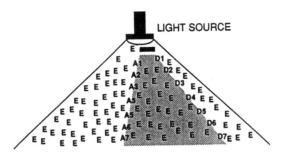

Figure 14.20
An object racing to the right casts a shadow on elements (*E*) with deletion (*D*) at its leading edge and accretion (*A*) at its trailing edge. The elements in the shadow are not illuminated and are invisible.

the foreground, and the wall is the background. At night, insects swarming in a beam of light accrete and delete at the beam's margins, contrasting with dark buildings in the background.

In a 1930s gangster movie set in Alcatraz, a spotlight running across a surface such a brick wall at night could bring elements into the optic array and then move on so they would fall back into darkness. Bricks accrete and delete revealing a continuous surface, with no foreground or background. Cagney or Bogey could run through the spotlight and cast a deep shadow on the ground that would delete elements at its leading edge, while elements would accrete at the trailing edge (figure 14.20).

Other cases are provided by motion and highlights. As we move past a series of small spots of water on a surface, a path of highlights can stretch from us towards the sun, especially if it is low in the sky. The path moves with us, staying aligned with the sun. The highlights accrete as we move forward and delete as we move too far. The sparkling lights accrete at the leading edge of the path and delete at its trailing edge. The accretion and deletion tell us about a continuous surface below us. This is vividly observed flying east-west past the thousands of kettle lakes of the Mississippi, with the sun to the south, or walking over a fresh dry sparkling Ontario snowfall on a sunny winter's day.

On a breezy day, lake water often reflects sunlight as rippling light patterns on boat hulls. The ripples run along the hull and delete at the surface's edge. The accretion and deletion tell us about the foreground surface.

In sum, like outline, accretion and deletion require grouping to tell us about a continuous border. Also like outline, they are ambiguous and can use context to tell us to see them with one foreground-background relation or another.

14.14 STEREO BORDERS

Stereo perception is also very capable of linking separated elements. In random-dot stereo displays, separated dots trip very effective percepts of continuous edges. As in misunderstandings of accretion and deletion, it might be thought that stereo-defined depth is fixed for each element. Context is unimportant, in this view. If so, the hypothesis that there is a role for grouping for all edges, and that outline shares this feature, is threatened.

In fact, stereo-defined elements are affected by context, as a cube based on figure 14.3's dotted-strip figure can show. A flat cube drawing can be defined in a random-dot stereogram. Each stereo-defined line in the drawing is, say, six or seven dots wide. The stereogram can have all the dots defining the lines be at the same depth. The lines are coplanar but stand out from the background of random dots. That is, if we only saw small sections of the lines of the stereo-defined figure all the lines would appear to be on one flat surface, like a mass of dots on a transparency, above a flat, dotted background.

The flat stereo-defined drawing does not just stay flat. In inverse projection, it goes into apparent depth, We see the flat sheet of lines (a stereo image that looks like a 2-D pattern) and we also see a depicted cube, its bars in 3-D. Further, at "+" intersections, the apparent depth of the bars depicted by the stereo-defined lines reverses, much as the depicted bars do in figures 14.2 and 14.3. That is, at the "+" junctions formed by the lines, the percept first causes, for example, the horizontal stereo-defined bar to be in the foreground and continuous, and then the vertical stereo-defined bar to be in the foreground and continuous. The dots in the center of the stereo-defined "+" first group with the other dots to left and right in the horizontal bar, and all these dots are in the foreground. After a reversal, the central dots group with the dots above and below, in keeping with the vertical bar, and all these dots are in the foreground.

In this example, the stereo information for the coplanar locations of the dots does not prevent outline depiction, grouping, occlusion, and reversals. Rather, it provides the conditions under which outline can operate.

The oblique bars, depicting corners, in the stereo-defined depicted cube change orientation as the "+" intersections reverse depth and overlap.

Evidently the referents of outline are available to stereo-defined lines. If outline is a grouping function, as hypothesized, the same functions should be available to pictures of cubes available via motion-defined lines.

14.15 CONCLUSION

Common features of lines and surface edges allow outline drawings to stand for edges of surfaces. An outline drawing generally uses a continuous, polarized border. But dots induce lines that have no polarization. These function as outline, even in stereo-defined lines, and, by hypothesis, in motion-defined lines too.

The referents of outline are edges of surfaces. These are also defined optically by continuous and discontinuous borders, and have no polarization. In sum, grouping effects in perception link physically separate elements of texture. These grouping effects serve surface perception and outline.

Chapter 15

Irreconcilable Views

Hermann Kalkofen

Multiple views in perspectival pictures have been considered both fashionable and irreconcilable. The history of such views deserves to be remembered. Most of the contradictive views have arisen from violations of the tacit "one-point-in-time-one-center-of-projection" canon of linear perspective depiction. Simply stated, this canon is characterized by three main ingredients: "The *three principal elements* of a perspective construction are," in the words of Gezienus Ten Doesschate, "*a* the *centre of perspective* (the *eye*); *b* the *picture plane*; *c* the *object*" (Ten Doesschate 1964, p. 24). This chapter deals with *a* and *c*; the terms "perspective" and "projection" will—unless otherwise declared—be used synonymously. I should beg pardon in advance for a now-and-then unmannerly treatment of works of art.

15.1 "VISUAL FIELDS"

Figure 15.1 may not exactly be considered a work of art; it is borrowed from an illustrated history of psychology and is of the physicist, philosopher, and psychologist Ernst Mach in his study in Prague, probably in the 1880s (Mach 1903). An ordinary photograph, a *faithful picture,* "erscheinungstreues Bild vom Typ der Photographie," as Karl Bühler (1925, p. 113) put it. Photography implies one point of view, one moment. A drawing is a handmade picture, a *chirograph* in the sense of James J. Gibson (1950), not inevitably faithful.

Figure 15.2 also depicts Mach in his study, about 1870. He was at that time concerned with his phenomenal ego, the *Selbstanschauung,* in the case of monocular vision. The outcome is this rather humorously meant self-portrait "from within." It was published by the draftsman in

Figure 15.1
Ernst Mach. From J. Brozek and J. Hoskovec (1993, p. 229).

1885 in his *Analysis of the Sensations* and it has been revived in Gibson's *Perception of the Visual World* (1950). Gibson explained the portrayal as a "literal representation" of Mach's "visual field, with his right eye closed, as he reclined in a nineteenth century chaise longue. His nose delimits the field on the right and his mustache appears below. His body and the room are drawn in detail, although he could not see them in detail without moving his eye" (Gibson 1950, p. 27). Mach's portrait from within represents what Hermann von Helmholtz called a *Blickfeld,* whereby the eye is allowed here to move in its socket. Figure 15.3 shows the visual field of an arrested eye—in Helmholtz's terms a *Sehfeld* (see Metzger 1975, p. 127)—on top of Mach's Blickfeld. The boundary lines indicate appearance change as a function of where in the visual field an object is placed. For example, a yellowish-green perimetric target

Figure 15.2
Self-portrait "from within." From Mach (1903, p. 15).

appears, when first detected, whitish (solid line) and thereafter yellow
(broken line), and not until it reaches the dot-surrounded region does it
appear yellowish green. The so-called functional visual field is defined as
the area wherein some pattern discrimination with an arrested eye is just
possible. It has a horizontal extension of about 15° (Ikeda and Takeuchi
1975).[1]

15.2 CORNELIUS ON CLOSE DISTANCE CONSTRUCTIONS

Mach's portrait from within comprises a generous viewing angle of 150°
horizontally. It is an extremely close-distance construction. Close distance
constructions of pictures have been firmly condemned as a kind of pro-
fessional blunder by Hans Cornelius, philosopher, psychologist, as well as

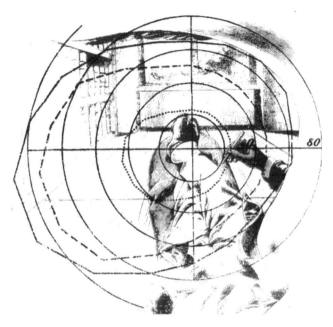

Figure 15.3
A *Sehfeld* on top of Mach's *Blickfeld*. From Mach (1903, p. 15) and Metzger (1975, p. 127).

art historian and educator. In his *Elementargesetze der bildenden Kunst* (Elementary laws of the visual arts) (1908),[2] such constructions came to be banned as they prevent the spectator from achieving a unified view, a *Fernbild,* in the sense of Adolf Hildebrand (1908). Instead they merely create a sum of disjointed impressions; they suffer from the flaw of multiple perspectives (*mehrfache Perspektive,* Cornelius 1908, pp. 23–24). For example, according to William Mackavey a picture as shown in figure 15.4 could just not create "a unitary and stable pictorial conception," because it provides "not only the intended impression of looking at or toward the subject but will contain downward and upward views as well" (Mackavey 1980, p. 215). This pinhole photograph by Maurice Pirenne (1970) of a Greek statuette covers (looked at from the projection center) a visual angle of 90°, as do the deterrent examples that Cornelius (1908, p. 25) constructed. What, then, is the visual angle that would in the eyes of authors such as Cornelius permit a unified view at one glance? Neither Cornelius nor Mackavey explicitly declared a number of degrees as the

Figure 15.4
Pinhole photograph of a Greek statuette (probably Aphrodite, second century
BC, according to Pirenne). From Pirenne (1970, p. 101).

limit. The value recently declared by Michael Bischoff (1998, pp. 143–144), how-ever, amounts to 36°. Outside this visual angle, according to him, objects are no longer clearly perceptible with an unmoving eye. Bischoff traces the 36° back to Hans Jantzen (1911), who asked for the limit up to which a picture can be clearly seen with an unmoving eye but beyond which several shifts of gaze are required to make it perceptible (ibid., p. 120). Jantzen's question remains, strictly speaking, unanswered; he suspected the region to ultimately extend inside the area beyond which increasing marginal distortions emerge. This area has been defined by Guido Hauck, to whom Jantzen referred. On the basis of his own perspective constructions, Hauck estimated it to be between 30° and, maximally, 36°.

15.3   HAUCK ON SUBJECTIVE PERSPECTIVE

Hauck was not actually concerned with gaze direction shifts. He stood out as a discerning critic of the geometrical-perspective teachings of his days, which were still based, as he saw it, on the physiology of the Kepplers (sic) and [Christoph] Scheiners. The latter considered the eye to be a *resting camera obscura,* and yet they were certain of a direct mental apprehension of the retinal image as an instantaneous whole (Hauck 1879, p. 4). The fact that this teaching, in 1879, had remained absolutely untouched by the recent achievements of physiological optics might have been, in Hauck's eyes, at least partly, explained by the accident that the alleged supreme fidelity of perspective received apparent confirmation by the camera obscura pictures of photography (ibid., p. 9).[3] Seeing, however, consists in the eye ceaselessly moving up and down, fixating, and flying over the integral object. According to Hauck, the skillfulness of the eye in this traveling activity is so great that we do not in the least realize the particulars of the process. In a trice, the total image *(Gesammtbild)* is created, which we believe to be a combination of *simultaneous* detail impressions, whereas in reality the same take place *in succession* (ibid., pp. 7–8). Seeing means a transference of the successive to simultaneity. The resulting mental visual image (Hauck's *Gesammt-Anschauungsbild*) would be composed of the received detail impressions, in part contradicting each other, whereas the duty to weigh and compare the importance of the distinct detail impressions fell upon the mind. This is necessary in order to even out the inconsistencies and to bring about an overall result that is

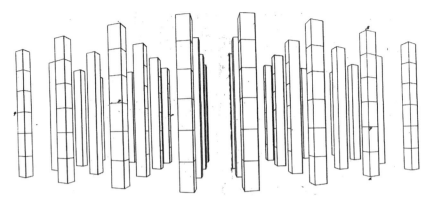

Figure 15.5
Fourfold row of pillars. From Hauck (1879).

consistent with itself and with the mind (ibid., p. 38). This is Helmholtzian "cognitivist" thinking at its best.

The *mathematician* Hauck considered it thinkable that central perspective might represent just one out of an entire order of imaginable and justifiable perspective systems (ibid., p. 6). However, he argued, "If we ... ask about the particular properties of our mental visual image two cardinal features turn out: 1) The *apparent size* of a length is proportional to the *angle of view.*—2) Any *straight line* appears again as *straight* line." The former feature would be called the *principle of conformity,* the latter the *principle of collinearity* (ibid., pp. 39–40).

Being the *aesthetician* that he was, Hauck suggested that a graphic representation, in order to equal the mental visual image as faithfully as possible, should be endowed with the following features: (1) two indispensable conditions to be fulfilled at all cost—the *principle of the linear horizon* and the *principle of verticality*; (2) two secondary conditions to be fulfilled if possible: the *principle of conformity* and the *principle of collinearity*.[4] The latter two conditions oppose each other and cannot be satisfied at the same time; the one excludes the other completely or in part (ibid., pp. 41–42).

Figure 15.5 shows a 95° view of a fourfold row of eight equidistant pillars, whose appearance follows the rules of conform perspective and is reshaped according to the verticality principle.[5] Mind the perceptible curvatures at top and bottom.

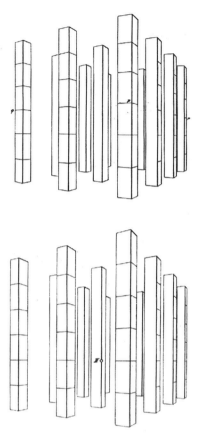

Figure 15.6
Varieties of perspective. From Hauck (1879).

15.4   HAUCK ON ABSOLUTE PERSPECTIVE

Figure 15.6 compares the twelve pillars at the left in figure 15.5 delineated in revised conform perspective (above) and in collinear perspective (below). In both cases, the visual angle is 36°. Up to this angle, the differences between conform and collinear pictures are so minute that it might be considered a region of *absolute* perspective. The deviations would further diminish if the angle becomes 30°. An angle of 30° corresponds, however, to an eye distance just 2 times the width of the picture, an angle of 36° to a distance of 1.5 picture widths,[6] distances generally used and recommended (ibid., p. 76). Is Hauck's estimate of the absolute perspec-

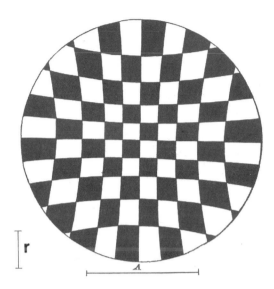

Figure 15.7
Hyperbolic checkerboard pattern. From Helmholtz (1910).

tive area, being based on a comparison of a linear perspective picture with a (no more than in its horizontal part) curvilinear perspective picture, an overestimation?

Figure 15.7 shows the so-called curvilinear checkerboard pattern, a well-known drawing by Helmholtz that is founded on a stereographic projection of the longitudinal and latitudinal meridians of the visual field, in the sense of Blickfeld.[7] The *A* is the appropriate eye distance (try to view the figure from that distance!) that corresponds to a visual angle of 90° or slightly more. The *r* (added by me) indicates the radius of that concentric circle that comprehends, again, Hauck's 36°. The answer to the question of whether linearity is upheld inside the region thereby enclosed may be a matter of taste; to me it tastes not too bad. So much for Hauck's estimate of the area in which artificial and natural perspective may peacefully coexist.

15.5   PIRENNE ON EYE ROTATION AROUND A PROJECTION CENTER

The Jantzen's question, however, needs further elaboration: Hauck's 36° area is still considerably larger than that of the functional visual field. Even a 30° projection cannot be grasped with one glimpse; "distinct detail impressions" have to be successively collected and integrated into a mental visual image here, too. Doing so clearly requires the apprehension of the vast majority of perspectival pictures (when looked at properly from their projection centers), that is, *multiple views*—but are they *irreconcilable* views? When dealing with this problem, Pirenne thinks of a certain window, commonly associated with the name of Leonardo da Vinci but probably invented by Alberti:

"Shutting one eye and keeping my head steady, I can, in principle at least, draw on my study window a picture, in exact linear perspective, of the view outside my window, by tracing (say, with a grease pencil) the outlines of all the objects I see on the glass pane of the window.—Note that, keeping my head steady, I could do this on different 'windows,' placed in different positions, or on windows whose shape is curved instead of plane. Yet, all these outlines in perspective would be seen to cover each other and to cover exactly the real objects, by virtue of their very construction.... This is so even though the eye is continually rotating around a fixed center of rotation, because the images projected successively on the retina, as the eye is rotating, always remain superimposed on one another for each position of the eye. Contrary to widespread misconceptions, *the physical and physiological basis of linear perspective does not in the least entail the immobility of the eye*" (Pirenne 1975, pp. 438–439; emphasis added). Let us, after Pirenne's authoritative plea, conclude this paragraph: even disjointed views may be considered reconcilable in the case that they originate in a selfsame projection center.

15.6   ZOOGRAPHY, SCENOGRAPHY

The third of Ten Doesschate's *principal elements* of perspectival construction, *c*, was the *object*, plainly "the object." Concerning *narrative* objects, Seymour Chatman recognizes in his book *Story and Discourse* first of all, a *what* and a *how*. "The story is the *what* in a narrative that is depicted,[8] discourse the *how*" (Chatman 1978, p. 19). Within the story Chatman discerns *events* and *existents*. Events comprise *actions* and *happenings;* existents are made up of *characters* and the *setting*.[9] In a more epistemological fashion, John Lyons (1977, p. 483) distinguishes between *static* and *dynamic* situations.[10] A static situation is one that is conceived of as *existing,* rather than happening, and as being homogeneous, continuous, and unchanging throughout its duration. A dynamic situation, on the other hand, is something that happens or *occurs*. It might be momentary or enduring, and it might or might not be under the control of an agent.[11] "If a dynamic situation is extended in time, it is a process ... if it is momentary, it is an event ... and, if it is under the control of an agent, it is an action.... Finally, a process that is under the control of an agent is an activity; and an event that is under the control of an agent is an act" (ibid., p. 483; asterisks omitted). Lyons's static situations equal Chatman's existents; Chatman's events resemble Lyons's dynamic situations.

Chatman's discernment of characters and setting within the class of existents brings us back to the notion of two originally separated artistic disciplines: *zoography,* which is accountable for the depiction of living beings, the characters, as Chatman puts it (or, the figures); and then *scenography,* which is obliged to the depiction of the scene, the setting, to use Chatman's term (or, the ground). The two disciplines appear connected first in Greece at the end of the third-century B.C.[12] The double-purpose utilization of pictorial space had begun. Characters (or, respectively, figures) and setting (respectively ground) were nonetheless disparately treated in Renaissance perspective painting, as has been pointed out by Pirenne (1970, p. 121 and n. 6). Margaret Hagen comments on the same issue: "Severe diminution occasionally may be tolerated across a scene, but almost never across an object, particularly not across the human figure" (Hagen 1986, pp. 136–137). This disparity is uniquely exemplified in Andrea Mantegna's impressive *Mourning of Dead Christ* (between 1485 and 1495). The photographic analysis of a secular model of the depicted scene has been carried out by Robert Smith (1974), who shows that "although the perspective diminution across the slab on which Christ's body rests is appropriate to a very close station point, approximately one-and-a-half meters, the figure of Christ is not similarly foreshortened. The proportions of the figure are consonant with a much longer [*sic*] station point" (Hagen 1986, p. 137). The viewing distance comes, according to Smith's diagram (1974, p. 241), to about 21 m. The *zoographic* view of the corpus Christi and the *scenographic* view of the slab are—in the prosaic sense of this chapter—irreconcilable views.

Figure 15.8 is a chronophotograph of Etienne Jules Marey (1882; cited after Ceram 1965, fig. 170). One is tempted to say that it reveals the ontological validity of Chatman's and Lyons's discernments. The chronophotograph was taken at ten equidistant points in time, t_1–t_{10}. We see *one* setting, the jumping posts and the bar, extending from t_1–t_{10}, and *ten* times the agent. The saying that perspective representation reduces the three dimensions of space to two and the dimension of time to a point

Figure 15.8
Chronophotograph of a high jump. From Ceram (1965, pp. 126–129).

is—considering time—apparently not equally valid for characters and
settings. Recording at multiple points in time, intentionally capturing
more than one moment, is not a chrono-*photographic* specificity. We shall
revisit this point in section 15.9.

15.7   PICTOGRAPHY, IDEOGRAPHY

What then is a faithful picture? Bühler's definition of "erscheinungstreues
Bild," translated here, faut de mieux, as "faithful," is met in the photograph as well as in "any picture constructed in accordance with the principles of photographic representation, that means first and foremost,
which takes perspective ('Formen-und Größenperspektive'), the distribution of light and shadow etc, into account" (Bühler 1925, p. 113). This
definition is possibly not in line with the thinking of Hauck (1879, p. 9);
quite noteworthy is, however, Bühler's continuation: "whether the object
depicted really exists or not, whether the artist draws it on the basis of a
perception or on the basis of an idea, whether he reproduces it, as he had

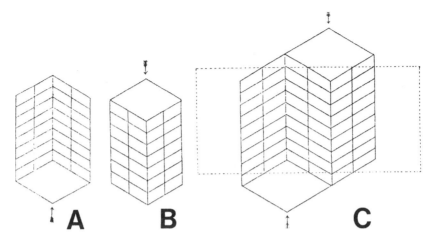

Figure 15.9
Prisms and double prism. From Thiéry (1895, p. 319).

seen it, or whether recreating imagination had been in the game—all that is insubstantial regarding the conception of pictorial faithfulness" (Bühler 1925, p. 113). Depictions of really existing (referent) objects are, semiotically spoken, *pictographs;* pictures of imaginary (referent) objects are *ideographs*.

15.8   GOMBRICH ON THIÉRY'S FIGURE

An unsettling example of a picture containing multiple views was devised by Armand Thiéry (1895) in his chirographic illustration shown in figure 15.9C (ibid., fig. 6). It is known as Thiéry's figure. It was probably not intended as a work of art but is nonetheless referred to in Gombrich's *Art and Illusion:* "It is practically impossible to keep this figure fixed because it presents contradictory cues. The result is that the frequent reversals force our attention to the plane. Thiéry's figure, I believe, presents the quintessence of cubism" (Gombrich 1983, p. 241). The name Armand Thiéry is pair-associated with the perspective theory of the geometrical size illusions. The theory posits that the illusion comes about when perspective suggests depth and thereby effects size changes (Gregory 1977, p. 150). Thiéry's *Pseudoskopisches Doppelprisma* (Wundt's term), is an improvement, as it were, of the Zöllner illusion, which Thiéry had attempted to explain. It is conceived as composed of drawings of two

Figure 15.10
From Theodor De Bry's *Collectiones peregrinatorum in Indiam Orientalem et Indiam Occidentalem* (1590–1634) (1990, p. 27). See plate 5 for color version.

prisms (figures 15.9A and 15.9B; figs. 4 and 5 in Thiéry 1895);[13] the one at the left seen from below, the right one seen from above. If both get combined and consequently have a lateral plane in common, an ambiguous pattern results, which can be interpreted in a twofold way: "If one moves one's eyes from the right to the left, the plane in common with its right edge comes to the fore and forms, with the plane at the right, the prism seen from above. The same right edge recedes, however, when the eyes run through the figure from the second to the third plane to the left. In this case, the planes located at the left apparently portray the prism seen from below" (ibid., p. 320). The two interpretations of Thiéry's figure go along with irreconcilable views.[14]

15.9   MULTIPLE MOMENTS

Prisms and double-prisms, too, are a variety of inanimate object, some sort of existent. The depiction of an existent may be called its presentation.

Figure 15.11
Noble Maiden from Segota. From De Bry (1990, p. 23).

Figure 15.10 (see also plate 5) shows an engraving from Theodor De Bry's *Collectiones peregrinatorum in Indiam Orientalem et Indiam Occidentalem* (1590–1634; see De Bry 1990). Is it the picture of two views of the same woman, or are there two women presented? The German title of the engraving may be translated as *How the Women of Dasamonquepeuc Are Accustomed to Carrying Their Children.* One is tempted to take it as an instructive illustration presenting the front and back of the same person. However, the differential coloring of skin and cloth casts doubt on the unity of the character.[15]

Figure 15.11 brings another example from De Bry's *Collectiones.* The two figures are differently colored, too, but according to the picture's title they depict *one Noble Maiden from Segota;* both are actually meant as presentations of the same character. The two views of the girl can be identified as one point-of-view (POV) shot, which, in this case, shows the canonical form of the object, and as one reverse angle (RVA) shot, which shows the rear view (Salt 1983). This opposition applies, however, to the character only and not to the setting, with its zoographic interspersions

Figure 15.12
Two Venetian Women, Albrecht Dürer (1495). From Strieder (1996, p. 150).

that are both contained in the POV shot.[16] This construction of the—then composite—picture requires *two* centers of projection—one for a zoographic view and one for a "holistic" view. The moment intended here corresponds to *one* point in time. The alternative construction assumes a *single* center of projection and *two* points in time.[17] Here the noble maiden had to change her statuary position during the time lapse between t_1 and t_2 exactly into its opposite.

Figure 15.12 is a drawing by Albrecht Dürer (1495). It is admittedly true that its caption reads as *Two Venetian Women*. The picture shall be nonetheless regarded as presentation of a single character. The sceno-

Figure 15.13
Angela Merkel. From *Die Zeit*, no. 19, 2000. Photographs by Uta Mahler with permission by Ostkreuz Agentur der Fotografen.

Figure 15.14
From De Bry (1990, p. 156).

Figure 15.15
From Stemberger (1990).

graphic cues denoting a unified pictorial space are minimally elaborated. The zoograph at the left presents the character in its canonical form; the one at the right shows its rear view. How is the distance in depth between the two views to be interpreted? Does it result from locomotion, that is, from an (ecliptically depicted) action performed by the character? And if so, how did the action proceed? Does the canonic view designate its beginning or rather the end? Either way, this construction assumes *two* points in time and *one* projection center. The alternative assumes, again, *one* point in time and *two* projection centers.

Figure 15.16
From Racinet (1888/1995, p. 85).

Figure 15.13 brings us a composite photograph presenting two zoo-graphic views of a contemporary German politician. Any scenographic cues have been obliterated here. Clearly, there are *two* points in time des-ignated. The difference in projective size of the views could in principle have been effected by locomotion of the object. More likely, however, it was achieved by traveling of the projection center, and even more likely by the surrogate manipulation of a zoom lens. The presentation comprises, anyhow, two points of view, two points in time. The order of the moments remains undecided.

Narration proper needs chronology. The heading of De Bry's engrav-ing presented in figure 15.14 reads: *The Wife of a King in the Province of Cumana Brings Gifts to the Landvogt Herrera* (1594). The temporal order of the two views suggested is from the right to the left. She approaches from the middle ground at the right, t_1, and has arrived in the foreground, t_2. Order in time and location in space are congruous here; remoteness in space corresponds in this case with remoteness in time passed. The per-spective may be named retrospective (Kalkofen 1993).

Figure 15.17
From Kratzsch (1983, p. 39).

However, future time, too, is remote and distant from the present. The picture *Serveto and His Execution* (Christof van Sichem, 1608) (figure 15.15) is an instance of what may be named prospective perspective (ibid.).

Figure 15.16 brings a detail from a Japanese woodcut *The Fitting out of an Archer*. It is the selfsame soldier indeed in both views, as can be deduced from the omitted context. The scenographic cues are minimized again. Pictorial space is reduced to the foreground. Thus, the depicted action proceeds from the left to the right.[18] Figure 15.17 shows a woodcut from the Luther Bible (Kratzsch 1983), *Samson Beats the Philistines,* 1534. This is another case of prospective perspective.

Pictorial narration may of course extend to more than two bare moments. For example, De Bry's engraving presented in figure 15.18 *(Indians want to try out whether the Spaniards be immortal folks and drown a Spaniard named Salsedo in the sea)* comprises three moments and is another example of prospective perspective. The instances of Wickhoff's *continuous* style with its characteristic figure repetitions could be enor-

Figure 15.18
From De Bry (1990, p. 158).

mously augmented by further examples. Suffice it to say that the rule of
the continuous style lasted, as stated by Franz Wickhoff, through one and
a half millennia, until the sixteenth century (Wickhoff 1912, p. 13). The
disappearance of continuous style began a long time before the invention of photography proper. Multiple use of scenographic space for zoographic purposes became unfashionable—for whatsoever reasons, not
necessarily aesthetic ones. Frescoes worked out by Sandro Botticelli,
Domenico Ghiralandaio, and Luca Signorelli in the continuous manner
beautify through today the walls of the Sistine Chapel.

15.10   EGYPTIAN VIEWS

The so-called Egyptian method (Arnheim 1974, p. 112) may be considered
as another, primordial, attempt in line of the multiple use of pictorial

Figure 15.19
From Lübke and Pernice (1921, fig. 71/51), *Sethos I. Offers a Picture to Truth* (Seth, Seti), nineteenth dynasty (1314–1200 B.C.).

space, which is here, of course, at most zoographical space. The famous drawing by Daniel Alain (Gombrich 1983, fig. 1; Gibson 1979, fig. 15.3) is a perceptive cartoon, perceptive also in that it represents the model's right arm as ending in a left hand. A similar case has been made by Pirenne (1970, p. 79) for an authentic papyrus drawing, where the left arm of the figure ends in a "wrong" hand. Unbeatable in this regard, however, is this presentation of Sethos I, (figure 15.19), the father of Ramses II. Let me conclude: not only the abolition of the one-point-in-time-one-center-of-projection canon leads to irreconcilable views.

Notes

1. The term has seemingly been coined by Sanders (1970); Ikeda and Takeuchi report that "the functional visual field varied greatly among subjects, and also changed for a particular subject when the data were collected on different occasions" (1975, p. 260).

2. The author was among the founding fathers of Gestalt theory (cf. Metzger 1975, p. 133). Jantzen (1911, p. 120) characterized Cornelius' book as "reich illustrierten Kommentar zu Adolf Hildebrands Problem der Form" ["richly illustrated commentary on Adolf Hildebrand's *Problem of Form*"] (Hildebrand 1908).

3. Compare Te Peerdt: "Vor Erfindung der Photographie ist nicht einmal der Gedanke einer wahrhaft einheitlichen optischen Darstellung gefasst gewesen" ["Before the invention of photography the thought of a truly consistent optical representation had not even existed"] (1899, p. 6).

4. I have reversed the order of the two principles from the order in which he gave them.

5. Hauck's "reconceived pictorial space"—one system of "curvilinear perspective" among others (Pirenne 1970, p. 148)—has been assessed by Ten Doesschate: "He introduced a new system of perspective which he called 'conform' in opposition to normal central perspective which is collinear.—Hauck is not consistent. He represents horizontal straight lines by arcs; verticals, however, he 'rectifies.' This he does according to our 'consciousness of verticality' (Vertikalitätsbewusstsein)" (1964, pp. 47–48). Hauck's semiconformity has already been criticized by Panofsky (1927, p. 262).

6. In the case of still smaller viewing distances, it would be feasible to begin the construction collinearily first and to reshape possible conformity distortions later on, according to conform perspective. Raphael always proceeded in this way, see, for example, the spheres at the right and the base of the column at the left in *The School of Athens,* 1510–11, (Hauck 1879, p. 75). Compare Pirenne: "The architecture which extends over most of the painting is drawn in perspective as one whole, from one main centre of projection. But the spheres (and the numerous human figures) are not drawn as projections from this centre. They are drawn from a number of subsidiary centres of projection, each in front of the position which the respective sphere or figure would occupy in the painting" (1970, p. 121).

7. "[D]ie Richtkreise des Blickfeldes, welche mit der durch den Fixationspunkt gehenden vertikalen und horizontalen Linie übereinstimmende Richtung haben, auf eine ebene Tafel projiziert" ["the reference circles that have a common direction with the vertical and horizontal lines that cross the fixation point, projected onto a plane"] (Helmholtz 1910, p. 150).

8. "[P]icture narratives have, of course, been common for centuries" (Chatman 1978, p. 34).

9. Chatman (1978) notes that this kind of distinction has been recognized since antiquity, that is, in Aristotle's *Poetics* (p. 19). Comparably, G. E. Lessing drew a distinction between characters *(Körper)* and actions *(Handlungen)* (Lessing 1964).

10. "The conceptual framework within which we organize and describe our perceptions of the physical world, whatever language we speak, is one in which we can identify not only states-of-affairs of shorter or longer duration, but also events, processes and actions.—There is, unfortunately, no satisfactory term that would cover states, on the one hand, and events, processes and actions, on the other" (Lyons 1977, p. 483). Lyons' opposition reminds us of L. von Bertalanffy's (1952) saying that "what are called structures are slow processes." Consistent with this opposition is Strawson's ontological distinction between first- and second-order entities (Lyons 1977, p. 443).

11. An agent is, in the sense of Chatman, an existent; in Lyons's sense he is a *static situation.* Lyons refrains—understandably—from naming agents situations.

12. In the words of Franz Wickhoff: "Endlich, für unsere gewohnte Vorstellung von der Kunstentwicklung spät genug, hatte sich auch im Bilde zusammengeschlossen, was man auf der Szene schon lange zu sehen gewohnt war: wandelnde Figuren vor einem geschlossenen Grund" ["Late enough for our accustomed idea of the development of art, something long familiar on the scene finally came together for the picture: changing figures in front of a closed ground"] (1912, p. 104).

13. This is a somewhat strange composition in that Thiéry's figures 4, 5, and 6 show nine, eight, and ten crossing transversals respectively.

14. The picture-prisms are, of course, *perspective projections:* Thiéry's drawing instructions for the prisms read as follows: "Man denke sich ein verticales Prisma, von dem bloß zwei Seitenflächen gesehen werden. Das Prisma ist um eine horizontale Achse beweglich. Auf jede der sichtbaren Flächen des Prismas zeichnet man eine verticale durch horizontale Striche eingetheilte Linie. Wenn das Prisma so gedreht worden ist, dass sein oberer Theil vom Beobachter entfernt liegt, dann wird das Prisma als Figur 4 und die wagerechten Striche werden als Transversalen erscheinen. Die eingetheilten Linien werden jetzt in Folge dessen nach oben convergent gesehen. Da das Auge des Beobachters in der Höhe der Achse liegt, so sind auch die oberen Eckpunkte der Linien dem Beobachter näher als die unteren; der Gesichtswinkel der Distanz zwischen den oberen Endpunkten ist also kleiner wie der zwischen den unteren. Ferner: wirklich nach oben divergirende Linien würden in diesem Fall als parallele Linien gezeichnet werden müssen" (Thiéry 1895, pp. 321–322).

15. The differential coloring is probably an indication of the advanced decay of what has been called by Wickhoff the *continuous* style, with its characteristic figure repetitions.

16. Or in the RVA shot: the picture can be "read" alternately.

17. Compare Vitz's nice analysis of Edouard Manet's *Bar at the Folies Bergère,* 1881 (Vitz 1979, p. 139).

18. The action proceeds with varying time intervals. Its depiction relates, in contrast to Marey's chronophotography of the jump, to an *intrinsic* segmentation.

References

Adams, P. A., and Haire, M. (1959). The effect of orientation on the reversal of one cube inscribed in another. *American Journal of Psychology, 72,* 296–299.

Adelson, E. H. (1993). Perceptual organization and the judgement of brightness. *Science, 262,* 2042–2044.

Alberti, L. B. (1436/1966). *On painting* (trans. J. R. Spencer). New Haven, Conn.: Yale University Press.

Alberti, L. B. (1436/1972). *On painting* (trans. C. Grayson). London: Phaidon.

Alhazen, I. (1039/1989). Book of optics. In A. I. Sabra (ed.), *The optics of Ibn Al-Haytham.* London: Warburg Institute, University of London. (Alhazen died about 1039 C. E. When he wrote this work is not known.)

Anderson, C. H., and Van Essen, D. C. (1987). Shifter circuits: A computational strategy for dynamic aspects of visual processing. *Proceedings of the National Academy of Science, 84,* 6297–6301.

Anderson, K. (1992). Brook Taylor's work on linear perspective. *Sources in the history of mathematics and physical sciences,* vol. 10. New York: Springer.

Arend, L., and Goldstein, R. (1987). Simultaneous constancy, lightness and brightness. *Journal of the Optical Society of America A, 4,* 2281–2285.

Arnheim, R. (1974). *Art and visual perception: A psychology of the creative eye.* Berkeley: University of California Press.

Atkins, J. E., Fiser, J., and Jacobs, R. A. (2001). Experience-dependent visual cue integration based on consistencies between visual and haptic percepts. *Vision Research, 41,* 449–461.

Attneave, F. (1954). Some informational aspects of visual perception. *Psychological Review, 61,* 183–193.

Bahn, P., and Vertut, J. (1997). *Journey through the Ice Age.* Berkeley: University of California Press.

Ballard, D. (1991). Animate vision, *Artificial Intelligence, 48,* 57–86.

Baxandall, M. (1985). *Patterns of intention: On the historical explanation of pictures.* London: Yale University Press.

Bazin, A. (1967). The ontology of the photographic image. In *What is cinema?*, vol. 1, selected and translated by Hugh Gray. Berkeley and Los Angeles: University of California Press.

Bechtel, W., and Abrahamsen, A. (1991). *Connectionism and the mind: An introduction to parallel processing in networks*. Cambridge, MA: Blackwell.

Belhumeur, P. N. (1996). A computational theory for binocular stereopsis. In D. C. Knill and W. Richards (eds.), *Perception as Bayesian inference* (pp. 323–364). New York: Cambridge University Press.

Belhumeur, P., Kriegman, D. J., and Yuille, A. L. (1999). The bas-relief ambiguity. *International Journal of Computer Vision, 35,* 33–44.

Berger, J. (1972). *Ways of seeing.* London: BBC and Penguin.

Berkeley, G. (1709/1975). An Essay toward a new theory of vision. In *Philosophical works,* introduction and notes by M. R. Ayers. London: J. M. Dent and Sons. (Original work appeared in 1709, Dublin.)

Bertalanffy, L. von (1952). *Problems of life: An evaluation of modern biological thought.* London: Watts & Co.

Biederman, I. (1985) Human image understanding: Recent research and a theory. *Computer Vision, Graphics and Image processing, 32,* 29–73.

Birnbaum, M. H. (1983). Scale convergence as a principle for the study of perception. In H. Geissler (ed.), *Modern issues in perception* (pp. 319–335). Amsterdam: North-Holland.

Bischoff, M. (1998). Nahdistanzkonstruktion und Bildwahrnehmung (Construction and Picture Perception). In K. Sachs-Hombach and K. Rehkämper (eds.), *Bild—Bildwahrnehmung—Bildverarbeitung* (image—picture perception—image processing) (pp. 143–151), Wiesbaden: Deutscher Universitätsverlag.

Bool, F. H., Kist, J. R., Locher, J. L., and Wierda, F. (1981). *M. C. Escher: His life and complete work.* New York: Harry Abrams.

Born, M., and Wolf, E. (1959). *Principles of optics.* London: Pergamon.

Bouret, J. (1950). *Picasso, dessins.* Paris: Diffusions Française.

Boyd, R. (1979). Metaphor and theory change: What is "metaphor" a metaphor for? In A. Ortony (ed.), *Metaphor and thought* (pp. 356–408). Cambridge: Cambridge University Press.

Brentano, F. von (1874). *Die Psychologie vom empirischen Standpunkte* (Psychology from an empirical standpoint). Leipzig, Germany: Duncker und Humbolt.

Brodatz, P. (1966). *Textures.* New York: Dover.

Brozek, J., and Hoskovec, J. (1993). Zur Geschichte der Prager deutschsprachigen Psychologie (Regarding the History of the German Speaking Psychology in Prague). In H. Lück and R. Miller (eds.), *Illustrierte Geschichte der Psychologie* (Illustrated History of Psychology) (pp. 227–232). Munich: Quintessenz.

Bruno, N., and Cutting, J. E. (1988). Minimodularity and the perception of layout. *Journal of Experimental Psychology: General, 117,* 161–170.

Buckley, D., Frisby, J. P., and Freeman, J. (1994). Lightness perception can be affected by surface curvature from stereopsis. *Perception, 23,* 869–881.

Bühler, K. (1922). Die Erscheinungsweisen der Farben (The appearance of the colors). In K. Bühler (ed.), *Handbuch der Psychologie,* part 1: Die Struktur der Wahrnehmungen (Handbook of Psychology, part 1: The structure of Perception) (pp. 1–201). Jena, Germany: Fischer.

Bühler, K. (1925). *Abriß der geistigen Entwicklung des Kindes* (Mental Development of the Child). Leipzig, Germany: Quelle and Meyer.

Bunge, W. (1966). *Theoretical geography.* Lund, Sweden: C. W. K. Gleerup.

Burton, H. E. (1945). The optics of Euclid. *Journal of the Optical Society of America, 35,* 357–372.

Busey, T. A., Brady, N. P., and Cutting, J. E. (1990). Compensation is unnecessary for the perception of faces in slanted pictures. *Perception and Psychophysics, 48,* 1–11.

Cabe, P. A., Abele, P. N., and Kennedy, J. M. (1999). Dominance of binocular depth information over competing kinetic occlusion information. Paper presented at the meeting of the Psychonomic Society, November 18–21, Los Angeles.

Cadiou, H., and Gilou (1989). *La peinture en trompe l'oeil* (Trompe l'oeil Painting). Paris: Dessain et Tolra.

Carani, M. (1998). The semiotics of perspective, *Semiotica, 119* (3/4), 309–357.

Carlbom, I., and Paciorek, J. (1978). Planar geometric projections and viewing transformations. *Computing Surveys, 10,* 465–502.

Carl Zeiss Jena (1907). Instrument zum beidäugigen Betrachten von Gemälden u.ggl (Instrument for the Binocular Viewing of Paintings). Kaiserliches Patentamt (patent no), Patentschrift no. 194480, Klasse 42h, Gruppe 34.

Carroll, N. (1988). *Mystifying movies: Fads and fallacies in contemporary film theory.* New York: Columbia University Press.

Cavanagh, P., and Kennedy, J. M. (2000). Close encounters: Small details veto depth from shadows. *Science, 287,* 2421.

Cavanagh, P., and Leclerc, Y. G. (1989). Shape from shadows. *Journal of Experimental Psychology: Human Perception and Performance, 15,* 3–27.

Cazeaux, C. (in press). Metaphor and the categorization of the senses. *Metaphor and Symbol.*

Cavanagh, P. (1987). Reconstructing the third dimension: Interactions between color, texture, motion, binocular disparity, and shape. *Computer Vision, Graphics, and Image Processing, 37,* 171–195.

Ceram, C. W. (1965). *Eine Archäologie des Kinos* (An Archeology of Cinema). Reinbek: Rowohlt.

Chatman, S. (1978). *Story and discourse: Narrative structure in fiction and film.* Ithaca, N.Y.: Cornell University Press.

Chauvet, J.-M., Brunel Deschamps, E., and Hillaire, C. (1995). *La Grotte Chauvet à Vallon-Pont-d'Arc*. Paris: Seuil.

Chomsky, N. (1957/1971). *Syntactic structures*. The Hague, Netherlands: Mouton.

Chomsky, N. (1995). *The minimalist program*. Cambridge, Mass.: MIT Press.

Chomsky, N. (1996). *Powers and prospects: Reflections on human nature and the social order*. London: Pluto Press

Chomsky, N. (2000). *New horizons in the study of language and mind*. Cambridge: Cambridge University Press.

Churchland, P. M. (1989). Perceptual plasticity and theoretical neutrality: A reply to Jerry Fodor, *Philosophy of Science, 55,* 167–187.

Churchland, P. M. (1992). *A neurocomputational perspective: The nature of mind and the structure of science*. Cambridge, MA: MIT Press.

Churchland, P. S., Ramachandran, V. S., and Sejnowski, T. J. (1994). A critique of pure vision. In C. Koch and J. C. Davis (eds.), *Large-scale neuronal theories of the brain* (pp. 23–60). Cambridge, Mass.: MIT Press.

Clottes, J. (2001). *La Grotte Chauvet: L'art des origines* (The Art of the Origins). Paris: Seuil.

Clowes, M. B. (1971). On seeing things. *Artificial Intelligence, 2* (1), 79–116.

Cook, M. (1978). Judgment of distance on a plane surface. *Perception and Psychophysics, 23,* 85–90.

Cornelius, H. (1908). *Elementargesetze der bildenden Kunst: Grundlagen einer praktischen Ästhetik* (Elementary Laws of Visual Art: Foundations of a Practical Aesthetics). Leipzig and Berlin: Teuber.

Costall, A. P. (1990). Seeing through pictures. *Word and Image, 6,* 273–277.

Cutting, J. E. (1986a). *Perception with an eye for motion*. Cambridge, Mass.: MIT Press.

Cutting, J. E. (1986b). The shape and psychophysics of cinematic space. *Behavior Research Methods, Instruments, and Computers, 18,* 551–558.

Cutting, J. E. (1987). Rigidity in cinema seen from the front row, side aisle. *Journal of Experimental Psychology: Human Perception and Performance, 13,* 323–334.

Cutting, J. E. (1988). Affine distortions in pictorial space: Some predictions for Goldstein (1987) that La Gournerie (1859) might have made. *Journal of Experimental Psychology: Human Perception and Performance, 14,* 305–311.

Cutting, J. E. (1997). How the eye measures reality and virtual reality. *Behavior Research Methods, Instruments, and Computers, 29,* 27–36.

Cutting, J. E. (1998). Information from the world around us. In J. Hochberg (ed.), *Perception and cognition at century's end* (pp. 69–93). New York: Academic Press.

Cutting, J. E., and Massironi, M. (1998). Pictures and their special status in perceptual and cognitive inquiry. In J. Hochberg (ed.), *Perception and cognition at century's end: History, philosophy, and theory* (pp. 137–168). San Diego: Academic Press.

Cutting, J. E., and Vishton, P. M. (1995). Perceiving layout and knowing distances: The integration, relative potency, and contextual use of different information about depth. In W. Epstein and S. Rogers (eds.), *Perception of space and motion* (pp. 69–117). San Diego, Calif.: Academic Press.

Damisch, H. (1994). *The origin of perspective* (trans. John Goodman). Cambridge, Mass.: MIT Press.

Danto, A. (2001). Seeing and showing. *Journal of Aesthetics and Art Criticism, 59,* 1–10.

Da Silva, J. A. (1985). Scales of perceived egocentric distance in a large open field: Comparison of three psychophysical methods. *American Journal of Psychology, 98,* 119–144.

De Bry, T. (1990). R*eisen in das östliche und westliche Indien: Reisen in das westliche Indien (Amerika)* (Travels to east and west Indies; Travels to the West Indies (America)), ed. G. Sievenich. Berlin and New York: Casablanca Verlag.

Denis, M. (1890/1976). In R. Goldwater and M. Treves (eds.) *Artists on art: From the 14th to the 20th century* (p. 380). London: John Murray.

Deregowski, J. B., Muldrow, E. S., and Muldrow, W. F. (1972). Pictorial recognition in a remote Ethiopian population. *Perception, 1,* 417–425.

Descartes, R. (1637/1965). *Discourse on method, optics, geometry, and meteorology* (trans. Paul J. Olscamp). New York: Bobbs-Merrill.

Diels, H. (1922). *Die Fragmente der Vorsokratiker*, 4th ed., vol. 1. Berlin: Weidmannsche Buchhandlung.

Doorn, A. J. van, Koenderink, J. J., Ridder, H. de (2001). Pictorial space correspondence in photographs of an object in different poses. In B. E. Rogowitz and T. N. Pappas (eds.), *Proceedings of SPIE: Human vision and electronic imaging VI. 4299,* 321–329.

Dosher, B. A., Sperling, G., and Wurst, S. A. (1986). Tradeoffs between stereopsis and proximity luminance covariance as determinants of perceived 3D structure, *Vision Research, 26,* 973–990.

Dubery, F., and Willats, J. (1972). *Drawing systems*. London: Studio Vista.

Dubery, F., and Willats, J. (1983). *Perspective and other drawing systems*. London: Herbert Press; New York: Van Nostrand Reinhold.

Eby, D. W., and Braunstein, M. L. (1995). The perceptual flattening of three-dimensional scenes enclosed by a frame. *Perception, 24,* 981–993.

Epstein, W. (1968). Modification of the disparity-depth relationship as a result of exposure to conflicting cues. *The American Journal of Psychology, 81,* 189–197.

Epstein, W. (1982). Percept-percept coupling. *Perception, 11,* 75–83.

Epstein, W., and Rogers, S. (in press). Percept-percept coupling revisited. In U. Savardi (ed.), *Festschrift in onore di Paolo Bozzi*. Padua, Italy: Cleup.

Erens, R. G. F., Kappers, A. M. L., and Koenderink, J. J. (1991). Limits on the perception of local shape from shading. In P. J. Beek, R. J. Bootsma, and P. C. W. van Wieringen (eds.), *Studies in perception and action* (pp. 65–71). Amsterdam: Rodopi.

Erens, R. G. F., Kappers, A. M. L., and Koenderink, J. J. (1993). Perception of local shape from shading. *Perception and Psychophysics, 54,* 145–156.

Evans, G. (1982). *The varieties of reference,* ed. J. McDowell. Oxford: Oxford University Press.

Farber, J., and Rosinski, R. R. (1978). Geometrical transformations of pictured space. *Perception, 7,* 269–282.

Faugeras, O. D. (1993). *Three dimensional computer vision: A geometric viewpoint.* Cambridge, Mass.: MIT Press.

Faul, F. (1997). *Theoretische und experimentelle Untersuchungen chromatischer Determinanten perzeptueller Transparenz* (Theoretical and experimental investigations of chromatic determinants of perceptual transparency). Dissertation thesis, University of Kiel.

Field, J. V. (1993). Mathematics and the craft of painting: Piero della Francesca and perspective. In J. V. Field and F. A. J. L. James (eds.), *Renaissance and revolution* (pp. 73–95). Cambridge: Cambridge University Press.

Flavell, J. H., Flavell, E. R., and Green, F. L. (1983). Development of the appearance-reality distinction. *Cognitive Psychology, 15,* 95–120.

Fleming, W. (1986). *Arts and ideas.* New York: Holt, Rinehart, and Winston.

Flückiger, M. (1991). La perception d'objets lointains. In M. Flückiger and K. Klaue (eds.), *La perception de l'environnement* (pp. 221–238). Lausanne, Switzerland: Delachaux et Niestlè.

Fodor, J. (1983). *The modularity of mind.* Cambridge, Mass.: MIT Press.

Freedberg, D. (1989). *The power of images.* Chicago: University of Chicago Press.

Fuchs, W. (1923a). Experimentelle Untersuchungen über das simultane Hintereinandersehen auf derselben Sehrichtung. *Zeitschrift für Psychologie, 91,* 145–235.

Fuchs, W. (1923b). Experimentelle Untersuchungen über die Änderung von Farben unter dem Einfluß von Gestalten ("Angleichungserscheinungen") (Experimental investigations about the influence of Gestalts on the change of color). *Zeitschrift für Psychologie, 92,* 249–325.

Gablik, S. (1985). *Magritte.* London: Thames and Hudson.

Galanter, E., and Galanter, P. (1973). Range estimates of distance visual stimuli. *Perception and Psychophysics, 14,* 301–306.

Gallistel, C. R. (1998). Symbolic processes in the brain: The case of insect navigation. In D. Scarborough and S. Sternberg (eds.), *Methods, models and conceptual issues: An invitation to cognitive science,* vol. 4 (pp. 1–51). Cambridge, Mass.: MIT Press.

Gallistel, C. R. (2000). The replacement of general-purpose learning models with adaptively specialized learning modules. In M. S. Gazzaniga (ed.), *The cognitive neurosciences,* 2d. ed. (pp. 1179–1191). Cambridge, Mass.: MIT Press.

Gårling, T. (1970). Studies in visual perception of architectural spaces and rooms, III: A relation of judged depth to judge size of space. *Scandinavian Journal of Psychology, 11,* 124–131.

Gelb, A. (1921). Grundfragen der Wahrnehmungspsychologie (Basic questions in perceptional psychology). In K. Bühler (ed.), *Bericht über den VII. Kongreß für experimentelle Psychologie* (Report on the 7th congress of experimental psychology) (pp. 114–115). Jena, Germany: Gustav Fischer.

Gelb, A. (1929). Die "Farbenkonstanz" der Sehdinge. In A. Bethe, G. v. Bergmann, G. Embden, and A. Ellinger (Eds.), *Handbuch der normalen und pathologischen Physiologie. Bd.12, 1.Hälfte. Receptionsorgane II. (pp. 594678)*. Berlin: Springer. [Transl: The color constancy of visual objects. Handbook of normal and pathological physiology, vol. 12: Organs of reception]

Gelb, A., and Granit, R. (1923). Die Bedeutung von "Figur" und "Grund" für die Farbenschwelle (The significance of figure and ground for the color threshold). *Zeitschrift für Psychologie, 93,* 83–118.

Gibson, J. J. (1947/1982). Pictures as substitutes for visual realities. In E. Reed and R. Jones (eds.), *Selected essays of James J. Gibson* (pp. 231–240). Hillsdale, N.J.: Erlbaum. (Original work appeared in 1947.)

Gibson, J. J. (1950). *The perception of the visual world.* Boston: Houghton Mifflin.

Gibson, J. J. (1954). The visual perception of objective motion and subjective movement. *Psychological Review, 61,* 304–314.

Gibson, J. J. (1954). A theory of pictorial perception. *Audio-visual Communications Review, 1* (3). (Gibson does not give any page nos. and I have been unable to track them down.)

Gibson, J. J. (1960). Pictures, perspective, and perception, *Dædalus, 89* (winter issue), 216–227.

Gibson, J. J. (1966). *The senses considered as perceptual systems.* Boston: Houghton Mifflin.

Gibson, J. J. (1971). The information available in pictures. *Leonardo, 4,* 27–35.

Gibson, J. J. (1979). *The ecological approach to visual perception.* Boston: Houghton Mifflin.

Gibson, E. J., and Bergman, R. (1954). The effect of training on absolute estimation of distance over the ground. *Journal of Experimental Psychology, 48,* 473–482.

Gibson, J. J., and Cornsweet, J. (1952). The perceived slant of visual surfaces— optical and geographical. *Journal of Experimental Psychology, 44,* 11–15.

Gilden, D. (1991). On the origins of dynamical awareness. *Psychological Review, 98,* 554–568.

Gilinsky, A. S. (1951). Perceived size and distance in visual space. *Psychological Review, 58,* 460–482.

Gillam, B. J. (1968). Perception of slant when perspective and stereopsis conflict: Experiments with aniseikonic lenses. *Journal of Experimental Psychology, 78,* 299–305.

Gillam, B. J. (1995). The perception of spatial layout from static optical information. In W. Epstein and S. Rogers (eds.), *Perception of space and motion.* New York: Academic Press.

Gillam, B., and Sedgwick, H. A. (1996). The interaction of stereopsis and perspective in the perception of depth. *Perception, 25 (supplement), 70.*

Gillam, B., Sedgwick, H. A., and Cook, M. (1993). The interaction of surfaces with each other and with discrete objects in stereoscopic depth. *Perception, 22 (supplement),* 35.

Glennerster, A., and McKee, S. P. (1999). Bias and sensitivity of stereo judgements in the presence of a slanted reference plane. *Vision Research, 39,* 3057–3069.

Gogel, W. C. (1993). The analysis of perceived space. In S. Masin (ed.), *Foundations of perceptual theory* (pp. 113–182). Amsterdam: North-Holland.

Gogh, V. van (1959). *The complete letters of Vincent van Gogh: With reproductions of all the drawings in the correspondence,* 2d ed., vol. 1. Greenwich, Conn.: New York Graphic Society.

Goldsmith, T. H. (1990). Optimization, constraint, and history in the evolution of eyes. *The Quarterly Review of Biology, 65,* 281–322.

Gombrich, E. (1956). *Art and illusion: A study in the psychology of pictorial representation.* Princeton, N.J.: Princeton University Press.

Gombrich, E. H. (1959). *Art and illusion,* part 3: The beholder's share. London: Phaidon Press.

Gombrich, E. H. (1960). *Art and illusion: A study in the psychology of pictorial representation.* New York: Pantheon.

Gombrich, E. H. (1960/1993). *Art and illusion: A study in the psychology of pictorial representation.* London: Phaidon.

Gombrich, E. H. (1974). "The sky is the limit": The vault of heaven and pictorial vision. In E. H. Gombrich, *The image and the eye: Further studies in the psychology of pictorial representation* (pp. 162–171). Ithaca, N.Y.: Cornell University Press.

Gombrich, E. H. (1982). *The image and the eye: Further studies in the psychology of pictorial representation.* Oxford: Phaidon.

Gombrich, E. H. (1983). *Art and illusion: A study in the psychology of pictorial representation.* Oxford: Phaidon Press.

Gombrich, E. H. (1987). The art of the Greeks. In R. Woodfield (ed.), *Reflections on the history of art* (pp. 11–17). Berkeley: University of California Press.

Goodman, N. (1968). *The Languages of art.* New York: Bobbs-Merrill.

Goodman, N. (1968/1976). *Languages of art: An approach to a theory of symbols.* Indianapolis: Hackett.

Goodman, N. (1969). *Languages of Art,* 2d ed. Oxford: Oxford University Press.

Gorea, A., and Julesz, B. (1990). Context superiority in a detection task with line-element stimuli: A low-level effect. *Perception, 19,* 5–16.

Gregory, R. L. (1977). *Eye and brain: The psychology of seeing.* London: Weidenfeld and Nicolson.

Grüsser, O. J., and Landis, T. (1991). Visual agnosias and related disorders. In J. Cronly-Dillon (ed.), *Vision and visual dysfunction.* Basingstoke, United Kingdom: MacMillan.

Haber, R. N. (1980). Perceiving space from pictures: A theoretical analysis. In M. A. Hagen (ed.), *The perception of pictures,* vol. 1 (pp. 3–31). New York: Academic Press.

Hagen, M. A. (1985). There is no development in art. In N. H. Freeman and M. V. Cox (eds.), *Visual order: The nature and development of pictorial representation* (pp. 59–77). Cambridge: Cambridge University Press.

Hagen, M. A. (1986). *Varieties of realism: Geometries of representational art.* Cambridge: Cambridge University Press.

Hagen, M. A., and Giorgi, R. (1993). Where's the camera? *Ecological Psychology, 5,* 65–84.

Hagen, M. A., and Jones, R. K. (1978). Cultural effects on pictorial perception: How many words is one picture really worth? In R. D. Walk and H. L. Pick Jr. (eds.), *Perception and experience* (pp. 171–212). New York: Plenum Press.

Harris, P. L., and Kavanaugh, R. D. (1993). Young children's understanding of pretense. *Monographs of the Society for Research in Child Development, 58.*

Harway, N. I. (1963). Judgment of distance in children and adults. *Journal of Experimental Psychology, 65,* 385–390.

Hauck, G. (1879). *Die subjektive Perspektive und die horizontalen Curvaturen des dorischen Styls: Eine perspektivisch-ästhetische Studie* (The subjective perspective and the horizontal curvatures of the doric style: A perspectival aesthetic study). Stuttgart, Germany: Wittwer.

Hawking, S. W. (1993). *A brief history of time: From the Big Bang to black holes.* London: Bantam Press.

Hecht, H., van Doorn, A., and Koenderink, J. J. (1999). Compression of visual space in natural scenes and in their photographic counterparts. *Perception and Psychophysics, 61,* 1269–1286.

Heider, F. (1926). Ding und Medium. *Symposium, 1,* 109–157.

Helmholtz, H. von (1867). *Handbuch der Physiologischen Optik.* Hamburg: Voss.

Helmholtz, H. von (1894). Über den Ursprung der richtigen Deutung unserer Sinneseindrücke (The origin and correct interpretation of our sense impressions). *Zeitschrift für Psychologie und Physiologie der Sinnesorgane, 7,* 81–91.

Helmholtz, H. von (1896). *Handbuch der physiologischen Optik,* 2d ed. Hamburg: Voss.

Helmholtz, H. von (1910). *Handbuch der Physiologischen Optik.* 3d ed., 3d vol. Hamburg/Leipzig: Voss. (Expanded and coedited with A. Gullstrand, J. v. Kries, and W. Nagel.)

Helmholtz, H. von (1911/1925). *Treatise on physiological optics,* 3d ed. (ed. and trans. J. P. C. Southall). Rochester, N.Y.: Optical Society of America.

Hel-Or, Y., and Edelman, S. (1994). A new approach to qualitative stereo. In S. Ullman and S. Peleg (eds.), *Proceedings of the 12th international conference on pattern recognition* (pp. 316–320). Washington, D.C.: IEEE Press.

Hildebrand, A. (1893/1945). The Problem of Form in Painting and Sculpture (trans. M. Meyer and R. M. Ogden). New York: G. E. Stechert. (Originally published 1893, Straßburg.)

Hildebrand, A. (1908). *Das Problem der Form in der bildenden Kunst.* Strasbourg, Germany: Heitz.

Hochberg. J. (1962). The psychophysics of picture perception. *Audio-Visual Communication Review, 10,* 22–54.

Hochberg, J. (1978). Art and perception. In E. C. Carterette and M. P. Friedman (eds.), *Handbook of perception,* vol. 10: Perceptual ecology (pp. 225–258). New York: Academic Press.

Hochberg, J., and Brooks, V. (1962). Pictorial recognition as an unlearned ability: A study of one child's performance. *American Journal of Psychology, 75,* 624–628.

Hoffman, D. (2003). Colour and contour from apparent motion. In R. Maus-feld and D. Heyer (eds.), *Colour perception: From light to object.* Oxford: Oxford University Press.

Holway, A. H., and Boring, E. G. (1941). Determinants of apparent visual size with distance variant. *American Journal of Psychology, 54,* 21–37.

Hopkins, R. (1998). *Picture, image and experience: A philosophical inquiry.* Cambridge: Cambridge University Press.

Hopkins, R. (2000). Touching pictures, *British Journal of Aesthetics, 40,* 149–167.

Hopkins, R. (2002). Thomas Reid on Molyneux's question. Manuscript in preparation.

Horn, B. K. P., and Brooks, M. J. (1989). *Shape from shading.* Cambridge, Mass.: MIT Press.

Hornbostel, E. M. von (1922). Über optische Inversion (About Optical Inversion). *Psychologische Forschung, 1,* 130–156.

Huffman, D. A. (1971). Impossible objects as nonsense sentences. In B. Meltzer and D. Mitchie (eds.), *Machine Intelligence,* vol. 6 (pp. 295–323). Edinburgh: Edinburgh University Press.

Huizinga, J. (1938/1986). *Homo Ludens.* Boston: Beacon Press.

Hurlbert, A. (1998). Illusions and reality-checking on the small screen. *Perception, 27,* 633–636.

Husserl, E. (1980). *Phantasie, Bildbewusstsein, Erinnerung. Zur Phänomenologie der anschaulichen Vergegenwärtigungen. Text aus dem Nachlass (1898–1925)* (Phantasy, image consciousness, memory. On the phenomenology of intuitive realizations. Text from the *bequest* estate 1898–1925), Husserliana, vol. 23, ed. E. Marbach. Dordrecht, Netherlands: Kluwer.

Hyman, J. (1992). Perspective. In D. Cooper (ed.), *A companion to aesthetics* (pp. 323–327). Oxford: Blackwell.

Ikeda, M., and Takeuchi, T. (1975). Influence of foveal load on the functional visual field. *Perception and Psychophysics, 18,* 255–260.

Indow, T. (1991). A critical review of Luneburg's model with regard to global structure of visual space. *Psychological Review, 98,* 430–453.

Ittelson, W. H. (1952). *The Ames demonstrations in perception.* Princeton, N.J.: Princeton University Press.

Ittleson, W. H. (1960). *Visual space perception.* New York: Springer.

Ittelson W. H. (1996). Visual perception of markings. *Psychonomic Bulletin and Review, 3,* 171–187.

Jackendoff, R. (1987). *Consciousness and the computational mind.* Cambridge, Mass.: MIT Press.

Jantzen, H. (1911). Die Raumdarstellung bei kleiner Augendistanz (Representation of space at near eye distance). *Zeitschrift für Ästhetik und allgemeine Kunstwissenschaft, 6,* 119–123.

Julesz, B. (1971). *Foundations of cyclopean perception.* Chicago: University of Chicago Press.

Kaila, E. (1928). Gegenstandsfarbe und Beleuchtung (Object color and illumination). *Psychologische Forschung, 3,* 18–59.

Kalkofen, H. (1993). *Szenengliederung und Szenenfolge im sogenannten Simultanbild* (Scene segmentation and scene order in the so-called simulations image). Paper presented at the 7th. Internationaler Kongreß der Deutschen Gesellschaft für Semiotik, Tübingen, Germany.

Katz, D. (1911). Die Erscheinungsweisen der Farben und ihre Beeinflussung durch die Individuelle Erfahrung. *Leipzig, Germany: J. A. Barth.*

Katz, D. (1935). *The world of color.* London: Kegan. (Translated in abridged form from the second German edition, 1930.)

Kemp, M. (1990). *The science of art: Optical themes in western art from Brunelleschi to Seurat.* New Haven, Conn.: Yale University Press.

Kennedy, J. M. (1974). *A psychology of picture perception.* San Francisco: Jossey-Bass.

Kennedy, J. M. (1993). *Drawing and the blind.* New Haven, Conn.: Yale University Press.

Kennedy, J. M. (1997). How the blind draw. *Scientific American, 276* (January), pp. 60–65.

Kennedy, J. M. (in press). Drawings by Gaia, a blind girl. *Perception.*

Kennedy, J. M., and Bai, J. (2000). Cavanagh and Leclerc shape-from-shadow pictures: Do line versions fail because of the polarity of the regions or the contours? *Perception, 29,* 399–407.

Kennedy, J. M., and Domander, R. (1985). Shape and contour: The points of maximum change are least useful for recognition *Perception, 14,* 367–370.

Kennedy, J. M., and Juricevic, I. (1999). Angular subtense and binocular vision: Worse than worst. In M. A. Grealey and J. A. Thomson (eds.), *Studies in perception and action,* vol. 5. (pp. 24–27). Mahwah, N.J.: L. Erlbaum.

Kennedy, J. M., and Merkas, C. (2000). Depictions of motion devised by a blind person. *Psychonomic Bulletin and Review, 7,* 700–706.

Kennedy, J. M., and Miyoshi, H. (1995). Combining illusions: A perfect additivity model fits imperfect additivity results. Paper presented at the meeting of the Psychonomic Society, November 10–12, Los Angeles.

Kennedy, J. M., Nicholls, A., and Desrochers, M. (1995). From line to outline. In C. Lange-Kuettner and G. V. Thomas (eds.), *Drawing and looking* (pp. 62–74). Hemel Hempstead, United Kingdom: Simon and Schuster.

Kepes, G. (1944). *The language of vision.* Chicago: Paul Theobold.

Kersten, D., Bülthoff, H. H., Schwartz, B. L., and Kurtz, K. J. (1992). Interaction between transparency and structure from motion. *Neural Computation, 4,* 573–589.

Kilpatrick, F. P., and Ittleson, W. H. (1953). The size-distance invariance hypothesis. *Psychological Review, 60,* 223–231.

Klee, P. (1925/1981). *Pädagogisches Skizzenbuch* (Pedagogical sketch book). Mainz and Berlin.

Klee, P. (1961). *Notebooks (The thinking eye),* vol. 1, ed. J. Spiller. London: Lund Humphries.

Klein, F. (1893). Vergleichende Betrachtungen über neuere geometrische Forschungen (the Erlanger Programm) (Comparative reflection on newer geometrical research). *Mathematische Annalen, 43,* 63–100.

Knill, D. C., and Kersten, D. (1991). Apparent surface curvature affects lightness perception. *Nature, 351,* 228–230.

Koenderink, J. J. (1990). *Solid shape.* Cambridge, Mass.: MIT Press.

Koenderink, J. J. (1998). Pictorial relief. *Philosophical Transactions of the Royal Society London, A, 356,* 1071–1086.

Koenderink, J. J. (1999). Virtual psychophysics. *Perception, 28,* 669–674.

Koenderink, J. J., and van Doorn, A. J. (1995). Relief: Pictorial and otherwise. *Image and Vision Computing, 13,* 321–331.

Koenderink, J. J., and Doorn, A. J. van (1997). The generic bilinear calibration-estimation problem. *International Journal of Computer Vision, 23,* 217–234.

Koenderink, J. J., and van Doorn, A. J. (1998). The Structure of Relief. *Advances in Imaging and Electron Physics, 103,* 65–150.

Koenderink, J. J., van Doorn, A. J., and Kappers, A. M. L. (1992). Surface perception in pictures. *Perception and Psychophysics, 52,* 487–496.

Koenderink, J. J., van Doorn, A. J., and Kappers, A. M. L. (1994). On so-called paradoxical monocular stereoscopy. *Perception, 23,* 583–594.

Koenderink, J. J., van Doorn, A. J., and Kappers, A. M. L. (1995). Depth relief. *Perception, 24*, 115–126.

Koenderink, J. J., van Doorn, A. J., and Kappers, A. M. L. (1996). Pictorial surface attitude and local depth comparisons. *Perception and Psychophysics, 58,* 163–173.

Koenderink, J. J., van Doorn, A. J., Kappers, A. M. L., and Todd, J. T. (2000a). Ambiguity and the "mental eye" in pictorial relief. *Investigative Ophthalmology and Visual Science, 41,* S36.

Koenderink, J. J., van Doorn, A. J., Kappers, A. M. L., and Todd, J. T. (2000b). Directing the mental eye in pictorial perception. In B. E. Rogowitz and T. N. Pappas (eds.), *Proceedings of SPIE: Human vision and electronic imaging, 3959,* 2–13.

Koenderink, J. J., van Doorn, A. J., Kappers, A. M. L., and Todd, J. T. (2001). Ambiguity and the "mental eye" in pictorial relief. *Percpetion, 30,* 431–448.

Koenderink, J. J., Kappers, A. M. L., Pollick, F. E., and Kawato, M. (1997). Correspondence in pictorial space. *Perception and Psychophysics, 59,* 813–827.

Koffka, K. (1935). *Principles of Gestalt psychology.* New York: Harcourt.

Koffka, K. (1953). *Principles of Gestalt psychology.* New York: Harcourt, Brace, and World.

Kosslyn, S. (1994). *Image and the Brain.* Cambridge, Mass.: MIT Press.

Kraft, R., and Green, J. S. (1989). Distance perception as a function of photographic area of view. *Perception and Psychophysics, 45,* 459–466.

Kratzsch, K. (ed.)(1983). *Illuminierte Holzschnitte der Luther-Bibel von 1534* (Illuminated wood cuts of the Luther-Bibel of 1534). Hanau, Germany: Dausien.

Kruskal, J. B. (1964). Multidimensional scaling by optimizing goodness of fit to a nonmetric hypothesis. *Psychometrika, 29,* 707–719.

Kubovy, M. (1986). *The Psychology of perspective and renaissance art.* Cambridge: University Press.

Kubovy, M., and Epstein, W. (in press). Internalization: A metaphor we can live without. *Behavioral and Brain Sciences, 24,* 618–625.

Künnapas, T. (1968). Distance perception as a function of available visual cues. *Journal of Experimental Psychology, 77,* 523–529.

Lakoff, G., and Johnson, M. (1999). *Philosophy in the flesh.* New York: Basic Books.

Landy, M. S., Maloney, L. T., Johnston, E. B., and Young, M. (1995). Measurement and modeling of depth cue combination: In defense of weak fusion. *Vision Research, 35,* 389–412.

Landy, M. S., Maloney, L. T., and Young, M. (1991). Psychophysical estimation of the human depth combination rule. In P. S. Shenker (ed.), *Proceedings of the SPIE, 1383, Sensor fusion III: 3-D perception and recognition,* 247–254.

Lee, M., and Bremner, G. (1987). The representation of depth in children's drawings of a table. *Quarterly Journal of Experimental Psychology, 39A,* 479–496.

Leeman, F., Elffers, J., and Schuyt, M. (1976). *Hidden images.* New York: Harry N. Abrams.

Lenk, E. (1926). Über die optische Auffassung geometrisch-regelmässiger Gestalten (On the optic prehension of geometric regular Gestalts). In F. Krueger (ed.), *Neue Psychologische Studien,* vol. 1 (pp. 577–612). Munich, Germany: Beck'sche Verlagsbuchhandlung.

Leonardo da Vinci (1989). *Leonardo on Painting* (trans. and ed. M. Kemp, M. Walker, and M. Kemp). New Haven, Conn.: Yale University Press.

Leslie, A. M. (1987). Pretense and representation: The origins of "theory of mind." *Psychological Review, 94,* 412–426.

Lessing, G. E. (1964). *Laokoon oder über die Grenzen der Malerei und Poesie* [Laokoon or on the limits of painting and poetry]. Originally published 1766. Stuttgart, Germany: Recclam.

Levelt, W. J. M. (1984). Some perceptual limitation in talking about space. In A. J. van Doorn, W. A. van de Grind, and J. J. Koenderink (eds.), *Limits in perception* (pp. 323–358). Utrecht, Netherlands: VNU Science Press.

Levin, C. A., and Haber, R. N. (1993). Visual angle as a determinant of perceived interobject distance. *Perception and Psychophysics, 54,* 250–259.

Lewis, D. (1969). *Convention: A philosophical study.* Oxford: Blackwell.

Lindberg, D. C. (1976). *Theories of vision from Al-Kindi to Kepler.* Chicago: University of Chicago Press.

Loomis, J. M., Da Silva, J. A., Philbeck, J. W., and Fukushima, S. S. (1996). Visual perception of location and distance. *Current Directions in Psychological Science, 5,* 72–77.

Loomis, J. M., and Philbeck, J. W. (1999). Is the anisotropy of perceived 3-D shape invariant across scale? *Perception and Psychophysics, 61,* 397–402.

Lopes, D. M. M. (1992). Pictures, styles and purposes, *British Journal of Aesthetics, 32* (4), 330–341.

Lopes, D. M. M. (1996). *Understanding pictures.* Oxford: Clarendon Press.

Lopes, D. M. M. (1997). Art media and the sense modalities: Tactile pictures. *Philosophical Quarterly, 47,* 425–440.

Lübke, W., and Pernice, E. (1921). *Die Kunst des Altertums* (The art of antiquity). Esslingen, Germany: Neff.

Luce, R. D., and Krumhansl, C. L. (1988). Measurement, scaling, and psychophysics. In R. C. Atkinson, R. J. Herrnstein, G. Lindzey, and R. D. Luce (eds.), *Stevens' handbook of experimental psychology* (pp. 3–74). New York: Wiley.

Lumsden, E. A. (1980). Problems of magnification and minification: An explanation of the distortions of distance, slant, and velocity. In M. Hagen (ed.), *The perception of pictures,* vol. 1 (pp. 91–135). New York: Academic Press.

Luneburg, R. K. (1947). *Mathematical analysis of binocular vision.* Princeton, N.J.: Princeton University Press.

Luo, R. C., and Kay, M. G. (1992). Data fusion and sensor integration: State-of-the-art 1990s. In M. A. Abidi and R. C. Gonzalez (eds.), *Data fusion in robotics and machine intelligence* (pp. 7–135). San Diego, Calif.: Academic Press.

Lyons, J. (1977). *Semantics,* 2 vols. Cambridge: University Press.

Lythgoe, J. N. (1979). *The ecology of vision.* Oxford: Clarendon Press.

Mach, E. (1903). *Analyse der Empfindungen* (The analysis of sensations). Jena, Germany: Fischer.

Mackavey, W. R. (1980). Exceptional cases of pictorial perspective. In M. A. Hagen (ed.), *The perception of pictures,* vol. 1 (pp. 213–223). New York: Academic Press.

Margerie, A. de (ed.) (1994). *Gustave Caillebotte, 1948–1894.* Paris: Réunion des Musées Nationaux.

Marler, P. (1999). On innateness: Are sparrow songs "learned" or "innate"? In M. D. Hauser and M. Konishi (eds.), *The design of animal communication* (pp. 293–318). Cambridge, Mass.: MIT Press.

Marr, D. (1982). *Vision: A computational investigation into the human representation and processing of visual information.* San Francisco: W.H. Freeman.

Marr, D., and Poggio, T. (1976). Cooperative computation of human stereo vision. *Science, 194,* 283–287.

Massaro, D. W., and Cohen, M. M. (1993). The paradigm and the fuzzy logical model of perception are alive and well. *Journal of Experimental Psychology: General, 122,* 115–124.

Maunsell, J., Sclar, G., Nealey, T., and DePriest, D. (1991). Extraretinal representations in area V4 in the macaque monkey. *Vision Neuroscience, 7,* 651–573.

Mauries, P. (1997). *Le trompe l'oeil.* Paris: Gallimard.

Mausfeld, R. (2002). The physicalistic trap in perception theory. In D. Heyer and R. Mausfeld (eds.), *Perception and the physical world* (pp. 75–112). Chichester, United Kingdom: Wiley.

Mausfeld, R. (2003). The dual coding of colour: "Surface colour" and "illumination colour" as constituents of the representational format of perceptual primitives. In R. Mausfeld and D. Heyer (eds.), *Colour perception: From light to object.* Oxford: Oxford University Press.

Mausfeld, R., and Andres, J. (2002). Second-order statistics of colour codes modulate transformations that effectuate varying degrees of scene invariance and illumination invariance. *Perception, 31,* 209–224.

Maynard, P. (1991). Real imaginings, *Philosophy and Phenomenological Research, 51* (2), 389–394.

Maynard, P. (1994). The contest of meaning (book review). *Journal of Aesthetics and Art Criticism, 49* (4), 390–392.

Maynard, P. (1996). Perspective's places. *Journal of Aesthetics and Art Criticism, 54* (1), 23–40.

Maynard, P. (1997a). *The engine of visualization: Thinking through photography.* Ithaca, N.Y.: Cornell University Press.

Maynard, P. (1997b). Rev. of Damisch 1994. *Journal of Aesthetics and Art Criticism, 55* (1), 84–85.

Maynard, P. (2001). "The time it takes." In J. Baetens (ed.), *The Graphic Novel* (pp. 191–210). Louvain, Belgium: Louvain University Press.

Meltzoff, A. N. (1995). Understanding the intentions of others: Re-enactment of intended acts by 18-month-old children. *Developmental Psychology, 31,* 838–850.

Meng, J. C., and Sedgwick, H. A. (2001). Distance perception mediated through nested contact relations among surfaces. *Perception and Psychophysics, 63,* 1–15.

Meng, J. C., and Sedgwick, H. A. (2002). Distance perception across spatial discontinuities. *Perception and Psychophysics, 64,* 1–14.

Messaris, P. (1994). *Visual literacy: Image, mind, and reality.* Boulder, Colo.: Westview Press.

Metz, C. (1974). *Film language.* New York: Oxford University Press.

Metzger, W. (1975). *Gesetze des Sehens.* Frankfurt/Main: Kramer.

Michalski, S. (1993). *The Reformation and the visual arts.* London: Routledge.

Michotte, A. (1948/1991). L'énigma psychologique de la perspective dans le dessin linéaire. *Bulletin de la Classe des Lettres de l'Académie Royale de Belgique, 34,* 268–288. Republished as The psychological enigma of perspective in outline pictures. In G. Thinès, A. Costall, and G. Butterworth (eds.), *Michotte's experimental phenomenology of perception* (pp. 174–187). Hillsdale, N.J.: Erlbaum.

Michotte, A. (1954/1991). Autobiographie. *Psychologica Belgica, 1,* 190–217. Republished as Autobiography. In G. Thinès, A. Costall, and G. Butterworth (eds.), *Michotte's experimental phenomenology of perception* (pp. 24–49). Hillsdale, N.J.: Erlbaum.

Michotte, A. (1960/1991). Le réel et l'irréel dans l'image. *Bulletin de la Classe des Lettres de l'Académie Royale de Belgique, 46,* 330–344. Republished as The real and the unreal in the image. In G. Thinès, A. Costall, and G. Butterworth (eds.), *Michotte's experimental phenomenology of perception* (pp. 187–197). Hillsdale, N.J.: Erlbaum.

Michotte, A., Thinès, G., and Crabbé, G. (1964/1991). Amodal completion of perceptual structures. In G. Thinès, A. Costall, and G. Butterworth (eds.), *Michotte's experimental phenomenology of perception* (pp. 140–167). Hillsdale, N.J.: Erlbaum. (French original appeared in 1964.)

Milbrath, C. (1998). *Patterns of artistic development in children: Comparative studies of talent.* Cambridge: Cambridge University Press, 1998.

Mingolla, E., and Todd, J. T. (1986). Perception of solid shape from shading. *Biological Cybernetics, 53,* 137–151.

Miskie, D., Dainoff, M., Sherman, R., and Johnson, L. (1975). Does distance perception change as the degree of enclosure changes? Some psychophysical studies under real and simulated conditions. *Man-Environment Systems, 5,* 317–320.

Mitchell, W. J. (1992). *The reconfigured eye: Visual truth in the post-photographic era.* Cambridge, Mass.: MIT Press.

Mitchison, G. J., and Westheimer, G. (1984). The perception of depth in simple figures. *Vision Research, 24,* 1063–1073.

Moskowitz, B. A. (1978). The acquisition of language. *Scientific American, 239,* 82–96.

Nagata, S. (1991). How to reinforce perception of depth in single two-dimensional pictures. In S. R. Ellis, M. K. Kaiser, and A. C. Grunwald (eds.), *Pictorial communication in virtual and real environments* (pp. 527–545). London: Taylor and Francis.

Nakayama, K., He, Z. J., and Shimojo, S. (1995). Visual surface representation: A critical link between lower-level and higher-level vision. In S. M. Kosslyn and D. N. Osherson (eds.), *Visual cognition. An invitation to cognitive sciences,* vol 2. (pp. 1–70). Cambridge, Mass.: MIT Press.

Nakayama, K., Shimojo, S., and Ramachandran, V. S. (1990). Transparency: Relation to depth, subjective contours, luminance, and neon color spreading. *Perception, 19,* 497–513.

Nicholls, A. L., and Kennedy, J. M. (1992). Drawing development: From similarity to direction. *Child Development, 63,* 227–241.

Nicholls, A. L., and Kennedy, J. M. (1995). Foreshortening in cube drawings by children and adults. *Perception, 24,* 1443–1456.

Nijhawan, R. (1997). Visual decomposition of colour through motion extrapolation. *Nature, 386,* 66–69.

Palmer, S. E. (1999). *Vision Science: Photons to Phenomenology.* Cambridge, Mass.: MIT Press.

Panofsky, E. (1924/1925). Die Perspektive als "symbolische Form." In *Vorträge der Bibliothek Warburg.* Leipzig and Berlin. (Translated in New York University samizdat typescript, n.d.)

Panofsky, E. (1927/1991). Die Perspektive als "symbolische Form." In *Vorträge der Bibliothek Warburg 1924/25* (pp. 258–330). Leipzig and Berlin. Republished as *Perspective as symbolic form* (trans. C. S. Wood). New York: Zone Books.

Peacocke, C. (1987). Depiction. *Philosophical Review, 96,* 383–410.

Peacocke, C. (1989). Perceptual content. In J. Lamog, J. Perry, and H. Wettstein (eds.), *Themes from Kaplan.* New York: Oxford University Press.

Pearson, D., Hanna, E., and Martinez, K. (1990). Computer generated cartoons. In H. Barlow, C. Blakemore, and M. Weston-smith (eds.), *Images and understanding* (pp. 46–50). Cambridge: Cambridge University Press.

Petersen, M. A. (1999). What's in a stage name? Comment on Vecera and O'Reilly (1998). *Journal of Experimental Psychology: Human Perception and Performance, 25,* 276–286.

Pinker, S. (1997). *How the mind works.* New York: W. W. Norton.

Pirenne, M. H. (1952/1953). The scientific basis of Leonardo da Vinci's theory of perspective. *British Journal for the Philosophy of Science, 3,* 169–185.

Pirenne, M. H. (1970). *Optics, painting and photography.* Cambridge: Cambridge University Press.

Pirenne, M. H. (1975). Vision and art. In E. C. Carterette and M. P. Friedman (eds.), *Handbook of perception,* vol. 5: Seeing (pp. 434–490). New York: Academic Press.

Polanyi, M. (1970a). What Is a painting? *The British Journal of Aesthetics, 10,* 225–236.

Polanyi, M. (1970b). What Is a painting? *American Scholar, 49,* 655–669.

Pollick, F. E., Giblin, P. J., Rycroft, J., and Wilson, L. L. (1992). Human recovery of shape from profiles. *Behaviormetrika, 19,* 65–79.

Posner, M. I., and Raichle, M. E. (1994). *Images of mind.* Scientific American Library. New York: Freeman & Co.

Prazdny, K. (1986). Three-dimensional structure from long-range apparent motion. *Perception, 15,* 619–625.

Racinet, A. (1888/1995). *Weltgeschichte der Kostüme* (World history of costumes). Cologne: Parkland.

Ramachandran, V. S. (1986). Capture of stereopsis and apparent motion by illusory contours. *Peception and Psychophysics, 39,* 361–373.

Ramachandran, V. S. (1990). Interactions between motion, depth, color, and form: The utilitarian theory of perception. In C. Blakemore (ed.), *Vision: Coding and efficiency* (pp. 346–360). Cambridge: Cambridge University Press.

Ramachandran, V. S., and Hirstein, W. (1999). The science of art: A neurological theory of aesthetic experience. *Journal of Consciousness Studies, 6,* 15–51.

Ratoosh, P. (1949). On interposition as a cue for the perception of distance. *Proceedings of the National Academy of Sciences, Washington, 35,* 257–259.

Rehkämper, K. (1995). Analoge Repräsentationen (Analog representations). In K. Sachs-Hombach (ed.), *Bilder im Geiste. Zur kognitiven und erkenntnistheoretischen Funktion piktorialer Repräsentationen* (Mental images: About the cognitive and epistemological function of pictorial representation) (pp. 63–105). Amsterdam and Atlanta, Ga.: Rodopi.

Reid, T. (1764). *An inquiry into the human mind, on the principles of common sense.* Edinburgh: A. Kincaid and J. Bell.

Reisberg, D., and Chambers, D. (1991). Neither pictures nor propositions: What can we learn from a mental image? *Canadian Journal of Psychology, 45,* 336–352.

Richter, J. P. (ed., and trans.) (1883). *The literary works of Leonardo da Vinci.* London: Samson, Low, Marston, Searle, and Rivington. Reprinted as *The notebooks of Leonardo da Vinci.* New York: Dover Press, 1970.

Riedl, R. (1988). *Biologie der Erkenntnis.* Munich: Deutscher Taschenbuch Verlag.

Rock, I. (1983). *The Logic of perception.* Cambridge, Mass.: MIT Press.

Rock, I. (1984). *Perception.* New York: Scientific American Books.

Rogers, B. J., and Collett, T. S. (1989). The appearance of surfaces specified by motion parallax and binocular disparity. *The Quarterly Journal of Experimental Psychology, 41A,* 697–717.

Rogers, S. (1995). Perceiving pictorial space. In W. Epstein and S. Rogers (eds.), *Handbook of perception and cognition,* 2d ed., vol. 5: Perception of space and motion (pp. 119–163). San Diego, Calif.: Academic Press.

Rogers, S. (1996). The horizon-ratio relation as information for relative size in pictures. *Perception and Psychophysics, 58,* 142–152.

Rogers, S. (1997). *Convention and constraint in pictorial perspective.* In G. L. Torenvliet and K. J. Vicente (eds.), *Perception and action.* Proceedings of the ninth international conference on perception and action, (p. 112). Mahwah, N.J.: L. Erlbaum.

Rogers, S. (2000). The emerging concept of information. *Ecological Psychology, 12* (4), 335–343.

Rogers, S. (in press). Through Alice's glass: The creation and perception of other worlds in movies, pictures and virtual reality. In J. D. Anderson and B. F. Anderson (eds.), *Moving image theory: Ecological considerations.* Carbondale IL: Southern Illinois University Press.

Rogers, S., and Costall, A. (1983). On the horizon: Picture perception and Gibson's concept of information. *Leonardo, 16* (3), 180–182.

Rogers, S., and Fichandler, C. E. (2000). Eye-height scaling of layout in pictures, trompe l'oeil, and real scenes. *Abstracts of the Psychonomic Society, 5,* 39.

Rogers, S., and Pollard, W. (1998). Perceived size and distance in real scenes and in photographs. *Abstracts of the Psychonomic Society, 3,* 59.

Rogers, S., and Watson, J. G. (1996a). Horizon-based relative size judgments in pictures, movies and virtual reality. *Investigative Ophthalmology and Visual Science, 37* (3), S519.

Rogers, S., and Watson, J. G. (1996b). The horizon-ratio: Size-distance invariance revisited. *Abstracts of the Psychonomic Society, 1,* 25.

Rubin, E. (1915). *Synsoplevede figurer* (Visually perceived figures). Copenhagen: Gyldendals.

Sachs, H. (1990). *Isotrope Geometrie des Raumes* (Isotropic geometry of space). Brunswick, Germany: Friedr. Vieweg and Sohn.

Sachs-Hombach, K. (1999). Bilder als wahrnehmungsnahe Zeichen. In J. Mittelstrass (ed.), *Die Zukunft des Wissens* (The future of knowledge) (pp. 1351–1358). Constance, Germany: Universitätsverlag Konstanz.

Sachs-Hombach, K., and Rehkämper, K. (1998). Thesen zu einer Theorie bildhafter Darstellung. In K. Sachs-Hombach and K. Rehkämper (eds.), *Bild—Bildwahrnehmung—Bildverarbeitung. Interdisziplinäre Beiträge zur Bildwissenschaft* (pp. 119–124). Wiesbaden, Germany: Deutscher Universitätsverlag.

Salt, B. (1983). *Film style and technology: History and analysis.* London: Starword.

Sanders, A. F. (1970). Some aspects of the selective process in the functional visual field. *Ergonomics, 13,* 101–117. (Cited in Ikeda and Takeuchi 1975).

Sartre, J.-P. (1940). *L'imaginaire. Psychologie phénoménologique d'imagination* (The imaginary: Phenomenal psychology of imagination). Paris: Gallimard.

Scharf, A. (1968). *Art and photography.* London: Penguin.

Schier, F. (1986). *Deeper into pictures.* Cambridge: Cambridge University Press.

Scholz, O. R. (1991): *Bild, Darstellung, Zeichen. Philosophische Theorien bildhafter Darstellung* (Image, representation, symbol: Philosophical theories of pictorial representation). Freiburg and Munich: Alber.

Schöne, W. (1954). *Über das Licht in der Malerei* (On the light in painting). Berlin: Gebr. Mann.

Schriever, W. (1925). Experimentelle Studien über stereoskopisches Sehen (Experimental studies of stereoscopic vision). *Zeitschrift für Psychologie, 96,* 113–170.

Schuster, D. H. (1964). A new ambiguous figure. *American Journal of Psychology, 77,* 673.

Schwartz, B. J., and Sperling, G. (1983). Luminance controls the perceived 3-D structure of dynamic 2-D displays. *Bulletin of the Psychonomic Society, 21,* 456–458.

Schwartz, R. (1994). *Vision: Variations on some Berkelian themes.* Cambridge, MA: Blackwell.

Schwartz, R. (1996). Directed Perception. *Philosophical Psychology, 9,* 81–91.

Searle, J. R. (1993). Metaphor. In A. Ortony (ed.), *Metaphor and thought,* 2d ed. (pp. 83–111). Cambridge: Cambridge University Press.

Sedgwick, H. A. (1973). The visible horizon: A potential source of visual information for the perception of size and distance. Doctoral dissertation, Cornell University. *Dissertation Abstracts International, 34,* 1301B–1302B. (University Microfilms No. 73–22,530.)

Sedgwick, H. A. (1980). The geometry of spatial layout in pictorial representations. In M. A. Hagen (ed.), *The Perception of Pictures*, vol. 1 (pp. 33–90). New York: Academic Press.

Sedgwick, H. A. (1983). Environment-centered representation of spatial layout: Available visual information from texture and perspective. In J. Beck, B. Hope, and A. Rosenfeld (eds.), *Human and machine vision* (pp. 425–458). New York: Academic Press.

Sedgwick, H. A. (1986). Space perception. In K. R. Boff, L. Kaufman, and J. P. Thomas (eds.), *Handbook of perception and performance*, vol. 1: Sensory processes and perception pp. 21.1–21.57. New York: Wiley.

Sedgwick, H. A. (1987a). Layout2: A production system modeling visual perspective information. In *Proceedings of the IEEE First International Conference on Computer Vision* (pp. 662–666). Washington, DC: IEEE Computer Society Press.

Sedgwick, H. A. (1987b). A production system modeling high-level visual perspective information for spatial layout. *Technical Report no. 298*, New York University Department of Computer Science.

Sedgwick, H. A. (1989). Combining multiple forms of visual information to specify contact relations in spatial layout. In P. S. Schenker (ed.), *Proceedings of SPIE*, vol. 1198: Sensor fusion II: Human and machine strategies (pp. 447–458). Bellingham, Wash.: SPIE.

Sedgwick, H. A. (1991). The effects of viewpoint on the virtual space of pictures. In S. R. Ellis (ed.), *Pictorial communication in virtual and real environments*, pp. 460–479. New York: Taylor and Francis.

Sedgwick, H. A. (2001). Visual space perception. In E. B. Goldstein (ed.), *Blackwell handbook of perception* (pp. 128–167). Oxford: Blackwell.

Sedgwick, H. A., and Gillam, B. (submitted). A non-modular approach to visual space perception.

Sedgwick, H. A., and Levy, S. (1985). Environment-centered and viewer-centered perception of surface orientation. *Computer Vision, Graphics, and Image Processing, 31*, 248–260.

Sedgwick, H. A., and Nicholls, A. L. (1993a). Cross talk between the picture surface and the pictured scene: Effects on perceived shape. *Perception, 22 (supplement)*, 109.

Sedgwick, H. A., and Nicholls, A. L. (1993b). Interaction between surface and depth in the Ponzo illusion. *Investigative Ophthalmology and Visual Science, 34*, 1184.

Sedgwick, H. A., and Nicholls, A. L. (1994). Distortions of pictorial space produced by optical minification. *Investigative Ophthalmology and Visual Science, 35*, 2111.

Sedgwick, H. A., and Nicholls, A. L. (1996). Picture perception in children: Interactions between the picture surface and the depicted scene. *Investigative Ophthalmology and Visual Science, 37*, S518.

Sedgwick, H. A., Nicholls, A. L., and Brehaut, J. (1995). Perceptual interaction of surface and depth in optically minified picture. *Investigative Ophthalmology and Visual Science, 36*, S667.

Sedgwick, H. A., Placide, F., Raul, C., and Flagg, T. (1991). Perceptual cross talk between pictured spatial layout and the picture surface. *Proceedings of the Seventh Annual Meeting of the International Society for Psychophysics*, Durham, N.C., October 17–21.

Shepard, R. N. (1980). Multidimensional scaling, tree-fitting, and clustering. *Science, 210*, 390–398.

Shepard, R. N. (1990). *Mindsights.* New York: W. H. Freeman.

Smith, R. (1974). Natural versus scientific vision: the foreshortened figure in the Renaissance. *Gazette des Beaux-arts, 84*, 239–248.

Speed, H. (1913). *The practice and science of drawing.* London: Seeley, Service, and Company.

Spencer, J. R. (1966). *Leon Battista Alberti on Painting.* New Haven, Conn.: Yale University Press.

Spivak, M. (1975). *Differential geometry,* vol. 3. Berkeley, CA: Publish or perish, Inc.

Steinberg, S. (1966). *Le masque.* Paris: Maeght Editeur.

Stemberger, G. (1990). *2000 Jahre Christentum–Illustrierte Kirchengeschichte in Farbe* (2000 years of Christianity—Illustrated ecclesiastic history in color). Erlangen, Germany: Karl Müller.

Stern, W. (1930). *Psychology of early childhood.* London: George Allen and Unwin.

Stevens, K. A., and Brookes, A. (1988). Integrating stereopsis with monocular interpretations of planar surfaces. *Vision Research, 28,* 371–386.

Stevens, K. A., Lees, M., and Brookes, A. (1991). Combining binocular and monocular curvature features. *Perception, 20,* 425–440.

Stevens, S. S. (1951). Mathematics, measurement, and psychophysics. In S. S. Stevens (ed.), *Handbook of Experimental Psychology* (pp. 1–49). New York: Wiley.

Stillings, N., Feinstein, M., Garfield, J., Rissland, E., Rosenbaum, D., Weisler, S., and Baker-Ward, L. (1987). *Cognitive Science: An Introduction.* Cambridge, Mass.: MIT Press.

Strieder, P. (ed.) (1996). *Dürer.* Augsburg, Germany: Bechtermünz.

Strubecker, K. (1956). *Einführung in die höhere Mathematik mit besonderer Berücksichtigung ihre Anwendungen auf Geometrie, Physik, Naturwissenschaften und Technik* (Introduction into higher mathematics with particular emphasis on its application to geometry, physics, natural science and technology), vol. 1: Grundlagen (Foundations). Munich: R. Oldenburg Verlag.

Swedlund, C. (1981). *Photography: A handbook of history, materials, and processes,* 2d ed. New York: Holt, Rinehart, and Winston.

Talbot, W. H. F. (1844–1846/1969). *The pencil of nature,* unpaginated reprint. New York: Da Capo.

Taylor, B. (1719). *New principles of linear perspective: Or the art of designing on a plane the representations of all sorts of objects, in a more general and simple method than has been done before.* London: Printed for R. Knaplock at the Bishop's Head in St. Paul's Churchyard.

Teghtsoonian, R. (1973). Range effects in psychophysical scaling and a revision of Stevens' law. *American Journal of Psychology, 86,* 3–27.

Ten Doesschate, G. (1964). *Perspective: Fundamentals, controversials, history.* Nieuwkoop, Netherlands: B. de Graaf.

Te Peerdt, E. (1899). *Das Problem der Darstellung des Momentes der Zeit in den Werken der malenden und zeichnenden Kunst* (The problem of representing a moment in time in paintings and drawings). Strasbourg, Germany: Heitz.

Terzopoulos, D. (1986). Integrating visual information from multiple sources. In A. Pentland (ed.), *From pixels to predicates* (pp. 111–142). Norwood, N.J.: Ablex.

Thiéry, A. (1895). Ueber geometrisch-optische Täuschungen (On geometric-optical illusions). *Philosophische Studien, 11,* 307–337.

Todorovic, D. (2002). Comparative overview of perception of distal and proximal visual attributes. In D. Heyer and R. Mausfeld (eds.), *Perception and the physical world* (pp. 37–74). New York: Wiley.

Tomasello, M., and Call, J. (1997). *Primate cognition.* Oxford: Oxford University Press.

Topper, D. (2000). On anamorphosis: Setting some things straight. *Leonardo, 33* (2), 115–124.

Trueswell, J. C., and Hayhoe, M. M. (1993). Surface segmentation mechanisms and motion perception. *Vision Research, 33,* 313–328.

Turhan, M. (1937). Über räumliche Wirkungen von Helligkeitsgefällen (About spatial impressions of contrast decrements). *Psychologische Forschung, 21,* 1–49.

Van Essen, D., and Anderson, C. A. (1990). Information processing strategies and the pathways in the primate retina and visual cortex. In S. F. Zornetzer, J. L. Davis, and C. Lau (eds.), Introduction to neural and electronic networks (pp. 43–52). Orlando, FL: Academic Press.

Van Essen, D., Anderson, C. A., and Olshausen, B. A. (1994). Dynamic routing strategies in sensory, motor, and cognitive processing. In C. Koch and J. L. Davis (eds.), *Large scale neuronal theories of the brain* (pp. 271–299), MIT Press.

Varnedoe, J. K. (1990) *A fine disregard: What makes modern art modern.* New York: Abrams.

Victoria, J. (1982). Correspondence between implied points of view and selected points of view in children's drawings of familiar and unfamiliar objects. *Review of Research in Visual Arts Education, 15,* 33–42.

Vitz, P. C. (1979). Visual science and modernist art: Historical parallels. In C. F. Nodine and D. F. Fisher (eds.), *Perception and pictorial presentation* (pp. 134–166). New York: Praeger.

Vollmer, G. (1990). *Evolutionäre Erkenntnistheorie* (Evolutionary epistemology). Stuttgart, Germany: S. Hirzel.

Wade, N. J., and Hughes, P. (1999). Fooling the eyes: Trompe l'oeil and reverse perspective. *Perception, 28,* 1115–1119.

Wagner, M. (1985). The metric of visual space. *Perception and Psychophysics, 38,* 483–495.

Wallach, H., and Karsh, E. B. (1963). The modification of stereoscopic depth-perception and the kinetic depth-effect. *American Journal of Psychology, 76,* 429–435.

Wallach, H., Moore, M. E., and Davidson, L. (1963). Modification of stereoscopic depth-perception. *American Journal of Psychology, 76,* 191–204.

Wallach, H., Weisz, A., and Adams, P. A. (1956). Circles and derived figures in rotation. *American Journal of Psychology, 69,* 48–59.

Walton, K. (1984). Transparent pictures: On the nature of photographic realism. *Critical Inquiry, 11,* 246–277.

Walton, K. (1990). *Mimesis as make-believe.* Cambridge, Mass.: Harvard University Press.

Waltz, D. (1975). Understanding line drawings of scenes with shadows. In P. H. Winston (ed.), *The psychology of computer vision* (pp. 19–91). New York: McGraw-Hill.

Ware, W. R. (1900). *Modern perspective,* rev. ed. New York: Macmillan.

Wehner, R. (1987). "Matched filters"—neural models of the external world. *Journal of Comparative Physiology A, 161,* 511–531

Weisstein, N., and Harris, C. S. (1974). Visual detection of line segments: An object superiority effect. *Science, 186,* 752–755.

Weisstein, N., and Wong, E. (1986). Figure-ground organization and the spatial and temporal responses of the visual system. In E. C. Schwab and H. C. Nusbaum (eds.), *Pattern recognition by humans and machines,* vol. 2: *Visual perception* (pp. 31–64) Orlando, Fla.: Academic Press.

Wheeler, M. E., Petersen, S. E., and Buckner, R. L. (2000). Memory's echo: vivid remembering reactivates sensory-specific cortex. *Proceedings of the National Academy of Sciences, 97,* 11125–11129.

White, J. (1967). *The birth and rebirth of pictorial space.* London: Faber and Faber.

White, J. (1987). *The birth and rebirth of pictorial space,* 3d ed. London: Faber.

Wickhoff, F. (1912). Römische Kunst (Die Wiener Genesis) (Roman art [the Viennese Genesis]). In M. Dvorak (ed.), *Die Schriften Franz Wickhoffs* (The writing of Franz Wickhoffs) (pp. 1–224). Berlin.

Wiesing, L. (2000). *Phänomene im Bild* (Phenomena in pictures). Munich: Fink.

Willats, J. (1977). How children learn to draw realistic pictures. *Quarterly Journal of Experimental Psychology, 29,* 367–382.

Willats, J. (1992a). The representation of extendedness in children's drawings of sticks and discs. *Child Development, 63,* 692–710.

Willats, J. (1992b). Seeing lumps, sticks and slabs in silhouettes. *Perception, 21,* 481–496.

Willats, J. (1997). *Art and representation: New principles in the analysis of pictures.* Princeton, N.J.: Princeton University Press.

Wimmer, H., and Perner, J. (1983). Beliefs about beliefs: Representation and constraining functions of wrong beliefs of young children's understanding of deception. *Cognition, 13,* 103–128.

Wittkower, R. (1977). *Sculpture, processes and principles.* New York: Harper and Row.

Wollheim, R. (1977). Representation: The philosophical contribution to psychology. In G. Butterworth (ed.), *The Child's representation of the world* (pp. 173–188). New York: Plenum Press.

Wollheim, R. (1980). Seeing-as, Seeing-in, and Pictorial Representation. In *Art and its Objects,* 2d ed. (pp. 205–226). Cambridge: Cambridge University Press.

Wollheim, R. (1973). *On art and the mind.* London: Allen Lane.

Wollheim, R. (1987). *Painting as an art.* London: Thames and Hudson.

Wood, C. S. (1995). Review of Damisch 1994, *Art Bulletin, 77* (December), 677–682.

Wundt, W. (1910). *Grundzüge der Physiologischen Psychologie* (The basics of physiological psychology), 6th rev. ed., vol. 2. Leipzig, Germany: Engelmann.

Wyszecki, G., and Stiles, W. S. (1967). *Color science: Concepts and methods, quantitative data and formulas.* New York: John Wiley and Sons.

Yaglom, I. M. (1979). *A simple non-euclidean geometry and its physical basis: An elementary account of Galilean geometry and the Galilean principle of relativity* (trans. from Russian by A. Shenitzer). Springer, N.Y.: Heidelberg Science Library.

Yaglom, I. M. (1988). *Felix Klein and Sophus Lie: Evolution of the idea of symmetry in the nineteenth century.* (Trans. from Russian by S. Sossinsky, eds. H. Grant and A. Shenitzer). Boston: Birkhäuser.

Yang, T., and Kubovy, M. (1999). Weakening the robustness of perspective: Evidence for a modified theory of compensation in picture perception. *Perception and Psychophysics, 61,* 456–467.

Yellott, J. I. (1981). Binocular depth inversion. *Scientific American, 245,* 148–159.

Youngs, W. M. (1976). The influence of perspective and disparity cues on the perception of slant. *Vision Research, 16,* 79–82.

Zacks, J. M., and Tversky, B. (2001). Event structure in perception and conception. *Psychological Bulletin, 127,* 3–21.

Zeki, S. (1993). *A Vision of the brain.* Oxford: Blackwell.

Contributors

Margaret Atherton
Department of Philosophy
University of Wisconsin at
Milwaukee
Milwaukee, Wisconsin

Juan Bai
University of Toronto
Department of Psychology
Scarborough, Ontario, Canada

James E. Cutting
Department of Psychology
Cornell University
Ithaca, New York

Andrea van Doorn
Helmholtz Instituut—Buys Ballot
Laboratory
Universiteit Utrecht
Utrecht, Netherlands

Heiko Hecht
Department of Experimental
Psychology
Johannes Gutenberg-Universität
Mainz
Mainz, Germany

Dieter Heyer
Martin-Luther-Universität Halle-
Wittenberg
Institut für Psychologie
Halle, Germany

Robert Hopkins
Department of Philosophy
University of Birmingham
Birmingham, United Kingdom

Igor Juricevic
Department of Psychology
University of Toronto
Scarborough, Ontario, Canada

Hermann Kalkofen
Universität Göttingen
Georg-Elias-Müller Institut für
Psychologie
Göttingen, Germany

John M. Kennedy
Department of Psychology
University of Toronto
Scarborough, Ontario, Canada

Jan J. Koenderink
Helmholtz Instituut, Buys Ballot
Laboratory
Universiteit Utrecht
Utrecht, Netherlands

Rainer Mausfeld
Christian-Alberchts-Universität zu
Kiel
Institut für Psychologie
Kiel, Germany

Patrick Maynard
Department of Philosophy, Talbot
College
University of Western Ontario
London, Ontario, Canada

Reinhard Niederée
Christian-Alberchts-Universität zu
Kiel
Institut für Psychologie
Kiel, Germany

Klaus Rehkämper
Carl von Ossietzky Universität
Oldenburg
Institut für Philosophie
Oldenburg, Germany

Sheena Rogers
Department of Psychology
James Madison University
Harrisonburg, Virginia

Mark Rollins
Department of Philosophy
Washington University
Saint Louis, Missouri

Klaus Sachs-Hombach
Otto-von-Guericke-Universität
Magdeburg
Interdisziplinäre Forschungsstelle
für Computervisualistik Institut
für Simulation und Graphik
Magdeburg, Germany

Robert Schwartz
Department of Philosophy
University of Wisconsin at
Milwaukee
Milwaukee, Wisconsin

H. A. Sedgwick
Department of Vision Sciences
SUNY College of Optometry
New York, New York

John Willats
The Gatehouse
Kingweston
Somerton, Somerset, United
Kingdom

Richard Wollheim
Department of Philosophy
University of California at
Berkeley
Berkeley, California

Index